The Family Welcom

THE
FAMILY WELCOME
GUIDE 1994

Jill Foster and Malcolm Hamer

HarperCollins*Publishers*

Our thanks
to our very efficient typist, Adrienne Fell
And our love to Polly

HarperCollins*Publishers*
77–85 Fulham Palace Road,
Hammersmith, London W6 8JB

Published by HarperCollins*Publishers* 1993

1 3 5 7 9 8 6 4 2

Whilst every effort has been made to ensure accuracy
throughout this work, the turbulent nature of the
international travel industry is such that the author and
publishers cannot be held liable for changes which occur
after the time of writing.

The Authors assert the moral right to
be identified as the authors of this work

A catalogue record for this book is
available from the British Library

ISBN 0 00 638112 X

Set in Linotron Ehrhardt

Photoset by Rowland Phototypesetting Ltd
Bury St Edmunds, Suffolk

Printed in Great Britain by
HarperCollinsManufacturing Glasgow

Contents

Introduction

The 11th edition of *The Family Welcome Guide* aims, as in all the previous editions, to provide families with a comprehensive choice of places to visit. You may want to break a journey for a short time at a pub or restaurant; or have a leisurely meal; or take a weekend break or a longer holiday together in a farmhouse, a grand hotel or in self-catering accommodation; or simply have a day out and visit a stately home, a theme park or an interesting museum.

Our guide will send you only to those places where all members of your family will be made welcome, and where the facilities which a family needs are provided.

These basic facilities are as follows:

1. Self-catering complexes: cots and high chairs are essential.
2. Hotels: cots and high chairs and free baby listening service must be available.
3. Pubs must have separate family rooms, i.e. rooms which do not have any facility for serving alcohol.
4. Restaurants must have at least one high chair and offer either smaller portions for children or a special menu. The presence of baby changing facilities is also monitored.
5. Leisure is the catch-all title for our final category and includes museums, theme parks, stately homes, country parks, zoos and wildlife parks. We include the best of these and they must have baby changing facilities, and high chairs in their cafés/restaurants.

Above we have listed the bare essentials, but we demand much more, particularly a real commitment to welcome families. Any establishment where we notice a half-hearted or grudging attitude towards families does not get a mention in *The Family Welcome Guide*.

We are invariably asked whether facilities for families are improving in Britain, and the answer is a guarded yes, because these improvements are gradual. But an encouraging sign is that there is a great deal more public awareness of the needs of families, more coverage of the subject in the newspapers and other parts of the media, and more public debate.

Readers of *The Family Welcome Guide* can help the cause of all families by asking for the facilities which they consider essential to their comfort and that of their families. If facilities which have been advertised by any 'family' establishment are absent, you should protest, politely but firmly, and ask that they be provided. But please make your point at the time; don't be typically British, put up with things and then complain later. Do something about it on the spot.

We mentioned earlier that our aim is to be as comprehensive as possible – within the limitations of the high standards we try to maintain. Apart from nearly 200 pubs and restaurants, we list around 150 hotels which vary from farmhouses with just a few rooms to grand seaside hotels. In addition, we recommend around 50 self-catering establishments. That is why we use the word comprehensive with justification.

THE ENTRIES

We try to present the information in the simplest form, without any of those confusing codes or symbols.

Name of the town or village, and its county or region.

Name of the establishment, and whether we recommend it as a self-catering place ⒮Ⓒ, an hotel Ⓗ, a pub Ⓟ, a restaurant Ⓡ, or a place in the leisure category Ⓛ. Sometimes establishments are entered in several categories.

Directions.

Description: we try to give you an impression of what the place is like and why we have included it and we summarise its facilities.

Food: we give you the serving times, and an idea of the price range and (if possible) type of food on offer. For restaurant meals (as opposed to bar snacks) we quote the price of a three-course meal and again an extract from a typical menu. Since prices are hard to forecast we have quoted to the nearest £, and have rounded figures upward. We tell you if special menus or smaller portions are available for children.

Credit Cards: we list the four major cards: Access, American Express, Diners Club and Visa.

Opening and closing times: except for pubs which, with rare exceptions, are open every day of the year. Pubs can remain open throughout the day, and when they do, we tell you in our report. Ale means real ale and we name the brands available.

Hotel information includes:

Price of rooms: we give two sets of information; first the lowest price for bed and breakfast for two people for one night, graded thus:

£ low = up to £40

£ medium = from £41 to £60

£ high = over £60

Best Bargain Break: every hotel offers bargain breaks, especially at weekends, and we have given these prices when they are available. There are great advantages in hunting these breaks out, since they really are bargains, especially out of season.

Children: we give you the terms for children and these are always on the basis that a child is sharing a room with its parents.

Facilities: we tell you how many cots and high chairs are available, and to what extent a baby listening service is offered.

Number of rooms: we give the total number of rooms in hotels, and the number of family rooms (i.e. which can sleep at least three people). We also mention suites, and interconnecting rooms. Apart from these, most hotels have other rooms which will take cots and/or extra beds.

We thank all those people who wrote in to us with recommendations and with comments about places already in the guide. These are invaluable; and we take your comments very seriously. Many establishments have been excluded, and many added, as a result. Please keep writing to us (the forms are at the back of the book).

West of England

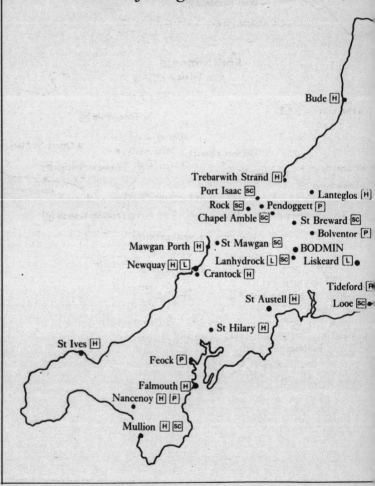

West of England

Bude [H]

Trebarwith Strand [H]

Port Isaac [SC]　　　　　　　　　　• Lanteglos [H]

Rock [SC]　• Pendoggett [P]

Chapel Amble [SC]　　　• St Breward [SC]

　　　　　　　　　• Bolventor [P]

Mawgan Porth [H]　• St Mawgan [SC]

Newquay [H] [L]　　　BODMIN

　　　Lanhydrock [L] [SC]　Liskeard [L]

Crantock [H]

　　　　　　　　　　　Tideford [P]

St Austell [H]　　　　Looe [SC]

• St Hilary [H]

St Ives [H]

Feock [P]

Falmouth [H]

Nancenoy [H] [P]

Mullion [H] [SC]

Ilfracombe [H]
Berrynarbor [P]
Woolacombe [H] [SC]
Saunton [H] [SC]
Barnstaple [L]
West Buckland [H]
South Molton [SC]
West Anstey [H]

King's Nympton [SC]
Tiverton [R] [L]
Cullompton [H]
Holsworthy [H] [SC]
Thorverton [SC]
Broadclyst [L]
Drewsteignton [L]
Whimple [P]
Ottery St Mary [H]
Bridestowe [H]
Chagford [H]
Exeter [L]
Colaton Raleigh [SC]
Launceston [SC]
Branscombe [H]
Lustleigh [P]
Widecombe-in-the-Moor [P]
Dawlish Warren [H]
Dawlish [H]
Holne [R]
Kingsteignton [P]
Buckfastleigh [L]
Torbryan [P]
Dartington [R]
Totnes [R]
Torquay [H]
PLYMOUTH [L]
Stoke Gabriel [H]
Mothecombe [SC]
Dartmouth [H]
Cawsand [H]
Churchstow [P]
East Allington [SC]
Bantham [H] [P] [SC]
Thurlestone [H]
Hope Cove [H]
East Portlemouth [H] [SC]

BANTHAM, DEVON
H P SC SLOOP INN, Bantham
Tel: 0548 560 489.
West of Kingsbridge off the A379/B3197.

Bantham is a pretty village in one of the loveliest parts of south Devon and the Sloop Inn fits in well, a 16th-century building which was once owned by a notorious smuggler and wrecker called John Widdon. It is a spacious pub with a separate family room where adults and children can eat and drink together and, on warmer days, you can head for the patio at the rear of the pub. Food is available every day and includes a good choice of local fish; there is a choice of real ale too, including Bass.

There are two family bedrooms, which have their own bathrooms, and include a double and a single bed.

Nearby: There is an excellent stretch of sandy beach a few hundred yards from the inn, which is patrolled by lifeguards during the summer because of the currents, but is safe as long as the warning notices are heeded. It is also a marvellous beach for surfing and there are other pleasant beaches, including Thurlestone, nearby. If you prefer dry land, the south Devon coast path goes from Bantham towards Hope Cove and offers a walk with some spectacular views. There are two golf courses, at Bigbury and Thurlestone, and there is plenty of sea and river fishing to be had, plus water sports of all kinds. There are many other attractions within reach: the National Shire Horse Centre and the Dartmoor Wildlife Park, the Torbay Aircraft Museum, Buckfast Abbey and the Dart Valley Railway.

✕ (12 to 2pm & 7 to 10pm) £2–9: local smoked salmon, plaice & chips, steaks, fresh crab salad, grilled lamb steak
Children: half portions
£ medium
Children: cot £2; half price thereafter up to 11 years
Facilities: 3 cots and 2 high chairs
5 rooms, 2 family
Open all year
P own car park
⊕ Ale: Bass, Usher's
Self-catering: There are three flats at the back of the pub. They

each have two bedrooms, a double and a twin; a sofa bed can also be used. The flats are equipped to a high standard with fridge/freezers, microwave ovens, dishwashers and utility rooms with washing machines and driers. Central heating is provided. There are lovely views of the bay and of Burgh Island.

The rents range from £190 to £560 a week; short breaks are available.

NR BARNSTAPLE, DEVON
Ⓛ ARLINGTON COURT, Shirwell
Tel: 0271 850 296.
On the A39, about 7 miles north-east of Barnstaple.

The Chichester family owned Arlington for over 500 years and the present house was built in 1820. It is pleasant enough, though not especially distinguished, and Arlington is notable mainly for other things.

The park and gardens are beautiful, and as you drive along the perimeter you will see masses of rhododendrons. Inside, there are peacocks, Shetland ponies and Jacob's sheep. It's a lovely place to relax.

The interior of the house is interesting because of the many collections made by the last owner, Rosalie Chichester, who left the house to the National Trust in 1949: paintings, porcelain, model ships (including one of Sir Francis Chichester's boat, *Gipsy Moth*) and pewter.

The walk to the church is delightful and the stables nearby have a superb collection of horse-drawn carriages: broughams, gigs, victorias and so on.

The restaurant, once the house kitchen, is light and bright and looks on to the lawns. There are two high chairs here and small portions of most meals can be made up for children. Hot and cold dishes are available from £1 to £5. Alongside, there is also a snack bar.

Open: 1 April to 31 October, 11am–5.30pm. Closed on Saturdays (except bank holidays)
Charges: adults £4.60; children £2.30

Baby changing: a shelf in the Ladies by the restaurant
Ⓟ ample

BERRYNARBOR, NR ILFRACOMBE, DEVON
Ⓟ YE OLDE GLOBE, Berrynarbor
Tel: 0271 882 465.
Off the A399 east of Ilfracombe.

This is a picturesque village of stone cottages, brightly decorated
with flowers, which has a handsome church, St Peter's. The pub
has been here since 1675 and was probably converted from a row
of cottages of an even earlier vintage. It now has pink-washed walls,
and the various rooms, which run off the bar, are packed with
antiques and curios – horse brasses and tackle, copper flasks, cases
of miniatures, etc. The beamed ceilings and timbered walls testify
to the age of the building, and there is a surprising amount of room
inside.

The family room is very large, with French windows at one end
which open on to the garden. There are plenty of wooden tables
and wheel-back chairs, a Wendy House, toys for younger children
and books and puzzles for older ones. There is an alternative,
smaller family room which has an open fireplace and a couple
of wooden tables. A couple of Christmases ago, we spent several
enjoyable lunchtimes here: the beer was excellent and the food of
good quality and generously served.

There is a small terrace at the front of the pub and, to the rear, a fairly large, enclosed garden with many bench tables on the lawn. A marvellous array of flowers greets your eyes: dahlias, fuchsias, sweet peas, petunias and many others. We were not surprised to learn that the pub has won its brewery's 'best kept garden' award.

✗ (12 to 2pm & 7 to 10pm) £1–10: spaghetti Bolognese, Cornish pasty, plaice & chips, steaks, lasagne, pizzas
Children: own menu, half portions
◲ Ale: Courage Directors, Usher's
Ⓟ limited, but large public car park nearby

NR BODMIN, CORNWALL
Ⓛ LANHYDROCK, Bodmin.
Tel: 0208 74281.
South of Bodmin on the B3268.

This magnificent house is one of the jewels in the National Trust's Cornish crown. Originally built in the 17th century, much of it was rebuilt by Lord Robartes in the 19th century after a fire. He adopted the florid, almost Gothic style of the time and added splendid mullioned windows. There are 36 rooms to see, the most notable being the gallery, which dates from the 17th century. It has a marvellous plaster ceiling with panels which illustrate Old Testament scenes such as the Creation.

This is primarily a place for adults and older children to appreciate but the huge expanse of formal gardens and park land is a great treat on a summer day. There is a lovely walk from the gatehouse through the woods down to the River Fowey.

Three places provide food and drink: the Stables Café offers drinks and snacks; the Servants' Hall does lunches from noon to 2pm (hot meals, such as lamb and tarragon casserole, from £2 to £6) and teas from 3pm; and the Housekeeper's Room does lunches and teas also. High chairs are available.

Open: 1 April to 31 October, 11am to 5.30pm. The house is closed on Monday, except bank holidays
Charges: adults £5; children £2.50

Baby changing: mother and baby room in the rear courtyard
P ample

BOLVENTOR, CORNWALL
P JAMAICA INN, Pipers Pool
Tel: 0566 86250.
On the A30 north of Bodmin.

Pop in to see this famous inn on rolling Bodmin Moor because it
was the setting for Daphne du Maurier's tale of villainy and
derring-do. She is commemorated with a special room here. The
inn was once owned by the thriller writer, Alistair MacLean.

If you are travelling down this busy main road in the summer
you will find food available here from just after 9am until about
10.30pm, and there are high chairs in the restaurant area. Children
are welcome there – and in the family room which also contains
the Joss Merlyn museum.

There is a large garden and the children's play area at the back
of the pub has swings, a slide, a climbing frame, etc. There are
also plenty of bench seats here. The Potter's Museum of Curiosity
is an added attraction.

✗ (9.30am to 10pm; until 9pm in winter) £1–11: smoked
mackerel, chicken Kiev, salmon steak, sirloin steak, roast duck
Children: own menu, half portions
⟁ Ale: Flowers and Guests
P own car park

BRANSCOMBE, NR SEATON, DEVON
H THE BULSTONE, Higher Bulstone
Tel: 029 780 446.
Off the A3052. Turn at the junction called Branscombe Cross.
It is signposted to Bulstone.

We continue to receive highly favourable reports of this hotel, which
is run specifically for families by the charming and indefatigable
Mr and Mrs Freeman. When we called in at the tail end of the
season a year or two ago, the hotel looked in pristine condition.

The hotel has been extended and the new stone walls fit in very well with the rest of the building, part of which dates back to the 16th century. The delightful sitting room with its fine fireplace testifies to the age of the original building – this is the only room which is for adults only.

The children have a large play room of their own and it is very well provided with toys and games including a very snazzy (and robust) lego table. The garden has loads of space for children to play and they can help to look after the chickens, the cats and Barney the rabbit. A large grassy play area contains slides, climbing frames, a sandpit, a football net, and a tree house; the nature garden, in the paddock and part of the orchard, is now established. This is a long-term project to attract the local wildlife into the grounds.

There is a pleasant conservatory in which to sit and parents on holiday will be glad of the laundry room and the well-equipped kitchen in which they can prepare drinks or snacks. Glad, too, of the way the family rooms are designed with separate bedrooms for the children.

Everything at this hotel is geared to the needs of families on holiday and this includes the provision of a cot for every room in the hotel and as many high chairs as could be required. It's a superb family hotel, which offers remarkable value, and makes you realize how poorly equipped are most other hotels to cope with the needs of families.

The food here is always made from fresh, local produce; and artificial flavourings and colourings are avoided. The children have their high teas between 4.45 and 5.30pm, so that the adults can enjoy their meals together later.

Nearby: The sea is very close with pleasant beaches, although some have pebbles underfoot. There is, however, a sandy beach at Sidmouth. It is a delightful part of the world with many benefits for holiday makers: the Donkey Sanctuary near Sidmouth, the Farway Country Park, Bicton Park, Killerton House, the nature reserve at Dawlish Warren, Castle Drogo, Powderham Castle, Pecorama and Crealy Working Farm are all an easy drive away.

✕ DINNER (7.45–8.45pm) £16: cheese & onion tartlet, paprika chicken, pudding and cheese
Children: own menu
£ medium

Best Bargain Break: £62 per person, 2 nights – dinner, b&b
Children: free up to 5 years, 50 per cent of adult rate from 5
to 12
Facilities: 15 cots and 8 high chairs; a baby listening system
12 rooms, all family
Closed mid-Nov to mid-Feb. No music
No credit cards accepted
No smoking in whole house, except lounge
⊿ Ale: Newquay Steam
ℙ own car park

BRIDESTOWE, NR OKEHAMPTON, DEVON
Ⓗ KNOLE FARM, Bridestowe
Tel: 0837 86241.
Off the A30 south-west of Okehampton.

The farmhouse, built as a gentleman's residence in the late 19th
century, is full of character with its attractive stone facade and
rambling design. The gardens are very appealing: in front there is
a large oval lawn surrounded by tall trees, and the rear garden,
grassy and well-maintained, also has lots of space where children
can play. You look out to the moors where there are plenty of
marked footpaths, and guests are welcome to walk the eighty-odd
acres of the farm.

You will receive a warm welcome from the Bickle family, and
traditional home cooking with fresh local produce is served in generous portions.

The comfortable lounge, which has a wood-burning stove, and the
dining room overlook the garden. The four bedrooms share a bathroom and include a family room, two doubles and a single. They are
attractively furnished and have lovely views of the countryside.

Knole Farm offers very reasonably priced accommodation in a
lovely part of Devon.

Nearby: This is an ideal base from which to explore Devon and
Dartmoor stretches away to the south and east of the farm in all
its splendour. There are delightful villages to see and many pubs
which welcome all the family. There are some excellent walks, good
fishing and golf, water sports, horse and pony riding, and much

else besides: Lydford Gorge, Becky Falls with its nature trail, the Parke Rare Breeds Farm and the remarkable Castle Drogo. Morwellham Quay is also a reasonable drive away.

� DINNER (6.30pm) £7
Children: half portions
£ low
Children: cot free; thereafter variable according to age.
Facilities: 1 cot and 1 high chair; and baby listening by arrangement
4 rooms, 1 family
Open Easter to November. No music
No credit cards. Unlicensed
🅿 own car park

BROADCLYST, NR EXETER, DEVON
🅛 KILLERTON HOUSE, Broadclyst
Tel: 0392 881 345.
Off the A396 north of Exeter.

The house, built in the late 18th century, was the home of the Acland family until it was given to the National Trust in 1944. It is an unremarkable building, but it houses a notable collection of 18th- and 19th-century costumes which were left to the Trust by Paulise de Bush. There are over 5000 items in the collection which are rotated on an annual basis. When we visited, the theme of the costume displays was family occasions.

The other notable feature of Killerton is the magnificent gardens and parkland – a delightful spot to wander.

The restaurant has several high chairs and smaller portions of the various dishes can be made available for children. The food ranges in price from £1 to £5 and includes salads, hot dishes of the day (including a vegetarian dish), quiches, etc.

Open 1 April to end of October, 11am to 5.30pm. Closed on Tuesday
Charges: adults £4.60; children £2.30 (1993 prices)
Baby changing: table and chair in the Ladies
🅿 ample

BUCKFASTLEIGH, DEVON

Ⓛ BUCKFAST ABBEY, Buckfastleigh

Tel: 0364 42519.

Just off the A38 between Exeter and Plymouth.

This Benedictine monastery was originally founded early in the 11th century but foundered after Henry VIII's dissolution of the monasteries in 1539. Several monks took it upon themselves to rebuild it and started work in 1907. They finished in 1938.

The building is a monument to their devotion and some of its notable features are the mosaic floors, the stained glass windows and the remarkable high altar. In the crypt, there is an exhibition which traces the history of the Abbey, and there are concerts every month.

Families are well catered for, especially in the new restaurant, the Grange. The self-service area is bright and airy under a high dome, and all the food is freshly made on the spot. The dining room is also spacious and appealing, with its high, curved ceiling and a glass wall and doors to a delightful stone terrace, where there are plenty of bench tables. Whether indoors or outdoors, you will have splendid views of the gardens and of the great Abbey itself. There is a wide range of snacks, cakes and sandwiches and the hot dishes of the day (lamb casserole, turkey pie and vegetable lasagne, for example) cost around £4.

The mother aand baby room, close to the entrance, is well equipped with tables, a couch, a chair and a wash basin.

Open: the Abbey church is open throughout the year, as are the restaurant and shops, 9am to 5.30pm (winter 10am to 4pm).
Exhibition open Easter to end of October.
Charges: £1 cars. Exhibition: adults 75p, children: first two free, then 30p
Baby changing: mother and baby room
Ⓟ plenty

BUDE, CORNWALL
Ⓗ CLIFF HOTEL, Bude
Tel: 0288 353 110.
Near Crooklets Beach, which is well signposted.

This small and unpretentious family hotel is situated at the top of a cul-de-sac in five acres of grounds. It is very safe for children and offers good facilities. A sandy beach lies only two hundred yards away; the golf course is about the same distance away.

The garden has extensive lawns, paddocks and a special play area for children with swings, slides, a seesaw and a sandpit. For adults and older children, there is a hard tennis court and a putting green. Everyone can enjoy the sizeable indoor swimming pool. There is also a spa bath in a separate building, darts and a pool table in the games room. Alternatively, you can just relax in a comfortable chair on the patio.

The hotel has several public rooms: a bar, a lounge, a separate wine bar and a sun lounge cum writing room, which has fine views of the cliff top and the sea. The food is freshly cooked and will always include a good choice of fish, and the roast of the day will be carved for you at your table.

This is a very friendly seaside hotel in a pleasant setting, and the owner can offer very special discounts to families in the off-season periods: April to the middle of May, but not Easter, and mid-September to October. Give Mr Sibley a call.

Nearby: Bude is well known as a surfing resort. There are other excellent beaches nearby including Sandy Mouth, Widemouth Sand and Crackington Haven. Further afield you can visit the Tamar Otter Park near Launceston, which has a famous castle, and nearby is the starting point for the Launceston Steam Railway.

✕ DINNER (6.30pm) £6: home-made soup, roast beef, profiteroles
Children: own menu, half portions
£ low
Children: cots from £3 a day, 25 per cent reduction up to 12 years
Facilities: 3 cots and 3 high chairs
15 rooms, 14 family, 1 set interconnecting
Open Easter to October. No credit cards
Ⓟ own car park

CAWSAND, CORNWALL
Ⓗ WRINGFORD DOWN, Cawsand
Tel: 0752 822 287.
From the B3247 south of Torpoint, follow the signs for Cawsand.
The hotel's brochure gives detailed directions.

Wringford Down is a rare hotel for Britain in that its owners, Harvey and Andrea Jay, provide only for families; even rarer, their hotel best suits families with children up to about six years of age. Needless to say there are plenty of cots and high chairs and an efficient baby listening service. The children all sit down to high tea at 5 o'clock (their meals are pre-ordered at breakfast). It was a remarkable sight to see nearly thirty young children, aged from one to five, with their parents in attendance, all seated at one long table and tucking into their nosh.

This unusual hotel is housed in a nice old stone house, the main part of which is 18th century, and has been extended over the years. The facilities include a small bar, a pool table in an adjoining room, and a restaurant. There is a spacious lounge, which has a TV and a video, and a playroom alongside; there are plenty of toys and games and blackboards on which the children can scribble. A very large conservatory has been built next to the dining room, a pleasant place to snatch some moments of relaxation with a drink or a book.

The enterprising owners provide loads of amusements both indoors and out for children. There is a huge play barn which would keep the children amused for days. It has some rabbits, a huge and very practical padded playpen, a sandpit, a trampoline and climbing ropes on a special safety surface, ride-on toys, table tennis, a collection of BMX bikes, which can be used on the paths outside, and roller skates.

Move outdoors and you can enjoy a large garden with lovely views over the surrounding countryside with a church spire on the horizon. There is a children's play area plus chickens, goats, pigs, angora rabbits and sheep for them to make friends with. Donkey rides are also organized. An indoor heated swimming pool and a paddling pool have been added to the facilities and were packed with children when we visited. There is also a hard tennis court.

On a practical level, a refrigerator is provided for guests, plus a microwave oven, bottle sterilizers, etc.

This hotel has splendid facilities for young families and if you fancy a gregarious holiday during which you can muck in with lots of other parents with young children in a 'family friendly' atmosphere, you should visit Wringford Down.

Nearby: There are many sandy and safe beaches and many other attractions within easy reach: Mount Edgcumbe Country Park is just up the road; there is a monkey sanctuary near Looe, the Shire Horse Centre east of Plymouth and Dartmoor Wildlife Park; Morwellham Quay, Cotehele House, Dobwalls Theme Park, Lanhydrock, and Restormel Castle.

✗ DINNER (7pm): crab salad, steak & mushroom pie, apple pie & cream
Children: high teas, small portions
£ low
Bargain Breaks: available in spring and autumn
Children: free
Facilities: 20 cots and 20 high chairs; baby listening system to every room
12 rooms, all family, 6 sets interconnecting
Open all year except Christmas
P own car park

CHAGFORD, DEVON
H MILL END HOTEL, Chagford
Tel: 0647 432 282.
On the A382 – not in Chagford itself.

This lovely hotel was once a flour mill and the wheel still turns in the courtyard. You are well shielded by walls in the gardens, and it is very peaceful in the back garden, shaded by enormous trees.

Children are accommodated free to a ripe old age. Indeed, a third person sharing a room with two others does not pay extra – an enlightened policy which more British hoteliers ought to follow.

The charming and hospitable owners now welcome children of all ages into the restaurant in the evenings, provided that reasonable standards of behaviour are met. High teas are still available at 6pm.

It's a lovely part of the country – on the edge of Dartmoor – and

Evelyn Waugh wrote *Brideshead Revisited* while staying in the village in 1944.

Nearby: Fishermen are well catered for here. They can fish for salmon and trout in the Upper Teign River which flows past the hotel, and also in some nearby reservoirs. Further stretches of the river are also available. There is a golf course about five miles away, and this is a lovely part of the world for walking and riding. The remarkable Castle Drogo is next door and you can quickly reach Killerton House, Powderham Castle, Becky Falls, Parke Rare Breeds Farm and the nature reserve at Dawlish Warren.

✗ LIGHT LUNCH (12–1.45pm) £2–9: soup, ploughman's, salads;
DINNER (7.30–9pm) £25: bouillabaise, lamb tagine, pudding, cheese
Children: high teas, half portions
£ high
Best Bargain Break: £114 per person, 2 nights – dinner, b & b
Children: free to any age
Facilities: 3 cots and 2 high chairs; a baby listening system to all rooms
17 rooms, 2 family.
Open all year except mid-December and mid-January
Access/AmEx/Diners/Visa. No music
⊞ Ale: Wadworth's
℗ own car park

CHAPEL AMBLE, NR WADEBRIDGE, CORNWALL
SC THE OLDE HOUSE, Chapel Amble
Tel: 0208 813 219.
The village is off the B3314 north of Wadebridge and The Old House is close to the village pub, the Maltsters Arms.

There are 30 cottages from which to choose at this enterprising holiday centre and farm. It all began in 1978 when Andrew and Janice Hawkey converted a couple of their old farm buildings and the venture has grown every year. The latest additions to the list were five new cottages, finished in 1989, but made of Cornish stone and with slate roofs.

The other cottages are all built from the old stone outbuildings and every effort has been made to insert all the comforts which families on holiday require while retaining the character of the buildings. They mostly accommodate four to six people, although Wheel cottage sleeps only two and three other cottages can take up to eight.

The cottages have been made from a barn, a mill, a stable and a cow house and grain store, but they have one thing in common: they have been converted with style and good taste, and are well-furnished and well-equipped. (It is also noticeable that most of the houses have their own gardens – a valuable asset for families).

One of the great advantages of staying here is the presence of an excellent, purpose-built leisure centre. Under its vaulted roof, it has a sizeable swimming pool, a children's pool, jacuzzi, sauna and solarium. It has its own lounge area with a snooker table. Outside, there is a splendid adventure playground, swings and a climbing frame, a fort, Wendy house and an old tractor. There is also an all-weather tennis court.

The Olde House is at the centre of a working farm of 500 acres and the guests are welcome to join in; and the farm animals are particularly appealing to the children. This is a marvellous place for a family holiday.

Nearby: there is no shortage of safe and sandy beaches in the area, and Damer and Polmeath offer surfing and swimming, while Rock has sailing, wind surfing and water skiing. You can follow the coastal footpath and there are plenty of stables from which to go riding. Fishermen and golfers are well catered for. If you like to see the sights you can head for Pencarrow House, Lanhydrock House, Dobwalls Theme Park, Trerice and the Lappa Valley Railway. The children will enjoy a visit to Newquay Zoo and the Tropical Bird Gardens at Padstow.

Units: 30

Rent: £120 to £759 a week

Other costs: linen at £2.50 a person; electricity is on a meter

Heating: central heating

As many cots & high chairs as required

Open all year

CHURCHSTOW, DEVON
P CHURCH HOUSE, Churchstow
Tel: 0548 852 237.
On the A379 west of Kingsbridge.

This building was a rest home for Benedictine monks in the 13th century. It was renovated in the 16th century and its basic structure remains to this day.

The delightful bar is long and narrow, with a large inglenook fireplace, black wooden beams holding the ceiling up and a number of wooden settles. There are two alcove rooms at one end of the bar.

The new family room is a stylish conservatory, a very pleasant place to sit. There is loads of space, a tiled floor and marble topped tables. The landlord asks that children be properly supervised – and so say all of us. Two high chairs are available.

The large terrace at the side of the pub is well provided with bench tables and sun umbrellas, and is bright with trailing flowers and greenery. When we called in last summer it was packed with families enjoying their food and drink together.

You will always find some food on the go including a carvery at Sunday lunchtimes at around £6 for two courses, which is also in operation from Wednesday to Saturday in the evening.

✗ (12–1.30pm & 6.30–9pm) £1–7: whitebait, fish pie, devilled chicken, mixed grill, rump steak
Children: smaller portions
🍺 Ale: Bass, Dartmoor. No music
P own car park

COLATON RALEIGH, NR SIDMOUTH, DEVON
SC DRUPE FARM, Colaton Raleigh
Tel: 0395 68838.
On the B3178 west of Sidmouth.

The conversion of old farm buildings (some dating back to the 16th century) was carried out in the late seventies with great success. The smart cottages, some built from the local pink-tinged stone and others painted white, form a natural courtyard around a lawned garden with lots of cheerful flowers and shrubs.

Drupe Farm is just off the main street of the attractive village and the shops and a smart-looking pub (The Otter) are within a short stroll.

Most of the fourteen properties sleep up to four people, while two can sleep six and two others can sleep up to seven people. There are plenty of high chairs and cots available. The properties have plenty of space and they are comfortably and unfussily furnished. Many of them, such as Bulverton Cottage, have open-plan living areas. We noticed how the old beams of the original buildings had been retained and used to good effect. One of the great bonuses of staying at Drupe Farm is the lovely view from the cottages.

The facilities here are excellent and include a laundry, a very well-equipped games room with table football, table tennis, a pool table, a dart board and some amusement machines; and a very safe and well-kept play area with swings, a seesaw, wooden climbing frames, a sandpit, and an old tractor on which children can play. Bats and balls are also provided. There are bench tables here and a barbecue; it's a lovely spot to have an *al fresco* meal while the children amuse themselves.

One of the cottages overlooks the picnic cum play area and its semi-circular living room is an unusual and charming conversion. With fourteen properties to look after, refurbishment is a continual process here and the manager told us that a complete programme of renovation will be finished by the beginning of next year.

Nearby: East Devon is a beautiful part of the country and Drupe Farm sits in an area of outstanding natural beauty. The countryside offers much to walkers, or you can enjoy it all from horseback. Fishermen have a good choice of river or sea fishing and there are golf courses within a few miles. There are many beaches including Budleigh Salterton, Sidmouth and Branscombe with attendant water sports. There are plenty of interesting places to see: Bicton Park, the donkey sanctuary near Sidmouth, the Farway Park, the Maritime Museum in Exeter, Killerton House, Powderham Castle and the nature reserve at Dawlish Warren.

Units: 12 cottages, 2 apartments
Rent: £133 to £412 a week (short breaks also available in winter)
Other costs: none
Heating: gas central heating

7 cots and 5 high chairs (stairgates also provided)
Open all year

CRANTOCK, NEWQUAY, CORNWALL
Ⓗ CRANTOCK BAY HOTEL (Minotels), Crantock
Tel: 0637 830 229.
Off the A3075 south of Newquay.

The hotel is along the road from Crantock and is probably in West
Pentire. But no matter: suffice to say that the hotel has one of the
best coastal positions we have seen. Its long grassy gardens, complete with hedges forming wind breaks and suntraps, slope down
towards the sea and afford you a magnificent view of the lovely
Crantock Bay – a good place to swim and loll, but you must be
careful at low tide (obey the signs). It is patrolled by Life Guards
during the summer; and is a great spot for surfers too.

The hotel is very much geared up to family holidays with plenty
of facilities to keep young and older occupied. The children have
an activity area with a very substantial wooden fort, swings and
climbing frames; there is a hard tennis court, and croquet and
putting on the lawns.

The excellent indoor swimming pool (plus paddling pool for
young children) is enclosed by a curved glass roof and outside there
is a sun terrace. The exercise room has some serious equipment,
including a static bicycle, jogging machine and multi-gym, and
you can recover on the sun terrace, in the sauna or in the spa
bath.

In the field alongside the hotel there are donkeys, pigs and
chickens which belong to the hotel and it is pleasing to report that
the owners grow a lot of their own vegetables (as well as providing
their own free-range eggs). Children are encouraged to eat smaller
versions of the adults' food – mini-dinners are served at 5pm.

Many of the rooms have fine views of the bay and beach, and
some of the ground floor rooms lead directly out to the gardens.

This is a delightful place and the prices charged are very reasonable indeed; the hotel represents outstanding value for families on
holiday.

Nearby: As well as Crantock Bay there are many good beaches for swimmers, surfers and deckchair huggers. There are many attractions around Newquay including the zoo, the Lappa Valley Railway, Dairyland Farm Park, St Agnes Leisure Park and the beautiful Elizabethan house of Trerice.

✗ LUNCH (12–2pm) £1–3: soup, cold buffet
DINNER (7–8pm) £14: salad Nicoise, soup, poached hake, pudding or cheese
Children: own menu
£ medium
Best Bargain Break: £75 per person – 2 nights, dinner, b&b (winter weekends)
Children: free up to 2 years; one third of adult rate from 2–5 years; half from 6–8 years; three quarters from 9–12 years
Facilities: many cots and high chairs, baby listening
35 rooms, 6 family. Closed end Nov to mid-March
Access/AmEx/Diners/Visa
No smoking in the dining room and garden lounge
Ⓟ own car park

NR CULLOMPTON, DEVON
Ⓗ WISHAY FARM, Trinity
Tel: 0884 33223.
On minor roads near Cullompton. The farm's brochure has excellent directions.

You will find peace and quiet in abundance at this long and well-proportioned 17th-century farmhouse. It is surrounded by rolling countryside, and there is a spacious lawn at the front of the house. The children can play happily here, and there is a swing and a slide for them to use.

Inside you will find sizeable, attractive rooms with wooden-shuttered windows. The sitting room is very comfortable and relaxing, with a large stone fireplace with alcoves at each side, and windows looking on to the garden. Each of the family rooms, which have plenty of space and are very nicely furnished, has a double and two single beds, and one of them has an en suite bathroom. The other has a separate bathroom which is shared with the one single room.

The owners also have a play room at the rear of the house and it is packed with toys and games. If the weather turns nasty the children will have plenty to occupy their day. Not that there is any lack of diversions in this part of the world.

Nearby: Bickleigh Mill and Bickleigh Castle are very close, as is Knightshayes Court and Killerton House. Also within easy reach are the Donkey Sanctuary near Sidmouth, Farway Countryside Park, Bicton Park, Powderham Castle, and Exeter's many museums. A whole line of excellent beaches stretches south to Torquay and includes Dawlish Warren, where there is a splendid nature reserve.

✗ DINNER (6.30pm) £8
Children: half portions
£ low
Children: cot £2; half price thereafter
Facilities: 1 cot, 1 high chair
3 rooms, 2 family. Open February to November
No credit cards. No music
🅿 ample. Unlicensed

DARTINGTON, DEVON
Ⓡ CRANKS HEALTH FOOD RESTAURANT,
Shinners Bridge
Tel: 0803 862 388.
Look out for the Cider Press sign on the A384.

Within this very interesting crafts centre you will find a Cranks self-service restaurant, one of the first of the chain of vegetarian restaurants, and it offers a good array of fresh and healthy vegetarian dishes, salads, quiches, fresh orange juice, homemade lemonade, and many other good things. There are many shops in which to browse – Dartington glass, farm food, pottery, clothes, toys, etc., and there is, of course, an old cider press.

There are plenty of grassy areas, with bench tables and shady trees – a pleasant spot to have a picnic.

There is a pull-down shelf for baby changing in the Ladies in the Cider Press Room.

✕ £1–4: baked potato, mixed salads, pizzas and quiches, cauliflower croustade
Children: small portions
Open 10am to 5pm Mon to Sat (and on Sundays during summer)
No credit cards accepted. Open all year
Ⓟ in the complex. Licensed

NR DARTMOUTH, DEVON
Ⓗ STOKE LODGE HOTEL, Stoke Fleming
Tel: 0803 770 523
Just off the A379 south of Dartmouth.

A cream-painted Georgian building, with some later additions, bay windows on the ground floor and a portico entrance. One of its many agreeable features is the large raised sun terrace with views across the gardens to the pretty village of Stoke Fleming, with its fine old church, and beyond to the sea.

The hotel has excellent facilities for families. Three acres of attractive gardens include a pond (once the village pond) where ducks gather, a top quality all-weather tennis court, a heated swimming pool and giant chess and draughts boards. Indoors you will find another swimming pool, a jacuzzi, a fitness room and a games room with table tennis, darts and a pool table.

There is an abiding impression of space at Stoke Lodge. A long and comfortable lounge, with a bar, overlooks the terrace and the gardens and there is another well-furnished lounge with lots of easy chairs, books on the shelves and a good selection of boxed games. The dining room, decorated in a dashing shade of pink, has wide windows on to the gardens.

The bedrooms are furnished and decorated to an excellent standard and include spacious family rooms with delightful views.

The hotel has everything a family needs for a relaxing stay in comfortable surroundings.

Nearby: There is a great selection of sandy beaches and bays, and the area offers all kinds of water sports, horse riding, fishing, golf, and many attractions, the National Shire Horse Centre, Dartmoor Wildlife Park and the Parke Rare Breeds Farm among them. You can also visit Buckfast Abbey and the Buckfast Steam Railway, Compton Castle, Morwellham Quay, the nature reserve at Dawlish Warren and of course the beauties of Dartmoor.

✗ LUNCH (12–2pm) £9: savoury peach & pineapple, liver and bacon, pudding or cheese
DINNER (7–9pm) £16: soup, goujons of plaice, rump steak chasseur, sherry trifle
Children: half portions
£ high
Best Bargain Break: £80 per person – 2 nights. dinner, b&b
Children: free up to 2 years; 25 per cent from 2 to 5; 50 per cent from 5 to 14; 75 per cent thereafter
Facilities: 4 cots and 4 high chairs; baby listening system
24 rooms, 4 family. Open all year
Access/Visa. No music
ℙ own car park

DAWLISH, DEVON
Ⓗ RADFORDS COUNTRY HOTEL, Lower Dawlish
Water
Tel: 0626 863 322.
In the countryside near Dawlish – the hotel provides an excellent
map.

This hotel, at the heart of which is an attractive, pink-washed
thatched building, has been in *The Family Welcome Guide* since the
first edition many years ago, and we have had nothing but good
reports of it ever since. It is everything a family hotel should be,
and is aimed at parents with young children. One of our readers,
Mrs Stepney from Surrey, wrote: 'Ten out of ten for child toler-
ance. My nine-year-old daughter thought it was wonderful . . .
Excellent value.'

Every room is a family room and there are masses of cots and
high chairs available. The owners are punctilious about the way in
which their guests are cared for: the indoor pool, for example, with
its separate children's pool, is always attended by a life-guard.

Similarly, two of the staff are on duty as baby-sitters every night
from 7pm to 11.30pm and will check each child at regular intervals.
What a relief for parents who, after all, need a holiday too!

The facilities are comprehensive: a games room with a pool table,
skittles, darts, table tennis, space invaders, etc; a play area with
swings, a slide, a wooden fort, a roundabout and a climbing frame;
a playroom with a selection of toys, an outdoor badminton court;
and, of course, the indoor pool. Entertainments for the children

are organized almost every day, and they have a chance to learn horse riding.

Nearby: Guests have the advantage not only of the hotel's spacious grounds but also of the glorious countryside surrounding it. There are many sandy beaches nearby, including Dawlish Warren, which has a nature reserve adjoining it, where a huge variety of birds can be seen. Nature lovers will also be interested in the Parke Rare Breeds Farm, while the Dartmoor Wildlife Park and the Shire Horse Centre are a bit further away (near Plymouth). Other nearby attractions include Powderham Castle, Bicton Park, the remarkable cottage of A La Ronde, Compton Castle and the Dart Valley Railway – plus the busy resort of Torquay.

✗ DINNER (6–7pm): trout mousse, carbonade of beef, fresh fruit salad
Children: own menu, half portions
£ medium
Best Bargain Break: £70 per person, 2 nights – dinner, b&b
Children: from no charge to half the adult cost, depending on season
Facilities: numerous cots and high chairs; a baby listening system to each room and a baby patrol from 7pm to 11.30pm
37 rooms, all family, 11 sets interconnecting
Closed mid-Nov to Mar (open in Feb at half term)
No credit cards accepted. No smoking in dining room
Ale: Courage
Ⓟ own car park

DAWLISH WARREN, DEVON
Ⓗ LANGSTONE CLIFF HOTEL (Consort), Dawlish Warren
Tel: 0626 865 155.
Take the signs for Dawlish Warren off the A379.

This is a large and well-organized hotel which is a bit reminiscent of the better Spanish resort hotels: it has very spacious public rooms and many of the rooms have balconies which overlook the grounds of the hotel with their wide lawns and woodland.

The facilities are plentiful with an outdoor and an indoor

swimming pool, both with paddling pools, a tennis court and a play area for children in the nineteen acres of gardens. You can also play snooker, table tennis, carpet bowls or darts, and there is a golf course next door.

With dozens of high chairs and cots available and over forty family rooms (including family suites with two bedrooms), the hotel is firmly in the family market and copes with its demands with great success.

Nearby: Right next door there is the Dawlish Warren Nature Reserve, with a multitude of Brent geese; other wildfowl can be viewed from a hide. There is a host of attractions within reach: Powderham Castle, Castle Drogo, Parke Rare Breeds Farm, Compton Castle, the Dart Valley Railway and Buckfast Abbey. There are many excellent beaches on which to loll, starting with Dawlish Warren, from which dogs are banned, and those around Torquay.

✕ COFFEE SHOP (10am–7pm) £1–3: soup, cottage pie, roast of the day, beef curry & rice, plaice & chips;
DINNER (7–9pm) £14: Brixham crab, mavarin of lamb, pudding and cheese
Children: high teas, half portions
£ high
Best Bargain Break: £90–£120 per person, 2 nights – dinner, b&b
Children: free up to 6 years; half price thereafter
Facilities: 15 cots and 15 high chairs; baby listening system to every room
68 rooms, 41 family. Open all year
Access/AmEx/Diners/Visa
Ⓟ own car park.

DREWSTEIGNTON, DEVON
Ⓛ CASTLE DROGO
Tel: 0647 433 306.
Off the A30 and the A382 between Okehampton and Exeter.

This extraordinary country house was built from granite blocks between 1910 and 1930 to the design of Sir Edwin Lutyens. It was commissioned by Julius Drewe, who made a huge fortune as a partner in the Home and Colonial Stores chain. The house is perched dramatically high above the River Teign and looks like a rather sombre fortress, even though the house was built for comfort, with its own sources of electricity and its own telephone system, for example.

It is fascinating to stroll around this extremely grand country house and you will notice that there is no shortage of portraits of the Drewe family, and especially of Julius himself. Shades of William Randolph Hearst, perhaps.

The restaurant is housed in two attractive rooms, with panelled walls, and is open from 11am to 5.30pm. There are several high chairs available and a children's menu. The dishes range in price from £1 to £5 and cream teas are also served.

Open: 1 April to end of October, 11am to 5.30pm. Closed on Friday.
Charges: adults £4.60; children £2.30
Baby changing: pull-down shelf in one of the Ladies'
P ample

EAST ALLINGTON, NR TOTNES, DEVON
SC FLEAR FARM COTTAGES, East Allington
Tel: 054 852 227.
Off the A381 north of Kingsbridge.

The original stone barns of Flear Farm have been converted to form eight holiday cottages, and the rich colour of the stone, which has some of the characteristics of slate and is called shillet, is an appealing sight.

The cottages are of varying sizes; the largest (The Granary) will accommodate eight people and the smallest (called 1843) will house three. Several are grouped around an open courtyard and have skylights in the steeply pitched slate roofs and solid wooden-framed windows of varying sizes.

The various cottages have been designed to emphasize their individuality; they are spacious, light and airy and the decoration and furnishings reach a very high standard. All have gas central heating, Neff kitchens, microwave ovens, fitted carpets, wood-burning stoves, colour televisions, good pine furniture and king-size double beds; most have dishwashers. The cottages are kept in pristine condition, helped in no small part by their being let only to non-smokers.

You can be sure of peace and seclusion at Flear Farm since it lies along a narrow lane a mile or so from a small village, and the farm sits in its own wooded valley. There are thirty acres of fields and woods, which all the members of the family can enjoy. Splendid facilities are laid on, including one of the best playrooms we have ever seen. It is housed in a huge barn and has an excellent adventure playground with a safe bark surface, a big trampoline, a Wendy House and table tennis. There is masses of space and children can have many hours of enjoyment here.

In addition, there is a sizeable, well-designed, indoor swimming pool. It looks smart surrounded by its pine roof and walls and is open at all times; it has excellent changing rooms and there is a playpen in one corner. Up above the pool there is a do-it-yourself barbecue area on a partly-roofed verandah. All the necessary equipment is provided and there are several bench tables; it is a pleasant place for guests to meet during those warm summer evenings.

We were most impressed by Flear Farm. The accommodation is first class and everything has been provided to ensure a happy family holiday.

Nearby: Plenty of safe and sandy beaches can be reached easily; sailing, fishing and golf are readily available (Thurlestone has an excellent course with lovely views). The children will no doubt vote for a visit to the National Shire Horse Centre and Dartmoor Wildlife Park and there are many other attractions within easy reach: Buckfast Abbey, Compton Castle, the nature reserve at Dawlish Warren, the Maritime Museum in Exeter, Castle Drogo and Morwellham Quay.

Units: 8
Rent: £220 to £820 a week (short breaks also available)
Other costs: none
Heating: central heating
Plenty of cots and high chairs
Open all year except January

EAST PORTLEMOUTH, NR SALCOMBE, DEVON

H SC GARA ROCK HOTEL, East Portlemouth
Tel: 0548 842 342.
Take the road to the coast from the A379 at Frogmore.

The hotel was originally a row of coastguard's cottages and there are glorious views of the cliffs, the sea and the surrounding National Trust land. You can see a sandy cove down below which can be reached via a footpath. Gara rock provides the flexibility families need: there are twenty self-contained suites which accommodate up to six people (some have bunk bedrooms), and the Balcony Suite, with its spectacular views, up to nine. The hotel also has a few twin-bedded, double and single rooms. Guests can therefore choose to prepare their own meals or use the hotel's catering facilities – bar snacks and dinner are available every evening.

Great care is taken here to make life as easy as possible for parents, with plenty of cots and high chairs and a baby listening system. There is a lot for the children to do – apart from the beach, there are acres of grassy garden in which there is a heated outdoor swimming pool and paddling pool, a hard tennis court and an exceptionally good adventure playground; skittles can also be played. There are swings and a roundabout for tiny children. Inside is a games room with table tennis and table football and the hotel organizes various entertainments like the weekly Magic Show and children's party. A play group is organized for two hours a day on five days of the week for under sixes (run by a trained nanny) and there is a 'Fit Kids Club' for older children. There is a sauna, sun bed and gymnasium, and a room for teenagers, aptly called the Wreck Room.

All the family can enjoy the superb walks in this beautiful part of Devon, even though there is so much to do at the hotel that you need never leave its grounds. On a sunny summer day you can have a relaxing lunch on the lawns and the barbecue is usually in full swing. Children's suppers are available at 5.45pm.

This hotel manages to care for families extremely well and offers outstanding value for money. All sorts of extra activities are organized: swimming galas, magic shows, children's parties, and quiz nights; and a clown is in attendance at Saturday lunchtimes.

Nearby: If you fancy some sightseeing, there is much to choose from within easy reach. The children will enjoy the National Shire Horse Centre and the Dartmoor Wildlife Centre; enthusiasts will head for the Dart Valley Railway; while the Dartington Cider Press Centre has an array of craft shops and a couple of restaurants. Buckfast Abbey, the Torbay Aircraft Museum, and Compton Castle are all nearby, as is the busy resort of Torquay.

Units: 23 suites
Rent: £140–£850 a week (short breaks available)
Other costs: linen £10 per person per week
Heating: central heating
Facilities: 20 cots and 15 high chairs
Open Easter to October.

EXETER, DEVON
Ⓛ MARITIME MUSEUM, The Haven
Tel: 0392 58075.
Near the centre of the city. Follow the signs.

The museum is housed in refurbished warehouses alongside the basin of the Exeter Canal. The museum was opened in 1969 with a couple of dozen boats, and now has nearly 200 on display.

It can claim with justification to be one of the world's finest collections of boats and it is a fascinating view of the history and development of small boats: a raft, reed boats, skin and bark boats, dug-outs and, of course, plank boats of different constructions.

The boats have been collected from all around the world and include a gondola, a prahu, a Victorian cygnet, jukungs, a sheure from Bahrain, a Portuguese sardine boat, and many others with exotic names. Some bigger boats are moored in the basin and include a steam tug, a dredger designed by Brunel and a sailing lighter.

This is very much a 'hands on' museum and it is entertaining to see the hordes of children climbing in and out of many of the boats, and operating the capstan, the windlass and other equipment.

The restaurant is on the ground floor of one of the buildings and is a spacious, pleasant and cheerful room with a couple of high chairs.

It is a splendid museum which can be enjoyed by people of all ages.

Open: every day, 10am to 5pm April to September; weekends in winter 10am to 4pm (though hours may vary, so please ring to check)
Charges: adults £3.80; OAPs £2.90; children £2.20
Baby changing: minimal – table and chair in the Ladies
P own car park

FALMOUTH, CORNWALL
H ROYAL DUCHY HOTEL, Cliff Road
Tel: 0326 313042.
Near the town centre and overlooking the bay.

The hotel, which celebrated its centenary in 1993, is in a superb situation overlooking the broad sweep of Falmouth Bay. Recently renovated, the hotel is in pristine order with very appealing public rooms. The spacious L-shaped bar looks over the terrace and the gardens and has the great bonus of views out to sea, as does the elegant dining room.

We looked at several family bedrooms and were impressed by the amount of space provided. Many of the rooms have panoramic views over the bay.

The facilities at the Royal Duchy are first class. The well-designed leisure centre (for the use only of guests) has a sizeable pool, a paddling pool and a whirlpool; alongside there is a games room with table tennis, snooker and a few amusement machines.

Nearby: Leisure facilities are readily available in the locality and include golf, tennis, squash, fishing, horse riding and every type of water sport. There are many safe and sandy beaches within easy reach. The attractions are many and varied and include Trelissick Garden, Pendennis Castle, the Seal Sanctuary, Goonhilly Earth Station, Flambards Theme Park, Godolphin House and St Michael's Mount.

✕ BAR SNACKS (12.30–2pm) £2–6: kiwi mussels, chicken tikka, Cornish plaice, mixed grill, vegetable moussaka;
LUNCH (12.30–2pm) £8: seafood platter, grilled mignon steak, pudding

DINNER (7–9pm) £16: crispy fried duck & noodles, barbecued spare ribs, grilled lemon sole, pudding or cheese
Children: own menu, half portions
£ high
Best Bargain Break: £92–139 per person, 2 nights – dinner, b&b
Children: free under 2 years; £5 from 2–5; £25 from 6–11; £35 thereafter
Facilities: 6 cots and 6 high chairs, baby listening system
46 rooms, 10 family
Access/AmEx/Diners/Visa
Open all year
P: ample

FEOCK, NR TRURO, CORNWALL
P PUNCH BOWL & LADLE INN, Feock
Tel: 0872 862 237.
On the B3289 south of Truro.

A marvellous job has been done in renovating this fine old pub, which looks so smart and appealing with its white-painted walls under a thatched roof. There is masses of space inside, and it is nicely arranged in various rooms and alcoves. The wooden beams, pillars and wood panelling are very much in character and there are good wooden tables and extremely comfortable armchairs and sofas scattered about.

Families are welcome to use three alcove rooms, which are all well away from the bar. They are very attractive, with their full complements of low black beams and thick plaster walls, and all are comfortably furnished with padded bench seats and easy chairs. Outside there is a terrace with a few tables and chairs.

It's a most attractive pub which also offers a good selection of food, which is available for most of the time that the pub is open.

✕ (11.30am to 2.30pm & 6.30pm to 10pm) £2–7: smoked salmon, halibut, lamb chops, pie of the day, steak teriyaki
Children: own menu, half portions
⊟ Ale: Bass, Whitbread
P ample

HOLNE, DEVON
Ⓡ OLD FORGE, Holne
Tel: 036 43 351.
Holne is well-signposted off the A38 near Ashburton. The Old
Forge is by the church.

You will find this attractive café sitting in front of the village church.
The walls of the Old Forge are painted a crisp white and offset the
black beams on the ceiling. The bellows and anvil which were used
by the last smith, Fred Pearse, are still here.

When we called in one cold spring day, it was a pleasure to sit
by the roaring fire. Families receive a warm welcome here and food
is available throughout the day. It's almost all homemade, too, and
children have a good range of snacks from which to choose.

At the front of the old Forge in the courtyard are some bench
tables and some of these are under a pretty wooden canopy which
is hung with flowers.

The café also sells some locally made craft goods and foods.

✕ £1–4: full breakfast, quiche & salad, burgers, jacket potatoes,
cream tea
Open: 10am to 5.30pm, daily. Closed Nov to Feb
Unlicensed. No credit cards accepted
Ⓟ own car park. No music

HOLSWORTHY, DEVON
Ⓗ SC LEWORTHY FARM, Holsworthy
Tel: 0409 253 488.
Three miles south of Holsworthy on minor roads.

The farmhouse dates back to Saxon times and is a large and
comfortable home. The sizeable lounge has a huge open fireplace
and wood-burning stove, bar and pianola, and the spacious dining
room has a small snooker table. There is a separate TV room and
as an antidote plenty of books and board games are available.

Everything here is done to ensure that a family can have an
active and gregarious holiday. Most evenings during the season, for
example, there will be an entertainment – a conjuror, a barn dance,
a fancy dress competition, or a sing-song. The excellent facilities

for families include several family rooms, two of which are suites with two bedrooms.

The very large, lawned garden contains a huge fig tree, which still bears fruit, and a good-sized lake on which guests can take a boat or do some fishing; anglers can also fish in the neighbouring river.

The children have their own play areas on the lawn and in the barns – skittles, table tennis, badminton and toys are all available, and there are even two ponies which they are allowed to ride under supervision. All sorts of other activities are organized: snooker and darts; pony trekking on Dartmoor; clay pigeon shoots which are arranged by Mr Cornish; croquet, a weekly hayride, and there is a nine-hole pitch and putt course and a tennis court.

This is also a wonderful spot for nature lovers: red deer, buzzards, pheasant, herons, kingfishers and many other species can be seen.

Nearby: The sandy Cornish beaches are not far away, including those at Bude which are so popular with surfers: Sandy Mouth and Widemouth Bay are particularly good for families. A sports centre at Holsworthy has a swimming pool and many other facilities. The Tamar Otter Park may also be part of the children's holiday programme, and there are castles to see at Launceston and Tintagel, plus Hartland Quay and Clovelly. Morwellham Quay is a little further away but worth the trip.

✗ DINNER (7pm) £10: leek & potato soup, roast lamb, raspberry pavlova, cheese

Children: own menu, half portions
£ low
Children: discounts from 75 per cent to 25 per cent
Facilities: 2 cots and 2 high chairs available; and a baby listening system
10 rooms, 3 family, 2 sets interconnecting
Open all year. Access/Visa
No smoking in dining room. Licensed
P ample
Self-catering: Leeside is a self-contained stone bungalow which sits alongside the house. It contains a lounge, separate kitchen, a twin-bedded room, a double room and bedroom with two bunk beds. The rental costs are from £50 to £350 a week.

NR HOLSWORTHY, DEVON
SC GLEBE HOUSE, Bridgerule
Tel: 028 881 272.
Off the B3254 south east of Bude.

A few years ago we spent an extremely happy Christmas in one of Don Dudley's and Marion Wakefield's cottages. The fond memories were rekindled when we visited it again last year and saw that the owners have forged on with their policy of improving (wherever possible) their immaculately maintained properties, all of which are Grade II listed.

The focal point of the estate is Glebe House itself, a lovely stone house which was built in 1800. It was once a vicarage. The regular proportions are as pleasing to the eye as the clematis that clings to the mellow stone walls. The Chancellry takes up the ground floor of the house and can sleep ten people in comfort. There are some fine and spacious rooms, including a bedroom with four single beds (ideal for a large family), an oak-panelled bedroom with its own bathroom, and an eccentrically shaped double bedroom.

The cottages have been formed from the original farm buildings and the original features have been retained wherever possible. The Old Stables still has its studded wooden door and the wooden pillars and beams; the Granary and the adjoining Little Barn have spacious open-plan living rooms on the upper floor, very appealing rooms with their whitewashed stone walls and their wooden rafters. These two cottages could be rented together by a large family group.

On our Christmas visit we rented the single storey Forge, which has now acquired an upper floor and has become two cottages, one of which sleeps four people and the other five. Each has a four-poster bed and a whirlpool spa bath. The conversion has been done with such skill that you cannot see the join; it is indicative of the owners' care and attention to detail.

The cottages are furnished to an extremely high standard; the accent is on comfort and style and every detail is taken into consideration. You will find everything you need and any cook would be happy to work in the well-equipped kitchens.

There are several acres of grounds with stately trees at both ends of the estate. At the back of the house there is a huge lawn; you can play skittles, badminton or croquet there and slides, swings and a climbing frame are provided for youngsters. It's a wonderful spot to sit and dream on a warm summer's day. There is woodland to explore and a paddock is home to a pony. In addition, there is a games room with table tennis and a mini-snooker table.

The owners have converted the cellars of Glebe House into a small, well-stocked bar, and alongside is a pleasant restaurant which is open on Tuesday, Thursday, Friday and Sunday evenings. A good range of dishes is offered at reasonable prices: fantail prawns, boeuf bourguignonne, cherry chicken, tipsy beef and seafood provençal. Children's meals are also provided.

Glebe House offers some of the best self-catering accommodation we have seen; it is in a delightful spot, with a profusion of wildlife, a few hundreds yards from the River Tamar, and has many attractions in the vicinity.

Nearby: Sportsmen are well provided for, there are three golf courses within a short drive, stables, tennis and squash courts, indoor swimming pools and fishing facilities (river, lake and sea) all readily available. The sandy beaches to the west are reached in minutes and to the south are the rugged attractions of Dartmoor. Sightseers can head for Clovelly, Tintagel Castle, Pencarrow, Wesley's Cottage and Dobwalls Theme Park; nature lovers will enjoy the nature reserve at Braunton Burrows, Tamar Otter Park and the Tropical Bird Gardens at Padstow.

Units: 8 (7 cottages and 1 apartment)
Rent: £140 to £725; a typical rent in May or September would
be £200–300
Other costs: none
Central heating: provided
7 cots and 7 high chairs
Open all year

HOPE COVE, KINGSBRIDGE, DEVON
Ⓗ THE COTTAGE HOTEL, Hope Cove
Tel: 0548 561 555.
Look for Hope Cove off the A381 and take Inner Hope Road.

A comfortable family hotel which has an idyllic position overlooking
two safe beaches, which are protected by a grassy headland on one
side. From the terrace and the two acres of sloping garden you look
out to Thurlestone across Bigbury Bay. There are swings in the
garden and a good-sized playroom upstairs with table tennis, space
invaders, a piano and a wide window overlooking the sea.

We have had several reports about this hotel praising the helpful
and hard-working staff, who clearly understand how to look after
families. By Easter 1994 all rooms will have their own bathrooms.

Nearby: This is one of the loveliest parts of Devon and not the
least of the attractions are the many sandy beaches; at Hope Cove
itself, Salcombe, Bantham Bay and Thurlestone, for instance. The
South Devon Coast Path runs through Hope Cove. The children
will certainly enjoy a visit to the National Shire Horse Centre and
the Dartmoor Wildlife Park; while Buckfast Abbey, the Dart Valley
Railway, the Torbay Aircraft Museum and Compton Castle are all
within reach. Golfers can take advantage of the special rates available to guests at Bigbury Golf Club.

✗ BAR SNACKS (12pm to 1.30pm) £1–9: steak, mushroom &
potato pie, plaice & chips, ravioli, lobster salad;
DINNER (7.30–8.30pm) £17: taramasalata, soup, macaroni au
gratin, escalope of veal, pudding and cheese
Children: own menu, half portions
£ medium
Best Bargain Break: £38 per person per night – dinner, b&b

Children: £2 under one year; £6 from 1 to 3 years; £10 from 4
to 8 years; £13.50 from 9 to 12 years (includes meals)
Facilities: 6 cots and 6 high chairs; a baby listening system
35 rooms, 5 family. No credit cards accepted
Closed Jan. No music
Ⓟ own car park

ILFRACOMBE, DEVON
Ⓗ SOUTHCLIFFE HOTEL, Torrs Park
Tel: 0271 862 958.
Near the centre of the town.

Once a Victorian gentleman's residence, this large building retains
its attractive stained glass windows and original marble fireplaces.
The owners, Mr and Mrs Anderson, have attacked the family
market with great resolve and everything here is geared up for
parents with young children.

Apart from the many cots and high chairs, there is a children's
playroom with all sorts of toys, a Wendy House and a small model
railway. Board games can also be made available, and cartoons are
shown on the video in the playroom. There are loads of books
around the hotel, plus a games room for older children with a pool
table and darts. Just as useful for parents is a kitchen where food
can be prepared for small children; and there is also a washing
machine, a spin drier, an iron, etc on the premises.

The attractive rear garden has a lawn on two levels, a fine display
of flowers and a couple of copper beech trees. You can sit happily
in the sun and there is room for the children to play. They have a
swing and the owners provide various garden games. The lounge,
with its comfortable chairs and sofas, overlooks the garden, as does
the dining room.

You can be assured that the food will be of good quality here,
because the owners used to run an excellent wholefood restaurant
in Shrewsbury – the Good Life, which is still recommended in *The
Family Welcome Guide*.

Nearby: Ilfracombe is a popular holiday resort with many attractions and if you fancy a change from the beaches there is a good
indoor swimming pool. The children will no doubt enjoy a visit

to Watermouth Castle, Exmoor Bird Gardens and Combe Martin Wildlife Park; while the adults will perhaps argue the case for Braunton Burrows nature reserve, Arlington Court and Dunster Castle. The beauty of Exmoor is on the doorstep, too.

✗ DINNER (6.30pm): melon & orange salad, diced pork in cider, pudding and cheese
Children: own menu, half portions
£ low
Best Bargain Break: £161 per person per week – dinner, b&b
Children: first child free up to 5 years (before mid–July and after the end of August); one third of full rate up to 2 years; half from 2 to 11; three quarters from 12 to 14
Facilities: plenty of cots and high chairs; baby listening system
14 rooms, 4 family, 4 sets interconnecting
Open Easter to September. No credit cards accepted
No smoking in dining room and play room
Ⓟ own car park

KING'S NYMPTON, DEVON
Ⓢ🄲 COLLACOTT FARM, King's Nympton
Tel: 07695 2491.
South of South Molton between George Nympton and King's Nympton.

Collacott Farm seems to us to have all the attributes necessary for a highly enjoyable family holiday. The peace and quiet of the farm, encircled by beautiful countryside, and the comfortable and well-equipped cottages will appeal to the adults; and there is much more for any family to enjoy.

For a start, horse-mad children will be in their element here since the smart riding stables house a number of ponies which will suit riders of varying ages and abilities. Apart from hacks through the delightful countryside there is an all-weather outdoor arena and qualified staff to oversee your offspring's equestrian efforts. Mrs Francis also organizes residential holidays for girls aged between 9 and 14 years. They are housed in a splendid converted barn, with resident staff.

In addition there is an all-weather tennis court and an outdoor swimming pool, enclosed and with its own little terrace where you can sit in the sun. Younger children have a play area with a sand pit, swings and a climbing frame and there are indoor facilities also. The games room has table tennis, pool and table football and there is a trampoline; it is set at floor level and is properly padded and therefore very safe.

The accommodation, in converted stone barns with partial wooden cladding, is grouped around the farmhouse and is of a very high standard. The four cottages on the one side sleep between five and eight people. The abiding impression is that Mr and Mrs Francis have taken no short cuts in furnishing and equipping the cottages. The kitchens are smart and have everything a cook needs including a microwave as well as conventional cookers and a dishwasher. The original features have been retained wherever possible: the old wooden beams, the sloping roofs of the bedrooms and the wooden doors all add to the charm. Above all, furniture of good quality has been provided; solid and comfortable easy chairs and attractive wooden tables and chairs. Wood-burning stoves have been installed. Each cottage has its own stone terrace and enclosed garden; you can sit at peace and enjoy the view across the rolling fields with the church spire of King's Nympton marking the horizon.

On the other side of the courtyard there are two adjoining stone cottages, the Granary which sleeps four people, and the Dovecote which sleeps six. The open-plan living areas and kitchens are on the top floor and the bedrooms below. They are delightful buildings, with their own enclosed gardens, and can be hired together by larger families. Finally, Cloam Cottage has been converted from one side of the farmhouse. It has its own entrance, a patio and a garden and will sleep four people (one bedroom has two bunk beds).

We were very impressed with the great care which has been taken to ensure that Collacott Farm provides everything necessary for all members of the family to have an enjoyable holiday.

Nearby: The beaches to the west and the north can be reached fairly quickly and all the beauties of Exmoor are on the doorstep. The Exmoor Centre at Dulverton is a good starting point for walks. Many attractions are within reach including Dunster Castle, Combe Sydenham Hall, the West Somerset Railway, Knightshayes Court, the Exmoor Bird Gardens, Arlington Court and the nature reserve at Braunton Burrows.

Units: 7
Rent: £130 to £720 (winter breaks available)
Other costs: heating is metered
Central heating: provided
4 cots and 4 high chairs
Open all year

KINGSTEIGNTON, NR NEWTON ABBOTT, DEVON

P OLD RYDON INN, Rydon Road
Tel: 0626 54626
Just north of Newton Abbot. If you follow the road to Teignmouth (A381) you will see the Bell Inn. Turn there and follow your nose for a few hundred yards.

Once a farmhouse, this is a handsome building, parts of which date back to the 13th century. A steeply pitched roof overhangs the building at the back, and the front is beautifully proportioned, white-painted, and with wisteria clinging to it.

Inside are a series of small rooms with hugely thick walls and black ceiling beams. Up some stairs above the bar is a room where families are welcome to go: it was once the hayloft, and is a lovely room with plenty of tables at which to park yourselves. On Sundays and Mondays and at lunchtimes families have alternative places to go: the restaurant and dining room are also available, and are very pleasant and cosy rooms. In the restaurant, there is a table with a glass centre and below it you can see an old well which should interest the children.

In addition there is an attractive conservatory alongside the terrace and a pretty lawned garden with a swing.

A wide range of original food is always available and all of it is freshly prepared and cooked; and there is a high chair. Close to the south-west end of the M5, and only a short detour off the A38, this is a pub which is well worth seeking out.

✗ (12–2pm & 7–10pm) £1–6: egg & smoked salmon mayonnaise, seafood casserole, beef & mushroom pie, butterbean & vegetable gratinée, Tandoori chicken
Children: own menu

🍺 Ale: Bass, Wadworth's and guests
🅿 own car park

LANHYDROCK, NR BODMIN, CORNWALL
🆂🅲 TREFFRY FARM COTTAGES, Lanhydrock
Tel: 0208 74405.
Just off the B3268 south of Bodmin.

Treffry was once the home farm of the Lanhydrock estate (the National Trust property is a few hundred yards away) and the 18th-century farm buildings have been converted with skill and sympathy. Treffry is still a dairy farm of around 200 acres and guests, especially the children, are encouraged to join in the farming activities – collecting eggs, feeding the calves, seeing the milking etc. Pat Smith, the owner, issues badges to the children and provides them with a countryside book.

The cottages have an air of privacy and seclusion, a result perhaps of the thick stone walls covered with clematis, roses, wisteria and Virginia creeper. Great efforts have been made to furnish them in a comfortable and traditional way: good furniture with cheerful fabrics, wood burning stoves, exposed wooden beams and baskets of flowers. The kitchens have excellent equipment, everything a cook might need is in place. There are unusual touches in several of the cottages: the upstairs studio in Swallows Cottage, the gallery bedroom in Churns Cottage and the Waterwheel in Cogwheels Cottage.

The accommodation is varied. The smallest cottage suits two adults and two children and the largest can take up to eight persons. Board games, cards and jigsaws are provided in all the cottages. On a practical level, there is a laundry room and a pre-cooked meal service.

There is lots of space around the cottages, and at the top of a large enclosed lawned garden there is a splendid play area with climbing frames and swings. The picnic area has a barbecue and there is both an adventure trail and a woodland trail, so that all the family can have their fun. The farm pony, Fred, will give the younger children rides during the week and the ducks and chickens wander about freely.

It is a lovely spot for a family holiday and is very well placed for many other activities.

Nearby: The splendid Lanhydrock House is on the doorstep and Pencarrow House is also very close, as are the ruins of Restormel Castle. The children will enjoy Dobwalls Theme Park and Newquay Zoo and the Dairyland Farm Park will also appeal to them. Bodmin Moor, a lovely spot for riding, walking and contemplation, is near and there is a wonderful choice of safe and sandy beaches on either coast: Newquay and Crantock Bay, Vault Beach and Lantic Bay. The coastal walks are magnificent. Bodmin has swimming, squash and tennis and there is excellent fishing and golf to be enjoyed; the Lanhydrock course is on the doorstep.

Units: 7
Rent: £100 to £495; short breaks available
Other costs: linen on hire; electricity on meters
Heating: central heating
4 cots & 4 high chairs
Open all year

LANTEGLOS, NR CAMELFORD, CORNWALL
Ⓗ HOTEL LANTEGLOS, Lanteglos
Tel: 0840 213 551.
Off the A39.

This hotel is run for families by a family who have taken the utmost care to provide everything necessary for parents and children to have a good holiday.

It's a lovely stone country house set in fifteen acres of delightful garden, sheltered by mature trees, and with its own stream. It was built as a rectory for the local church by the famous architect, Augustus Pugin. There are splendid facilities – plenty of indoor and outdoor play areas, a woodland fort, and a spacious heated swimming pool and paddling pool in the lawned gardens.

A splendid conservatory has been built alongside the bar and its great advantage is that it looks over a play area. So the adults can sit there in peace and still keep an eye on their offspring. There is a hard tennis court, a squash court and two badminton courts. Bowood Park golf course is next door to the hotel: guests have direct access, priority tee times and reduced green fees, and the hotel has concessionary rates at ten other golf courses. There is a children's entertainer at peak times.

Nearby: If you should wish to venture forth for other entertainment, there are safe and sandy beaches close at hand: Daymer Bay and Trebarwith Strand, for example. The famous Bodmin Moor is a few miles south, and nature lovers will perhaps head for the Tamar Otter Park. Wesley's Cottage, Pencarrow, Lanhydrock and the Farm Park near Bodmin are other nearby attractions.

✕ BAR SNACKS (12pm to 2pm & 6pm to 10pm) £1–6: Cornish fish pie, chicken curry, scampi, sirloin steaks;
DINNER (7.30–9.30pm) £13: egg mayonnaise, chicken Indienne, pudding or cheese
Children: high teas
£ medium
Best Bargain Break: £33 per person per night – dinner, b & b
Children: first child under 5 is free, and the second one at certain times; thereafter, children are charged on a sliding scale from £4 to £20 a day

Facilities: over 20 cots and over 20 high chairs; a baby listening
system
17 rooms, 11 family. Access/Visa
Closed Nov-Feb
Ⓟ own car park

LAUNCESTON, CORNWALL
ⓈⒸ HIGHER BAMHAM FARM
Tel: 0566 772141.
Follow the Polson road (old A30) from Launceston.

The first thing to note about Higher Banham Farm is its location on
high ground outside Launceston and the views of the surrounding
countryside are superb. Second, the facilities make it an ideal place
for a family holiday. Above all, there is an indoor swimming pool,
with a paddling pool for younger children, and a sauna for the
adults. It is all very well designed and the pool is of a reasonable
size; a lawn and pleasant terrace await you after your swim.

The enclosed lawned garden runs alongside the old farmhouse
and includes a play area for the children and a swing. On the other
side there is yet another lawn, fringed by trees, for impromptu
games of football or cricket or whatever. In addition there is a
games room where you can play table tennis, table football or pool
and there are plenty of books available.

To match all these excellent amenities (and on a practical level
there is a laundry room) the eight cottages are furnished and
equipped to the highest standards. They have been converted from
the original farmhouse and its outbuildings, which are of 18th-
century vintage, and made from local stone with some of the outside
walls clad with slate.

The cottages can accommodate from four to eight people. The
largest is Tamara, a detached single-storey cottage, which has two
double bedrooms and another bedroom with bunks to sleep four
children. Ancona can sleep four adults and three children, as can
Welsummer. The other five cottages can sleep from four to six
people.

We were impressed by the care which has been taken with the
conversions. Wherever possible the original materials have been

retained, such as the old wooden beams, and they are complemented by nice wooden doors and ceilings. The living rooms are mostly open plan with an integral kitchen and the cottages, with one exception, have their own patios.

Higher Bamham Farm offers high quality accommodation and excellent facilities for families in a lovely part of Cornwall.

Nearby: Launceston has a fine old Norman castle and a steam railway and the Tamar Otter Park is close by. Wesley's Cottage, Cotehele House, Dobwalls Theme Park, Lydford Gorge and Morwellham Quay can all be reached with ease. The natural delights of Bodmin Moor are on the doorstep and there are many fine beaches within easy reach. Golf, tennis, squash, swimming, riding and fishing are all readily available.

Units: 8
Rent: £125 to £465 (short breaks available off peak)
Other costs: electricity is metered at some of the cottages
Heating: night storage
Facilities: cots and high chairs available
Open all year

LISKEARD, CORNWALL
Ⓛ DOBWALLS FAMILY ADVENTURE PARK,
Liskeard
Tel: 0579 20325.
On the A38 at Dobwalls, a few miles west of Liskeard.

Dobwalls own description, a family adventure park, suits it well since much of the park is given over to a series of adventure playgrounds. They are very well designed and spread out among a heavily wooded area. All the equipment is in pristine condition, with safe surfaces for children to land on: they will be amused for hours in the Stockade, the Timber Tumble, High Jinks, the Play Port, the Rattlesnake (a long tube slide) and Babes in the Wood for younger children.

Another great attraction for children is the collection of ten miniature steam and diesel locomotives, which travel around the park every quarter of an hour. The two routes, the Union Pacific and the Rio Grande, are perfect replicas of real sections in the

USA and the names of the locomotives reflect their origins: Queen of Wyoming, Spirit of America, and so on.

While the children tear around in the adventure playgrounds, the adults can relax in one of the picnic areas or take in Mr Thorburn's Edwardian Countryside, which is devoted to the works of the wildlife painter, Archibald Thorburn. The exhibition, which includes a light and sound display, won the 1987 Sotheby's award.

There are two restaurants. The Denver Diner is like an enlarged railway carriage and serves fast foods, salads and homemade cakes. The Edwardian Tea Rooms is attractively done out with portraits of Queen Victoria and her family on the walls. There is a good range of food on offer: baked potatoes, beef in ale, chicken curry and spaghetti Provençal, for example. There are high chairs available here and children's meals such as egg on toast.

The smart new toilet block near the Edwardian Tea Rooms contains a mother and baby room. There is always a trained 'first aider' on duty during the summer.

This is a well organised park and we noticed how smart and new everything looked. The children can have hours of fun here, while the adults can also enjoy the place, especially on a summer day.

Open: Easter to end of September, 10am–6pm, last entries at 4.30pm. Weekends only in October, 10am–5pm (but daily during half-term holidays)
Charges: adults £6.50; children and OAPs £4.50; under 3s free; Family car ticket £20 (1993 prices)
Baby changing: mother and baby room
P ample

NR LOOE, CORNWALL
SC TRENANT PARK COTTAGES, Sandplace
Tel: 0503 263 639.
Off the A387 at Sandplace (just north of Looe).

It would be difficult to find a more delightful and attractive place than Trenant Park, which is bounded by the East Looe River. The four cottages have been converted from the coach houses of Trenant Park Manor and the mellow stone walls are loaded with clematis, roses and honeysuckle.

The cottages each have their own gardens but the guests can also enjoy the spacious grounds which encompass smooth lawns and splendid mature trees: copper beeches, limes and Aylex oaks. It is a blaze of colour in spring and summer and a dovecote adds to the effect. Guests are also very welcome to stroll in the surrounding parkland and watch the great variety of wildlife.

We were very impressed by the care which has been exercised in converting these cottages. There is plenty of space and the decorations (Sanderson and Laura Ashley) are of excellent quality, with good wooden doors, attractive farmhouse tables and very well-equipped kitchens with pine units, microwave ovens as well as conventional cookers, and dishwashers and washing machines.

Lord Offerd's Cottage is the largest and can accommodate five people in its two bedrooms, plus another two if the bed-settee is used. It has an attractive open-plan sitting room and kitchen area. The lawned garden is complemented by a secluded cobbled courtyard which is a sun trap.

Squire Peel's Cottage and Sir John Buller's Cottage can both sleep from four to six people (two bedrooms each plus sofa-beds) and Lady Pamela's Cottage sleeps two people in its double bedroom.

If you want self-catering accommodation of an exceptionally high standard, in beautiful and tranquil surroundings, you need look no further than Trenant Park.

Nearby: The Chapmans, who own the cottages, have a boat which can be borrowed and there are riding stables on the estate. There is no shortage of beaches in the vicinity and every type of water sport is readily available, as is golf, tennis, squash, badminton and other sports. Sightseers have a great deal of choice, including the Monkey Sanctuary, Cotehele House, Dobwalls Theme Park, Lanhydrock and Pencarrow, and all the natural delights of Bodmin Moor.

Units: 4
Rent: £155 to £495 (short breaks available November to Easter)
Other costs: electricity on a meter
Heating: night storage
Facilities: cots and high chairs available
Open all year

LUSTLEIGH, DEVON
Ⓟ CLEAVE, Lustleigh
Tel: 064 77 223.
Just off the A382 north of Bovey Tracey. Watch for the sign.

The village is largely composed of lovely, thatched, granite cottages and is famous for its May Day festival. The 15th-century pub, thatched like most of its neighbours, suits the village perfectly. You can sit at peace in the lawned garden at the front of the pub. It is a secluded spot, sheltered by trees and with a fine array of greenery and flowers all around. There are two sizeable bars inside and an attractive dining room and families are made welcome in a pleasant wood-panelled room at the back of the pub. There are several tables, some padded chairs and a high chair, and only one amusement machine; it is a no-smoking area.

It is useful to know that the Cleave is open all day (Monday to Saturday) during the summer months, and there is a very good choice of food available.

✕ (12pm to 2pm & 7pm to 9pm) £2–11: whole lemon sole, steak & kidney & Guinness pie, rump steak, chilli con carne, lasagne
Children: smaller portions
Ⓟ on street (can be difficult)
🍺 Ale: Bass, Castle Eden, Flowers

MAWGAN PORTH, CORNWALL
Ⓗ BEDRUTHAN STEPS HOTEL, Mawgan Porth
Tel: 0637 860 555.
On the B3276 – the main coast road from Newquay to Padstow.

The hotel takes its name from the array of huge rocks by the beach said to be the stepping stones of the legendary giant Bedruthan. It is a modern and spacious hotel which is totally geared to the holiday needs of families; there are masses of cots and high chairs, and almost all the rooms are family rooms. The facilities for adults are excellent including two squash courts, indoor and outdoor heated swimming pools, a short tennis and full-size tennis court, snooker, table tennis, carpet bowls, giant chess and skittles. Golfers can take advantage of a concessionary rate at St Mellion.

The facilities for children are outstanding: as well as the swimming pools there are various play areas (including adventure playgrounds, swings and an area for football), children's films, etc. The 'jungle tumble' play area has a ball pool, tube slide, rope ladders and biff bags; it is indoors and is supervised and has a special toddlers' area. To take the younger children off your hands there is a play group every morning except Sundays. The children's entertainment programme is extensive and includes treasure hunts, craft workshops, cookery classes and painting.

The hotel has a farm and a large market garden so it is not surprising that most of the vegetables and quite a lot of fruit are grown by the hotel. The fish is caught locally, and the bread is made on the spot too. As at its sister hotel, the Trevelgue near Newquay (q.v.), there are some excellent wines at remarkably good prices and a good selection of vegetarian dishes. The hotel provides a range of homemade puréed foods for babies. All round you get astonishing value for money.

Nearby: You need never leave the hotel, but there is no shortage of outside attractions. Mawgan Porth beach, right in front of the hotel, is safe and sandy and there are several excellent beaches at Newquay, a busy resort about six miles away. It has an excellent zoo. The Lappa Valley Railway will appeal to many families, as will the Dairyland Farm Park and Trerice, a superb Elizabethan manor house. Bedruthan Steps itself, a National Trust beauty spot, is only a short walk away.

✗ LUNCH (1–2pm) £9: soup, cold buffet, pudding or cheese;
DINNER (7.45–9.30pm) £11: pheasant terrine, poached salmon, pudding or cheese
£ medium
Best Bargain Break: £27 per person per day – dinner, b&b
Children: a quarter to three quarters of the adult rate; free of charge in some off-peak periods
Facilities: 50 cots and 50 high chairs; and a baby listening system in every room
75 rooms, 70 family, 26 sets interconnecting
Closed Nov to March. Access/Visa
🍺 Ale: Bass. No music
No smoking in restaurant, lounge and children's play area
🅿 own car park

MOTHECOMBE, DEVON
[SC] THE FLETE ESTATE, Mothecombe
Tel: 075 530 253.
Off the A379 east of Plymouth. Follow the signs to Mothecombe.

Superlatives flow trippingly off the pen when describing the Flete Estate, which comprises 5000 acres of extraordinarily beautiful terrain: rolling fields and woodland, the estuary of the River Erme with a profusion of bird life, safe and sandy beaches. It is an unspoiled haven of peace and tranquillity where you might be a world away from the normal cares of everyday existence.

Three of the cottages sit in a row above the estuary. Flat-fronted and with a tile-hung upper floor, they were once home to the local coastguards and, as one would expect, have clear views of the estuary and the two headlands. Most of the rooms have the same magnificent outlook, as has the terrace, a fine place to sit and doze contentedly. To the right are the private beaches, where families can play and swim in safety and there are also other beaches on the other side of the estuary.

Each of the coastguards' cottages has three or four bedrooms and can sleep six to eight people. The ground floor contains a well-equipped kitchen, a dining room, a sitting room and a study, which can be used as a fourth bedroom. There is a games room with a table tennis table.

Nepean's Cottage, once the abode of the estate's last gamekeeper, is a most appealing stone building with arched windows and doors, and dormer windows in the steep slate roof. Guests have a soothing outlook to the estuary and the various beaches are within easy reach: a few minutes by car to Mothecombe and the coastguards' beaches and on foot to Pamflete Beach.

Nepean's Cottage sleeps ten people. Inside, there is a spacious sitting room cum dining room, with two twin-bedded bedrooms at one side. Upstairs, there are two twin-bedded rooms and a double. Surrounded by gentle hills and woodland and with its views of the estuary, the cottage is an unparalleled delight.

A large family would be admirably suited by Efford House, a lovely Georgian stone building which offers space and comfort in a series of beautifully proportioned rooms. The seven bedrooms can sleep up to twelve people and there is ample room on the ground floor for everyone. The two large sitting rooms are well provided with comfortable easy chairs and sofas and, on an upper level, there is a sizeable dining room with a long pine table. The house has its own table tennis table. Encircled by undulating fields and woodland, the house has an entrancing view, down the long and grassy garden, to the estuary. The various beaches are just over a mile away.

As well as the beaches, guests can roam the 5000 acres of the estate and enjoy all that it offers: the wildlife, the woodland and the flowers. It is an enchanting place where anyone's spirits will be revived.

Nearby: Should you fancy a change there are many other beaches in the vicinity and a whole range of places to visit. Wildlife enthusiasts should visit the National Shire Horse Centre and the Dartmoor Wildlife Park. Mount Edgcumbe Country Park, the great houses of Saltram and Cotehele, Morwellham Quay, Buckland Abbey, the Buckfast Steam Railway and the adjoining Abbey, and Compton Castle are all within easy reach.

Units: 5 (4 cottages and a large house)
Rent: £180 to £800
Other costs: linen can be hired and electricity is metered
Cots and high chairs are available for all the houses
Heating: electric (Efford House has partial central heating); all the properties have log fires
Open all year

MULLION, CORNWALL
H SC **POLURRIAN HOTEL**, Polurrian Cove
Tel: 0326 240 421.
Follow your nose through Mullion, past the cricket ground – you may have to ask, although there is a hotel sign.

The roof blew off this excellent hotel at the beginning of 1990 but it is good to report that all is now well again. From the expansive gardens of the Edwardian building you will have some breathtaking views down to the sea. If it is action rather than contemplation that you require, there is plenty to divert you: a putting green, hard tennis court, squash court and a superbly equipped grassy play area with a slide, trampoline, sandpit and swings – all enclosed for the parents' peace of mind. Down below is a sandy cove where you can do some surfing.

There is a games area indoors with snooker, bar billiards and table tennis. The leisure club has an indoor swimming pool with a paddling pool and a mini-gym, plus a sauna and a solarium. There is also an outdoor heated swimming pool.

There is a warm and relaxing atmosphere at this hotel, which has everything necessary for a happy family holiday, including children's outings to local attractions.

Nearby: Most of the surrounding land is owned by the National Trust, and there are delightful walks to take. Mullion golf course is just a couple of miles away and there are many attractions within reach: Goonhilly Earth Station, the Flambards Theme Park, Poldark Mine, the Seal Sanctuary at Gweek and St Michael's Mount.

✗ BUFFET LUNCH (12–2pm) £2–8: chicken & chips, cold buffet, scampi, fisherman's pie, moussaka;
DINNER (7–9pm) £21: quenelle of sole, soup, roast leg of pork, pudding or cheese
Children: own menu, half portions
£ high
Best Bargain Break: £290–320 per person 4 nights – dinner, b&b
Children: free up to 14 years
Facilities: 12 cots and 10 high chairs, and baby listening system
40 rooms, 4 family. Access/AmEx/Diners/Visa
Open March to November. No music
Ⓟ own car park
Self-catering: The hotel has seven bungalows, two cottages and two apartments and they can accommodate from four to seven people. The rents very from £150 to £545 a week and guests can use all the facilities of the hotel.

NANCENOY, NR HELSTON, CORNWALL

Ⓗ Ⓟ TRENGILLY WARTHA, Nancenoy

Tel: 0326 40332.

Between Constantine and Gweek.

The inn is situated down the narrow country lanes east of Helston and not far from the Helford River where it cuts deep into the Cornish landscape. There are signs here and there which point the way to the place and, eventually, you will find a long, cream-painted building with a conservatory at the front. The latter room, a no smoking area, is where families are welcome to settle if they have young children in tow and it is a no smoking area; the adjoining entrance hall contains a pool table. Behind is a pleasant and spacious bar and real ale enthusiasts will be glad to hear that there is always a wide choice of beers available and the choice is rotated on a regular basis.

At the back of the bar there is a comfortable and pleasantly furnished lounge with an open fire; and the restaurant is a very pretty and relaxing place. We had a really excellent dinner and a nicely cooked breakfast and greatly enjoyed our stay at this well-run inn.

There are six bedrooms in the pub and some of them can accommodate two parents and a child. On summer days, you can take advantage of the covered patio and the very pretty garden with its array of flowers and bushes. The gardens have recently been extended and now include a lake. It's a quiet and peaceful spot with a view across the lush valley of a distant village church.

Nearby: There are many sandy beaches nearby and the pick of them for families are perhaps Kennack Sands, Towan and Pendower beaches and the Lizard Peninsula is one of the most attractive parts of Cornwall. There is no end of attractions for holiday makers within easy reach: the Seal Sanctuary at Gweek, Flambards Theme Park near Helston, the Poldark Mine, Godolphin House, St Michael's Mount, Paradise Park and the Shire Horse Farm near Camborne.

✗ BAR SNACKS (12pm to 2.15pm & 6.15pm to 9.30pm) £1–9: smoked salmon trout, dressed crab salad, Trengilly sausage, sirloin steak, lasagne;

DINNER (7.30 to 9.30pm) £18: grilled goat's cheese, poached salmon, pudding

Children: own menu, half portions
£ medium
Best Bargain Break: £70 per person, 2 nights – dinner, b&b
Children: cots £2; £8 thereafter
Facilities: 1 cot and 1 high chair; all rooms have baby listening through the phones
6 rooms. Access/AmEx/Visa
Open all year
🍺 Ale: a varying choice
🅿 own car park

NEWQUAY, CORNWALL
Ⓗ TREVELGUE HOTEL, Newquay
Tel: 0637 872 864.
On the B3276 Newquay–Padstow road.

The brochure of the hotel proclaims it as a 'parents' haven – children's paradise' and that is an apt description since it is a hotel dedicated to family holidays and everything is provided to ensure every member of a family is properly looked after. It is a modern, purpose-built hotel with very spacious rooms: the majority of them are suites with a separate twin-bedded room for children. The views over the bay are delightful.

Even if it is pouring with rain the superb indoor facilities will keep anyone amused: they include a snooker room, a swimming pool with separate children's pool, table tennis, pool, games machines and lots of space where children can play. There is a playroom and a hobby club and an indoor jungle trail for young children. For the older children, there is a special disco. Nearby in Newquay itself is the Fun Factory, which is an indoor play area for under 12s. Play groups are organised every day by the childcare staff who also run other entertainments; and the hotel will hire buggies, pushchairs, baby walkers and so on to guests.

When the sun shines, there is another excellent swimming pool in its own grassy garden; a hard tennis court, paddler, tennis court and squash court, a boule pitch, giant chess, a badminton court, a golf net and practice hole and mini-football pitches. There's an adventure playground, a sandpit and a pirate ship, all within easy viewing and shouting distance of the terrace, upon which you can enjoy your drinks with an easy mind. There are nine acres of grounds in which the children can roam and three acres of garden. A barbecue area has now been added to the facilities and families can cook their own food here.

Below the hotel are some lovely sandy beaches. Under-6s can be abandoned to the play group each morning from Monday to Friday and over-6s are taken on various outings and offered Punch and Judy shows, parties, galas, games and magic shows, etc. Parents will be interested in the wine list, which has some real bargains.

Entertainments are put on every evening, so it is just the place for an active, gregarious holiday for families with young children. The food, by the way, is bound to be fresh – the hotel has its own market garden, makes its own bread and pasta, etc. When we visited recently our dinner was first class.

The Trevelgue offers tremendous value for money.

Nearby: The busy resort of Newquay is just down the road and has safe, sandy beaches. It is one of the main surfing centres in Britain. The children may want to visit the zoo, the Dairyland Farm Park and the World in Miniature; the Lappa Valley Railway and the lovely Elizabethan house at Trerice are within easy reach.

✕ BAR LUNCH (12 to 2pm) £1–4: burgers, baked potatoes, pizzas, salad;
DINNER (7.30 to 9pm) £10: potted crab, chicken bonne femme, pudding or cheese
Children: own menu
£ medium
Best Bargain Break: £33 per person per night – dinner, b&b
Children: varies from free to 20 per cent discount
Facilities: 70 cots and 70 high chairs; baby listening
70 rooms, 60 family. Access/Visa
Closed Nov to Mar
Ⓟ own car park

NR NEWQUAY, CORNWALL

H SC WATERGATE BAY HOTEL, St Mawgan

Tel: 0637 860 543.

On the B3276 north of Newquay.

This substantial family hotel is not too far away from the busy resort of Newquay. Not that you need venture there, since there are loads of facilities at the hotel itself, including a sandy beach, part of which actually belongs to the hotel. The coastal footpath runs close by.

The garden has swings, sandpits, a junior 'assault course' and a trampoline and many activities are organised for the children here and on the beach. In addition, there are Punch and Judy shows, fancy dress parties, swimming galas, table tennis and other sporting competitions, and conjurors every week. Adults have dancing and entertainments every evening.

Indoors, there is a spacious playroom for young children with plenty of toys and games, a slide and a pirate ship; alongside, there is a pool table for older children. The snooker room is confined to adults or children supervised by adults. In addition, there is a tennis court and a separate sports hall which has a skittle alley, a fitness room, a squash court and a court on which to play badminton, short tennis, etc adjoins the hotel. There is a putting green on one of the terraces which overlooks the bay and loads of room for families to relax, including a lounge or quiet room for adults only.

The Coffee Shop (open from 10am to 6pm) offers a good range of snacks and dishes of the day. It overlooks the outdoor swimming pool and paddling pool and alongside it is a small indoor pool.

Nearby: Newquay itself is a busy and lively resort and, apart from Watergate Bay, there are many safe, sandy beaches in the near vicinity. There are many places to visit. Children will certainly be interested in the zoo, which has a large play area and a leisure centre attached to it with swimming pools, squash and tennis courts and a golf driving range. There is a leisure park at St Agnes, a farm park (Dairyland) near Newquay and a World in Miniature at Goonhavern, five miles from Newquay. Add the Lappa Valley Railway and the Elizabethan manor house at Trerice, and there is something for everyone.

✗ COFFEE SHOP (10am-6pm) £1–4: soup, salads, ploughman's, hot dish of the day;
LUNCH (12.30–1.45pm) £8: soup, cold buffet or dish of the day, pudding or cheese;
DINNER (7–8.30pm) £15: smoked mackerel paté, roast leg of lamb, pudding or cheese
Children: own menu, half portions
£ low
Best Bargain Break: £35 per person per night – dinner, b&b
Children: free at certain times; 25 per cent of adult rate up to 3 years; 50 per cent from 4 to 7 years; 66 per cent from 8 to 10; 75 per cent from 11 to 14
Facilities: as many cots and high chairs as required; baby listening system to every room
70 rooms, 35 family, 17 sets interconnecting. Access/Visa
Open March to November. No smoking in restaurant
⊕ Ale: Bass. No music
℗ ample
Self-catering: Close to the hotel there are three villa flats. One of them is very large and can sleep up to ten people; the others can accommodate four to five. They are well-equipped and the garden has a sandpit, a trampoline and other play equipment. There is a launderette. In addition, there are two houses which are a

couple of miles from the hotel. The large one can sleep nine or ten people and the smaller one four.

The facilities of the hotel are available to guests, and cots and high chairs, central heating and bed linen is provided. The electricity is metered and you must provide your own towels. The rents vary from £130 to £870 a week.

NR NEWQUAY, CORNWALL
Ⓛ TRERICE, Newquay
Tel: 0637 875 404.
Off the A3058 south east of Newquay.

Trerice was acquired by the National Trust in 1953 and is a beautiful Elizabethan stone manor house. Most of the building was constructed in 1572 and it has been left largely unaltered ever since. It was the home for several centuries of one of the most powerful Cornish families, the Arundells.

The house lies in a little valley through which the River Gannel flows. It is set among trees and surrounded by its own formal gardens.

There are, of course, some impressive rooms, with interesting plasterwork. One of the prominent features of the hall, which rises through two storeys, is the huge, leaded window with its 576 panes of glass. The house is not overwhelming in the way so many grand houses are, since it is on a smaller scale and has great charm.

The self-service restaurant is housed in a huge barn, possibly of 15th-century origin. It is an attractive room, with white-washed stone walls and wooden rafters. There is a choice of salads, ploughman's and dishes of the day from £2 to £5. It is open from 11am, is licensed and is a no smoking area. High chairs are available.

The mother and baby room is through an unmarked door in the Great Hall and has a chair and a table with a changing mat. Baby wipes are also provided.

Open: 1 April to 31 October, 11am to 5.30pm (to 5pm in October). Closed on Tuesdays.
Charges: adults £3.60; children £1.80

Baby changing: excellent mother and baby room off the hall
P own car park

OTTERY ST MARY, DEVON
H FLUXTON FARM HOTEL, Ottery St Mary
Tel: 0404 812 818.
On the Tipton St John Road, which runs south of Ottery St Mary.

This is a handsome 16th-century Devon longhouse situated in the Otter valley, and most of the rooms have splendid views to friendly wooded hills across the valley. Although it is no longer a farm, the owners keep some ducks, chickens and several cats.

The delightful gardens spread across a couple of acres, with a stream running through, and are partly enclosed by an old stone wall. Adults can take their ease on the wide lawns, shaded perhaps by one of the many stately trees. The owner has a miniature train on which he occasionally runs round the grounds; there is a putting green and a trout pond and a license can be bought for fishing on the Otter.

There are two charming and comfortable lounges; the one in the older part of the house has a low ceiling and splendid crooked windows. The dining room has a fine open fireplace and a beamed ceiling, and there is a small bar.

We looked at several bedrooms, nicely proportioned with lovely views. The two family rooms (both with a double and two single beds) have plenty of space, and one has a single room alongside and can be used as a family suite.

Nearby: It is an attractive area for holiday makers, with pretty countryside, and the coast is very close with an excellent choice of clean, sandy beaches. Children will be interested in nearby Bicton Park, the Donkey Sanctuary and Farway Countryside Park. The amazing building, 'A la Ronde', near Exmouth is also well worth a visit, as are the Maritime Museum in Exeter and Killerton House. On the other side of the Exe Estuary, you can visit the Dawlish Warren Nature Reserve.

✗ DINNER (6.45pm) £7
Children: own menu, half portions
£ medium
Children: babies free; one third of full rate up to 5 years; half price thereafter
Facilities: 2 cots and 1 high chair; baby listening by arrangement
12 rooms, 2 family. Open all year
No smoking in the lounge and the dining room
No credit cards. No music
Ⓟ own car park

PENDOGGETT, CORNWALL
Ⓟ CORNISH ARMS, Pendoggett
Tel: 0208 880 263.
On the B3314 north of Wadebridge.

This attractive 16th-century pub has an exterior partly covered by slate and the floors inside are of the same material, probably from the local Delabole quarries.

As you enter there are three low-ceilinged rooms adjoining each other, all comfortably and attractively furnished. The smallest of them has a padded settle curving around the walls; the Coffee Room is a delightful and cosy room, with padded benches around its walls. There are leaded windows and pictures of the inn in former years on the walls.

Families with children are welcome to use the Coffee Room at lunchtimes and the restaurant is also available to them in the evenings. When the sun shines, the pleasant garden, with views across the fields towards Port Isaac, is the place to enjoy a drink and some food. There are plenty of bench tables and it is safe for children.

For the unencumbered adult drinker the spacious back bar, with more padded settles and a good array of wooden tables, is the place to be. There's a good, friendly atmosphere here in which to sup a couple of glasses of the strong Pendoggett Special.

The pub is open all day from Monday to Saturday.

✕ (12pm to 2pm & 6pm to 10.30pm) £2–11: lemon sole, beef & ale casserole, salmon fishcakes, entrecote steak, kidney kebab
Children: own menu
Ale: Bass, Flowers, Pendoggett Special
[P] own car park

NR PLYMOUTH, DEVON

[L] DARTMOOR WILDLIFE PARK, Cornwood
Tel: 0752 837 209.
Off the A38 at Sparkwell. Well signposted from the main road.

The park covers a site of around thirty acres and one of the great attractions for children is 'close encounters of the animal kind', when they can learn a little about animals and actually handle lambs, rabbits and even snakes and raccoons. There is quite a collection of birds of prey and some of these are flown each day: falcons, kestrels, hawks, buzzards and owls.

The bigger animals include tigers, brown bears, panthers, bison, pumas, lions and deer; other species (over a hundred) include seals, otters, monkeys and many varieties of wild fowl.

The restaurant is huge, with its tables laid out in uniform rows, and the food is of the 'chips with everything' variety: sausages, burgers, pasties, etc. There is a children's menu and there are lots of high chairs.

The restaurant contains a spacious mother and baby room; it has a changing mat on a table and a padded bench.

The best plan would be to take your own food and take advantage of the picnic area alongside the restaurant. Alongside, there is an excellent play area which would keep any child amused.

Parents with young children should note that the main car park is a walk of several hundred yards from the park.

Open: every day 10am to dusk

Charges: adults £4.95; OAPs £4.45; children £3.30 (1993 prices)
Baby changing: mother and baby room
P̄ own car park

PORT ISAAC, CORNWALL
SC TREVATHAN FARM, St Endellion
Tel: 0208 880 248.
Off the B3314 just south of St Endellion.

Down a leafy lane or two, south of Port Isaac, you will find a delightful farmhouse where a series of cottages have been constructed from 18th-century stone outbuildings. Even though we saw the properties on a dismal, rainy day last summer, their charm and appeal shone through undimmed.

A noticeable feature of all the cottages is the amount of space which is at the guests' disposal. The living areas, usuallly open plan with a kitchen at one side, are generously proportioned and the furnishings and equipment are as good as any we have seen. It is good to report that there is nothing uniform about the furniture; attractive pieces have been collected and there are some lovely wooden tables and chests to be seen. The various wooden doors greatly add to the appeal of the cottages. They all have their own gardens.

Most of the cottages accommodate four people, usually in one double and one twin bedroom. Rose Cottage has an extra bedroom with bunk beds for children; it also has a separate kitchen and a beautifully furnished dining room with a wood-burning stove. Clover Cottage has an extra bedroom with bunk beds and is a detached cottage with an extremely spacious living room. Like the other cottages, it has its own garden and terrace as well as magnificent views of the surrounding countryside.

The peace and beauty of the Cornish fields is there to be enjoyed and there are many animals on Mr and Mrs Symons' 250-acre farm. The children can make friends with the cows, ducks, goats, dogs, cats, rabbits and a pot-bellied pig.

As well as the splendid cottages, the owners provide many extra amenities to keep holidaymakers amused. There is a huge games room which has table tennis, table football, pool tables and a Hammond organ. The fitness room (for adults only) is as well-equipped as any we have seen outside a leisure centre; it has several static cycles, a multi-gym machine, weights, a rowing machine and a treadmill.

Out of doors, there is a hard tennis court, and swings and slides for the children. There is a tea room on the farm where you can indulge yourselves with cream teas; alongside, the Symons family have a self-pick fruit and vegetable field.

Just up the lane Mr and Mrs Symons have another charming detached stone cottage. Myrtle Grove has a children's twin bedroom on the ground floor and a double and a twin on the first floor. French doors lead to a patio and a sizeable grassy garden.

A really large family party would be suited to Polmear House, which is near the hamlet of Tregoodwell on the outskirts of Camelford. The house, which belonged to the grandparents of Mrs Symons, can sleep twelve people in the five bedrooms. There are two lounges, a dining room and a games room. A large lawn runs along the front of the house and there are 60 acres of land to enjoy.

Nearby: All kinds of water sports are available – sailing, surfing, water skiing from the safe, sandy beaches. Fishing, golf and horse riding can easily be arranged and there are wonderful walks along the Cornish coastal paths, for example. Nature lovers can visit Newquay Zoo, Dairyland Farm Park and the Tropical Bird Gardens at Padstow. There are many other intriguing places to see: Pencarrow; Lanhydrock; Trerice; the Lappa Valley Railway and Dobwalls Theme Park.

Units: 10
Rent: £120 to £800 (short breaks available)
Other costs: electricity is metered
Heating: electric storage heaters
Facilities: plenty of cots and high chairs
Open all year

NR PORT ISAAC, CORNWALL
SC GREEN DOOR COTTAGES, Port Gaverne
Tel: 0208 880 244.
Follow the B3267 beyond Port Isaac.

You would be hard pressed to find a more attractive spot than the cove at Port Gaverne. Alongside sits the charming 17th-century Port Gaverne Hotel; opposite is a row of fishermen's cottages, built in the middle of the 18th century. They have been converted into self-catering accommodation of a very high standard.

Your first impression of the cottages will not prepare you for the roomy interiors. From the outside, they look small but inside there is a lot of space, an impression which is enhanced by the high ceilings, wooden beams and rafters. For colder evenings, there is a wood-burning stove, even though all the properties are double glazed and have central heating. The open-plan living room, kitchen and dining area is usually on the top floor and is comfortable and well equipped. The kitchen has everything a cook will need and we noticed how carefully the furniture had been chosen: solid wooden chairs and tables are provided in the dining areas, not standard, chain store products.

In most of the cottages, the bedrooms, a twin and a double, are on the ground floor. They too are furnished simply and stylishly, with wooden furniture. Not all the cottages are designed in the same way. Rose Cottage is on a single storey and Little Shrub is conventionally laid out, with the bedrooms on the upper floor. With one exception (Jasmine, which sleeps three), all the cottages sleep four guests.

The cottages are grouped around a central courtyard and each has a little terrace where you can enjoy the sunshine. The cottages have their own club with a bar and a pool table. Alternatively, you could head for the welcoming bars in the Port Gaverne Hotel, which also offers a wide range of food: bar meals, a lunchtime buffet and an excellent choice of locally caught fish in the restaurant.

Nearby: You can swim and sail from the cove a few yards away and there are many other excellent beaches within reach. Fishing, surfing and horse riding are all readily available and there are several fine golf courses, including Trevose and St Enodoc's. Much of the encircling area is owned by the National Trust and there are splendid walks to enjoy, especially on the North Cornwall Coast Path. Many attractions are a short drive away: the Tropical Bird Gardens at Padstow, the zoo at Newquay and the farm park at Bodmin, Pencarrow, Lanhydrock and Dobwalls Theme Park.

Units: 7
Rent: £150 to £500 (short breaks available)
Other costs: none
Central heating: provided
7 cots and 7 high chairs; baby listening through to the hotel
Open all year

ROCK, CORNWALL
[SC] CANT FARM
Tel: 0208 862 841.
On the outskirts of Rock (the brochure has a clear map)

Only a full range of superlatives can do justice to the charms and excellence of Cant Farm. The group of six spacious stone houses lies in an idyllic situation on high ground overlooking the waters of the Camel Estuary with the slopes of Cant Hill on the other side. At low tide you can see the wrecks of the 19th-century ketches which lie in Cant Cove.

The six houses can accommodate from five to eight people, are models of good design and are well equipped and well furnished. It is no surprise to learn that Cant Farm has earned the Tourist Board's highest classification: five keys de luxe.

The Old Granary has four bedrooms. French windows lead out from the magnificent lounge on to a large terrace with barbecue and large garden. The other houses also have terraces and gardens, high quality bathrooms, extensively equipped kitchens which include microwaves and dishwashers, and utility rooms with washing machines and tumble dryers. The Old Granary and the Farmhouse have saunas.

Cant Farm has 70 acres of land, a hard tennis court and golf practice area.

Nearby: Rock is a delightful village and is well known as a sailing centre. Water-skiing is available, there is surf at Polzeath beach, or you can walk along the sands of Daymer Bay or the North Cornwall coastal path. Fishing and pony trekking are both available locally and bicycles can be hired. Golfers have several courses to choose from, and among the many attractions within reach are Pencarrow, Lanhydrock, Trerice, Newquay Zoo and Tintagel Castle.

Units: 6
Rent: £210 to £1280 (short breaks available)
Other costs: none
Heating: central heating and log fires
Facilities: Cots and high chairs available
Open all year

ST AUSTELL, CORNWALL
H CARLYON BAY HOTEL, St Austell
Tel: 0726 812 304.
Off the A390 east of St Austell.

The hotel was built in 1930 and has a marvellous location in 250 acres of grounds, which include an excellent golf course of 6500 yards, and a well-established nine-hole short course. The extensive landscaped gardens are a delight, due in no small part to the excellent climate of the Cornish Riviera, and they have marvellous views of the bay. The coastal path and Crinnis Woods, part of the hotel grounds, are lovely spots to explore.

The facilities here are superb. As well as the golf courses, there are two hard tennis courts and an outdoor heated swimming pool. Children are catered for with an adventure paddock which has a tree house, a slide and a trampoline. If the weather is unkind you can enjoy the splendid indoor leisure centre which has an excellent swimming pool, a children's pool, sauna, solarium and spa bath. There are two snooker tables, table tennis and a children's play room.

This excellent hotel offers a high standard of service and comfort to give a relaxing and agreeable family holiday. It is good to report that there is an extensive and healthy menu for children and a good choice of vegetarian dishes, all served in the refurbished Bay View Restaurant.

Nearby: The coastline is dotted with lovely, sandy bays, including one below the golf course. If you fancy seeing the sights,

Charlestown, an 18th-century port is on the doorstep and has a visitor centre; Mevagissey has a folk museum. There are many other attractions within an easy drive: the ruined Restormel Castle, Lanhydrock, the farm park at Bodmin, Dobwalls Theme Park, Trelissick Garden, the Dairyland Farm Park, Trerice and the Newquay Zoo.

✕ LUNCH (12.30pm to 2pm) £11: four courses
DINNER (7.30pm to 9pm) £19: four courses
Children: own menu
£ high
Best Bargain Break: £100 per person, 2 nights – dinner, b&b
Children: from £3 a day to 70 per cent of the adult rate
Facilities: as many cots and high chairs as required; baby listening system
73 rooms, 2 family, 14 sets interconnecting
Open all year. Access/AmEx/Diners/Visa
P own car park

ST BREWARD, NR BODMIN, CORNWALL
SC COOMBE MILL, St Breward
Tel: 0208 850 344.
Off the B3266 south of Camelford. The brochure has clear directions.

The village sits on the edge of Bodmin Moor and the thirty acres of the Coombe Mill estate shelters in the Camel valley below. The river runs right through Coombe Mill, and provides superb salmon and trout fishing. The valley is a home to a wide variety of birds, animals and plant life.

The properties comprise six stone cottages and twelve log cabins. Four of the cottages have been converted from old farm buildings: a mill, a granary, a stable and a barn. One of them is suitable for only two people while the others will accommodate four. The best features of the old buildings – exposed beams and stone internal walls – have been retained and augmented by excellent furnishings and equipment. They all have wood-burning stoves and the Old Mill has a minstrel's gallery over the spacious living room.

Two cottages have recently been built and, with their granite walls and slate roofs, they fit in with grand style. Each has one double and two twin bedrooms and is superbly equipped.

These cottages all look out over a beautiful lawned garden surrounded by old trees, the ground scattered with bluebells and other wild flowers. There are some rockeries and a children's seesaw. When we visited one spring day we were struck by the tranquillity of the place.

One of the great advantages for families of staying at Coombe Hill is the presence of the animals. There is a herd of red deer, Jacob sheep, pigmy goats, Vietnamese pot-bellied pigs, Highland cows and donkeys plus the ducks, geese, swans and many wild birds.

It is a great spot for children, who also have the benefit of an excellent adventure playground. There is a huge covered barbecue and, on a practical level, a well-equipped laundry room.

Nearby: Apart from all the opportunities for fishermen, the delights of Bodmin Moor lie on the doorstep. There is a long run of safe, sandy beaches on the nearby coast, including Newquay and Bedruthan Steps. All sorts of sports are available: surfing, sailing, swimming, tennis, golf and horse riding. The other attractions are diverse. Famous houses such as Pencarrow, Trerice and Lanhydrock are close; the children will be keen to see the Tamar Otter Park and Newquay Zoo; and Dobwalls Theme Park and the Dairyland Farm Park are not too far away.

Units: 18
Rent: £140 to £660 a week (short breaks available)
Other costs: electricity by meter; high chairs & cots with linen £10 a set
Heating: central heating
Cots & high chairs: 12 of each
Open all year

ST HILARY, NR PENZANCE, CORNWALL
Ⓗ ENNYS, St Hilary
Tel: 0736 740 262.
Off the A30 or A394 east of Penzance.

You must traverse a few hundred yards of a narrow lane, its banks loaded in spring with bluebells, before you arrive at Ennys, a beautiful Cornish manor house, which was built in 1688. Its stone walls, covered in wisteria and Virginia creeper, look over a peaceful sunken garden. It is a delightful spot and you walk through to an open-air heated swimming pool with encircling terrace. Alongside there is an excellent grass tennis court, and a further stretch of garden; part of it is a herb garden, and there is also a children's swing on the grass.

The house itself has beautifully proportioned rooms, including a wood-panelled dining room and a comfortable lounge with open fireplace. The three bedrooms in the main house are stylishly decorated and furnished and have their own bathrooms and lovely views.

A barn alongside the house has been converted to provide two attractive suites, each with a double bedroom, twin-bedded room and bathroom. They are ideal for family occupation.

Ennys is a small working farm, and guests are welcome to walk the fields which stretch down to the River Hayle.

This is a delightful base for a family holiday, in a lovely rural setting, but with the beaches and the towns within easy reach. The food is mostly cooked from home-grown ingredients, with fresh fish and shellfish often available – even the bread is baked daily on the premises. The children have their high teas at 5.30pm, so that the adults can relax over their candle-lit dinner.

Nearby: There are numbers of excellent beaches within easy reach – Prussia Cove, Whitesand Bay, Praa Sands, etc – and St Michael's Mount and Land's End are a short drive away. You can easily reach Paradise Park, Poldark Mine, the Flambards Theme Park, Godolphin House and the Seal Sanctuary near Helston. Fishing, pony trekking and golf can all be arranged and there is a wind-surfing school nearby at Marazion. The Minack open-air theatre stages plays in Lamorna.

✕ DINNER (7pm) £14: avocado mousseline with prawns, supreme of chicken, iced nut cake
Children: own menu, half portions
£ medium
Best Bargain Break: £80 per person, 2 nights: dinner, b&b
Children: two thirds of adult rate up to 10 years
Facilities: 1 cot and 1 high chair; and baby listening
5 rooms, 2 family suites. Open all year

No credit cards. No smoking in bedrooms
Ⓟ own car park

ST IVES, CORNWALL
Ⓗ PORTHMINSTER HOTEL (Best Western), The
Terrace
Tel: 0736 795 221.
On the main road into the town (A3074).

This substantial and traditional seaside hotel has a wonderful location high above the steep and twisting streets of the town, which has distinct artistic association since its inhabitants have included Whistler, Walter Sickert and Barbara Hepworth.

When we visited one sunny spring morning the views over the bay were spectacular and the hotel's own gardens lead down to the sea and a lovely safe and sandy beach. The sizeable heated outdoor swimming pool has a children's paddling area and a terrace on which to loll, and the playground has a climbing frame, slide and seesaw. During the summer season table tennis, pool and darts can be played indoors.

If the weather is unkind you can head for the excellent indoor leisure centre which has a very smart swimming pool, gymnasium, sauna and solarium, and cocktail bar.

The stately lounge, well provided with comfortable chairs, spacious bar and dining room have dazzling views, as do many of the bedrooms.

The Porthminster is an excellent family hotel in a splendid seaside spot.

Nearby: The town has several museums including the Barbara Hepworth museum; Bernard Leach's pottery is well worth a look. Land's End and St Michael's Mount are quite close, with Paradise Park even closer. South toward the Lizard you can visit the Poldark Mine, Flambards Theme Park, the Seal Sanctuary and Goonhilly Earth Station.

✗ BAR LUNCH (12.15pm to 2pm) £2–6: chef's special, ploughman's, cold buffet, roast of the day;
DINNER (7.15pm to 8.30pm) £16: shellfish cocktail, soup, tournedos Rossini, pudding or cheese

Children: own menu, half portions
£ high
Best Bargain Break: £92 per person, 2 nights – dinner, b&b
Children: free up to 2 years; one third of adult rate from 2–7
years; half the adult rate from 8–12 years
Facilities: 4 cots and 4 high chairs; 2 baby listening lines
49 rooms, 11 family, 7 sets interconnecting
Open all year. Access/AmEx/Diners/Visa
P own car park opposite

ST MAWGAN, CORNWALL
SC LANVEAN FARM COTTAGES, St Mawgan
Tel: 0637 860 555.
Directions are given at the Bedruthan Steps Hotel in Mawgan
Porth: the cottages are owned by them.

St Mawgan is a delightful little village which has an agreeable
16th-century pub with a splendid garden. The three cottages have
all been converted from stone farm buildings and offer comfortable
accommodation for families in a quiet setting. They overlook the
village and have particularly good views of the ancient church and
the surrounding countryside.

Sampson Cottage was a farm house and can sleep four people
in a double and a twin bedroom. Bryher Cottage can accommodate
five people in a double, a twin and a single bedroom and the cot
can be put in the double room. It has a spiral staircase. Barn Cottage
was converted from a traditional grain barn and has three bedrooms
to accommodate six people.

The cottages are all comfortably furnished, attractively decorated
and have well-equipped kitchens. Each cottage has its own lawn
with a picnic table and a small barbecue. They all have dishwashers.

There is a great bonus for guests in that all the facilities of the
Bedruthan Steps Hotel and the Trevelgue Hotel (at Newquay) are
at their disposal. Both hotels have been in *The Family Welcome Guide*
since the very first edition and have unrivalled facilities for families.
There are comprehensive leisure facilities and full entertainment
programmes (see under Mawgan Porth and Newquay in the Guide).

Nearby: Safe, sandy beaches abound in this part of Cornwall and include the one at Mawgan Porth. Newquay has several excellent beaches and has become a notable surfing centre. Alternatively, you can walk along the North Cornwall Coast Path. Newquay also has an excellent zoo and the children will also enjoy the Leisure Park at St Agnes and the Dairyland Farm Park. Trerice is a wonderful Elizabethan mansion, while Dobwalls Theme Park and Lanhydrock are a little further afield.

Units: 3
Rent: £190 to £620 a week
Other costs: none
Heating: central heating & wood-burning stoves
Cots & high chairs provided for Bryher and Barn cottages
Open all year

SAUNTON, NR BARNSTAPLE, DEVON
H SC SAUNTON SANDS HOTEL
Tel: 0271 890 212.
On the B3231.

This large and impressive hotel, prominently situated above the rolling expanse of Saunton Sands, has an excellent range of facilities for families and succeeds in looking after them well.

There is an indoor swimming pool, with a paddling pool for the children, and a sauna; there is a squash court, a mini-cinema, a pool table and table tennis. The sizeable outdoor pool also has a paddling area for children and sublime views over the sands and the sea; there is a putting green, a hard tennis court, swings and a children's play area and a path down to a long stretch of sandy beach. Horse-riding, sailing, wind-surfing and fishing can all be arranged by the hotel staff; just down the road is Saunton Golf Club, a splendid links course which offers a stern test for any golfer.

One of the great bonuses of this hotel is the presence of a nanny, who is in attendance from 10am to 5pm every day and until 3pm on Sunday. There are plenty of toys here and lots of organized activities.

The bedrooms are comfortable and well-appointed, some with little terraces or balconies and many with enchanting views over the bay.

Nearby: Saunton Sands spreads below the hotel and there are

many other fine beaches including Woolacombe and Croyde Bay. Nature lovers should see Braunton Burrows, one of the largest nature reserves in Britain, and the children will enjoy a visit to Exmoor Bird Gardens. They will have fun, too, at Watermouth Castle, and Arlington Court is well worth a visit.

✖: LUNCH (12.30–2pm) £11: four courses
DINNER (7.30–9pm) £17: four courses
Children: own menu, half portions
£ high
Best Bargain Break £120 per person 2 nights - dinner, b&b
Children: free up to 2 years; 60% discount from 2–5; 40% discount from 6–11 years
Facilities: 20 cots and 7 high chairs; baby listening line for every room
94 rooms, 7 family, 12 suites Access/AmEx/Diners/Visa
Open all year
P: own car park
Self-catering: Seventeen apartments are let on a self-catering basis, and the occupants can use all the hotel facilities. The apartments are well-equipped and spacious and many of them look out over the dunes and the estuary. They vary in size and can be rented at prices ranging from £95 to £185 per night.

NR SOUTH MOLTON, DEVON
SC VENN FARM, King's Nympton
Tel: 0769 572 448.
The farm is south of South Molton between George Nympton and King's Nympton.

The attractive stone barns of this farm in peaceful Devon country-side were converted into four cottages a couple of years ago by Mr and Mrs Martin. The cottages, named after birds, vary slightly in size and can each sleep from four to six people.

Without exception the four cottages have been converted and equipped to a very high standard. They all have open-plan living areas, with very comfortable furnishings and well-equipped kitchens which include microwave as well as conventional cookers. There is plenty of space and the stripped-pine dining tables and chairs add to the cheerful atmosphere. A couple of the cottages have bunk beds which can also be used as separate singles. The bedrooms, some with skylights and some with windows set low down the walls, are most appealing.

Each cottage has a small terrace at the back, sheltered by a bank of flowers and shrubs. It's a lovely spot to have a drink or a meal, and barbecues are provided.

Around the cottages there is plenty of space for all the family and there are swings and a climbing frame on one of the lawns. The farm runs to about 50 acres and there are all sorts of animals with which the children can make friends: sheep, goats, ducks, geese, chickens, cats and dogs. Mrs Martin encourages the children to join in and feeding times are jolly affairs.

Delightful countryside encircles the farm and the views down the rolling, wooded valleys, through which the rivers Taw and Mole run, are sheer joy. There are some superb walks.

In addition to the cottages, an annexe to Venn Farm, Pond Cottage, can be rented. This is a spacious, if rather more functional, cottage and it has two bedrooms, a double and a twin. Guests also have the use of a large lawned garden.

Nearby: There is no shortage of leisure facilities, with horse riding, golf, swimming and fishing readily available. Mr Martin organizes clay pigeon shooting at the farm. The beaches both to the north and the west are easily reached and there are many places to visit, including Watermouth Castle, the Exmoor Bird Gardens, Arlington Court, the nature reserve at Braunton Burrows, Knightshayes Court, Dunster Castle, Combe Sydenham Hall and the Exmoor National Park Centre, a starting point for many excellent walks.

Units: 5
Rent: £110 to £370 (short breaks available off peak)
Other costs: electricity is metered in summer
Central heating: night storage and gas heaters (included in the winter price)
3 cots and 2 high chairs
Open all year

STOKE GABRIEL, NR TOTNES, DEVON
Ⓗ GABRIEL COURT HOTEL, Stoke Gabriel
Tel: 0803 782 206.
Go to the village and you'll find a signpost to the hotel.

We are always happy to visit this very pretty 16th-century manor house. It's an elegant, white-painted building with an ornamental balustrade and a square tower, in a quiet village between Paignton and Totnes. It is set in three acres of lovely, tranquil, sloping land which boasts one of the oldest pink magnolias in England, ancient yews, an old-fashioned knot garden, a vegetable garden and an orchard just made for visiting youngsters to play in. There's also a heated outdoor swimming pool, a croquet lawn and an outdoor play area.

The kitchen uses local produce as much as possible – fruit and vegetables from the garden, salmon and trout from the Dart, poultry and venison from nearby farms and woods. There are separate meal times for children, who are not allowed in the dining room in the evenings.

Nearby: This part of Devon has so many attractions for visitors, especially families. There is an array of excellent beaches surrounding the busy resort of Torquay and many places to visit, including Compton Castle, Buckfast Abbey and its neighbour, the Dart Valley Railway. Further afield, the children can visit the Dartmoor Wildlife Park and the National Shire Horse Centre. The ruins of Berry Pomeroy Castle, haunted, of course, are not far from the hotel. Golf is available and trips on the River Dart can also be arranged.

✗ DINNER (from 7.30pm) £21: egg baked with cream & cheese, soup, fresh Dart salmon, pudding and cheese
Children: high teas
£ high
Best Bargain Break: £228 per person, 4 nights – dinner, b&b
Children: cot £6.50; £9.50 from 3 to 10 years; £15 thereafter
Facilities: plenty of cots and high chairs; baby listening to every room
20 rooms, 5 sets interconnecting. Access/AmEx/Diners/Visa
Open all year, except February. No music
Ⓟ own car park

THORVERTON, NR EXETER, DEVON
sc FURSDON, Thorverton
Tel: 0392 860 860.
Off the A396 north of Exeter.

Anyone who craves the peace and tranquillity of the countryside
will be well suited by Fursdon, a small country estate in delightful
Devon countryside. At the heart of the estate is the manor house
of Fursdon itself, a most appealing building which was re-designed
in the 18th century but whose origins lie as far back as the 13th
century.

One of the most attractive aspects of the self-catering accommodation at Fursdon, apart from the lovely surroundings, is the opportunity to live within the walls of an ancient house with its own
historical associations. Three of the properties are within Fursdon
House itself. The East Wing is the largest apartment and sleeps
six people; the comfortable and well-proportioned sitting room
looks out over the gardens and the park to the rolling countryside
beyond. The North Wing sleeps four: the adults in a double bedroom and two children in bunk beds. The panelled sitting room
has a view of the terraced gardens behind the house. Both properties
have their own entrances.

The third property, full of interest with its sloping ceilings also
overlooks the rear gardens, and sleeps two people.

Two of the cottages are close to the main house. The Lime
House was converted from a granary store and has the bonus of
its own quiet and enclosed garden. It sleeps eight people in one
double, two twin and two single bedrooms.

Close by there is Fursdon Cottage, its facade covered in wisteria
and roses, which also has its own garden. It can sleep six people.
Fursdon Barton has been converted from the wing of the home
farmhouse and sleeps up to six people. Like all the properties, it
has splendid views over the estate and the countryside.

At Fursdon there are 700 acres in which to roam, including
nearly a hundred acres of woodland. Wildlife enthusiasts will find
much of interest here, and there are beautiful stretches of garden
in which to browse, smooth lawns sheltered by shady trees and old
stone walls. If you are feeling athletic there is a grass tennis court,
and you can play badminton, croquet and table tennis. Board games

and table tennis are also available. A children's play area includes swings and a slide. Guests can also fish on the estate, as long as a licence is bought. Guided tours of Fursdon are conducted at various times through the summer.

Nearby: Golf and riding are readily available in the locality and there are many good beaches within easy reach. There is no lack of attractions for holiday makers to enjoy: the Maritime Museum in Exeter, the nature reserve at Dawlish Warren, Powderham Castle, Bicton Park, the donkey sanctuary near Sidmouth, Killerton House, Bickleigh Castle, Knightshayes Court and the remarkable Castle Drogo.

Units: 6
Rent: £100 to £325
Other costs: electricity is metered
Heating: a mixture of central heating and electric heaters
6 cots and 6 high chairs
Open all year

THURLESTONE, DEVON
Ⓗ THURLESTONE HOTEL, Thurlestone
Tel: 0548 560 382.
In the centre of the village.

This has long been a favourite hotel of ours and on our various visits we have always found that the Grose family, who have owned and run this hotel since before the turn of the century, get most things right. When we last stayed we had a delightful room which overlooked the gardens and the sweep of Bigbury Bay, and we found the staff as friendly and efficient as always. The food was of excellent quality and cooked with skill.

All this makes a pretty good starting point for a family holiday. But, in addition, this hotel, which is in one of the loveliest spots in south Devon, has wonderful facilities including two hard tennis courts, two squash courts, a badminton court, a swimming pool and a play area with a climbing net, swings, a playhouse and a slide. The well-designed indoor pool has a paddling pool for very young children. There is also a fitness room. With table tennis and snooker, an excellent par-three course at the hotel and golf at

Thurlestone and Bigbury all aspiring and perspiring superstars are wonderfully well catered for.

On a practical level, playpens are provided at both swimming pools and there is a well-equipped laundry room (washing and drying machines, ironing board and iron).

Good news for real ale fans: the baby listening service extends to the hotel's pub next door.

Nearby: There are plenty of sandy beaches all along this stretch of coast, including one at Thurlestone. Inland, you can visit the National Shire Horse Centre and the Dartmoor Wildlife Centre, Buckfast Abbey and the adjacent Dart Valley Railway, and the castles at Compton and Totnes.

�ం BAR SNACKS (12.30pm to 2pm & 7pm to 9pm)) £2–8: Danish open sandwiches, smoked salmon, Torbay crab & prawns, ravioli;
LUNCH (12.30pm to 2pm) £14: Cornish scallops, mixed grill, fresh fruit salad;
DINNER (7.30pm to 9pm) £23: crab & avocado cocktail, soup, rosette of Devon lamb, pudding and cheese
Children: own menu
£ high
Best Bargain Break: £72–110 per person, 2 nights – dinner, b&b
Children: free up to 2 years; £11 to 12 years (includes breakfast and high tea)
Facilities: 6 cots and 6 high chairs; baby listening lines to all rooms
Open all year (except for a week in January)
68 rooms, 15 family, 3 sets interconnecting
Access/Visa. No smoking in restaurant
⊞ Ale: Bass, Palmers, Wadworth's
ℙ own car park

TIDEFORD, CORNWALL
ℝ HESKYN MILL, Tideford
Tel: 0752 851 481.
By the A38 west of Saltash. Look for the sign and take the turning to St Germans.

The old mill wheel is still attached to the wall of this beautiful stone building, and inside you can see the rest of the machinery on each floor. Downstairs, there is a small bar and under the low beams a nice mixture of wooden tables, sofas and settles and a wood-burning stove. The restaurant is up the open wooden staircase and is another delightful room, with a mix of differing wooden tables.

You will always find fresh Cornish fish on the menu; indeed, the owners try to use local sources for their food whenever possible.

There is a little terrace by the front door and lawns at the back where you can sit on warmer days.

✗ LUNCH SNACK MENU £3–12: fish soup, game pie, fish of the day, rack of lamb, fillet of salmon;
DINNER £18: prawn Waldorf, rosette of lamb, pudding or cheese
Children: small portions
Open 12pm to 2pm & 7pm to 10pm. Closed Sunday and Monday
Access/AmEx/Visa
⊕ Ale: St Austell
ℙ own car park

TIVERTON, DEVON
Ⓡ Ⓛ KNIGHTSHAYES COURT, Tiverton
Tel: 0884 254 665.
Just off the A396 North of Tiverton.

All the confidence of the Victorian age went into the flamboyant style of this mansion, built in the 1870s to the design of the architect, William Burges. The richly decorated interior has been restored and there are some notable paintings by Constable and Turner on display, as well as a Rembrandt self-portrait.

Knightshayes Court is the home of Lady Heathcoat Amory, formerly Joyce Wethered, who is reckoned to be the greatest of all lady golfers. One of the glories of the place is the gardens, which are immense and beautiful. The immaculate lawns, fine trees and arrays of flowers and shrubs make it interesting at any time of the year.

The restaurant was constructed in the old stable block, built in the same Gothic style as the main house, and the National Trust shop and a garden shop are also here. The restaurant is spacious and attractively designed; the two rooms have polished brick floors, stone walls with wood panelling and wooden tables, smartly painted red. You can get something to eat here throughout the day, while lunches are served from 12 till 2pm, and there are plenty of high chairs. Hot and cold meals are available at prices up to £5.

The lavatories are roomy and the Ladies has a chair and plenty of space, alongside the wash basins, on which you can change a baby.

✗ £1–5: Devon paté, fresh trout, ploughman's, cream teas
Children: half portions
Access/AmEx/Visa. Licensed
No smoking. No music
Open Easter to 31 October; gardens 10.30am to 5.30pm; house 1.30 to 5.30pm (4.30 in October); closed on Fridays
Charges: adults £4.80; children £2.40 (1993 prices)
Baby changing: facilities in the Ladies
ⓟ ample

TORBRYAN, DEVON
ⓟ OLD CHURCH HOUSE INN, Torbryan
Tel: 0803 812 372.
From the A381 follow signs to Ipplepen and then to the village.

Take a drive through Devon lanes to this ancient pub and see the fine church of Saxon origin opposite and the Saxon oak door embedded in the pub wall. With the history taken care of, you can relax with a drink in the comfortable oak-furnished children's room, one of the five rooms in this pub of beamed ceilings, dark panelling and stone walls. The pub has recently been extended into the old cellars, and presumably the three ghosts which inhabit the building have no objections to this.

There are a dozen or so real ales on offer and the landlord varies his selection; the menu, which is very comprehensive, includes fresh fish from Brixham and Dartmouth. A three-course lunch is served on Sundays at around £5.

There is a grassy bank where wild flowers grow and where you may sit on warm days.

✗ (12pm to 2.30pm & 7pm to 10.30pm) £1–9: salads, Dart salmon, Brixham plaice, country pie, steaks, hare & venison pie
Children: half portions
🍺 Ale: Bishop's Tipple, Hall & Woodhouse and umpteen others
🅿 own car park

TORQUAY, DEVON
Ⓗ CRAIG COURT HOTEL, 10 Ash Hill Road
Tel: 0803 294 400.
Not far from the town centre and close to Castle Circus.

This well-maintained hotel is in a handsome Victorian building with spacious public rooms which include a comfortable lounge whose bay windows look out over the gardens, the town and bay. There is a bar alongside. A secluded lawned garden sheltered by trees is a real sun trap, and you can enjoy panoramic views from the little terrace, shaded by a canopy, above the garden.

The brightly decorated bedrooms have ample space and include two family rooms, one with a double and two single beds and the other with a double bed and bunk beds for two children. These have their own bathrooms, as have four of the other bedrooms.

The hotel faces south and is in a reasonably quiet road, yet it is within walking distance of the beaches, the main shopping centre and most of the attractions of the town. This comfortable and moderately priced hotel is a good base for a holiday in this part of the world, which has so much to offer to families.

Nearby: There is a host of things to do and see in this popular resort, with a wide selection of beaches – Blackpool Sands, Paignton, Anstey's Cove, Oddicombe Beach, Ness Cove, and Dawlish Warren, to name but a few. There are many other attractions for the holiday maker: museums at Brixham, Torbay and Dartmouth; the Dart Valley railway; castles at Totnes and Compton; Buckfast Abbey; and the Dartmoor Wildlife Park and the National Shire Horse Centre are near Plymouth.

✗ DINNER (6pm) £9
Children: half portions
£ medium

Best Bargain Break: £64 per person, 3 days – dinner, b&b
Children: £2 up to 3 years, half price to 11 years; 25 per cent off
from 11 to 14 years
Facilities: 1 cot and 1 high chair
10 rooms, 2 family. Open Easter to October
Ⓟ own car park. No credit cards. No music

TOTNES, DEVON
Ⓡ WILLOW, 87 High Street
Tel: 0803 862 605.
At the top of the town, in the Narrows.

This self-service vegetarian restaurant is sited at the top of the hill
in the attractive main street of Totnes, a town which is notable for
its large number of public car parks. It is a plain and simple restaurant with several nice wooden tables, and a family room with
some settees and cane chairs at the back. This leads out to a little
patio, with a few tables. It is very peaceful there on summer days.
   The dishes are imaginative, and very good value, and are cooked
from organically grown vegetables.
   The lavatory off the patio has some padded benches on which
babies can be changed.

✗ £1–6: aubergine bake, homity pie, cheesy shepherd's pie,
vegetable thali, gypsy casserole
Children: small portions
Open 10am to 5pm Mon to Sat & 6.30 to 10pm Wed to Sat
No smoking in restaurant area. Licensed
One high chair only
Ⓟ public car park nearby

TREBARWITH STRAND, TINTAGEL, CORNWALL
Ⓗ OLD MILLFLOOR, Tintagel
Tel: 0840 770 234.
Off the B3263, south of Tintagel. Take the road to Trebarwith
Strand.

Idyllic is the adjective which immediately springs to mind as, from the road above, you gaze down at this delightful 16th-century house with its leaded windows. It is set in ten acres in a little valley and the garden is so appealing and peaceful. You can sit at the bench tables and look around you at the wooded slopes with their profusion of ferns and flowers, trees and trailing greenery. A small stream meanders through the garden and, when the rain comes, rushes through, so you must keep an eagle eye on your offspring.

Keep a wary eye on them too, and on where you place your own feet, when you approach the house, because the entrance can only be reached down a steepish gravel path and some steps. You must park your car in the spaces provided on the roadside.

The inside of the house lives up to its surroundings. The living room has four wooden dining tables and the sitting area is furnished with comfort and style; there are deep armchairs and a sofa on which to relax and a beautiful old padded wooden settle. The three bedrooms, one of which is a family room, are lovely high-ceilinged rooms and are quiet and peaceful.

This is definitely the place to 'get away from it all', and for a very reasonable price too.

Nearby: Down the road is the little beach of Trebarwith Strand, with Gull Rock rising impressively from the sea. You must exercise care on this beach as the rising tide can cut off the unwary. There are many alternatives nearby: for example, Crackington Haven, Harlyn Bay and Constantine Bay. There are superb walks along the coastal path. There are many attractions within easy reach, especially around Newquay: the zoo, the Lappa Valley Railway, Dairyland farm park and the lovely house at Trerice. The Tropical Bird Gardens at Padstow, Tintagel Castle, Pencarrow and Bodmin Moor are not too far away.

✗ DINNER (7pm to 8pm) £11
Children: high teas
£ low
Children: free if sharing with parents
Facilities: 2 cots and a high chair
3 rooms, 1 family. Open March to October
No smoking. Unlicensed
Ⓟ spaces on the road above

WEST ANSTEY, YEO MILL, NR SOUTH MOLTON, DEVON

Ⓗ PARTRIDGE ARMS FARM, Yeo Mill

Tel: 039 84 217.

Off the B3227 east of South Molton.

Once a coaching inn, where the last pint was served in 1905, the farm has been in the same family since the early years of this century. It now consists of 200 acres, and sits on the southern slopes of Exmoor. The charming building dates back to the 14th century and has rough cast walls, painted pale pink, with honeysuckle climbing over them and the lawned gardens sport several apple trees and a lily pond.

The cosy sitting room has comfortable chairs and a sofa, a large stone fireplace with a wood-burning stove, and paintings of wildlife and hunting scenes adorn the walls. There are no less than three charming dining rooms; one has a huge open fireplace decorated with old farm implements and cider jars and the low ceiling is cross-hatched with wooden beams; the next room has another open fireplace and a long wooden table; and the third dining room also contains a small bar, which has been kept as it was in the 19th century.

Everything overlooks the encircling farm land and guests are welcome to wander around among the cows, sheep, pigs, geese, hens, dogs, cats and ponies. The farm, by the way, has its own stretch of trout fishing.

All of the bedrooms are pleasing. One has a four-poster, one double bedroom has a separate room with bunk beds, and there is a family room with double bed and two bunk beds. Most of the rooms have their own bathrooms.

Partridge Arms Farm is run entirely by the Milton family and is a most appealing and welcoming place to stay in the heart of the Devon countryside.

Nearby: You are not too far from the north Devon and Somerset coastal resorts, including Woolacombe Sand and Croyde Bay. The whole of Exmoor is also at your feet – lovely for nature lovers, walkers, and pony trekkers. There is much else for the holiday maker within easy reach: the nature reserve at Braunton Burrows and the Exmoor Bird Gardens; the Maritime Museum at Appledore; Arlington Court; the Dartington Glass factory; Watermouth Castle and the Combat Vehicles Museum near South Molton.

✕ DINNER (7.15pm) £8
Children: own menu, half portions
£ low
Children: nominal charge up to 5 years; then according to age
Facilities: 2 cots and 2 high chairs
7 rooms, 2 family, 1 set interconnecting. Open all year
No credit cards. No music
Ⓟ ample

WEST BUCKLAND, NR BARNSTAPLE, DEVON
Ⓗ HUXTABLE FARM, West Buckland
Tel: 0598 760 254.
Off the A361 east of Barnstaple. The farm entrance is opposite West Buckland School.

This is a delightful listed building which dates back to the 16th century, a Devon longhouse built of stone and with climbing jasmine over the walls. The house has been restored with care by the owners, and antique furniture complements the original features. The sitting room has fine proportions and looks on to an enclosed garden; it is a comfortable and very inviting room with a wood-burning stove and some pleasing corner cupboards. Across the corridor, with its ancient black beams and screen panelling, there is a splendid dining room which has a large open fireplace with a stove, a dresser and a lovely wooden table around which the guests gather to enjoy Jackie Payne's excellent food (and home-made wine). The extensive gardens provide most of the produce used in the house. Children have their own small dining room for breakfast and high teas, and there is also a television room where there are children's games and a good selection of books.

There is a games room in the garden, with table tennis and darts, and a quarter-size snooker table and lots of toys. There is loads of room for children to play, and swings, slides, a sandpit, Wendy house and seesaw are set up in the garden. Sheep are reared on the 80 acres of farmland and children are welcome to help to feed the pet lambs, rabbits, Shetland ponies and pygmy goats.

The bedrooms are furnished and decorated to a very high standard and are full of character, with views over the tranquil gardens and encircling countryside. The family rooms are very spacious, especially a secluded one on one side of the house which has double and two single beds and a bathroom. The two bedrooms in the converted barn also have loads of space. A laundry room is available.

This welcoming and well-equipped farmhouse offers an excellent base for a family holiday.

Nearby: The coastal resorts of north Devon are fairly close and there are some excellent beaches to visit, especially at Woolacombe and Croyde Bay. The natural splendours of Exmoor are close and the Exmoor Centre is near Dulverton, a good starting point for walks. The Tarka Trail runs past the entrance to the farm. There is much else to see: Braunton Burrows, one of the largest nature reserves in Britain; Arlington Court; Watermouth Castle; Exmoor Bird Gardens; the Maritime Museum at Appledore; Dunster Castle, Combe Sydenham Hall and Rosemoor Royal Horticultural Garden.

✗ DINNER (7.30pm) £12: herb & liver paté, lamb korma, pudding and cheese

Children: own menu
£ low
Children: cot £6; extra bed £9
Facilities: 2 cots and a high chair; baby alarms provided
6 rooms, 2 family. Open all year except Xmas
No music
No smoking in dining room. Unlicensed
P ample

WHIMPLE, DEVON
P PADDOCK INN, Whimple
Tel: 0404 822 356.
On the A30 (eastbound side) between Exeter and Honiton.

This large pub, its brick now painted white, sits on the busy A30 and began life in the 18th century as a farmhouse. One of its attributes is an outstanding stock of bottled beers from all over the world and there is always a good choice of real ale.

It is an agreeable pub, with its dark wooden panels and beams and brass decorations, and has excellent facilities for families. There is a sizeable family room with plenty of wooden tables, padded chairs and benches; alongside, there is a games room with a pool table.

The family room leads out to a grassy area with bench tables and a children's play area with a tree house, swing and a climbing frame.

The pub is usually open all day during the summer months (Monday to Saturday) and food is available at all times.

✗ (11am to 2.30pm & 6pm to 10pm; all day during summer) £2–10: burgers, plaice & chips, steaks, vegetable curry, chicken Kiev
Children: own menu, half portions
⊕ Ale: Courage, Golden Hill and Guests
P own car park

WIDECOMBE IN THE MOOR, DEVON

P OLD INN, Widecombe
Tel: 036 42 207.
North of Ashburton on the minor roads, and can be reached from
the A38 or the B3212.

This famous village has a pub to match. It is part of a row of
14th-century stone buildings which also house gift and craft shops.
It has several rooms with thick stone walls and lots of oak, and the
family room has a large open fire, a floor of worn flagstones, oak
benches and settles.

Children are also welcome in the long, narrow dining room which
has several tables and padded bench seats, and in the other eating
areas within the pub.

The way to the car park is not immediately obvious – take the
road to the right of the stone buildings and the car park is on your
left. Next to it is a large grassy garden with a tiny brook, picnic
benches and a terrace.

There's a good choice of food at reasonable prices, with daily
specials, several vegetarian dishes and a Sunday lunch for around
£5.

✕ (11am to 2pm & 6.30pm to 10.15pm) £2–10: Moorland smokie,
turkey & ham pie, steaks, beef in red wine, bean casserole
Children: half portions
⊞ Ale: Usher's. No music
P own car park

WOOLACOMBE, DEVON

H SC DEVON BEACH HOTEL, The Esplanade
Tel: 0271 870 449.
On the coast road.

The hotel is housed in a substantial building, painted white with a
blue trim, and it stands high above Woolacombe Bay with its sheltered sandy beaches. It has an indoor heated swimming pool and
a games room with a pool table, table tennis and various machines.
A washing machine and tumble dryer are also available.

The views from the hotel windows are magnificent: a panorama of sand, rocks and sea that you can enjoy from the sun terrace. Most of the bedrooms have the same view, and those we looked at were nicely decorated and functional. There are plenty of family rooms, and the Devon Beach is a decent, reasonably priced hotel.

Nearby: The beaches are wide and sandy; lifeguards patrol both Woolacombe and Croyde Bay during the summer. There is a great range of other attractions within easy reach: Watermouth Castle and Arlington Court; the nature reserve at Braunton Burrows and Exmoor Bird Gardens; the Exmoor Park Centre; Dartington Glass; and the Combat Vehicles Museum near Barnstaple.

✗ BAR SNACKS (12.30pm to 2pm) £1–3: ploughman's, jacket potatoes, salads, scampi & chips;
DINNER (7pm to 8.15pm) £11: salmon ramekin, soup, roast turkey, pudding and cheese
Children: own menu, half portions
£ medium
Best Bargain Break: £39 per person per night – dinner, b&b
Children: from £5 to £20 per day (including meals)
Facilities: as many cots and high chairs as needed; baby listening system in every room
32 rooms, 17 family, 2 sets interconnecting
Closed end Oct to Easter. Access/Visa
No smoking in one lounge
Ⓟ car park
Self-catering: The hotel has a penthouse apartment which can accommodate up to seven people. The lounge and one bedroom have sun terraces and every room has lovely views out to sea. The terms, which include linen, heating etc, range from £200 to £500 per week for four people (an extra person is charged at £50 a week).

WOOLACOMBE, DEVON
Ⓗ SC WOOLACOMBE BAY HOTEL (Best Western)
Tel: 0271 870 388.

This resort has a magnificent stretch of beach and a lovely setting amid rolling hills. This stately seaside hotel is in pristine condition both inside and out and has some fine public rooms, including comfortable lounges, a welcoming, high-ceilinged restaurant, two bars with real ale, and very agreeable and well-furnished bedrooms, many of them with sea views. The bathrooms are of very high quality.

The array of facilities includes a sizeable indoor pool with paddling pool (and galas organized for children), a steam room, jacuzzi and sauna, three squash courts, including a glass-backed court, table tennis and pool, a very well-equipped fitness room with some serious apparatus, and a very congenial snooker room with wood-panelling and a high ceiling (for adults only).

The children have their own spacious play area indoors with table tennis, pool, amusement machines, big screen videos and lots of organized activities.

Everyone can enjoy the large outdoor swimming pool with its flume slide, around which there are lots of reclining seats. In addition the hotel has two hard tennis courts, an expansive stretch of grass in front of the hotel which runs down to the sea, and a play area to the side which has croquet, swingball, and a pitch and putt course. The hotel also has a motor yacht which can be chartered.

All kinds of games and sports are organized during the summer, and entertainments – dances and discos in the large ballroom – are laid on in the evenings.

The bistro and coffee shop is open all day for meals and snacks, and serves a three-course menus in the evening for around £10. The full dinner menu in the restaurant is excellent value, too.

The Woolacombe Bay is an impressive hotel in a delightful location and has all the amenities any family could desire.

Nearby: Woolacombe has a three mile stretch of sands and there are other excellent beaches nearby, including Croyde Bay and Saunton, where there is a superb golf course. If you are interested in the natural world you should visit Braunton Burrows, one of Britain's largest nature reserves and the Exmoor Bird Gardens should also appeal to children. Watermouth Castle is great fun for youngsters, while the adults will perhaps favour a visit to Arlington Court. The beauties of Exmoor are not far away and the Exmoor Centre near Dulverton is a good starting point for walks.

✖ BISTRO (10am to 10pm) £1–4: selection of hot & cold snacks;
DINNER (7.30pm to 9pm) £17: 7 course menu, eg, hors d'oeuvres,
soup, seafood vol au vent, roast venison, cheese, fruit
Children: own menu, half portions
£ high
Best Bargain Break: £103 per person, 2 nights – dinner, b&b
Children: from free to £49 depending on age and season
Facilities: as many cots and high chairs as required; baby listening
to every room
59 rooms, 13 family, 11 sets interconnecting
Closed January. Access/AmEx/Diners/Visa
🚹 Ale: Bass. No music
🄿 own car park
Self-catering: The hotel can also offer nearly forty apartments
on self-catering basis. They sleep from two to eight people and
range in price from £150 to £1170 per week. All the facilities of
the hotel can be used, and cots and high chairs and baby listening
are made available.

Mid-West England

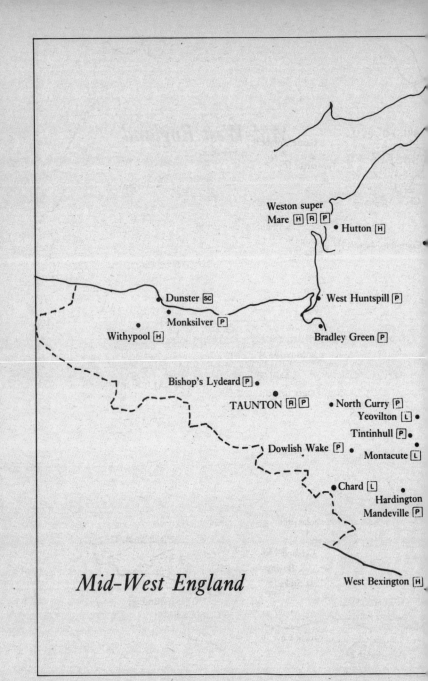

Weston super
Mare Ⓗ Ⓡ Ⓟ
● Hutton Ⓗ

Dunster ⓈⒸ
● West Huntspill Ⓟ
Monksilver Ⓟ
Withypool Ⓗ
Bradley Green Ⓟ

Bishop's Lydeard Ⓟ ●
●
TAUNTON Ⓡ Ⓟ   ● North Curry Ⓟ
Yeovilton Ⓛ ●
Tintinhull Ⓟ ●
Dowlish Wake Ⓟ ●   ●
Montacute Ⓛ

● Chard Ⓛ   ●
Hardington
Mandeville Ⓟ

Mid-West England

West Bexington Ⓗ

BRISTOL R L

Castle Combe P
Tormarton P • Pewsham P

Calne L • Avebury R

Chew Magna SC
• Bathford P

BATH R • Bradford-on-Avon H

• Compton Martin P • Norton St
Philip P

• Erlestoke H SC

• Wells H R L

• Stourton L

Semley P
Shaftesbury H SC • • Ansty H P SALISBURY R P

• Trent P

Lydlinch H •

• Sydling St Nicholas H Spetisbury R

• Plush P BOURNEMOUTH H
Lytchett Minster R P •
Dorchester SC Bovington Camp L
East Stoke H • Sandford R
Osmington Mills P Studland H
Moonfleet • • Corfe Castle L
H SC Lulworth Cove H
Weymouth
H L

BRIAN R. ANDREWS

ANSTY, DORSET
HP THE FOX, Ansty
Tel: 0258 880 328.
Signposted in the minor roads near Milton Abbas and south-west
of Blandford.

In its dual role as both a medium-sized hotel and a pub, the Fox
has outstanding facilities for families. The building itself is very
appealing with its brick and flint facade and it has two attractive
bars with a remarkable collection of Toby jugs and china plates.
Alongside the food service area there is a pleasant dining room
with good wooden tables and a little alcove at one end with wide
windows which overlook the garden. There is also an attractive
restaurant, which is open in the evening, with french windows that
lead out to the enclosed garden.

The pub is notable for its large family area (no smoking here)
with plenty of tables and chairs, and has a pool table and table
football. Alongside is a sizeable playroom with slide, rocking rabbit,
toys and children's books, and a skittle alley. High chairs are
available.

The bedrooms have excellent standards of decoration and comfort, and the family rooms are very spacious indeed. We looked at
several: two with a double bed and two single beds, and another

which could accommodate a family of five without any strain at all. The rooms are light and bright and have lovely views.

There is plenty of room in the rear garden where there is an enclosed lawned area with bench tables and a Wendy house, and a sizeable swimming pool with a surrounding terrace. The front garden, under some mature trees, has another Wendy house and some slides and a few bench tables.

This is an exceptional family inn in a lovely part of Dorset.

Nearby: A number of interesting places are within easy reach, not least the coast, which runs east and west from Weymouth, and the Sea Life Centre. Athelhampton House and Kingston Lacy, Milton Abbey, Hardy's Cottage, The Tutankhamun Exhibition, the Tank Museum at Bovington, Corfe Castle and Brownsea Island are also close by.

✕ BAR MEALS (12pm to 2pm & 7pm to 10pm) £2–8: Dorset paté, lamb chops, swordfish steaks, Madras curry;
DINNER (7–9pm) £12: seafood pancake, chicken romana, pudding or cheese
Children: small portions
£ medium
Best Bargain Break: £33 per person, per night – dinner, b&b
Children: free up to 3 years; £10 from 4 to 11; £12 from 12 to 16
Facilities: 4 cots, 3 high chairs; baby listening system
14 rooms, 5 family
Open all year. Access/Visa
🍺 Ale: Hall & Woodhouse, Tetley & guest beer
Ⓟ own car park

AVEBURY, WILTS
Ⓡ STONES RESTAURANT, Avebury
Tel: 067 23 514.
Off the main street of the village.

The village is encircled by the famous Neolithic stones which brood across the landscape in their twin circles, and were thought by John Aubrey in the 17th century to be of more historical importance than Stonehenge. He wrote of the stones as looking 'like a flocke of sheep. One might fancy it to have been the scene, where the giants fought with huge stones against the gods.'

The restaurant is housed in a fine old stone barn next to the National Trust Shop and the Tourist Information Centre. There's a cobbled patio outside, a large grassy area with pond, a dovecote, a backdrop of lime trees, and across the way is the manor house. Inside, the restaurant is long and spacious, plainly and attractively furnished with pine tables, chairs and settles.

All the food is homemade including the bread and cakes (from organic flours), the jams and the chutneys. The herbs and much of the organic produce are grown in the village and do not contain any artificial additives. There are plenty of morning snacks available, including rolls, quiches, salads, cakes and various savouries; after-noon teas are served from 2.30pm, and there is an excellent choice of teas.

A chair and a table has been provided in the Ladies, albeit the space is limited.

✕ £1–5: soup, salads, hot savoury dishes, cream tea
Children: smaller portions
Open 10am to 6pm every day during summer; weekends only in winter
Closed in Jan. No credit cards accepted
🍺 Ale: Bunce's. No smoking area.
Licensed. No music
🅿 in the village

BATH, AVON
🆁 SALLY LUNN'S HOUSE, 4 North Parade Passage
Tel: 0225 461 634.
In the town centre, not far from Abbey Green.

This is one of the oldest houses in Bath and dates from 1482. Excavations in the cellar revealed items such as pottery, pieces of mosaic from Roman times, and a series of figures which depict people through the ages: these are on display in the little museum, along with an ancient oven. Sally Lunn started baking her famous buns in the latter part of the 17th century and buns made from the

same recipe are still sold here – both the savoury and the sweet variety.

The café is on two floors: there is a pretty, chintzy room on the first floor with a large fireplace; and the larger ground floor room is an attractive beamed area with an archway in the middle. Dinners are now served from six o'clock in the evening and the early sittings are popular with families. It is advisable to book ahead.

Space is at a premium here, and there is nowhere to change a baby.

✗ £1–5: Sally Lunn buns – Welsh rarebit, chicken curry, smoked salmon paté, baked beans, salads;
DINNER (6pm to 11pm) £11: crudités, stuffed breast of chicken, apple pie & cream
Open 10am to 11pm (from noon on Sunday & until 6pm on Monday)
Licensed. Access/Visa
No smoking

BATHFORD, NR BATH, AVON
P THE CROWN, 2 Bathford Hill
Tel: 0225 852 297.
At the junction of the A4 and A363 east of Bath.

This stately stone pub dates back to the 18th century but was substantially altered in the early years of this century. Its fine Georgian facade is enlivened by lovely displays of flowers.

There is plenty of space inside, with a large bar area, but the interior is well designed to give the effect of a number of small rooms. One of these is for families: the smartly furnished Garden Room is a no smoking area; a door leads out to a terrace and on to a large lawned garden, which is safely enclosed. There are plenty of bench tables and in summer toys are put out for young children.

An alternative to the Garden Room for families is the Burgundy Room on the other side of the pub. This is a spacious and well-proportioned room with plenty of tables and chairs and it particularly comes into play at weekends. There are several high chairs available and a changing table in the Ladies.

It is good to report that the enterprising range of food is freshly prepared, so you must be prepared to wait at busy times (weekends, for example). Even better to report that chips do not sully the premises, and that children are offered smaller portions of the adult dishes – not the inevitable things and chips. They also have their own range of cocktails: Blue Lagoon, Dragon's Blood, Purple People Eater and so on.

This is an admirable and very welcoming pub where the licensees hold a balance between their various customers with great success; it is a real pub in the traditional sense (good food and a choice of real ales) and it also has excellent facilities for families.

✕ (12pm to 2pm & 7pm to 9.30pm, not Mon lunch) £1–9: rump steak, Thai chicken & brown rice, steak & mushroom & ale pie, lentil nut casserole, Indian chicken parcel
Children: own menu, small portions
ℚ Ale: Bass, Ruddles, Usher's
P own car park

BISHOP'S LYDEARD, SOMERSET
P BELL INN, Bishop's Lydeard
Tel: 0823 432 968.
In the village off the A358 north west of Taunton. Head for the church.

The lovely garden gives visitors a good introduction to this old pub. It has a terrace with some bench tables and is ringed with bright flowers and greenery. The pub, built in the 15th century, is alongside the ancient village church.

Inside, the stone walls and beamed ceilings give an appealing atmosphere to the place and families are welcome either in the Cellar Bar, which has a pool table and various amusement machines, or in the restaurant area, a lovely bright room on the far side of the lounge bar.

Food is served every day and a Sunday lunch is also available at under £4 for a main course. There is an excellent range of real ales to be tried.

✕ (12pm to 2pm & 6.30pm to 10pm) £1–9: devilled whitebait, chicken Kiev, steaks, mixed grill, plaice & chips
Children: own menu, half portions
⌁ Ale: Golden Hill, Wadworth's, Websters & guest beer
P own car park

BOURNEMOUTH, DORSET
H HINTON FIRS HOTEL (Exec Hotels), Manor Road, East Cliff
Tel: 0202 555 409.
Follow the signs for East Cliff.

This welcoming hotel, built in the late 19th century as a seaside villa, occupies a corner site in the heart of the hotel area of the town, and is just a hundred yards or so from the cliff top. Lifts and paths go down to the beach.

The hotel is in pristine condition and one of its merits is the large amount of space at the guests' disposal: a large and smartly decorated dining room, a very comfortable, large lounge which overlooks the garden, a no-smoking television lounge and a very

agreeable cocktail bar, rich pink in colour with padded green furniture.

The facilities are excellent here. There is a heated outdoor pool
with a children's play pool in a sheltered spot in the attractive
lawned garden, which is enclosed and has some fine trees, a rockery
and rhododendron bushes. It is a real sun trap and lunch can be
enjoyed on the terrace. Sliding doors lead to the indoor pool, there
is also a sauna and jacuzzi, and the games room has table tennis
and a pool table.

Just as the public rooms are spacious and bright, so are the many
family rooms, usually equipped with a double and a single bed
(every bedroom has its own bathroom). The decorations and furnishings are first class. The annexe also contains two family rooms,
including a large family suite which has a double and a single bed
in one room and a separate single room.

The Hinton Firs is a very appealing hotel which offers excellent
value in a popular holiday area.

Nearby: Apart from the many attractions of Bournemouth itself
you have easy access to the rest of Dorset: to Corfe Castle, the
Swanage Railway and Durlston Country Park; to Brownsea Island
and Merley Bird Gardens, and to Kingston Lacy and Wimborne
Minster. A bit further afield you can visit the Tank Museum at
Bovington Camp, the Tutankhamen Exhibition, Clouds Hill and
Hardy's Cottage.

✕ BAR LUNCH (12.30–2pm) £2–6: grilled plaice, seafood
platter, chicken goujons, steak & kidney & mushroom pie

DINNER (7–8.30pm) £12: canneloni Rossini, soup, grilled sirloin steak, pudding & cheese
Children: own menu
£ high
Best Bargain Break: £36 per person per night – dinner, b&b
Children: babies free; one third up to 5 years; half price from 5 to 11 years; two thirds over 11 years
Facilities: plenty of cots and high chairs, and a baby listening system
52 rooms, 12 family. Open all year
No smoking in dining room & one lounge. Access/Visa
P own car park

BOVINGTON CAMP, NR WAREHAM, DORSET
L TANK MUSEUM, Bovington Camp
Tel: 0929 403 329.
Just off the A352 west of Wareham.

The museum was founded in 1923 and the story goes that Rudyard Kipling suggested it when he saw several First World War tanks at the camp and learned that they were about to be dismantled.

Today those tanks are still there amongst a remarkable collection of ironclad engines of warfare which range from those used in both the World Wars – British, German, Russian and American – to post-war and modern vehicles, including experimental tanks and carriers and a Centurion which has been cut down its length to show all the secrets of its interior.

The simulators are great draws for children and adults alike and you can pretend that you are driving a tank or firing a missile. The museum is full of interest with collections of other militaria in addition to the tanks. There are four free video theatres, and an excellent adventure playground out of doors, a costume collection (dedicated to the Army wife) and a T.E. Lawrence room. The gift shop has an unrivalled selection of military books and model kits, in addition to an excellent choice of souvenirs.

The bright and cheerful Gauntlet self-service restaurant has high chairs available and a children's menu and the food is fresh and well presented. Outside there is a terrace with plenty of bench tables.

This is an extremely well-organized and entertaining museum.

Open: every day, 10am to 5pm. Closed for 10 days over Christmas.
Charges: adults £4; OAPs £2; chidren £2; under 5s free (1993
prices)
Baby changing: a changing table and chair in the Ladies
Ⓟ ample

NR BRADFORD-ON-AVON, WILTS
Ⓗ WOOLLEY GRANGE, Bradford-on-Avon
Tel: 0225 864 705.
At Woolley Green, off the B3105 north east of Bradford-on-Avon.

This 17th-century manor house is an engaging sight, built as it is
from a warm-looking limestone and with its pointed gables and tall
chimneys. It was a family home for several hundred years until Mr
and Mrs Chapman adapted it a couple of years back as a country
house hotel. Style is the keynote from the moment you step into
the wood-panelled hall with its patterned plaster ceiling and
comfortable chairs and sofas.

The original decor is maintained in the sitting rooms and the
attractive dining room; the Long Room, which is part library, part
television room and part games room is a delight. So are the bedrooms which are all differently furnished and decorated but in
every case reflect the owners' wishes to provide their guests with
comfortable and elegant surroundings.

The huge Victorian conservatory, with its excellent cane furniture, is a lovely place to sit over coffee or something stronger. Outside, there are stretches of garden and a stone-paved terrace where you can have *al fresco* meals. Through a gate, you will find a heated swimming pool, a croquet lawn in an enclosed area, two grass tennis courts (by this year more all-weather courts will have been added), and a badminton court. There are fourteen acres of garden in which to relax, and children can enjoy the 'Bear Garden', which has swings, a slide, a climbing frame and a small enclosed football pitch. As well as the Moulton bicycles provided at the hotel, guests can try an authentic Indian trishaw.

Amid all these comforts and excellent facilities it has been remembered that many adults have young children who also have to be cared for. This is done with a will, too. There are plenty of cots and high chairs and certain rooms are interconnecting and can form family suites.

Woolley Bear's Den occupies a large barn and it is packed with toys and games for younger children; and there is a pool table, table tennis and table football for older children. A nanny is in attendance every day (from 10am to 6pm) and the children can be fed in the nursery off the play room; lunch is at noon and tea at 5pm. What a boon for parents, who can enjoy their food in peace!

The hotel has a notably good chef and the same attention to detail goes into the buying of the raw ingredients for the dining room. The hotel has a two-acre kitchen garden which provides the fruit and the vegetables.

This is a really splendid hotel which provides marvellous facilities, and a proper welcome, for all the family. It well deserved its 1992 'Parent Friendly' Award.

Nearby: If you can tear yourself away from the comforts of Woolley Grange there is a range of places to visit. The beautiful city of Bath is very close, as are Corsham Court, Sheldon Manor, Lacock Abbey and Bowood House, which has a wonderful adventure playground. Longleat Safari Park is also within reach, with Stourhead a little further south. Riding and clay pigeon shooting can be arranged and the hotel provides bicycles and local maps to guide you. The route along the Kennet and Avon canal is recommended.

✗ TERRACE MENU (12–2.30pm & 7–10pm) £3–8: omelette Arnold Bennett, smoked salmon, hamburger, griddled fish & salad; DINNER (7pm to 10pm) £28: grilled scallops with leeks & ham, best end of spring lamb, rhubarb & orange crème brulé or farmhouse cheeses
Children: own menu
£ high
Best Bargain Break: £180 per person, 2 nights – dinner, b&b
Children: free
Facilities: 15 cots and 12 high chairs; a baby listening system; and a nursery with a nanny
20 rooms, 8 family, 5 sets interconnecting. Open all year
Access/AmEx/Diners/Visa. No music
Ⓟ own car park

BRADLEY GREEN, NR CANNINGTON, SOMERSET
Ⓟ MALT SHOVEL INN, Bradley Green
Tel: 0278 653 432.
Just off the A39 west of Bridgwater. Look for the sign (to Bradley Green).

This friendly and unpretentious country pub has an appealing atmosphere, with wooden tables and settles under the low wooden beams, cream-painted stone walls, on which are hung photographs of the Bridgewater Canal, some window seats and a wood-burning stove.

There are three bars to give plenty of space, and families are welcome to use a room separated from the main bar. It has several tables and is furnished and decorated in the same agreeable style as the rest of the pub.

The family room opens on to a large lawned garden with several tables and chairs. A high chair is available and there is a good choice of food.

✗ (12pm to 2pm & 7pm to 9.30pm) £1–9: fisherman's pie, steaks, smoked haddock cheesy bake, nut crumble, lamb & potato provençale
Children: own menu

🍺 Ale: Butcombe, John Smith's & guests
🅿 own car park

BRISTOL, AVON
🆁 BROWNS RESTAURANT, 38 Queens Road
Tel: 0272 304 777
Next to the Bristol Museum and opposite the triangle.

This is the most recent offspring of the excellent Browns' chain (there are others in Brighton, Cambridge and Oxford, *q.v.*) and it is housed in a wonderful and stately building which began life as the town library and then became the Students' Union refectory. There are tables on the terraces at the front among the substantial stone pillars and inside you will find a huge high-ceilinged room with tables set out on two different levels.

Plenty of space is left around a long wooden bar and there are alcoves here and there, one with padded benches and Lloyd Loom chairs. The main restaurant has ceiling fans, wide windows, a profusion of potted plants and nice wooden furniture. It is a lively place, with youthful and cheerful staff, and it offers an excellent range of food at reasonable prices.

Families are made very welcome and there are plenty of high chairs, a children's menu and a well-equipped mother and baby room.

✗ (11am–11.30pm; from noon on Sunday) £2–10: salad frisée, pasta with various sauces, fisherman's pie, roast pork ribs, fresh vegetable bake
Children: own menu, half portions
No smoking in over half the restaurant. Access/Visa.
Licensed
🅿: meters or public car parks

BRISTOL, AVON
Ⓛ CITY MUSEUM AND ART GALLERY, Queen's
Road
Tel: 0272 223 571.
Close to the city centre and adjoining the university.

A highly successful businessman donated this building to the city
in 1903. It is a spacious stone building with marble staircases and
mosaic flooring and houses superb collections of ceramics, pottery,
and displays of archaeology and Egyptology. The natural history
exhibits are particular favourites with children.

Train enthusiasts can browse among the collection of replicas of
GWR rolling stock, while there is also a wide selection of classical
and modern art.

The café is at the back of the museum and is pleasantly furnished
and made more agreeable by the paintings on the walls. High chairs
are available and there is a children's menu here, as well as snacks,
salads and hot meals.

The museum has an excellent range of things to see, of interest
to the whole family, young and old.

Open: 10am to 5pm, every day
Charges: adults £2; free up to 16 years
Baby changing: mother and baby room
Ⓟ on street or public car parks

BRISTOL, AVON
Ⓛ THE EXPLORATORY, Bristol Old Station, Temple
Meads
Tel: 0272 252 008.
In the centre of the city.

The Exploratory is a splendid concept, a 'hands on science centre'
as the organizers describe it. You can find the answers to many
natural and scientific problems by doing the experiments yourselves.

There are ten scientific categories, and nearly 150 experiments
to try, without a 'do not touch' notice anywhere. On the contrary,
this is the place to investigate light and lenses, mirrors and magnets,
bridges and bubbles, sound, electricity, illusions and chemistry at
first hand. It is enormous fun for everyone.

The Exploratory is housed in what was originally the terminus for the Great Western Railway. It is a spacious, stone building and was designed by Isambard Kingdom Brunel. There is a neat and pleasant café at one end where you can buy a snack or a drink. There are high chairs.

Open: every day, 10am to 5pm
Charges: adults £3.75; children and OAPs £2.50; under 5s free (1993 prices)
Baby changing: a table in the disabled toilet area
P several public car parks

CASTLE COMBE, WILTS
P WHITE HART, Castle Combe
Tel: 0249 782 295.
Directly opposite the cross in the centre of the village.

The lovely old pub, sprucely painted white, sits opposite the church in this famous village. The pub has small wooden mullioned windows under its steep roof of Cotswold stone tiles.

As you enter, the bar is on one side and quite a sizeable family room on the other. It has a low ceiling, with wooden beams, plenty of tables and chairs and wooden settles, and the walls are decorated with prints of hunting scenes.

If the weather is warm, you should head for the secluded garden terrace, enclosed by stone walls, and with a paved floor. There are picnic seats, and shrubs and trees around the walls. You have a good view from here of the eccentrically shaped roofs of the surrounding cottages.

There are barbecues during the summer months and the pub is open throughout the day from Monday to Saturday.

✗ (12pm to 2.30pm & 7pm to 9.30pm) £2–7: filled jacket potatoes, lasagne, garlic mushrooms, steaks, chicken Kiev
Children: own menu, half portions
🍺 Ale: Bass, Butcombe, Ruddles, Usher's, Wadworth's
P public car park

CHARD, SOMERSET
Ⓛ CRICKET ST THOMAS WILDLIFE PARK, Chard
Tel: 0460 30755.
On the A30 just east of Chard.

A family can have an interesting day out in the 1000 acres of this very attractive and well-organized park.

It began as a wildlife park in 1967 and the animals still make up a large part of its appeal. There are leopards and lynx, monkeys, elephants, penguins, lemurs, reptiles, a large collection of birds, and the sealions are immensely popular with everyone.

The walk along the valley (or you can take the scenic railway) is a delight as you look down at the expanse of lakes below, which were made by damming a tributary of the River Axe. There are many waterfowl to admire and the deer, llamas, wallabies, emus and Bactrian camels also live here. At the end, there is the Heavy Horse Centre and the children's farm.

The gardens are delightful and there is an excellent play area with swings and a splendid wooden fort.

Food and drink is provided at various points around the park. The Pavilion restaurant is a fine wooden building, surrounded by a terrace and lawns. It is very spacious inside and provides a good range of food and nearby is the Tythe Barn, a restaurant with waitress service. Carvery meals are served from noon until 3pm, and teas from 3pm to 5.30pm. High chairs are available in both these places.

There is a café at the Heavy Horse Centre and a Coffee Shop near the house; and the Black Swan pub is conveniently situated by the sealions' pool.

The many attractions add up to a full day's entertainment for the whole family.

Open: 10am to 6pm, every day (earlier in winter)
Charges: adults £5.80; OAPs £4.80; children £4; under 3s free (1993 prices)
Baby changing: mother and baby rooms at the Pavilion and near the Heavy Horse Centre
Ⓟ ample

CHEW MAGNA, NR BRISTOL, AVON
SC CHEW HILL FARM, Chew Magna
Tel: 0275 332 496.
Off the B3130 south of Bristol.

Chew Hill Farm has an unrivalled location nearly 500 feet above the village on the south slopes of Dundry Hill. From there you have wonderful views over the Chew Valley and to the Mendips beyond.

There are three properties on the farm and they have one very important characteristic in common, especially for a family on holiday who need plenty of space. West Lodge is an agreeable Victorian lodge with three bedrooms and it has its own lawned garden and a garage. East Lodge was built in 1963 and has three bedrooms, a spacious lawned garden and a garage. Finally, the Bailiff's House, built in 1955, provides the same facilities as East Lodge but with a smaller garden.

Each house is comfortably furnished and carpeted and has a well-equipped kitchen. Above all, it is the peace and tranquillity of the place and the wonderful views which will appeal to the holiday maker. So will the rental charges, which are reasonable.

Nearby: Chew Hill is an excellent base for a holiday with so much to see and do in the vicinity. Bristol and Bath, and Wells with its magnificent cathedral are close. Fishermen are well looked after, with trout to catch at Blagdon Lake and Chew Valley Lake and the latter is also a nature reserve. If you head south to the

Mendips you can visit Wookey Hole Caves, Cheddar Gorge and Ebbor Gorge; and a little further afield Nunney Castle, Montacute House, the Fleet Air Museum, Ham Hill Country Park and the wildlife park at Cricket St Thomas.

Units: 3
Rent: £200 to £295 a week
Other costs: electricity on a meter
Heating: night storage heaters
2 cots and 1 high chair available
Open all year

COMPTON MARTIN, AVON
Ⓟ RING O'BELLS, Compton Martin
Tel: 0761 221 284.
On the A368.

This excellent family pub – long, low and white-painted – sprawls welcomingly against a backdrop of wooded hills, and has a large and splendid garden. It is well-grassed with plenty of log tables and benches and has a slide, a log climbing frame, an activity unit, swings (all on safe bark surfaces) and a scattering of apple trees. There is also a boule pitch for the adults. It is a delightful spot, which we singled out for special praise in the very first edition of the *Guide*.

The interior of the pub is spacious and welcoming. The main bar has good wooden tables and pews and wooden screens, and there is a huge inglenook fireplace in the other bar.

The family room, a no-smoking area is extremely well organized: spacious and attractive with stone walls topped by a high vaulted ceiling and with a good array of wooden tables, chairs and settles and a rocking horse.

It is a rare pub which boasts more than one token high chair – but this one has three.

There's a very extensive menu for the adults, and a particularly good choice of salads. There is always a good range of real ales, too.

✕ (12pm to 2pm & 7pm to 10pm) £2–9: Somerset smokies, ham & eggs, plaice & chips, sirloin steak, mariner's pie
Children: own menu, half portions

🍺 Ale: Bass, Butcombe, Wadworth's and guest beer
🅿 own car park

CORFE CASTLE, DORSET
🏰 CORFE CASTLE
Tel: 0929 481 294.
On the A351 south of Wareham.

The famous castle, a romantic ruin which broods above the attractive town, has a remarkable and bloody history. In 978 the young King Edward was murdered so that Ethelred, 'the Unready', could gain the throne. The castle was reduced to its present state of ruin during the Civil War, when Lady Bankes defied the Cromwellian forces for two years, until the castle fell in 1645.

You can spend an interesting hour or so in exploring the ruins and there is a restaurant near the entrance of the castle. There is a high chair available, plus a limited children's menu. Hot and cold meals and snacks range in price from £1 to £4 and a three course Sunday lunch can be booked, too.

You can change a baby in the Ladies, where there is plenty of space; the top of a large cupboard acts as a table and there is also a chair.

Open: 10am to 5.30pm, 8 February to end of October; 12 to 3.30pm, weekends only, from 10 November to 9 February
Charges: adults £2.80; children: £1.40; under 5s free (1993 prices)
Baby changing: a changing table and chair in the Ladies
🅿 public car parks in the village

DOWLISH WAKE, NR ILMINSTER, SOMERSET
🅿 NEW INN, Dowlish Wake
Tel: 0460 52413.
The village is south-east of Ilminster. Head for Kingstone and it is nearby.

This very appealing village has many fine stone buildings and a lovely church, but is probably most notable as the home of Perry cider: the mill is well worth a visit.

The New Inn is a well-proportioned stone building with a very pleasant and quite spacious bar: the beams are decorated with hops, there is good wooden furniture including some old settles, and a large ingle-nook fireplace with a seat in it alongside the iron stove.

The family room is at the back of the pub, relatively new, and with wide windows which look out to the lawned garden which stretches back alongside the skittle alley. There are plenty of bench tables on the grass, and for the children a wooden climbing frame and a slide.

✕ (12pm to 2pm & 6.30pm to 9.15pm) £2–11: soft roes on toast, Bellew sausage & rosti, fish of the day, nut roast, braised duck
Children: own menu, smaller portions
⌑ Ale: Butcombe, Theakston's, Wadworth's
Ⓟ own car park

NR DUNSTER, SOMERSET
SC DUDDINGS COUNTRY HOLIDAYS,
Timberscombe
Tel: 0643 841 123.
On the A396 on the Dunster side of the village.

Duddings has an enviable location alongside the valley created by the River Avill; from the cottages you have a delightful view of the gentle wooded hills and scattered fields.

The cottages have been built from the old barns, whose walls were made from the attractive local stone, which is reddish-brown in colour. The smallest properties can accommodate two people and the largest seven, with half a dozen cottages able to sleep between four and six people.

We were impressed with the care which has clearly been exercised in converting the buildings. The original features, the ancient beams and stone walls, have been retained and enhanced by the provision of comfortable and stylish furniture and excellent decorations. There are fitted carpets throughout the cottages and the kitchens have everything a cook would need, including microwave ovens. The proprietors are on the spot to ensure that the guests are well looked after.

The cottages have the great advantage of a lovely setting, and there are little picnic areas with bench tables, set amongst the trees in the immaculately maintained gardens. The cottages also have their own little patios where you can have a quiet drink or an *al fresco* meal.

The other facilities are excellent, too. There is loads of space for the children to play in the paddock and in the fields and alongside the river; Duddings has the bonus of a hard tennis court, an indoor heated swimming pool, which is four feet in depth and suitable for most members of a family, a putting green, pool room and a table tennis table. There are many pets with whom the children can make friends: dogs, kittens, ducks and peacocks. This is a marvellous spot for a family holiday in an area which has so much to offer.

Nearby: Fishermen are well catered for on the local rivers, the Exe and the Barle, and there are brown trout in the Avill, which flows through the Duddings' grounds. It is a superb part of the world to see from the back of a horse or pony and there are several riding centres in the vicinity. The beaches of the north Somerset coast are close and a new leisure pool has been built in Minehead. There are many attractions to see: Dunster Castle, Combe Sydenham Hall, the West Somerset Railway, the Exmoor National Park Centre, Fyne Court, Poundisford Park, while Cricket St Thomas Wildlife Park is just a little further afield.

Units: 11
Rent: £100 to £550 a week (off peak breaks available – a minimum of 3 nights)
Other costs: electricity (at cost)
Heating: convector heaters in all rooms
4 cots and 4 high chairs
Open: March to December

EAST STOKE, NR WAREHAM, DORSET
田 KEMPS COUNTRY HOUSE HOTEL, East Stoke
Tel: 0929 462 563.
On the A352 West of Wareham.

Facing south to the Purbeck Hills, this Victorian rectory, built, according to a stone plaque on the facade, in 1874, is marked at the entrance by some towering pine trees.

The interior is handsome, with well-proportioned rooms, which are stylishly decorated. The restaurant, with its bright flowered wallpaper, is particularly attractive as is the conservatory, which opens out to a terrace and lawned garden with a pond. There is a well-proportioned and comfortable lounge, a welcoming bar with stained glass panels above the serving area, and a second lounge with several sofas and armchairs.

In the main building we looked at a nicely decorated family room (with a double and single bed) which has wide windows giving excellent views of the Dorset countryside. A new block of rooms has been built in the garden and these are very spacious and bright with furniture and decorations of excellent quality. They could all accommodate a cot or an extra bed without any strain.

Nearby: The coast is not far away and the best sandy beaches are at Swanage and Studland. Railway buffs could take in a ride on the Swanage Railway and Durlston Country Park also lies in that direction. There are many other attractions within reach: Corfe Castle, the Tank Museum, the Tutankhamun Exhibition and the Sea Life Centre at Weymouth. There are excellent amenities in the vicinity including a leisure centre, squash and tennis courts, fishing, riding and water sports.

✗ BAR SNACKS (12–1.30pm) £2–10: chicken liver terrine, smoked salmon & crab pancake, supreme of chicken, calves liver & onionsLUNCH (12–1.30pm) £9: whitebait, grilled local plaice, pudding or cheese;
DINNER (7pm to 9.30pm) £17: ham & celeriac salad, soup, noisette of lamb, pudding or cheese.
Children: own menu, half portions
£ medium
Best Bargain Break: £90 per person, 2 nights – dinner, b&b
Children: free up to 7 years; £5 from 7 to 12
Facilities: 2 cots and 1 high chair; baby listening to every room
15 rooms, 4 family. Access/AmEx/Diners/Visa
No smoking in dining room
Ⓟ own car park

ERLESTOKE, NR DEVIZES, WILTS
Ⓗ ⓈⒸ LONGWATER, Erlestoke
Tel: 0380 830 095.
On the B3098 west of Market Lavington. Turn off at Erlestoke
Post Office.

This modern brick farmhouse was built in 1980 in a very agreeable
style, and is the focal point of the farm of about 160 acres. This is
an organic farm and there are some rare breeds of sheep and
longhorn cattle here. The farm's produce will be served to you for
dinner, and wines from a local vineyard are available.

A great amount of space is given over to the guests at Longwater.
A huge and very comfortable sitting room with wide windows over
the lake is adjoined by a conservatory which runs the length of the
house, and there is a terrace in front. In these rooms and the pleasant
dining room, the owner's remarkable collection of china (Blue
Italian Spode) is on display.

The bedrooms (all with their own bathrooms) are also generous
in size, very bright and furnished to a high standard; most of them
have a double and a single bed but are let only to two people at a
time. There is a splendid family room on the upper floor which
contains a double bed in the main room and a separate twin-bedded
room. The views of the lake are delightful.

The farm has its own area of parkland and two lakes, one of
which is stocked with roach, perch, carp etc. Guests are welcome
to fish here. The little valley has been made into a conservation
area, and several types of wild fowl breed there. It is a lovely spot
and the charming village is just a short walk away.

A separate bungalow houses two more very spacious bedrooms and a larger family could take them both and have a self-contained suite.

Nearby: There is much to interest the holiday maker; the whole of Salisbury Plain lies at your feet, with the fine cities of Bath and Salisbury within reach. There are many interesting sights to see: Stonehenge, Longleat Safari Park, Avebury, Bowood House, the fascinating village of Lacock and its abbey, and Barton Farm Country Park. Erlestoke Sands golf course is on the doorstep and welcomes visitors.

✗ DINNER (7pm) £11: herb tomato soup, local trout, pudding & cheese
Children: half portions
£ low
Children: nominal charge for cot; half price thereafter
Facilities: 2 cots and 2 high chairs
5 rooms, 2 family
Open all year, except Christmas & New Year
No smoking in dining room and conservatory
No credit cards. No music.
Ⓟ ample
Self-catering: Mr and Mrs Hampton also let Park Farm House which is a few hundred yards away. A pretty, double-fronted farmhouse, it overlooks the lake and has three bedrooms to accommodate up to six people. There is a large lawned garden and all the facilities a holidaymaker needs including a washing machine and dryer, dishwasher and a fully equipped kitchen. The price per week varies from £150 to £350 and short breaks are available.

HARDINGTON MANDEVILLE, SOMERSET
Ⓟ MANDEVILLE ARMS, Hardington Mandeville
Tel: 0935 862 418.
Off the A30 between Crewkerne and Yeovil.

This pub has been enlarged and completely refurbished and now looks very smart and comfortable. The spacious open-plan bar still has its low ceilings, old wooden beams and pillars, good wooden tables and brick walls as well as a good quality carpet.

The family room, at one end of the pub, is done in the same style and doubles as a restaurant. The licencees make the valid point that parents should stay with their children and not leave them to their own devices while they prop up the bar.

There is a delightful garden at the front of the pub. It is surrounded by a small stone wall and looks very cheerful with its collection of sun umbrellas and colourful flowers.

Food is served every day from a wide-ranging and enterprising bar menu and, in the winter, a three-course Sunday lunch is available for around £7.

✕ (12pm to 1.45pm & 7.30pm to 10pm) £1–11: fresh vegetable pancake, seafood au gratin, steaks, spicy pork in ginger, moussaka
Children: own menu, half portions
🍺 Ale: Boddington's, Flowers, Marston's, Wadworth's
🅿 own car park

HUTTON, NR WESTON-SUPER-MARE, AVON
Ⓗ MOORLANDS, Hutton
Tel: 0934 812 283.
In the village, which is south of Weston-super-Mare and can be reached from the A371 or A370.

This is a most attractive Georgian house in a village which sits at the foot of the Mendip Hills. The garden spreads over two secluded acres with lawns, trees, rockeries, a lovely display of flowers, a kitchen garden and a paddock where pony rides are arranged. It is relaxing and safe for children to play; there is a slide, a climbing frame and a garden badminton set. Both the dining room and the comfortable lounge look over the gardens and beyond to the wooded hills.

The outlook of Mr and Mrs Holt is stated in their brochure: that they receive visitors into their own home as guests and try to make them feel at home. That certainly includes children, since there are five rooms which can accommodate two adults and a child. Two of them have a double and two single beds.

There is a vegetable garden and the owners use as much of their own, and local, produce as possible.

Nearby: If you like an active holiday you could hardly be in a better spot: golf, fishing and a dry ski slope are available in the locality. The traditional seaside resort of Weston-super-Mare is quite close and it has an excellent leisure centre. Glastonbury and Wells are nearby; as are Cheddar Gorge, the Wookey Hole caves, Ebbor Gorge and the East Somerset railway. A bit further afield, nature lovers can head for Chew Valley Lake and Cricket St Thomas Wildlife Park.

✕ DINNER (6.30pm) £9: home-made carrot soup, beef Italien, pudding & cheese
Children: half portions
£ low
Children: under 2 years £4; half price thereafter
Facilities: 4 cots and 3 high chairs; and a baby listening system
7 rooms, 5 family. Open January to October
Access/AmEx/Visa. No music
No smoking in dining room
Ⓟ own car park

LULWORTH COVE, DORSET
Ⓗ MILL HOUSE HOTEL AND BISHOP'S
COTTAGE HOTEL, West Lulworth
Tel: 0929 41404.
At Lulworth Cove.

Lulworth Cove is a very popular tourist spot and these two related hotels are in the heart of it, on the one and only main street, which is traffic free.

The two hotels sit side by side and share their various facilities. Bishop's Cottage was once the home of Bishop Wordsworth of Salisbury, and is an appealing small hotel, which sits comfortably in the shelter of Bindon Hill. The nice little bar and the spacious dining room both look out to the small enclosed garden, and down some steps there is the sister hotel.

The Mill House is a pleasant old stone building; it seems to have grown in higgledy-piggledy fashion and that is part of its charm. There is a café/restaurant on the ground floor, and the residents' lounge and dining room are on the first floor, along with some of the bedrooms. The latter have a cottagey feel with their sloping walls and dormer windows. The attractive terraced gardens are well sheltered by the surrounding hills and, at the far end, there is an excellent swimming pool, surrounded by grass on which to loll. There are wonderful views of the famous cove from here.

The kitchen produces fresh food for the hotel and the café: local fresh shellfish is a speciality and vegetarian meals are also available. Meals can be taken either in the Bishop's Cottage restaurant or the Mill House restaurant, which has an extensive menu, so the whole environment is very flexible for families.

Nearby: This is a splendid holiday area with lots of interesting coastline to see and particularly good sandy beaches at Swanage, Weymouth and Studland. The Dorset coastal path runs past Swanage and there is a nature reserve at Studland. Inland, there is superb countryside to explore, as well as the Sea Life Centre at Weymouth and Durlston Country Park. Other places to visit include Corfe Castle, the Swanage Railway, the Tutankhamun Exhibition, Thomas Hardy's Cottage, the prehistoric Maiden Castle and Athelhampton.

✕ BAR MEALS (12pm to 2.30pm & 6pm to 9.30pm) £1–11: lasagne, crab salad, plaice & chips, lentil crumble, steak & kidney pie
DINNER (6pm to 10pm) £11: garlic mushrooms, baked bream, pudding & cheese
Children: own menu, half portions
£ medium
Best Bargain Break: £65 per person, 2 nights – dinner, b&b
Children: free up to 3 years; £8 from 3 to 7 years; £10 from 8 to 11 years
Facilities: 5 cots and 4 high chairs; and a baby listening system
26 rooms, 5 family, 2 sets interconnecting
Open all year. Access/Visa
Ⓟ limited, but public car park nearby

LYDLINCH, NR STURMINSTER NEWTON, DORSET
Ⓗ ⓈⒸ HOLEBROOK FARM, Lydlinch
Tel: 0258 817 348.
Just off the A357 two miles west of Sturminster Newton.

You will find this very attractive Georgian farmhouse, built of light-coloured stone, in a quiet setting and surrounded by the green fields of the family-run farm.

One of the benefits of staying at Holebrook Farm is that you can elect to use the rooms either on a bed and breakfast or on a self-catering basis since they all have well-equipped kitchens and plenty of space. The accommodation, contained within converted stables and the old dairy, is furnished to a high standard and many of the original features have been used to good effect: the wooden beams and the stall partitions, for instance.

Two of the rooms in the stables can interconnect, if desired, to form a suite for a family of four; another larger unit contains two twin-bedded rooms and a sizeable sitting-cum-dining room with an integral kitchen.

The dairy has been converted in fine style to give four cottages, each with a sitting room and kitchen and a bedroom made even more attractive by the sloping ceiling. These cottages are suitable for two adults and a baby only.

The flexibility inherent in the accommodation will suit many families and so will the excellent facilities and all the freedom which the gardens and the surrounding open spaces allow, especially to the children. At one side of the house there is a sizeable and well-maintained lawn bordered by hedges and shrubs and, in another part of the garden, there is a small swimming pool. There are other activities laid on for guests: clay pigeon shooting, with tuition, can be arranged, for example; one of the outbuildings has been converted into a games room with a pool table, table tennis and other games. There are also two exercise machines.

Nearby: Sherborne Abbey and the neighbouring ruined castle are close, as are the butterfly gardens at Compton House. Montacute House, Ham Hill Country Park, the Fleet Air Arm Museum and Hambleden Hill can all be reached with ease. A little further away in various directions you can reach Cricket St Thomas Wildlife Park and Longleat, Stourhead and Kingston Lacy, and the Rare Breeds Centre near Gillingham.

✗ DINNER (7pm) £11
Children: half portions
£ medium
Children: half price

Facilities: 3 cots and 3 high chairs
6 rooms, 1 set interconnecting. Open all year
No credit cards. Licensed
ℙ plenty. No music
Self-catering: When the suites or the cottages are rented on this
basis they cost from £130 to £360 depending on the season.

LYTCHETT MINSTER, NR. POOLE, DORSET
ℙℝ BAKERS ARMS
Tel: 0202 622 900.
On the A35 at the roundabout where it meets the A351 west of
Poole.

The Bakers Arms was listed in several early editions of the *Guide*
and has now become a part of the Brewers Fayre chain.

It offers considerable facilities for families within its spacious
rooms: there is an indoor play area with lots of equipment, nappy
changing facilities, plenty of high chairs and a large outdoor adventure playground, which is safely enclosed and has a bark surface.

The pub is open throughout the day and food is available for
most of the time. The family dining area is spacious and is of course
a no smoking room. The interior is welcoming and is sensibly
divided up into a number of small rooms and alcoves, with wooden
tables and pews, padded chairs and benches. The brick walls, glass
screens and wooden pillars add to the agreeable atmosphere.

✗ (11.30am—10pm; from noon on Sunday) £2–8: seafood crêpes,
sirloin steak, fish pie, vegetable crumble, steak & kidney pie
Children: own menu
⌂ Ale: Boddington's, Wadworth's
ℙ: own car park

MONKSILVER, SOMERSET
ℙ NOTLEY ARMS, Monksilver
Tel: 0984 56217.
On the B3188, south of Williton.

This attractive white-walled village pub has a light and clean family
room, well furnished with tables and chairs and plenty of toys. The

relaxing and comfortable bar has some good wooden tables and wood-burning stoves at either end.

There is a delightful large garden, with plenty of tables and chairs, lovely shrubbery and flower beds and, to add to the interest, a stream running through.

The pub offers a good choice of freshly-made, home-cooked dishes, which are more enterprising than normal pub food and very reasonably priced. Their ice cream is also homemade.

✗ (12–2pm & 7–9.30pm) £1–5: vegetable curry, whole prawns, poorman's pocket, shepherd's purse & richman's pouch (pitta bread with various fillings), pork & veg goulash with rice
Children: half portions
🍺 Ale: Usher's, Ruddles, Theakston's, Wadworth's
🅿 own car park

MONTACUTE, SOMERSET
🅛 MONTACUTE HOUSE, Montacute
Tel: 0935 823 289.
Off the A3088 west of Yeovil.

This beautiful house was built towards the end of the 16th century and stayed in the Pheilps family until 1931, when it was saved from demolition by the National Trust.

The character of the house owes much to its honey-coloured stone, from Ham Hill, and the dozens of stone, mullioned windows. Inside, the rooms have superb wooden panelling and elaborate fireplaces and the house is notable for the collection of 16th- and 17th-century paintings. The Long Gallery measures 172 feet and houses a great array of Tudor portraits.

The walled formal gardens are immaculately kept and the whole place has a very special atmosphere.

The restaurant is housed in a long, low, stone building, one of several around a grassed courtyard. It may have been the laundry room and has old settles and pine tables set out on the flagged floor. There are a couple of high chairs and half portions can be served up for children.

Open: noon to 5.30pm, 1 April to 31 October. Closed on Tuesdays .

Charges: adults £4.60; children £2.30; under 5s free (1993 prices)
Baby changing: a table in the Ladies
P ample

MOONFLEET, NR WEYMOUTH, DORSET
Ⓗ ⓈⒸ MOONFLEET MANOR, Moonfleet
Tel: 0305 786 948.
Off the B3157 north-west of Weymouth.

The owners rightly describe Moonfleet Manor as an hotel and
sports resort, since the sporting facilities are exceptional. Many of
them are housed in the Ball Park which has two squash courts,
table tennis, a full-sized indoor bowls pitch, a snooker table, two
automated 9-pin bowling lanes and two bars. There is a pool table,
table football and amusement machines. It is a wonderful place,
with lots of space and you could spend all day there.

There are many other facilities too: two hard tennis courts, an
indoor swimming pool with a children's pool, a gymnasium with
serious equipment (and it is properly supervised), a short tennis
court, and a sandpit and an adventure playground for the children.

The core of the hotel is a very handsome Georgian manor house
which was restored near the end of the 19th century. It sits right
by Chesil Beach in a beautiful location and has its own pleasant
lawned gardens.

One of the many virtues of the hotel is the amount of space
put at the guests' disposal: a large lounge and bar with nice cane
furniture and sofas and a sizeable dining room with a conservatory
where children have their suppers at 6 o'clock.

The bedrooms are similarly generous in size, especially the family
rooms: three of them are suites with interconnecting double and
twin bedrooms and some have double beds with bunk beds for
children. All of them have enchanting views.

This is a really splendid family hotel with exceptional facilities
where everyone, from grandparents to grandchildren, will find
much to enjoy.

Nearby: The huge expanse of Chesil Beach is shingle, but
nearby Weymouth has a sandy beach and a Sea Life Centre, which
will attract the children. In the other direction lies Abbotsbury, with

its ruined abbey and famous gardens and swannery. If you go inland, the lovely town of Dorchester is quite close and Thomas Hardy's cottage and the Tutankhamun Exhibition can be seen. If you are in the mood for sightseeing you can visit the country house of Athelhampton, the tank museum at Bovington Camp and Clouds Hill, the memorial to T.E. Lawrence.

✗ COFFEE SHOP (12.30–2.30pm) £2–5: vegetable samosas, salads, ploughman's, lentil crumble, lasagne;
DINNER (7–9pm) £14: smoked mackerel, medallions of beef, pudding or cheese
Children: own menu, half portions
£ high
Best Bargain Break: £88 per person, 2 nights – dinner, b&b
Children: from 15 per cent to 80 per cent of the adult rate, depending on age
Facilities: 8 cots and 6 high chairs; a baby listening system
37 rooms, 10 family, 3 sets interconnecting
Open all year. Access/AmEx/Diners/Visa
⚏ Ale: Hall & Woodhouse. No smoking in one lounge
🅿 own car park
Self-catering: Three self-contained cottages are now available and were recently converted from the coach house, which was built in 1806. Each cottage has a double and a twin-bedded room on the ground floor and an open-plan living room above: lounge, dining area and kitchen. The hotel facilities are available to guests and the baby listening system extends to the cottages. The rents vary between £200 and £350 but the cottages are only let on a self-catering basis outside the school holidays.

NORTH CURRY, SOMERSET
🅿 THE RISING SUN, Knapp
Tel: 0823 490 436.
Between the A361 and the A378 east of Taunton. Look for the North Curry sign.

It is well worth the effort to seek out this 16th-century inn, which was once licensed for cider only. If you head for North Curry, you

will find some well-placed signs just outside the village to point you
to the pub.

It has been renovated and expanded, and very smart it looks in its
coat of white paint, with baskets of bright flowers and honeysuckle
adorning the front walls. There is a little terrace at the front and
another one at the back of the pub.

The bar is a most attractive room with ancient wooden beams
which form a square pattern in the ceiling; wooden pillars make an
open screen to the dining room. Very smart and comfortable chairs
and banquettes furnish the bar, where there is a huge open fireplace
with an iron stove.

The family room, with its stone walls and old oak panelling is a
delight. There are padded settles and several tables and another
huge walk-in fireplace with an iron cooking range.

Although you have a wide choice of food here (and we had an
enjoyable lunch at the Rising Sun a summer or two ago) the owner
specialises in fish. There are some unusual varieties here; talapia,
black bream, Indian Ocean bass and gurnard, as well as plaice,
Dover sole, brill and monkfish. The three-course Sunday lunch is
great value at under £8.

Seek out the Rising Sun: it is only a very short drive from junction
25 of the M5.

✗ LUNCH (12pm to 2pm) £1–8: cauliflower au gratin, Welsh
rarebit, grilled plaice, spicey pork sausages, grilled rib eye steak;
DINNER (7pm to 9.30pm) £2–11: bouillabaise, whole Brixham
plaice, hot spiced crab, beef Stroganoff, supreme of chicken aioli
Children: half portions
Ⓐ Ale: Bass, Boddington's Exmoor
Ⓟ own car park

NORTON ST PHILIP, SOMERSET
Ⓟ GEORGE INN, Norton St Philip
Tel: 0373 834 224.
On the A366.

A magnificent and classic old inn dating from the 13th century
and possibly even earlier, where little has been done to spoil an
oak-beamed and wood-panelled interior with its old tables and

wooden settles. The landlord, thank goodness, has no music in the pub nor any of those ghastly games machines with their hideous electronic noises.

Children are welcome in one of the lounges, which is large and very much in character with a good array of tables and chairs, and a huge stone fireplace. Another children's room comes into play at the weekend when the 'Dungeon Bar', which held a group of the rebel Duke of Monmouth's men prisoner in 1685, is open. Take a look at the splendid wooden ceiling. The 'Monmouth Room' is also available at times for families.

On sunny days you can sit in a small courtyard, with a part-paved, part-cobbled floor, and surrounded by thick stone walls and heavy roofs. Alternatively there is a pretty lawned garden with several apple trees, and from there you look out across playing fields to the local church.

There is a good choice of hot and cold food available throughout the day, both at the bar and in the restaurant, and a traditional three-course lunch is served on Sundays for around £8. There are two high chairs available.

✕ (10am to 2pm & 6.30pm to 10.30pm) £1–4: ploughman's, hot pasty, vegetarian lasagne, baked potato with ham & cheese
Children: small portions
⌑ Ale: Bass, Wadworth's. No music
Ⓟ own car park

OSMINGTON MILLS, NR WEYMOUTH, DORSET
Ⓟ SMUGGLERS INN, Osmington Mills
Tel: 0305 833 125.
Off the A353 north-east of Weymouth.

This partly thatched 13th-century inn has a delightful setting in a valley on the Dorset coastal path. It has recently been renovated with great care by the licensee; although the interior is now open plan, there are plenty of nooks and crannies to keep it cosy. Huge old timbers have been used and the black panelling has been retained. There is a restaurant at one end of the pub.

The family room is housed in a thatched extension and has a

pool table, video game and a piano. It is comfortably furnished. One of the seats is made from an upturned rowing boat and there are a couple of small saddles (on secure stands) for children to sit on.

On warm days you can sit on the paved terrace and keep a watch on the children while they enjoy the swings and the slide.

✕ (12pm to 2pm & 7pm to 9.30pm) £1–13: lasagne, meat & vegetable pie, plaice & chips, steaks, rack of lamb
Children: own menu, half portions
⊟ Ale: Courage, Ringwood
ℙ own car park

PEWSHAM, NR CHIPPENHAM, WILTS
ℙ LYSLEY ARMS, Pewsham
Tel: 0249 652 864.
A couple of miles east of Chippenham on the A4 at the junction with the A342.

This very large and busy roadside inn is smoothly painted white under its steep roof with dormer windows. A long bar greets you as you enter and on the other side of a large fireplace there is a very comfortable sitting room with a huge and welcoming log fire.

The other end of the pub comprises an eating area and off this is the Garden Room, and families are welcome to use this to eat together or just to have a drink. It's really a large conservatory and it leads out to an enclosed and secluded garden. Alongside is another very large garden with plenty of bench tables and a children's play area which includes slides, swings, a climbing frame and a seesaw. It has recently been extended and now includes a Fun Trail.

This pub has excellent facilities and families are made particularly welcome by the licensees, Roy and Hilma Skinner.

✕ (12pm to 2pm & 6pm to 9.30pm) £2–9: garlic mushrooms, local trout, vegetable gratin, swordfish, steaks
Children: own menu, half portions
⊟ Ale: Bass, Boddington's, Eldridge Pope, Whitbread
ℙ own car park

PLUSH, DORSET
ℙ BRACE OF PHEASANTS, Piddletrenthide
Tel: 030 04 357.
Signposted from the B3143 near Piddletrenthide.

This is a super pub in every way and well worth a short drive along country lanes. In fact you can reach it very easily from Cerne Abbas if you turn into Piddle Lane and go straight across country.

It is a most attractive building, made by amalgamating two cottages and the village forge, and now sits under its thatched roof. The bar takes up one side of the pub, and is a long room with a beamed ceiling and an open brick fireplace at one end and a wood-burning stove at the other.

The family room, the old kitchen, is to one side of the bar and is a bright and cheerful place, with chequered tablecloths on the tables.

To add to the pleasure of a visit here, the garden is really lovely with a sloping lawn against a backcloth of trees, a rockery and an iron seat encircling a large tree. A children's play area has also been installed with a climbing frame, etc.

The food (available every day) is enterprising and there is a very good choice of real ales which are rotated at regular intervals.

It's a lovely spot – but please note the opening hours – in the evening, especially in winter, it is often not open until 7pm.

✕ (12pm to 1.45pm & 7pm to 9.45pm) £2–13: crab savoury, bouillabaisse, liver with bacon & onions, rosettes of lamb, fish pie
Children: own menu, half portions
🍺 Ale: Bass, Greene King, Smiles, Tetley, Wadworth's and guests
No music
ℙ own car park

SALISBURY, WILTS
ℙ OLD CASTLE, Castle Road
Tel: 0722 328 703.
Opposite Old Sarum, on the A345, a couple of miles from the city centre.

The pub stands on a hill on the outskirts of this famous city with its many fine buildings and magnificent cathedral. Across the road is Old Sarum, the original site of Salisbury and before that a Roman camp and Iron Age fort.

There is masses of space inside the pub, but it is broken up into interconnected rooms, with alcoves here and there.

Families are welcome to settle in the Garden Room which is off the main bar. It is a large conservatory and has a touch of the British Raj with its tiled floor, plants, overhead fan and old-fashioned radiators. It is light, bright and attractive. The Ladies has a large powder room with a counter and baby changing mat and another shelf on which to lay a baby.

The garden has lawns on various levels, with picnic tables and umbrellas, and overlooks Salisbury and a wide valley. There is a slide in one part of the garden.

✗ (12pm to 3pm & 5.30pm to 10pm) £1–6: a range of traditional English pub food
Children: own menu, half portions
🍺 Ale: Courage
🅿 own car park

NR SALISBURY, WILTS
🅿🆁 PHEASANT HOTEL, Winterslow
Tel: 0980 862 374.
Six miles north east of Salisbury on the A30 at Winterslow.

Any regular traveller along the A30 will have seen the Pheasant Hotel; it is a prominent building, very smart in its coat of cream paint with a wooden-clad facade and an array of flowers in window boxes and hanging baskets. It looks like a 1920s roadhouse and is now a very large family pub/restaurant.

Open all day and every day, with food available most of the time, it is a very useful place for families, especially if they want to break a journey.

When we visited there was a children's party in full swing at the family end of the pub. There is a children's play area here with a ball swamp, toys and a lego table. Parents of small children will find a nappy changing facility and plenty of high chairs, and in the pleasant lawned garden (safely enclosed) there is an excellent wooden play unit.

The interior of the pub is nicely designed with wood panelling and beams much in evidence and comfortable padded benches and seats. It is split into a series of inter-connected rooms and one of them, with a wooden floor, a brick fireplace and a bar billiards table, resembles an old-style snug.

It all adds up to a very agreeable family pub with excellent facilities.

✗ (1.30am–10pm; from noon on Sunday) £2–8: smoked trout, gammon steak, fillet of salmon, vegetable crumble, lasagne verde
Children: own menu
🍺 Ale: Boddington's, Flowers, Wadworth's
Ⓟ lots

SANDFORD, NR WAREHAM, DORSET
Ⓡ WOODS EDGE RESTAURANT, Sandford
Tel: 0929 556 959.
On the A351, north-east of Wareham.

This agreeable restaurant is tucked into the dense trees alongside the main road, and the bright-green awnings over the windows give it a cheerful air.

It is a sunny and appealing place with masses of space: an open-plan design incorporating three eating areas. The cream walls, Laura Ashley curtains and the greenery to be seen through most of the windows adds up to a pleasant place to have a meal. There is also a small lounge area with comfortable settees. Outside is a smart little patio with sun umbrellas over the tables.

The Ladies is spacious and includes a table where a baby can be changed; there is a supply of paper towels.

This is an excellent family restaurant, which we are happy to recommend.

✗ £2–11: vegetable lasagne, plaice & chips, ham & eggs, chicken chasseur, steak Bordelaise
Children: own menu, half portions
Open 10.30am to 2.15pm & 6.30pm to 10pm Mon to Sat; 10.30am to 10pm Sun (winter hours may vary slightly)

Open all year. Licensed
No smoking in part of the restaurant. Access/Visa
P own car park

SEMLEY, NR SHAFTESBURY, DORSET
H P BENETT ARMS, Semley
Tel: 0747 830 221.
Off the A350 north of Shaftesbury.

The pub was built from the local Chilmark stone in the 16th century
by a local landowner, who wanted a village inn where his estate
workers could enjoy themselves. It has stood the test of time and
is a handsome sight, situated, as is right and proper, on the village
green close to the church, with a small garden to the rear where
there are swings and a slide.

   If you have children in tow it is nice to know that you are welcome
in various parts of the pub; for example, there is a separate family
room–cum–dining room up some steps from the bar. With its
wooden tables, mullioned window and some interesting prints on
the walls it is an agreeable place to settle. There is also a restaurant
for more elaborate meals, and the bar itself is a delightful room
with a large brick fireplace, a nice old leather sofa, and stone walls
decorated with horse brasses.

   Most of the food on the enterprising menu is cooked on the spot
from fresh produce which might include fresh fish from Poole and
salmon shipped overnight from Scotland. The traditional Sunday
lunch is good value at around £10.

   Although we list the Benett Arms as a pub there are five pleasant
bedrooms here: none of them qualifies as a family room but some
are large enough to accommodate a cot or an extra bed.

✗ BAR SNACKS (12pm to 2pm & 7pm to 10pm) £2–9: scampi
royale, trout, steaks, Wiltshire ham with egg & chips, lasagne;
DINNER (7pm to 10pm) £15: Cajun prawns, rack of lamb,
pudding or cheese
Children: half portions
⊟ Ale: Gibbs Mew
P own car park

NR SHAFTESBURY, DORSET

Ⓗ ⓈⒸMELBURY MILL, Melbury Abbas

Tel: 0747 52163.

From Shaftesbury, take the B3081; after a Fiat garage on the left there is a right turn with a sign to the mill.

Down a few hundred yards of narrow country lane you will find peace and tranquillity in the form of Melbury Mill, a dignified and charming stone house with its mill alongside. The buildings date from the late 18th century and the house has the classic four-square Georgian mien, the facade bright with roses, wisteria and clematis. Alongside, the mighty wheel still turns and the mechanism in the mill grinds endlessly on.

Spreading in front of the house there is an inviting garden with an immaculate lawn; it gives plenty of space for guests and children can also play in the adjoining field.

Inside the house you will find a handsome dining room, with a flagstone floor and a large table where the guests eat together (24 hours notice for evening meals). Alongside there is an agreeable and comfortable sitting room, with windows on to the garden and the millpond, and with books and games available.

There is one bedroom in the house, a charming and spacious family room, with a double and a single bed and its own separate bathroom. The views over the gardens are a delight to the eye. The other two bedrooms (both with their own bathrooms) are in the mill building adjoining the house and are notable for the old wooden beams which are still in place. The larger of the two can easily accommodate an extra bed or a cot, and all the bedrooms are decorated and furnished to very high standards.

Melbury Mill is an idyllic place with top-class facilities at a very reasonable price.

Nearby: Shaftesbury is an excellent base for many activities. Stourhead, Longleat, Wilton House, the Fleet Air Arm Museum, Montacute House and Hambledon Hill are all within easy reach. There are wonderful walks nearby and all types of recreational facilities including golf, fishing, tennis and squash, and horse riding.

✕ DINNER (7–9pm) £12.50 (by arrangement)

£ low

Children: cot £5; thereafter £10

Facilities: 2 cots and a high chair
3 rooms, 2 family
No credit cards
Unlicensed. Open all year
No music
P own car park
Self-catering: Melbury Mill also has a charming apartment in the Mill building. It contains a spacious living room with an integral kitchen; a window set into one wall looks into the millhouse itself. Down some stairs there is a bedroom with a double and a single bed and a bathroom. The apartment is suitable for a family of three and costs between £140 and £215 a week: a very reasonable rent.

SPETISBURY, NR BLANDFORD FORUM, DORSET
R MARIGOLD COTTAGE TEAROOMS, Spetisbury
Tel: 0258 452 468.
On the A350 south of Blandford Forum.

You will first be struck by the immaculate condition of this lovely 16th-century English cottage, long and low and painted white below the thatched roof. The interior confirms one's first impressions, and on summer days you should head for the pretty garden, shaded by apple trees. There are also extra tables in a summer house alongside a collection of colourful caged birds.

There is plenty to choose from on the menu and it is all home-made and very good value, with English breakfasts available up to 11am, lunch from 12 to 2pm, afternoon teas and a variety of snacks available at any time.

The Ladies has adequate space if a baby needs to be changed.

✕ £2–6: cheese on toast, cream teas, various roasts with vegetables, fried plaice, filled jacket potatoes
Children: small portions
Open 9.30am to 5.30pm, Tues to Sun; 7.30pm to 9.30pm, Fri & Sat
Closed Mondays and from 25 Dec to 1 Feb
Access/Visa. Licensed. No smoking

One high chair only. No music
℗ 15 spaces

STOURTON, NR MERE, WILTS
Ⓛ STOURHEAD HOUSE AND GARDEN, Stourton
Tel: 0747 840 348.
Just off the B3092.

The Palladian-style house was built in the 1720s and its interior is mainly notable for a comprehensive collection of Chippendale furniture and some fine paintings.

The great glory of Stourhead is the garden which was created by the banker, Henry Hoare, in the 1740s. In some ways he was a forerunner of Capability Brown. Following his Grand Tour, Henry Hoare was devoted to the elaborate Italianate style and he set out to realise his romantic vision. He first created a lake by damming springs from the River Stour and then built a series of classical structures around it: the Temple of Flora, a grotto with a figure of Ariadne, a Gothic cottage, a Pantheon and a Temple of Apollo. With the many magnificent trees, a huge range of shrubs and flowers and Hoare's remarkable design, the garden is an extraordinary creation.

When you have walked the two-mile circuit you might well require a cup of tea. You can buy this as well as snacks, salads and hot food in the spacious self-service café in the courtyard. There are a couple of high chairs here.

If you fancy something stronger head for the Spread Eagle opposite. This lovely old pub has two comfortable bars and, if you have children in tow, you can take them into the dining room. There is a good range of food on offer here, including vegetarian dishes.

Open: Garden – every day, 8am to 7pm (or sunset); House – noon to 5.30pm, 3 April to 31 October. Closed Thursdays and Fridays
Charges: adults £4; children £2; under 5s free (1993 prices)
Baby changing: parents' room in the new visitor reception area
℗ ample

STUDLAND, DORSET
Ⓗ KNOLL HOUSE HOTEL, Studland
Tel: 092 944 251.
On the B3351 east of Corfe Castle and north of Swanage.

The Ferguson family have owned the Knoll House since 1959 and adhere to their philosophy of holding the balance between the differing requirements of their guests: on the one hand it has a location and an array of facilities which appeal greatly to families (and it continues to be one of our favourite family hotels), and on the other it also has many regular guests who are unencumbered by children. The philosophy is easy to express but difficult to achieve; in our opinion the Fergusons achieve it with style and aplomb.

Everyone is well looked after here. The children have their own dining room, with decent wooden furniture and cheerfully decorated with animal murals and colourful blinds. As well as their breakfast the children can have their lunch (there is an excellent menu which includes dishes such as grilled fish and roast beef) at 12.30 and are then supervised in the well-equipped play room (Wendy House, play-pens, video cartoons, toys, etc.) while the parents have their meal in peace. Similarly, children under 8 are not permitted in the dining room at night, but have high tea from 5 o'clock.

The facilities within the hotel and the 100 acres of grounds are extensive and include a heated swimming pool and paddling pool, safely enclosed, with a terrace, lawn and bar; a huge play area shaded by tall pines, with a pirate ship and a wonderful and ingenious 'Hag' adventure playground; and a par-3 golf course and two hard tennis courts. Indoors there are games such as table tennis, pool, table football, etc. Finally the well-designed leisure centre has a small indoor pool, a fitness room with serious equipment, a sauna, steam room and solarium, and a health juice bar. This is primarily a place for adults, but children are allowed in from 11am to midday, and for an hour in the afternoon if the weather is foul.

There is a feeling of spaciousness in the hotel, not least in the dining room where the tables are set well apart and a wall of windows overlooks the gardens. Similarly, the family suites offer plenty of space, with separate single or twin bedrooms for the children.

The location of the hotel, with its expansive grounds, encircled by National Trust land, and with one of the best beaches in Britain on the doorstep is outstanding. It is a top class family hotel in a superb holiday area.

Nearby: The beaches in this area are splendid and indeed the Studland beach, with over three miles of sand, is one of the best and cleanest in Britain. Behind it lies the Studland Heath Nature Reserve, and its neighbour, Swanage Beach, is also clean and sandy. The Swanage Railway is on the doorstep, as is Durlston Country Park and Corfe Castle. Brownsea Island is delightful and has many sandy beaches, too. Sightseers can easily reach the Tank Museum at Bovington, Hardy's cottage and the Tutankhamun Exhibition at Dorchester; and the children will enjoy a visit to the Sea Life Centre at Weymouth.

✗ LUNCH (1pm onwards) £15: hors d'oeuvres, soup, grilled whole local plaice, pudding or cheese;
DINNER (7.30pm onwards) £17: creamed smokies with prawns, roast Dorset lamb, pudding, cheese
Children: own menu
£ high
Best Bargain Break: £242 per person, 5 nights – full board
Children: a sliding scale depending on age
Facilities: plenty of cots and high chairs; and a baby patrol from 7.30pm to 11pm
80 rooms including 30 family suites
No credit cards accepted. Closed Nov to end Mar
No music except in leisure centre
Ⓟ own car park

SYDLING ST NICHOLAS, NR DORCHESTER, DORSET
Ⓗ Ⓢ Ⓒ LAMPERTS FARMHOUSE, Sydling St Nicholas
Tel: 0300 341 790.
Off the A37 and the A352 north of Dorchester.

The village of Sydling St Nicholas nestles in a beautiful and unspoilt valley, surrounded by fields and woods. The attractive farmhouse, built about 400 years ago of brick and flint under a thatched roof, stands hard by the approach road to the village, about three miles from the A37, the Dorchester to Yeovil road.

The bedrooms are nicely furnished and have their own bathrooms; the family room has an antique brass double bed and an unusual old Swedish pine bed which can be adjusted to suit the size of the child. There is plenty of room for a cot or another bed.

The comfortable lounge has an inglenook fireplace with all the fittings for smoking bacon still in place. Board games, cards and toys are available. Meals are taken at the huge pine table in the farmhouse kitchen.

The spacious garden is safely encircled by hedges and there is loads of room for children to play on the lawns. Mrs Bown is delighted to have families to stay, and the children can meet the farm's many animals – cows, chickens, ponies and dogs. There is much to do and see in the immediate vicinity.

Nearby: The attractive port of Weymouth is not far away. It has an excellent sandy beach, from which dogs are banned. Lodmoor Country Park is close to the beach, as is the nature reserve at Radipole Lake. This is Thomas Hardy country, and his cottage is nearby; also within easy reach are the Tutankhamun Exhibition, Maiden Castle, Athelhampton and T.E. Lawrence's cottage, Clouds Hill. The children may enjoy the Sea Life Centre at Weymouth.

✖ DINNER (6.30pm to 8pm) £10
Children: half portions
£ low
Children: cot £2; £9 up to 13 years
Facilities: 2 cots and 1 high chair; baby listening by arrangement
3 rooms, 1 family. Open all year
No credit cards. Unlicensed. No music
℗ ample
Self-catering: One wing of the farmhouse has been restored as a cottage for two people and a child (a cot is available). The charming bedroom is under the eaves and the sitting room has french windows which lead out to the garden. The rent varies from £80 to £190 a week.

NR TAUNTON, SOMERSET

ℙℝ BATHPOOL, Bridgewater Road
Tel: 0823 272 545.
Near junction 25 of the M5; on the A38 north east of Taunton.

Behind the long, low facade of this pub, smartly painted in cream, you will find an extremely spacious and well-organized operation which has all the facilities a family might require. The Bathpool is open throughout the day and serves food right through until 10 o'clock in the evening; there are plenty of high chairs and a nappy changing facility, and a children's menu.

In addition, the pub has a splendid indoor play area with a ball swamp, all kinds of things to climb on or over, and plenty of games; it is located alongside the family eating area, where smoking is forbidden. Outside, there is another sturdy play unit on a safe bark surface; it is within the enclosed lawned garden where there are bench tables for the adults.

The interior is very spacious but not overwhelming by dint of the many alcoves and little rooms. The wood panelling (some of it painted a dashing green), stripped wooden floors, the padded benches and seats and cheerful decor add up to a very agreeable pub/restaurant.

✗ (11.30am–10 pm) £2–8: hot mushrooms, chilli con carne, sirloin steak, plaice & chips, vegetable crumble
Children: own menu, half portions
🍺 Ale: Boddington's, Flowers and guests (e.g. Wadworth's, Bateman's)
ℙ: own car park

TINTINHULL, NR YEOVIL, SOMERSET

ℙ CROWN & VICTORIA, Tintinhull
Tel: 0935 823 341.
Off the A303 – follow the signs to Tintinhull House.

The owners of this nicely-proportioned stone pub with shuttered windows have children of their own and, therefore, make due allowance for families, who are welcome in the skittle alley, with its few tables and piano.

On summery days, you can head for the splendid, large garden. There is a lot of lawn on which to relax, with swings and a slide, a climbing frame and a football net.

Nearby is the National Trust property of Tintinhull House with its celebrated gardens.

✕ (12.30pm to 2.30pm & 7.30pm to 9.30pm) £1–6: lasagne, trout & vegetables, salads, sirloin steak, chicken in cream & cider
Children: half portions
⊟ Ale: Fuller's, Courage and guest beer
Ⓟ own car park

TORMARTON, NR BADMINTON, AVON
Ⓟ COMPASS INN, Tormarton
Tel: 0454 218 242.
Half a mile north from Junction 18 of the M4 – take the first right turn off the A46 going towards Stroud.

This fine old creeper-covered pub of 18th-century origin is in a useful spot – only a minute or so from the motorway. The main bar, with a good selection of real ale, leads down to the food bar. On from there is a huge, glass-roofed orangery which is always pleasantly warm and bedecked with hanging plants. Children are welcome in the food bar or the orangery. A patio and a lawned garden offer pleasant spots to sit on summer days.

There is always a good display of food here, from the cold buffet to the daily specials, and it is served seven days a week. There is also an excellent vegetarian menu. The pub is open throughout the day and it is good to report that food is available at all times – from 7 o'clock in the morning until 10 o'clock at night.

✕ (7am to 10pm) £2–7: fresh poached salmon, chicken curry, dressed crab, lasagne, ratatouille au gratin
Children: own menu, half portions
⊟ Ale: Archer, Bass, Smiles
Ⓟ own car park

TRENT, NR SHERBORNE, DORSET
P ROSE AND CROWN, Trent
Tel: 0935 850 776.
Four miles north-west of Sherborne off the B3148.

A couple of decades ago this was a farmhouse, built from two 15th-century stone cottages, which stands up a short drive in this delightful village. Anyone who enjoys real pubs will feel at home here, because the Rose and Crown has not been messed about by insensitive 'designers'. It has retained its simply decorated bar with a tiled floor, open fire, low ceilings and curved settles. The pub houses a collection of antique brass and copper cooking utensils.

To the right of the entrance, you will find a small family room, with a stone-flagged floor, large fireplace and an early Victorian dresser. An alternative for families with older children is the attractive conservatory dining room. There is a varied choice of real ales to be had here, and some very interesting food, especially Creole and Cajun dishes from Louisiana, which was the landlady's home.

Outside, the skittle alley borders one side of the garden with plenty of bench tables on the lawn. There is a good display of flowers and you will have a lovely view over the hills of Blackmore Vale and Elizabethan Compton House. The village church is only about fifty yards away. Both the church and Compton House were used as hiding places by Charles II, when he was on the run from Cromwellian soldiers. The story is documented in Samuel Pepys' diaries.

It is agreeable to report that there is a total absence of music and games machines here – it's a very charming pub, and long may it remain so.

✗ (12pm to 2pm & 7pm to 9.30pm) £2–10: samosas, cold duck pie & salad, barbecued chicken, Indonesian pork sate with peanut sauce, beef & Burgundy casserole
Children: own menu, small portions
Ale: Oakhill, Wadworth's and guest beers
P own car park. No music

WELLS, SOMERSET
® THE GOOD EARTH, 4 Priory Road
Tel: 0749 678 600.
On the A371 west of the Cathedral, a few hundred yards from
the High Street.

When you have uplifted your soul by gazing at the magnificent
cathedral in this lovely town, attend to the inner self at this attractive
wholefood restaurant. It is based in a series of bright and airy rooms
with pine floors and solid oak tables and benches. You can also eat
in a little paved courtyard with barrel tables and chairs.

There's a pleasing ambience to this restaurant, and the prices
are very pleasing too – a very substantial three-course meal will set
you back around £5. A baby can be changed in the Ladies, where
there is a table, and paper towels are supplied.

The wholefood store which is a part of the Good Earth has a
full range of unrefined foods: newly baked bread, stoneground
flour, local cheeses, free range eggs, sugar free jams and so on.

✗ £1–3: soups, pizza, jacket potato with cheese, dish of the day
(e.g. mushroom & cashew nut pie, or cauliflower cheese), salads
Children: own menu, half portions
Open 9.30am to 5.30pm Mon to Sat
Closed Sun. Access/Visa
Licensed. Several no smoking rooms
℗ free car park at rear. No music

WELLS, SOMERSET
®Ⓛ WELLS CATHEDRAL
Tel: 0749 674 483.
In the centre of the town.

Wells Cathedral represents one of the great glories of ecclesiastical
architecture. It was begun in the 12th century; the remarkable West
Front was begun in 1230 and is notable for the 293 sculptures
which adorn it; the famous astronomical clock, made in 1390, is in
the north transept.

You can stroll around the cathedral close and visit the Chapter
House, the Library and the Bishop's Palace.

When you have seen all these beautiful buildings you might well be hungry and thirsty, so head for the Cloister Restaurant, which has been recommended in *The Family Welcome Guide* for many years. The long room has a double row of plain wooden tables, overlooked by memorial plaques on the walls. You can sit in peace and contentment under the carved stone roof and look out through the mullioned windows to the cathedral.

A good selection of salads, snacks and dishes of the day is on offer, plus a choice of pastries and cakes. It is all reasonably priced: eat heartily because the profits go to the cathedral. High chairs are available, and there is a mother and baby room in the nearby Cathedral lavatories.

Open: Cathedral – daily from 7.15am to 6pm, later in the summer; Palace – every Sunday and Thursday from Easter to end October and every bank holiday Monday, 2pm to 6pm; some Wednesdays and Fridays from May to September; daily in August, 11am to 6pm
Charges: voluntary donation
Baby changing: mother and baby room
✗ £1–3: jacket potatoes, quiches, salads, hot dishes of the day
Children: smaller portions
Open 10am to 5pm, Sun from 2pm to 5pm. Closed for 2 weeks at Christmas
No credit cards accepted. No smoking
Licensed. No music
P public car parks

NR WELLS, SOMERSET
H GLENCOT HOUSE, Glencot Lane, Wookey Hole
Tel: 0749 677 160.
North-west of Wells off the A371. Follow the signs for Wookey Hole. The hotel is signposted.

Glencot House is a stylish Victorian mansion, in a splendid location in 18 acres of gardens and parkland alongside the River Axe. There is plenty of space for children to play and for adults to relax. It is a quiet and peaceful place.

The building has been faithfully restored during the last few years and the interior has been decorated and furnished with great care. There is lovely oak panelling throughout the house and fine views through the large mullioned windows. The library is a comfortable and quiet room and the spacious lounge has an unusual patterned wood ceiling; the bay windows overlook the gardens and the river and there is a vast inglenook fireplace which can seat six people with ease. A charming little bar with a verandah, and a stately dining room, oak panelled and with a splendid chandelier, complete the picture. Antique pieces abound and some discretion must be exercised by younger children. The bedrooms have been furnished and decorated in varying styles and to very high standards, and many of them have idyllic views across the gardens to the water. Plenty of space is provided for guests and especially so in the family rooms.

The extensive gardens are a delight and guests can fish for trout in the river. Indoors, there is a small plunge pool and a sauna, a full size snooker table and table tennis.

Glencot House is an outstanding hotel in a superb location, where families are made very welcome.

Nearby: The charming city of Wells with its great cathedral is just over a mile away and the famous Wookey Hole Caves are just down the road. The Mendips offer superb walks and you can take in Cheddar Gorge and the less popular Ebbor Gorge. The nature reserve at the Chew Valley Lake is of great interest, as are the Tropical Bird Gardens north of Frome. Nunney Castle, the Fleet Air Arm Museum, Montacute House, Ham Hill Country Park, Cricket St Thomas Wildlife park and the cities of Bath and Bristol are all within easy reach.

✂ DINNER (7pm to 9pm) £16: smoked fish salad, peppered rump steak with red wine sauce, pudding
Children: own menu, half portions
£ medium
Best Bargain Break: £80 per person, 2 nights – dinner, b&b
Children: free up to 4 years: £12 from 4 to 10 years
Facilities: 2 cots and 2 high chairs; baby listening on 3 lines
12 rooms, 2 family, 1 set interconnecting
Open all year. Access/Visa

No smoking in restaurant. No music
Ⓟ own car park

NR WELLS, SOMERSET
Ⓛ WOOKEY HOLE CAVES AND PAPER MILL, Wells
Tel: 0749 672 243.
Off the A39 or A371 north-west of Wells.

The focal point of the place is the amazing formation of limestone caves. The major chambers are linked to provide a circular tour for visitors. You will also see a weirdly shaped stalagmite, which the local legend says is a witch turned to stone.

You can see paper being made by hand in the mill, and it is said that there was a mill on this site in the 11th century. The Old Penny Arcade has a display of end-of-pier machines and you can buy the old pennies with which to operate them. The butler didn't really see much, did he! Other attractions include a Fairground by Night exhibition and a Magical Mirror Maze.

There is a large, nicely decorated self-service restaurant in which several high chairs are provided. The menu is extensive and reasonably priced, including snacks and sandwiches, steak and kidney pie, lasagne, roast chicken and filled jacket potatoes. Alternatively, bring your own food and take advantage of the picnic area.

All the family can enjoy this famous tourist attraction.

Open: 9.30am to 5.30pm, March to October; 10.30am to 4.30pm in the winter months
Charges: adults £5.20; OAPs £4.50; children £3 from 4 to 16 years; under 4s free
Baby changing: a pull-down shelf in the Ladies
Ⓟ plenty (and a buggy park near the entrance)

WEST BEXINGTON, NR DORCHESTER, DORSET
Ⓗ MANOR HOTEL, West Bexington
Tel: 0308 897 785.
Signposted off the B3157 coastal road between Bridport and Weymouth.

This 16th-century stone manor house has a marvellous position in a small village in the lee of rolling downland overlooking Chesil Beach and Lyme Bay – popular for fishing but dangerous for swimming. There is safe swimming to be had at Weymouth's sandy beach, which is also patrolled by lifeguards during the summer season. Rowing and motor boats can be hired, and there are traditional children's attractions such as Punch and Judy shows and a children's beach club.

The hotel's interior is handsome with its Jacobean panelling and flagstone floors, and the owner, a racing fan, has a multitude of paintings and prints of the sport of kings on the walls.

The appealing restaurant, with large windows overlooking the terrace and gardens, has a huge inglenook fireplace decorated with horse brasses and copper kettles and pans. There are two very comfortable lounges with fine views.

On the floor below you will find a splendid bar; it has a real pubby feel to it with its wooden tables, recessed window seats, white-washed walls, beamed ceiling and horse brasses and harness. Up some steps is a large conservatory that can be used by families; it opens on to a lawned garden with bench tables. The bar always has a good choice of real ales.

We looked at several bedrooms, all decorated and furnished in fine style; a family room (with a double and a single bed) at the top of the house is particularly attractive with its sloping ceilings and it has terrific views.

The gardens include a lawned area in front of the hotel with bench tables, and a bigger stretch, overlooking the sea in the distance, which has a children's play unit.

Nearby: You are on the verge of the lovely Dorset countryside, made famous by Thomas Hardy. His cottage can be seen near Dorchester. The Tutankhamun Exhibition is near there too, as is Athelhampton, the Tank Museum at Bovington Camp, T.E. Lawrence's cottage (Clouds Hill) and Maiden Castle. Nature lovers will head for Abbotsbury, with its famous swannery and the sea life centre at Weymouth.

✗ BAR SNACKS (12pm to 2pm & 6.30pm to 10pm) £2–13: crab pancake, liver & bacon, Dover sole, game pie, rack of lamb
LUNCH (12pm to 2pm) £15: fresh sardines, chicken supreme, pudding;
DINNER (7pm to 10pm) £20: Abbotsbury oysters, escalope of veal, pudding or cheese
Children: own menu, half portions
£ high
Best Bargain Break: £111 per person, 2 nights – dinner, b&b
Children: half price for under 10s
Facilities: 5 cots and 5 high chairs, and a baby listening system
13 rooms, 1 family. Access/AmEx/Diners
Open all year. No smoking in conservatory
⊟ Ale: Wadworth's, Palmer's, Eldridge Pope
ℙ own car park

WEST HUNTSPILL, SOMERSET
ℙ CROSSWAYS INN, West Huntspill
Tel: 0278 783 756.
On the A38 just south of Highbridge.

This pub is not very far from the M5 between Bridgewater and Burnham-on-Sea (Junction 22 or 23). Built in the 17th century, it is quite a large place and looks very smart with the lower half of the facade painted white and a tiled upper half. Inside, there are several rooms around the bar which have their fair share of wooden beams, exposed brickwork, wooden tables and settles. There is an open fireplace with a stove at one end of the main bar and an alcove with wooden settles formed into booths.

Families are welcome in a high-ceilinged room with plenty of tables and chairs, and a skittle alley at one end. There is a high chair available.

For warm days, there is a little patio by the entrance as well as a quite large enclosed grassy garden with fruit trees and plenty of bench tables.

✖ (12pm to 2pm & 6.30pm to 10pm) £2–10: broccoli & chicken & ham Mornay, curried vegetarian nut roast, beef Stroganoff, smoked salmon
Children: own menu, half portions
🍺 Ale: Eldridge Pope, Flowers, Smiles and guests
🅿 own car park

NR WESTON-SUPER-MARE, AVON
Ⓗ PURN HOUSE FARM, Bleadon
Tel: 0934 812 324.
Off the A370 south of Weston-super-Mare. Turn opposite the Anchor Inn at Bleadon. (The owners suggest leaving the M5 at J.22 to avoid heavy traffic around Weston-super-Mare.)

Weston-super-Mare is a busy place, but you will find peace and quiet at this handsome, creeper-clad 17th century farmhouse situated at the foot of Purn Hill at the western end of the Mendips. There are splendid views of the surrounding countryside and across to the Bristol Channel.

There are excellent facilities for families, including four family sized rooms, high chairs and cots. The bedrooms have plenty of space, especially the four family rooms, which have double beds and either one or two single beds for the children. The family room on the top floor under the eaves is charming, and there is a family suite on the ground floor which has a double bed and a second bedroom through an archway which can accommodate either a single bed or bunk beds.

Much of the food served by the friendly owner is grown on the farm's 700 acres, and visitors are welcome to walk around and watch the various farming activities. Children must of course be supervised. There is a games room ('The Cave') with pool, table tennis, darts and board games, and there are plenty of books and information about the locality.

The large lawn is encircled by a drive and there is a rockery and a small garden pond. You can sit in the sun in a secluded walled area and even have a picnic there, perhaps in the shade of the ancient weeping ash tree.

Nearby: There is plenty to do and see in the area. Guests can fish in the River Axe which flows through the grounds of the farm and trout fishing can be had at Chew Valley and Blagdon Lakes; riding and pony trekking can be arranged at local riding schools. Nearby attractions include Cheddar Gorge, Wookey Hole Caves, Wells and Glastonbury, and the East Somerset Railway near Shepton Mallet. There are plenty of sandy beaches within easy reach: at Uphill, Burnham and Berow for example.

✗ DINNER (6.30pm) £7
Children: half portions
£ low
Children: half price under 3 years; two thirds price 3 to 11 years
Facilities: 2 cots and 2 high chairs; and a baby listening system
6 rooms, 4 family
Open February to November. No credit cards
No smoking in dining room and bedrooms. Unlicensed
Ⓟ own car park

NR WESTON-SUPER-MARE, SOMERSET
⒫Ⓡ HOBBS BOAT, Bridgewater Road, Lympsham
Tel: 0934 812 782.
On the A370, three miles south of Weston-super-Mare.

When we visited the Hobbs Boat one sunny lunchtime, the garden was packed with children enjoying the adventure playground and the bouncy castle, while the adults looked on and enjoyed their food and drinks.

The large indoor playroom was just as popular and it has an array of things for children to crawl on or under, to ride on and fall on, including a ball swamp. Alongside there is the family eating area (no smoking) and there are several high chairs and a nappy changing facility.

The pub is divided up into alcoves and rooms on different levels and this masks its size. Smart wallpaper, richly coloured carpets, wooden furniture and padded benches and chairs make this a comfortable and appealing pub/restaurant with excellent family amenities.

✗ 11.30am–10pm: £2–8: fish dippers, steak & kidney pie, sirloin steak, chicken escalopes, fillet of salmon
Children: own menu, half portions
🍺 Ale: Bass, Boddington's, Flowers
Ⓟ own car park

WEYMOUTH, DORSET
Ⓗ STREAMSIDE HOTEL, 29 Preston Road
Tel: 0305 833 121.
On the A354, just before the sea front.

The hotel was built in the 1930s in mock-Tudor style. The black and white facade, ablaze with flowers in tubs, window boxes and hanging baskets, is a cheerful sight. You will find a fresh, attractive interior and the Tudor theme is continued with beamed ceilings.

The garden has both lawned and terraced areas, with plenty of picnic tables, chairs and bench tables. It overlooks a nature reserve. There is a swing in the garden. Indoors, there is a pool table, table tennis and darts.

Nearby: Weymouth has one of the safest beaches in the area (patrolled by lifeguards throughout the summer), a broad sweep of sand which is overlooked by the fine Georgian houses on the esplanade. Dogs are rightly banned from the main beach areas. At the back of the beach is Lodmoor Country Park and nature reserve. There is a Sea Life Centre in the town and many attractions within an easy drive: the Tutankhamun Exhibition, Hardy's Cottage, the Tank Museum at Bovington Camp, Athelhampton House, Corfe Castle and the Swanage Railway.

✗ BAR SNACKS (12pm to 2pm) £2–6: Cumberland sausage, grilled trout, minute stake, brunch, salmon fishcake

DINNER (7pm to 9pm) £10: pork & live terrine, poached salmon, sherry trifle
Children: own menu, half portions
£ high
Best Bargain Break: £60 per person, 2 nights – dinner, b&b
Children: cot £4; £7 from 4 to 7 years; £13 from 8 to 12 years
Facilities: 2 cots and 2 high chairs; baby listening to each room
15 rooms, 4 family. Open all year
Access/AmEx/Diners/Visa.
ⓟ own car park

WEYMOUTH, DORSET
Ⓛ SEA LIFE CENTRE, Weymouth
Tel: 0305 788 255.
On the A353 in Weymouth.

The Centre is situated in Lodmoor Country Park and offers a fascinating insight into all that lives beneath the waves. Several buildings house different types of fish in their varying environments and you can view them from all angles. There are octopus, giant rays, flatfish and dozens of other species. The giant whale splash pool is especially popular, as is the touch pool, where you can pick up and examine the small marine creatures which lie there.

There are enough attractions here to keep a family amused for several hours: an audio visual show; a simulator in which you can travel on a roller coaster, a bob sleigh, or in a jet fighter; a miniature railway; a picnic area; and a play area.

The restaurant has several high chairs and serves a wide range of food: sandwiches and cream teas, plaice and chips, scampi and even curry with chips. It's certainly chips with everything on the children's menu too. In addition, a beach barbecue operates during the summer months.

This is a well-organized place with something of interest for all the family and, dare one say it, with an excellent educational content also.

Open: 10am to 5pm, every day
Charges: adults £4.50; children & OAPs £3.25 (1993 prices)
Baby changing: excellent facilities in the disabled toilet area – a

table with changing mat, a bin for nappies and paper towels
P plenty

WITHYPOOL, SOMERSET
H WESTERCLOSE COUNTRY HOUSE HOTEL,
Withypool
Tel: 064 383 302.
Off the B3223, south west of Minehead. The hotel is signposted
in the village.

The hotel sits just above a pretty village in nine acres of gardens –
plenty of space in which the children can roam. It is an agreeable,
white-painted building, which began life as a hunting lodge in the
1920s and has now assumed the mantle of a very comfortable and
relaxing hotel.

If peace and quiet is what you seek this is an excellent place to
be, surrounded by lovely countryside and with the whole of Exmoor,
its moorland teeming with wildlife, to explore.

We were impressed by the standard of the public rooms. There
are two spacious lounges; one doubles as the reception area and
the other has a good selection of books and a writing desk. They
are nicely decorated and well furnished. The large conservatory is
another agreeable place to sit; it is a comfortable spot and the bar
is alongside. There is also a little terrace outside the windows.

We looked at several bedrooms, which have been decorated in a
stylish and attractive way. They include a nice little single room
which would suit an older child, and a splendid family room with

a double bed built in an ingenious way against an old wooden pillar. This room also has a sofa-bed.

The gardens around the hotel are well maintained, with smooth lawns and mature trees. There are lots of animals in evidence – cats, chickens and donkeys – which should please the children; and the hotel has stables, so you can arrive on horseback, if you wish.

It is clear that the owners have put a great deal of care into this very appealing hotel, where families will be welcomed and where they will be very comfortable. There is, by the way, an excellent vegetarian menu, and the Sunday lunch is marvellous value at £11 for three courses.

Nearby: The hotel is right in the middle of Exmoor, a wonderful place to explore on foot or horseback. Birdwatching is a favourite pastime here and fishermen are very well catered for. The Exmoor Centre is just down the road at Dulverton. You can reach the coast to the north quite easily. If you like to see the sights there is plenty of choice: Combe Sydenham Hall, the West Somerset Railway, Dunster Castle, Fyne Court, Gaulden Manor, Knightshayes Court and Orchard Mill are all within easy reach.

✕ BAR SNACKS (12.30pm to 2.30pm) £3–9: smoked fish paté, Exe Valley trout, spicy bean casserole, steak & kidney pie, pork casserole
DINNER (7.30pm to 9.15pm) £19: smoked haddock, fillet of beef, pudding & cheese
Children: own menu
£ medium
Best Bargain Break: 5 per cent discount from Sunday to Thursday, October to March
Children: free up to 3 years; £10 for an extra bed
Facilities: 2 cots and 2 high chairs; a baby listening system
10 rooms, 1 set interconnecting, 2 family. Open all year
Access/AmEx/Visa. No music (except in the dining room)
No smoking in dining room.
Ⓟ own car park

YEOVILTON, SOMERSET
Ⓛ **FLEET AIR ARM MUSEUM**, Yeovilton
Tel: 0935 840 565.
Off the A303/A37 and on the B3151 near Ilchester. Well
signposted.

The museum contains a remarkable collection of aircraft with an
emphasis, naturally, on naval aircraft: the famous Fairey Swordfish,
the Seafire, Corsair, Hellcat and Avenger, and even a Japanese
Kamikaze suicide bomber. There are First World War aircraft such
as a Sopwith Pup and Camel and jets such as the Sea Vampire,
the Buccaneer and the Phantom.

One of the great attractions is one of the prototype Concordes;
you can walk through the aircraft and also see how supersonic flight
developed.

There are many exhibitions in the museum and they tell the story
of naval aviation: between and during the World Wars, through the
Falklands War and up to the present day. A Korean War Exhibition
was opened last year and features a MiG fighter, and at Easter
1994 an Aircraft Carrier Exhibition opens. It will include a section
of a flight deck and a dozen aircraft from the late Sixties and early
Seventies.

The Swordfish Restaurant is a well-organized self-service cafeteria which serves hot and cold meals and snacks; fish and chips,
burgers and salads, for example. Two high chairs are provided.

Outside, there are bench tables on a grassy picnic area and alongside is an excellent adventure playground where the children can
amuse themselves.

Open: 10am to 5.30pm (4.30pm in winter), every day 24–26
December
Charges: adults £4.80; OAPs £3.50; children £2.70; under 5s free
(1993 prices)
Baby changing: mother and baby room
Ⓟ ample

London, South and South-East

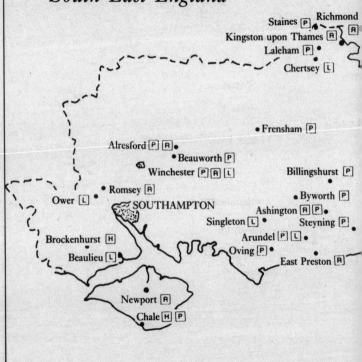

London, South and
South-East England

Staines [P] Richmond
Kingston upon Thames [R] [R]
Laleham [P]
Chertsey [L]

• Frensham [P]

Alresford [P] [R]
• Beauworth [P]
Winchester [P] [R] [L]

Billingshurst [P]

• Byworth [P]

Romsey [R]
Ower [L] • SOUTHAMPTON
Ashington [R] [P]
Singleton [L] Steyning [P]
Arundel [P] [L]
Brockenhurst [H] Oving [P]
Beaulieu [L]
East Preston [R]

Newport [R]
Chale [H] [P]

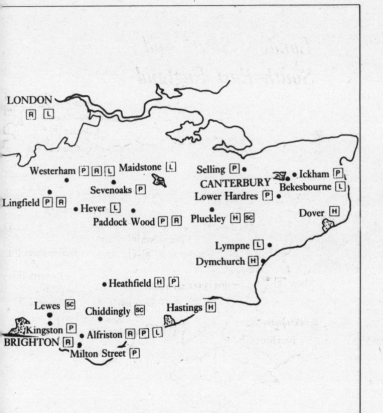

LONDON
R L

Westerham P R L Maidstone L   Selling P •
        •   Lingfield P R   Sevenoaks P   CANTERBURY
Lingfield P R   Lower Hardres P •
        • Hever L   •
     Paddock Wood P R Pluckley H SC

                                    Lympne L •
                             Dymchurch H

        • Heathfield H P

Lewes SC   Chiddingly SC   Hastings H
      •   •
  Kingston P   Alfriston R P L
BRIGHTON R
    Milton Street P

Ickham P
Bekesbourne L

Dover H

ALFRISTON, EAST SUSSEX
PRL DRUSILLAS PARK, Alfriston
Tel: 0323 870 234.
Just off the A27 near Alfriston.

It was no surprise that Drusillas won one of the English Tourist Board's top awards in 1991 (the Family Welcome of the Year award) since adults and children of all ages can have a lot of fun at this excellent park; the focal point is the zoo, but there are many more attractions available.

The zoo is designed with children in mind, and indeed the Board of Directors comprises seventeen children. For example, low level viewing panels, for very small children, are let into the cages, and all the signs are sizeable and use plain and simple words.

There are lots of activities scattered throughout the zoo: 'termite mounds' to be climbed, a zoolimpics with jumps and swings, and a huge play area with all sorts of equipment to amuse the children; if the weather turns nasty there is a well-equipped play barn. A miniature train runs through the animal paddocks and it includes a carriage for the disabled.

Adults are well cared for too. Apart from the wide range of birds and animals to see, there are eight shops on the site, including a pottery shop and a garden centre. There are some lovely gardens in which to relax, including the quiet Japanese Garden and a very large and well-maintained picnic area, a part of which is under cover.

There is a good range of food and drink on offer, and the restaurant, now called Toucans, has been recommended for many years in *The Family Welcome Guide*. It is open at weekends and during the school holidays and has high chairs, plenty of space and a varied menu; it is especially popular on Sundays when entertainments for the children are laid on, and it is a favoured place for birthday parties. Next door is a spacious pub, the Inn at the Zoo; it has two family rooms and is open every day.

There is also a new Family Food Bar in the zoo park where you can buy inexpensive snacks (burgers, hot dogs, etc). The bar contains a baby's play area at one end, so the adults can enjoy a snack while the baby entertains itself.

This is an extremely well run and entertaining place where the whole family can have an enjoyable day. A number of special events are held through the year, for example, family barbecues, an American Indian camp, birds of prey displays, world of owls week, and so on.

✕ (12 noon to 6pm) £2–6: spaghetti Bolognese, fish & chips, burgers, vegetable crumble bake
Children: own menu
Access/Visa. No smoking in various areas
🍺 Ale: Harvey's
Open every day, except the Christmas period, 10am to 5pm (or dusk)
Charges: adults £5; OAPs £3.50; children £4.50; under 3s free
Baby changing: two mother and baby rooms
🅿 ample

ALRESFORD, NR WINCHESTER, HANTS
🅿 PERCY HOBBS, Alresford
Tel. 0962 849 631.
Three miles from junction 9 of the M3 on the A31.

This agreeable country pub has a good collection of facilities for families, including several high chairs, a family dining room (no smoking), a small indoor play area with lego tables and toys and a nappy changing facility.

The Percy Hobbs has a very pleasant interior, with a long, bar area with windows on to the paved terrace. Off the bar there is a series of rooms and alcoves with wooden furniture and padded benches and chairs, wooden panelling and screens here and there and Laura Ashley-style wallpaper.

At the back you will find a pretty enclosed garden, shaded by tall trees and there is a children's play area on a safe bark surface.

✕ (11.30am to 10pm; Sunday 12pm to 10pm) £2–8: paté, plaice & chips, sirloin steak, vegetable harlequin, chicken Masala
Children: own menu
🍺 Ale: Flower's, Strong's
🅿 own car park

ARUNDEL, WEST SUSSEX
Ⓛ WILDFOWL AND WETLANDS CENTRE,
Mill Road
Tel: 0903 883 355.
One mile north of the town centre and close to the railway station.
Signposted from the A27.

Arundel is one of seven centres run by the Wildfowl and Wetlands
Trust, and the famous castle provides a splendid backdrop. The
Centre was developed on water meadows which are drained by
ditches and provide a home for a wide variety of ducks, geese and
swans plus a wide cross section of other birds. There are five hides
in the grounds from which you can observe them at close quarters.

Alternatively, you can stroll along the paved walkways, where lots
of information is provided and, on some days join a guided tour.
The birds are fed between 3pm and 5pm and this can best be seen
from the viewing gallery.

Special events are arranged throughout the year, including many
for children, and there are film shows and lectures, regular exhibitions of prints, plus a gift shop and a book shop.

The well-designed restaurant and coffee shop has wonderful
views over the Centre, and if the weather was really bad you could
sit here and watch the birds. There are a couple of high chairs,
and the food includes such dishes as vegetable pasta, jacket potatoes
and salads.

The Centre is a beautiful and tranquil place and most rewarding
for anyone with an interest in wildlife.

Open: summer 9.30am to 5.30pm. Closes at 4.30pm in winter
Charges: adults £3.75; OAPs £2.80; children £1.90; under 4s free
(1993 prices)
Baby changing: changing table in the Ladies
Ⓟ own car park

NR ARUNDEL, WEST SUSSEX
P BLACK RABBIT, Arundel
Tel: 0903 882 828.
From Arundel follow the signs to the Wildfowl Trust and keep going.

The pub has the great bonus of a superb position on the River Arun, and next door to the Wildfowl Trust. You have a lovely view of Arundel Castle, too.

The Black Rabbit is housed in an extremely attractive 18th-century building and offers excellent facilities for families, including several high chairs and a nappy changing unit in the Ladies. A family room, nicely furnished with wicker chairs, adjoins the main bar and both have the same lovely view of the river. A verandah runs the length of the building and is a fine sight with its many hanging baskets.

There is a very spacious restaurant at one end of the building, which includes a dining area which specializes in fish.

On summer days you can settle in the extensive garden and enjoy the delightful view. There are bench tables on the lawns, and cheerful baskets of flowers are hung here and there. A playboat has been installed to amuse the children.

During the summer months you can take a trip by boat from Arundel Quay to the Black Rabbit (at lunchtimes). The pub is open all day from Monday to Saturday, and food is available at all times (during the summer).

✗ (12pm to 10.30pm in summer; 12pm to 3pm & 7pm to 10.30pm otherwise) £2–9: crudités, lamb kebab, seafood enchilada, Hawaiian chicken
Children: own menu, small portions
⌐ Ale: Hall & Woodhouse
P own car park

ASHINGTON, NR PULBOROUGH, WEST SUSSEX
ℙℝ RED LION, Ashington
Tel: 0903 892 226.
On the A24 in the village of Ashington.

This large family pub and restaurant is housed in a substantial three-storey building, which is partly faced with tiles in the traditional Sussex manner and also has a good covering of Virginia creeper.

The façade gives one very little idea of the vast amount of space inside the pub, but sensibly the designers have split the interior into a series of small interconnecting rooms and alcoves. They are divided by screens of wood and glass, and wood is much in evidence in the form of beams and pillars. Comfortable padded seats and benches, wooden tables, nice brick fireplaces, prints on the walls and baskets of dried flowers add to the agreeable atmosphere.

Families are very well catered for with their own no-smoking dining areas and there is a sizeable children's play area indoors with lego, videos, a ball swamp and other equipment. There are several high chairs and a baby-changing facility. In addition, there is an enclosed outdoor play area with a bouncy castle and various rides, including a seesaw.

The Red Lion is a well-equipped family pub which is open throughout the day and serves food from morning through to evening.

✗ (11.30am to 10pm; Sundays 12pm to 10pm) £1–8: smoked trout, steak & kidney pie, sirloin steak, fish pie, vegetable crumble
Children: own menu, half portions
🍺 Ale: Boddingtons, Flowers
ℙ own car park

BEAULIEU, HANTS
Ⓛ BEAULIEU NATIONAL MOTOR MUSEUM,
Palace House and Gardens
Tel: 0590 612 345.
On the B3054 north east of Lymington.

Lord Montagu is one of the pioneers of the stately home business and Beaulieu is a well-organized and thriving enterprise.

The hub of Beaulieu (no pun intended) is clearly the Motor Museum which is a magnificent display of vehicles through the ages. What elegance, what nostalgia! And when you look at Donald Campbell's amazing Bluebird you wonder how he had the courage even to get into the tiny cockpit, let alone rev it up and let it go. 'Wheels', on the ground floor of the museum, is an excellent depiction of the impact that the car has had on our lives.

You can travel through Beaulieu on the monorail or on a vintage London bus to view the 13th-century Abbey and, alongside, the Palace House. Two of the ground floor rooms – the dining room and a drawing room – have superb fan-vaulted ceilings and pictures of the Montagu family adorn the walls. The portrait of the present Lord Montagu, by Patrick Proktor, is of particular interest.

Families with young children are well cared for and the mother and baby room is superbly equipped – a model for other similar establishments. There are two changing tables, chairs, a sofa, a bottle warmer, baby food, nappies, powder and ointment.

The Brabazon food court has bars and a very large cafeteria, designed in the most functional way to cope with the large numbers of visitors. Sandwiches and salads, and hot dishes such as scampi, lasagne, steak and kidney pie, etc are available at prices up to £4.

Despite our reservations about the style of some of the modern buildings, Beaulieu is a really slick enterprise, with fascinating exhibits. There are excellent facilities for families, who could easily spend a day here in comfort. The staff are, of course, well trained and friendly.

Open: every day except Christmas Day, 10am to 6pm, May to September (until 5pm other months)
Charges: adults £7; children (4 to 16) £5; OAPs £5.50
Baby changing: excellent mother and baby room
Ⓟ plenty

BEAUWORTH, NR ALRESFORD, HANTS
P THE MILBURY'S, Beauworth
Tel: 0962 771 248.
About two miles south of the A272, and one mile beyond the
hamlet of Beauworth.

Standing alone on top of the hill, the 17th-century pub is built in
soft, warm Hampshire brick with hung tiles, flint walls and dormer
windows set in a many-angled roof line. It is good to report that
families are welcome in various areas, so that adults can still enjoy
the real ales which are available and the excellent range of food. A
notable feature of the pub is the well in the bar. It is three hundred
feet deep and an ice cube, dropped from the safety grid, takes eight
seconds to hit the water. There is also a huge treadmill to be seen.

The two family rooms sit one above the other alongside the large
mill wheel. There are several tables on the ground floor and up
above you will find the gallery, an interesting room with a beamed,
sloping ceiling and wooden tables. There is also a skittle alley with
several tables.

There is a grassy garden with superb views of the wide open
countryside. There are plenty of picnic tables and barbecues are
held during summer weekends. Two swings make up a play area
in a corner of the garden.

✗ BAR SNACKS (12pm to 2pm & 6.30pm to 10.30pm) £1–10:
smoked salmon, cod fillet Mornay, steaks, plaice, chilli con carne;
Children: own menu, half portions
⚏ Ale: Courage, Greene King, Tetley and guest beer
P own car park

BEKESBOURNE, NR CANTERBURY, KENT
L HOWLETTS WILD ANIMAL PARK, Bekesbourne
Tel: 0891 800 605 (Infoline, 38p/45p per minute).
South-east of Canterbury off the A2. Well signposted.

Anyone who is interested in animals will enjoy a day out at Howletts,
an attractive and well-designed wild animal park which was the first
of John Aspinall's animal ventures. It covers over fifty acres of
woodland and you can see a wide variety of animals: the tigers,

leopards, lynx, panthers, elephants etc have plenty of space and the big animals – such as deer, bison and buffalo – are in large, grassy enclosures. Howletts is most famous for its large colony of gorillas.

There are plenty of kiosks which sell soft drinks and ice creams, and the new Pavilion Café is now open. A barbecue is also in action during the summer. You can enjoy the excellent picnic area. High chairs are made available at the café.

The park is well-run, clean and tidy, and any litter is cleaned up quickly by the friendly and helpful staff. Howlett's offers a good day's entertainment (plus some education) for all the family.

Open: every day except Christmas Day, 10am to 5pm or dusk
Charges: adults £6.50; children and OAPs £4.50; under 4s free
Baby changing: mother and baby room
P ample

NR BILLINGSHURST, WEST SUSSEX
P BLUE SHIP, The Haven
Tel: 0403 822 709.

Off the A29 just north of the junction with the A264. There is a sign to The Haven and you should then take the turning to Garlands and Okehurst.

This 15th-century pub is a lovely sight with its half-tiled brick walls, and dormer windows above, all festooned with Virginia creeper. There is a timeless look to the place, especially as you see the superb low-ceilinged bar, with a collection of wooden tables, scrubbed white, the old brick floor, and the large inglenook fireplace. There is just a serving hatch, and the beer is served direct from the barrels.

There are a couple of rooms away from the bar where families can sit; one has a pool table and the other is comfortable enough with its various wooden tables.

There is a very large grassy garden at the back of the pub and it includes some swings and a climbing frame for the children. From here you will see some of the landlord's Newfoundland dogs. There is more garden alongside the pub, with bench tables and a pretty display of roses, snapdragons and other flowers, plus a small patio at the front.

✕ (12pm to 2pm & 7pm to 9.15pm, not Sun or Mon pm) £2–5:
scampi, ham & eggs, plaice & chips, cheesy cottage pie, ratatouille
Children: half portions
🍺 Ale: King & Barnes. No music
🅿 own car park

BRIGHTON, EAST SUSSEX
🆁 BROWNS RESTAURANT, 3/4 Duke Street
Tel: 0273 323 501.
On the western side of The Lanes, not far from the Old Ship
Hotel.

This is very much in the same style as their Cambridge and Oxford
restaurants (qv) and is a busy, gregarious place in the centre of a
seaside town which continues to retain its charm and style.

The restaurant serves an excellent range of food, with the emphasis on pastas, salads and grills. We have invariably enjoyed our
meals here, as well as the lively atmosphere. Families are well cared
for: for example, there were half a dozen high chairs at the last
count; the toilet area is spacious and a pull-down shelf has been
installed in the Ladies.

✕ £2–10: spaghetti with various sauces, fisherman's pie, pot roast,
chicken, burgers, poached salmon
Children: own menu, half portions
Open 11am to 11.30pm (from noon on Sundays)
Closed at Christmas. Access/AmEx/Visa
🅿 multi-storey nearby

BROCKENHURST, HANTS
🅷 WATERSPLASH HOTEL, The Rise, Brockenhurst
Tel: 0590 22344.
On the B3055.

This hotel is situated in a quiet road, and the various extensions
do not hide the original Victorian building with its high roofs and
dormer windows. The elegant dining room overlooks the garden,

as does the welcoming lounge bar; another comfortable lounge, with a bay window, is nearby.

The family bedrooms (usually with a double and two single beds) are at the top of the house and have the benefit of plenty of space. With their sloping ceilings and wide dormer windows, they are light and bright and furnished in an appealing style.

The large gardens are sheltered by mature trees and are beautifully kept. The sizeable heated outdoor swimming pool has a terrace with picnic tables and is located by the kitchen garden which supplies fresh fruit and vegetables for the hotel. Other facilities include a games room with a snooker table; and a cards and board games area can be used by guests.

The Watersplash is an excellent family hotel in a most attractive area of the country.

Nearby: This is the heart of the New Forest with beautiful countryside and pleasant villages all around; a lovely place to walk and browse. There are many places to visit within easy reach: the famous motor museum and stately home at Beaulieu, the Bucklers Hard Maritime Museum, the New Forest Butterfly Farm, the Bolderwood Arboretum with its delightful walks, Paultons Park which offers splendid entertainment for families, and Broadlands, the home of Palmerston and later of Lord Mountbatten. In addition, there are some excellent sandy beaches less than half an hour's drive away.

✗ BAR SNACKS (12pm to 2pm) £2–5: scampi & chips, fried chicken & chips, ploughman's, filled baked potatoes;
DINNER (7.30pm to 8.30pm) £17: sweet pickled herrings, fresh local duckling, pudding and cheese
Children: high teas, half portions
[P] high
Best Bargain Break: £90 per person, 2 nights – dinner, b&b
Children: cots free; one third of adult rate from 4 to 10 years; half the adult rate from 10 to 16 years
Facilities: 3 cots and 3 high chairs; baby listening to all rooms
23 rooms, 5 family. Access/Visa
Open all year
[P] own car park

BYWORTH, WEST SUSSEX
Ⓟ **BLACK HORSE**, Byworth
Tel: 0928 42424.
Close to Petworth – look for the sign off the A283.

This fine old pub was built on the site of an ancient friary and has a charming tall brick front. Inside the overwhelming impression is of wood: wooden floors, scrubbed wooden tables of varying shapes and sizes, and black pillars and beams. The interior has great charm because it has not been messed about.

Families are welcome to use the three interconnecting rooms at the rear of the pub, a delightful spot which is primarily intended for eating and where an enterprising range of food is available seven days a week and includes a Sunday lunch for under £6. The menu changes every two months.

The garden is also a lovely spot to spend some time. Little verandahs and grassy areas go in steps down a slope (keep a wary eye on young children here) and you look across a valley to the woodlands beyond. At the bottom of the hill is a large lawned area.

The pub is only a mile or so from Petworth House with its magnificent collection of paintings by Turner, Van Dyck, Holbein, Rembrandt, Gainsborough et al, and is a good place to repair to after the rigours of sightseeing.

✗ (11.30am to 1.45pm & 6.30pm to 9.45pm) £2–10: seafood crêpe, broccoli and walnut au gratin, lemon sole, braised steak Bordelaise, roast rack of lamb

🍺 Ale: Young's, Ballard's, Eldridge Pope. No music

Ⓟ own car park

CHALE, ISLE OF WIGHT
ⒽⓅ CLARENDON HOTEL & WIGHT MOUSE INN,
Chale
Tel: 0983 730 431.
Just off the A3055 in the south of the island.

The hotel began life as a coaching inn in the 17th century and the stone building, with its dormer windows, is full of character.

The owners, John and Jean Bradshaw, have extended the hotel over the years and offer an excellent array of facilities for families. There are eight family-sized rooms (including two attractive family suite) and they are comfortable, spacious and well-furnished. There are always plenty of cots and high chairs available for very young children.

The dining room is nicely furnished with wicker-backed chairs and the hanging plants give it a relaxing look. Large windows give wonderful views out to sea.

The hotel has its own pub, the Wight Mouse Inn, which is also geared up for families with several areas where they can sit together. The family rooms are full of character with an eclectic collection of musical instruments, antique bottles, prints, maps and pictures.

The pub is open all day and has an extensive menu and a good choice of real ales. The list of whiskies, a different brand for every day of the year, is amazing.

Outside you will find a large and grassy garden which looks out to sea. There are plenty of tables and chairs and a separate play area for children with swings, slides, climbing frames, a petanque pitch and a pets corner with rabbits, chickens and lambs. There are Punch and Judy shows, rides for the children and entertainments are laid on.

The hotel offers splendid facilities (including live entertainment each evening in the inn) for families and is run in an enterprising and well-organized manner.

Nearby: Sandy beaches are easy to find on the island and there are lovely walks close to the hotel. There is a great deal to see and do and none of the attractions are difficult to reach. The nearest to the hotel is Blackgang Chine, a theme park which has long been recommended in *The Family Welcome Guide*. Yafford Mill, Carisbrooke Castle, Arreton Manor, Haseley Manor, the Needles Pleasure Park, Robin Hill Park and Flamingo Park are all within easy reach. Golf, fishing and horse riding can all be arranged.

✗ BAR MEALS (11am to 10pm, Mon to Sat; 12pm to 3pm & 7pm to 9.30pm Sun) £2–10: gravadlax, steaks, crab & prawn mornay, burgers, vegetable lasagne;
DINNER (7pm onwards) £10: quiche Lorraine, grilled lemon sole, fresh fruit meringue and cheese
Children: own menu, half portions
Ⓟ medium
Children: £2 up to 2 years; £5 from 3 to 5 years ; half price from 6 to 12 years; two thirds from 13 to 16 years
Facilities: 8 cots and 8 high chairs; baby listening system
13 rooms, 8 family, 2 suites. Open all year
⌘ Ale: Boddington's, Fuller's, Marston's, Wadworth's, Castle Eden
Ⓟ own car park. Access/Visa

CHERTSEY, SURREY
Ⓛ THORPE PARK, Staines Road
Tel: 0932 569 393.
On the A320 between Staines and Chertsey. Signposted from the M25.

Thorpe Park is a theme park on a grand scale since it covers around 500 acres, much of it water, and attracts well in excess of a million visitors each year. The entry fee covers all the rides and attractions.

There are many 'white knuckle' rides to attract the teenagers including the Flying Fish roller coaster, Thunder River, Logger's Leap, the Tea Cup Ride and the Calgary Stampede.

There are gentler rides and attractions for younger children; the Magic Mill Boat Ride, Treasure Island (complete with real pirates), the Carousel Kingdom which is a huge under-cover play area, Octopus Garden, Model World, and Thorpe Farm, which has some lovely animals, many of which are rare breeds. The Depth Charge, a giant water slide, looked a lot of fun and so did the Viking Rowers on the lake. Fantasy Reef, a man-made beach and a pool with little slides, would be a great haven for young children on a summer day.

There are eight different places to eat and drink; these are mostly fast food outlets including a Burger King, the Crown and Anchor pub, fish and chips, Southern Fried Chicken, and a French café which serves crêpes.

Thorpe Park is an extremely popular and successful tourist attraction and you must be prepared to wait patiently for many of the rides, especially at peak periods – just as you would at Disneyland. It is a wonderful place for children and the adults must assume the expression of the Sphinx and join in the young ones' fun.

Open: 10am to 6pm, Easter to end of October
Charges: adults £9.95; OAPs £7; children £8.95; children under a metre high free; family ticket £28 (1993 prices; telephone for current prices)
Baby changing: excellent facilities with plenty of mother and baby rooms; and disposable nappies on sale
Ⓟ ample

CHIDDINGLY, NR HAILSHAM, EAST SUSSEX

SC PEKES, Chiddingly

Tel: (for bookings) Mrs Eva Morris 071–352 8088; fax 071–352 8125.

Off the A22 north of Hailsham.

If you hanker for a bit of style, try Pekes, a Tudor manor house with grounds covering nearly thirty acres. It is a quiet and secluded spot and comprises four properties for letting.

The Wing, as the name suggests, is attached to the main house. It started life as a cowshed and was converted just after the turn of the century to serve as a drawing room and library for the main house. It is a most attractive building, long and low, with a large bay window. The main L-shaped room is very large and serves as both a living area and dining room. The one bedroom adjoins this, but there are two divans in the main room. A family of four could be accommodated here.

Tudor View looks like a cottage but is actually a bungalow. It was built in the late 1930s but fits into the general scheme of things very well. There are two bedrooms, a double and a twin, a sitting room and a dining room. It is the nearest property to the swimming pool and has its own little fenced garden.

The Gate Cottage is a delightful tile-hung cottage on two floors and was originally built (in 1911) for the coachman. There are two bedrooms, a living room and a dining room.

The Oast House is a most appealing building, its focal point being the two large round towers which were once used for drying hops. It was converted in 1911 and there are two circular bedrooms upstairs and two large reception rooms below. A further two bedrooms (one double and one single) have been built. A family of eight can easily be accommodated.

In addition to the lovely and peaceful grounds, parts of which can be used by guests, there are other excellent facilities, including the use of a tennis court and splendid new covered swimming pool. A sauna, solarium, spa bath and some exercise equipment is also available (50p meter). A badminton net is also provided.

The properties are all well-equipped and have central heating. The only extra is the hire of linen; and Tudor View has a meter for its electricity.

Nearby: Apart from the appealing countryside of Sussex there is no lack of things to do and see in the vicinity. Mitchelham Priory, Firle Place and Herstmonceux Castle are close; while the children will no doubt beat a path to Drusillas and the Seven Sisters Country Park, which has a Living World exhibition. There is a leisure centre at nearby Hailsham and another one at Eastbourne.

Units: 4
Rent: the three cottages £250 to £528 per week; the Oast House £650 to £995 per week (short breaks available)
Other costs: linen, and electricity at Tudor View and the Oast House
Central heating: provided
Two cots and two high chairs; baby sitting by arrangement
Open all year

DOVER, KENT
🅷 TOWER GUEST HOUSE, 98 Priory Hill
Tel: 0304 208 212.
Near the town centre. The brochure includes a detailed map.

When we last stayed at the Tower Guest House we were delighted with the attractively furnished and comfortable rooms. Delighted, too, by the warm and friendly welcome extended by Mrs Wraight.

Although evening meals are not available, and this would normally preclude the Tower from being recommended in the *Guide*, Dover is a special case, since many families need accommodation here if they have booked an early ferry. Also there is a very good choice of restaurants nearby in the town. This guest house, situated at the back of the Wraights' own home (the Old Water Tower) and built into a hillside, would suit such travellers very well. The house sits high above Dover and once was a notable landmark. Although other houses now surround it, the views of the town remain.

The family room, which has twin beds and bunk beds, is on the ground floor, and a kitchen is available to guests where they can heat baby food and make hot drinks and snacks.

Nearby: If you envisage a longer stay in Dover there are many things to do and see: the zoos at Port Lympne and Howlett for example; the theme park at Margate; the castles at Walmer, Deal and Dover itself; and challenging golf at Deal and Sandwich.

P low
Children: £8 per child
Facilities: 2 cots and 1 high chair
5 rooms, 2 family. Open all year except Christmas
No credit cards. No music
P garages, and on street. No smoking in dining room

DYMCHURCH, KENT
H CHANTRY HOTEL, 21 Sycamore Gardens
Tel: 0303 873 137.
Close to the centre of the village.

The hotel has a wonderful position overlooking a long, sandy beach and the wide open sea. Some of the rooms have the advantage of delightful views and a little verandah also faces seawards. To get to the beach you cross a little bridge and a traffic-free promenade and it is very safe since the sea is shallow; you can wade out a long way. The hotel has a boat for the use of guests. The garden offers plenty of space and there are swings on the lawn.

The building dates from the 19th century, is half timbered with weather boarding over the brick, and has some dormer windows. Most of its rooms are suitable for families and the suites have bunk beds for children in a separate bedroom.

It is a friendly and comfortable hotel which is well organized to look after families and does not cost the earth.

Nearby: Apart from the beaches which stretch along this part of the coast there is an array of things to do and see. Golfers have many fine courses within reach including those at Deal and Sandwich; wildlife enthusiasts can head for Port Lympne and Howletts zoo parks; there are castles to see at Dover, Deal and Walmer; and railway buffs can travel on the Romney, Hythe and Dymchurch and the Kent and East Sussex railways. Canterbury, with its famous cathedral, is not too far away.

✗ DINNER (6.30pm to 8pm) £11: mushrooms in garlic, lamb Shrewsbury, pudding and cheese
Children: own menu, half portions

P low
Best Bargain Break: £52 per person, 2 nights – dinner, b&b
Children: half price up to 12 years
Facilities: 2 cots and 2 high chairs; baby listening by arrangement
6 rooms, 2 family, 3 suites. Open all year
No smoking in dining room. Access/AmEx/Visa
P own car park

EAST PRESTON, WEST SUSSEX
R OLD FORGE RESTAURANT, The Street, East Preston
0903 782 040.
Off the A259 and in the centre of the village.

This very appealing brick and flint building, its walls festooned with
ivy, is of 17th-century vintage and was once a forge. Inside you will
find a very attractive and comfortable restaurant; its array of oak
beams and gnarled pillars testify to its long history and the brass
and copper *objets d'art* enhance the appeal of the place. There
is a remarkable collection of Toby jugs and miniature bottles of
spirits.

The emphasis is very much on fresh food, and especially fish; you will often have a choice of locally caught lobsters, scallops and crab. We think the three-course lunch offers particularly good value.

The Ladies is spacious and a baby can be changed in comfort on the table; there is a chair and a good supply of paper towels. Several high chairs are made available.

✗ LUNCH (12pm to 2pm) £10: seafood salad, baked chicken supreme, pudding or cheese;
DINNER (7pm to 10pm) £15: egg & smoked mackerel salad, lamb cutlets with plum sauce, pudding or cheese
Children: half portions
Closed Sun dinner/all day Mon. Access/AmEx/Diners/Visa
Ⓟ own car park. Licensed

FRENSHAM, SURREY
Ⓟ MARINERS HOTEL, Mill Bridge
Tel: 0252 792 050.
On the A287 south of Farnham, and close to Frensham Ponds.

You cannot miss this large Victorian building, painted in its smart trim of cream and white, on the main road south. The name of the pub suggests definite nautical connections, and the story is that the original house, which burnt down in the last century, was used as a depot for smugglers en route between the south coast and London.

It is a very spacious and cheerful place with a large bar area. Off to one side is a room with a vaulted ceiling and plenty of wooden tables and families are welcome to park themselves here. There are several high chairs available and the Mariners is open all day from Monday to Sunday, when you can get something to eat throughout the day.

There are two large patios on each side of the pub and a small lawned area with bench tables.

✗ (12pm to 2pm & 6pm to 10pm) £2–12: canelloni, plaice & chips, vegetarian pizzas, fillet steak, local trout
Children: own menu

🍺 Ale: Courage, Gale's, Marston's and guest beer
Access/AmEx/Diners/Visa
Ⓟ own car park

HASTINGS, EAST SUSSEX
Ⓗ BEAUPORT PARK HOTEL (Best Western), Battle Road
Tel: 0424 851 222.
On the A2100 between Battle and Hastings.

The regular lines and warm red brick of this splendid Georgian
mansion make a most appealing sight, especially when you take in
the pillared main entrance and the dormer windows in the steep
roof. It is a wonderful setting for this elegant hotel and was once
the home of Sir James Murray, who was second in command to
General Wolfe at Quebec. It has a lovely setting in about thirty
acres of parkland, which includes a formal Italian garden with
superb trees, and a tranquil sunken garden, partly enclosed by an
old stone wall.

The smooth lawn at the front contains a putting green, and beyond
there is a hard tennis court and a grass badminton court. At the back
of the hotel is a giant chess board, a boule pitch and a croquet lawn.
Above all there is an outdoor heated swimming pool, surrounded by
pleasant lawns on which to loll. Next door, there is a riding school
and six squash courts; and golfers should be in their element since
there is both a 9-hole and an 18-hole golf course.

Nearby: Hastings Castle and Battle Abbey, which is actually built
on the land where William the Conqueror defeated Harold. Parents
will perhaps favour a visit to the Carr Taylor vineyards; and within a
reasonable radius you can visit Rudyard Kipling's home, Bateman's,
Herstmonceaux Castle and Drusillas, with its zoo, miniature railway,
large adventure playground, restaurant and pub.

✗ BAR SNACKS (10am to 10pm) £1–5: soup, paté, vegetarian
pancake, coquille fruits de mer, ploughman's;
LUNCH (12.30pm to 2pm) £14: hors d'oeuvres, roast loin of pork,
pudding or cheese;
DINNER (7pm to 9.30pm) £16: chicken liver paté, grilled Scotch
salmon, pudding or cheese.
Children: own menu, half portions

P high
Best Bargain Break: £100 per person, 2 nights – dinner, b&b
Children: free up to 16 years
Facilities: 4 cots and 2 high chairs, and a baby listening service
on three lines
23 rooms, 1 family. Access/AmEx/Diners/Visa
Open all year. No music
P own car park

NR HEATHFIELD, EAST SUSSEX
H WEST STREET FARMHOUSE, Maynards Green
Tel: 04353 2516.
On the B2203 just south of Heathfield in the village of Maynards
Green.

This is a delightful brick farmhouse, built in an L-shape, parts of
which date back to the 17th century. It is surrounded by nearly
four acres of grounds, a large part of which comprise smooth lawns:
a lovely spot for the children to play (there are some swings) and
for the adults to relax. The views of the surrounding countryside
are superb.

The two bedrooms, one with a double and the other with twin
beds, are most attractive with their low-beamed ceilings and they
overlook the garden. A bathroom is shared between them and they
can both accommodate a cot.

Down below, there is a pleasant and cosy lounge with a television
and a wood-burning stove and the compact dining room is next
door. A family could rent both bedrooms and have their own very
peaceful self-contained unit.

Nearby: This is a delightful part of England, with glorious
countryside all around and with the coastline from Brighton east-
wards within easy reach. Nature lovers will head for Drusillas Park,
the Seven Sisters Country Park and the Bentley Wildfowl Trust
(there is also a motor museum here). Bateman's, where Rudyard
Kipling wrote many of his books, is nearby, as is Herstmonceux
Castle, Michelham Priory and the Bluebell Railway.

✕ DINNER (7pm) £9
Children: half portions

£ low
Children: no charge
Facilities: 1 cot and 1 high chair; baby listening by arrangement
2 rooms. Open all year
No credit cards. Unlicensed
Ⓟ own car park

NR HEATHFIELD, EAST SUSSEX
Ⓟ THREE CUPS, Punnetts Town
Tel: 0435 830 252.
East of Heathfield on the B2096 at Punnetts Town.

This is a delightful old pub, of 17th-century vintage; low slung,
with square bay windows, it has a weather-boarded upper storey.
There is a stretch of grassy garden at the side of the pub and
another enclosed garden with shady trees at the back. There are
some bench tables here and it is safe for children.

It is a real pleasure to sit inside the Three Cups with its low
ceilings with their black beams, on which are hung an eclectic range
of old coins, earthenware jars and mugs, brasses and even some
old golf clubs. The walls are panelled in wood and there is a huge
inglenook fireplace and several window alcoves.

It is a relaxing and welcoming place with a good choice of real
ales and good value food.

The family room is at the back of the pub and leads out to the
verandah and the garden.

✕ (12pm to 2pm and 7pm to 9pm) £2–12: leek & potato bake,
steaks, lemon sole, chili con carne, chicken cordon bleu
Children: own menu, half portions
🍺 Ale: Harvey's and guest beer
Ⓟ own car park

HEVER, NR EDENBRIDGE, KENT
Ⓛ HEVER CASTLE AND GARDENS, Edenbridge
Tel: 0732 865 224.
Three miles south-east of Edenbridge, off the B2026. Signposted
from the M25, A21, and A264.

Hever Castle dates back to the 13th century and is most famous
as the home of Anne Boleyn, Henry VIII's second wife, and mother
of Elizabeth I. The castle was restored by William Waldorf Astor
in the early years of this century. He built the Tudor Village and
created the huge lake and the delightful gardens.

There is a loggia on the lake, an Italian garden and a maze.
When your children emerge from the maze they can enjoy the
adventure playground, which is well equipped and also has swings
for younger children.

Hever Castle has a gift shop, a bookshop and a garden shop.
There are two self-service restaurants which open at 11am and
offer hot and cold dishes ranging from cod and chips to a cold
buffet (£1 to £5 approx). High chairs are made available.

The castle is a magnificent sight and the grounds are immaculately
kept, with plenty of signs and litter bins. It all adds up to an entertaining visit for all members of the family, with the Tudor Long Gallery
which commemorates the Henry VIII/Anne Boleyn courtship as a
special attraction. There is lots of space for the children to roam, and
you can have a picnic by the lake and then feed the ducks. There is
also an open-air theatre by the lake in the summer.

Open: 16 March to 7 November, gardens 11am to 5pm, castle
12pm to 5pm
Charges: adults £5; OAPs £4.50; children £2.50; under 5s free
Baby changing: well-equipped mother and baby room
Ⓟ own car park

ICKHAM, KENT
Ⓟ DUKE WILLIAM, Ickham
Tel: 0227 721 308.
Off the A257 about five miles east of Canterbury.

Set in a pleasant village, this roomy and attractive 17th-century pub
has a cheerful air. The style is set by the ebullient and friendly

landlord who was a professional chef for twenty years or so and who produces a very wide choice of freshly cooked dishes, both at the bar and in the spacious restaurant. The set menu is very good value at under £13 and high chairs are available.

Families can take advantage of a room at the back of the pub, which leads out to a delightful lawned garden, crowded with plants and flowers, or of the conservatory which was built recently and is a no-smoking area. To one side is a patio and some swings; there is more patio with goldfish ponds at the back – all this is lit up on summer evenings. From here you look out on rolling farmland.

✗ (12pm to 2pm & 7pm to 10pm, not Sun pm or Mon am) £1–7: Duke William brunch, plaice & chips, crab salad, spaghetti carbonara, steak & kidney pie
Children: small portions
🍺 Ale: Adnams, Fuller's, Shepherd Neame, Young's and guest beer
Ⓟ ample street parking

KINGSTON, NR LEWES, EAST SUSSEX
Ⓟ THE JUGGS, The Street
Tel: 0273 472 523
South of Lewes and signposted off the A27.

This delightful pub, with a half-tiled facade, dates from the 15th century and has a splendid bar with a low beamed ceiling and a big open fireplace; there are prints on the walls, an array of wooden tables and padded benches. The owners emphasize that they try to cater for a wide spectrum of customers, and their facilities for families are first class.

The sizeable family room (a no-smoking area) is particularly attractive with brick floor and walls, lots of wood in view and with wide windows to a patio. Alongside there is another agreeable room with a low ceiling, an old pew against one wall and a collection of brass pans and china jugs.

On the other side of the pub there is a charming little eating area, which used to be the kitchen (and was once a stable) and has a slanting beamed roof, white-washed walls and smart furniture. Families are very welcome here, too, and it can be reserved in

advance. The rest of the bar can also be used for casual eating. An enterprising range of food is on offer here and the landlord takes great pains to offer a wide range of non-alcholic drinks, which include fruit juices.

A long, brick-floored terrace runs outside the pub. There is a fine display of flowers and plenty of bench tables. A further patio area is enclosed by hedge on one side and a wall on the other and children cna have fun on the sturdy timber climbing frame. With a little patch of lawn as well, this is a lovely spot to have a drink or an *al fresco* meal.

✖ (12pm to 2pm & 6pm to 9.30pm) £2–9: haddock & chips, vegetable savoury, fillet steak, salt beef sandwich, chicken tikka Children: extra plate
⊟ Ale: Harvey's, King & Barnes. No music
Ⓟ own car park

KINGSTON UPON THAMES, SURREY
Ⓡ CLOUDS CAFE, 6/8 Kingston Hill
Tel: 081 546 0559
On the old Kingston to Putney road just before Kingston Hospital.

This is an appealing, well-run restaurant with efficient and cheerful staff. The decor, centred on wooden tables, old advertising signs and hanging plants, is simple and effective; and the food, although of the 'fast' variety, is as fresh and healthy as possible with pasta, salads, jacket potatoes and a few vegetarian dishes on the menu, while artificial flavourings are avoided.

You would not be able to change a baby in the Ladies, but the staff can find a quiet corner upstairs. The children's menu at £3.50 is very good value and includes an ice cream and a drink, and balloons and sparklers are provided too.

✗ £2–10: chicken satay, vegetable lasagne, barbecued chicken, steaks, tiger prawns
Children: own menu, half portions
Open 12am to 11.30pm; Sunday to 11pm. Open all year
Access/Visa
🍺 Ale: Adnam's
Ⓟ on street

LALEHAM, MIDDX
Ⓟ THREE HORSESHOES, Laleham
Tel: 0784 452 617.
Near the centre of the village, on the B377.

The pub has great charm, with wisteria and other greenery covering its white-painted walls, while baskets of flowers add a further cheerful touch. The building has a long history, since some of it dates back to the 13th century.

There is plenty of space inside, with smart carpets and comfortable padded furniture. On the walls, copper and brass artefacts, prints and china cluster together and there is a large open fireplace.

Families should head for the very pleasant conservatory, which has a tiled floor, some nice wooden tables and chairs and lots of plants. Alongside there is an enclosed lawned garden, bright with flowers and with plenty of bench tables.

It is an appealing pub with good facilities for everyone, including families. It is also good to report that English country wines are sold and you can have a glass of damson or parsnip wine, as well as a choice of real ales, to accompany one of the enterprising bar meals.

The pub is open all day from Monday to Saturday and food is available from noon to 9pm.

✗ (12pm to 9pm) £2–7: avocado & crab, corned beef hash, filled baked potatoes, steak in French bread, smoked salmon & salad
⚑ Ale: Fuller's, Ruddles, Webster's
Ⓟ own car park

NR LEWES, EAST SUSSEX
ⓈⒸ DUCK BARN HOLIDAYS, Telscombe
Tel: 0273 858 221.
South of Lewes off the A26. The brochure has detailed directions.

Telscombe village is one of those idyllic Sussex hamlets which sits quietly in a fold of the downs less than two miles from the sea. Finn and Anne Kennedy have converted three delightful cottages, which are full of character and offer peace and seclusion in a beautiful part of the country.

Duck Barn was once a part of Telscombe Manor and it is said that the garden was originally planted by staff from Kew Gardens. Romantic and informal, the garden is one of the many charms of staying in Duck Barn, with its mature trees and profusion of plants and flowers, a paved area where you can dwell over a meal, a lawn, an ornamental pond, a rockery and a terrace from which you have splendid views of the surrounding countryside, and a little woodland area.

Duck Barn can accommodate up to eight people in its four bedrooms and has been furnished and decorated to the highest standards. The kitchen has everything a cook would need, including a dishwasher and a microwave oven, as well as an electric cooker. The Great Hall, with its high beamed and vaulted ceiling, is a splendid room and has French windows on to the terrace. All the bedrooms have fitted carpets and the pine beds, which can be stacked as bunks, allow for flexibility.

Gardeners Cottage is a tiny flint building, which sits in the front garden of Duck Barn, and also has its own enclosed garden. With its one bedroom and open-plan living area, it is most suitable for a couple.

The Coach House has been converted with a sure touch and the same high standards as the other properties. It can sleep four people in two bedrooms and the bright and airy living area has floor to ceiling windows and French doors on to a terrace. There is a small lawned garden, which is enclosed by walls. The furniture is attractive and comfortable and the equipment is first class.

These are delightful properties, which have been converted with great care and some style. Duck Barn is eminently suitable for a family on holiday, as is the Coach House, and a large group (up to a maximum of twenty) could hire all three properties. Well-behaved pets are welcome for a charge of £10 per week.

Nearby: The beautiful countryside is a haven for walkers and strollers but, if you want a change of pace, the busy resort of Brighton, 'London by the sea', is only a few minutes away, as are the interesting towns of Lewes and Newhaven. Sightseers should head for Kipling's home, Bateman's, Mitchelham Priory, Firle Place and Wakehurst Place. The children will lobby for a trip to Drusillas, which has been recommended in the *Guide* since its very first edition, Seven Sisters Country Park and the Wildfowl Trust at Arundel. There are ample facilities for swimming, golf, fishing, tennis etc, in the locality.

Units: 3
Rent: £120 to £550 (short breaks available)
Other costs: electricity is metered
Heating: central heating and wood burning stoves
Several cots and high chairs
Open all year

NR LINGFIELD, SURREY
ℙℝ RED BARN, Blindley Heath
Tel: 0342 834 272.
On the B2029 near Lingfield.

An old farmhouse, a lovely brick building with a tile-hung upper storey, and a splendid old barn have been used as the core of this substantial pub which has excellent facilities for families.

The large family dining room is a fine sight with its wooden beams and pillars, and one end sits under a vaulted wooden ceiling and has a large brick fireplace. There is a little play area with a slide, an amusement machine, Lego, etc. This is a no smoking area and there are plenty of high chairs available plus a nappy-changing facility.

The main part of the pub comprises a long bar with many comfortable chairs and benches. The barn has been turned into a huge dining area and has a remarkable interior with old wooden pillars and cross-hatched beams under its vaulted roof; there are farm implements and horse brasses on the walls, colourful prints, stags' heads and sets of antlers, wooden pews and dressers and a large fireplace.

The garden is delightful with fine displays of flowers and an enclosed lawned area with bench tables and a large adventure playground for the children.

The pub is open throughout the day and food is available at all times.

✗ (11.30am to 10pm; from 12pm on Sunday) £2–8: smoked trout, sirloin steak, fried scampi, vegetable crumble, rogan josh
Children: own menu
🍺 Ale: Boddington's, Flower's
Ⓟ own car park

CENTRAL LONDON
Ⓡ CRANKS, 8 Marshall Street, W1
Tel: 071 437 2915
Nearest Underground: Oxford Circus

The Marshall Street branch of the well-known vegetarian restaurant chain is in a pleasant modern building quite close to the once famous Carnaby Street. There's a good range of salads, hot vegetarian dishes, baked potatoes and so on. There is a retail and a take-away shop attached to the restaurant.

As we went to press, we learned that the restaurant would be open later on Friday and Saturday evenings (until around 10.30pm) and would also have waiter service.

There are several other Cranks restaurants in London, in Adelaide Street and Covent Garden, Barrett Street and Tottenham Street.

✗ £1–5: salads, baked potato, pizzas and quiches, hot dishes of

the day e.g. casserole of broccoli and black-eyed beans in cheese sauce
Children: own menu
Open 8am to 8pm, Mon to Fri (from 9am Sat). Closed bank holidays
Access/Visa. Licensed
No smoking

CENTRAL LONDON
Ⓡ JOHN LEWIS, THE PLACE TO EAT, Oxford Street, W1
Tel: 071 629 7711.
Nearest Underground: Bond Street, Oxford Circus.

This exceptionally bright and well-organized self-service restaurant on the third floor has seven different sections offering different kinds of food – Breakfast All Day, Crock Pot, Patisserie, Cold Table, Crêperie, Seafood and the Soda Fountain. Something to suit most palates and at reasonable prices – nothing above £7. The Cold Table has an excellent range of salads and the Crock Pot offers various daily specials. The staff are extremely helpful and seem to take a great pride in the place. It gets very busy though – the best advice is to lunch before noon. The Coffee Shop also has high chairs and serves light meals all day, as well as lunchtime specials.

There is an excellent mother and baby room, or perhaps it should be called a parents and baby room, since fathers are not denied access. It has separate breast feeding and nappy changing areas, a bottle warming facility, and plenty of space. It is on the fourth floor, near the children's shoe department, and is accessible by lift.

✗ RESTAURANT £1–7: salads, lamb hot pot, chicken chasseur, seafood Mornay;
COFFEE SHOP £1–3: croissant, soup, salads
Children: own menu in Place To Eat
Open Mon to Sat 9am to 5pm, Thurs to 7.30pm
No credit cards accepted. Licensed
No smoking in any part of the store
No music

CENTRAL LONDON
R MILBURNS at the Victoria and Albert Museum, Cromwell Road, SW7
Tel: 071 581 2159.
Nearest Underground: South Kensington.

A couple of years or so ago, after many delays, Milburns opened their new restaurant in the Henry Cole Wing of the museum. It was worth waiting for because it is a lovely spot – very spacious with a York stone floor, exposed brickwork and good wooden tables. It is usually busy at lunchtimes, but don't be put off because the queue moves quickly.

The menus concentrate on salads, quiches, etc and a hot dish of the day, and the serve-yourself salads are good. There is, thank goodness, no canned music in the restaurant but there is the bonus of real live piano music on Saturdays.

You can change or feed a baby in the Ladies – there is a chair and a substantial table.

✗ LUNCH (12pm to 2.45pm) £1–4: soup, baked potato, salads, quiche, hot dishes of the day
Children: own menu
Open Tues to Sun 10am to 5pm, Mon 12pm to 5pm
Access/AmEx/Diners/Visa. Licensed
No music. No smoking in over half the restaurant

CENTRAL LONDON
R SELFRIDGES, Oxford Street
Tel: 071 629 1234.

The famous store has around a dozen food outlets of various kinds, from an ice-cream parlour to a smart restaurant; there is something here to suit the taste of any family.

The Food Garden Café on the fourth floor is a bright and cheerful self-service restaurant, which offers something to suit the palate at all times of the day including an all-day breakfast and a number of outlets which serve oriental food, pasta, salads, griddles, crepes and so on.

The mother and baby room is on the floor below (third), and

here also is the Selfridges restaurant, quiet, smart and comfortable, and with waitress service. You can eat breakfast, lunch and afternoon tea.

Of the other coffee shops and restaurants, the Arena restaurant in the basement is probably the most suitable for families. It has a couple of high chairs and a good choice of food. It is very close to the ice cream parlour.

✗ FOOD GARDEN CAFÉ £2—6: salads, spaghetti Bolognese, beef in oyster sauce, burgers, breakfast;
SELFRIDGES RESTAURANT: lunch, 2 courses: £13: potted shrimps, roast beef & Yorkshire pudding;
ARENA £2–7: paté, smoked trout, lasagne, roast chicken, spaghetti Bolognese
Children: own menu
Open Mon to Sat 9.30am to 7pm (Thur to 8pm)
Access/AmEx/Diners/Visa
Licensed. Mostly no smoking

CENTRAL LONDON
Ⓛ BRITISH MUSEUM, Great Russell Street, WC1
Tel: 071 636 1555.
Nearest Underground: Tottenham Court Road, Russell Square and Holborn.

The museum, founded in 1753, is one of the great museums of the world. You could spend months there in order to appreciate its scope which ranges from prehistoric times to the present day.

One of the best ways of seeing the Museum is on a guided tour which lasts about an hour and a half in the care of an expert and costs £5.

It would be pointless to try to list the remarkable treasures which the Museum contains but some of the most notable are: the Rosetta Stone, the reliefs in the Assyrian gallery, the sculptures from the Parthenon (the famous Elgin Marbles), the Portland Vase, the Sutton Hoo Burial Ship and the Franks Casket, the Mildenhall Treasure, the Egyptian mummies, the Magna Carta and so on. There are millions of exhibits and a constantly changing variety of exhibitions.

When you pause for a drink or a meal you can choose between the self-service cafeteria, with basic snacks for sale, or the restaurant, which has a splendid selection of food in delightful surroundings. Prices range up to £5 and smaller portions are served to children. High chairs are provided.

Open: 10am to 5pm, Monday to Saturday; 2.30 to 6pm, Sunday
Charges: admission free
Baby changing: good facilities in the First Aid room
Ⓟ public car park nearby, but better to use public transport

CENTRAL LONDON
Ⓛ IMPERIAL WAR MUSEUM, Lambeth Road, SE1
Tel: 071 416 5000.
Nearest tube: Lambeth North.

The museum was re-organized and extended a year or so ago and now covers four floors in a large building which long ago was a lunatic asylum. Now two huge naval guns, which could project a shell over a distance of 18 miles, mark the entrance.

The lower ground floor is devoted to the First and Second World Wars with a series of exhibits which cover most aspects of those conflicts by the use of static displays, video films and commentaries. You can experience the Blitz, and see the Victoria Cross and George Cross rooms. It is all put together with great verve and clarity.

The Large Exhibits Gallery occupies the central space of the building, a huge atrium, and you can see tanks and armoured cars, field guns and a whole range of aircraft including a Sopwith Camel, a Spitfire and a Mustang, and missiles including a V2 rocket. The art gallery is on the top floor.

The café is a pleasant and bright room which overlooks a garden. Hot meals and snacks are served and one high chair is available.

This is a superbly organized and fascinating museum, full of historical and human interest. A number of special events are organized through the year, including gallery talks, children's quizzes and holiday events for children.

Open: 10am to 6pm, every day

Charges: adults £3.70; children £1.85; OAPs £2.65; under 5s free (1993 prices). Entry is free after 4.30pm every day
Baby changing: a very well-equipped mother and baby room on the lower ground floor; there are chairs, two changing tables and a play pen
P meters

CENTRAL LONDON
L LONDON ZOO, Regent's Park, NW1
Tel: 071 722 3333.
Nearest Underground: Camden Town, Regent's Park and Baker Street.

This is the oldest and most famous of all zoos, which opened in 1826, mainly due to the drive and vision of Stamford Raffles. It was known as the 'Ark in the Park' then, and has survived many crises, usually financial, since that time.

Home to thousands of wild and wonderful animals such as gorillas, penguins, giraffes, snakes and huge spiders, there are also many rare and endangered species including Asiatic lions, Arabian oryx, Sumatran tigers and golden lion tamarins.

There's lots to see and do – daily 'Animals in Action' shows take place in the amphitheatre, and you can hear more about some of the animals from their keepers in the Animal Encounter sessions. Feeding times are ever popular and the children can help weigh the elephants and have a ride on a pony.

Don't miss Ming Ming and Bao Bao the giant pandas, on loan to London Zoo as part of the zoo's worldwide animal conservation breeding programme. In the Moonlight World, day and night are reversed so that its nocturnal occupants are out and about for you to see. Look out for spiny anteaters, bats and fennec foxes. Leave time to look around the Aquarium with its sharks and piranhas, and the Reptile House which has huge snakes and crocodiles. There is also a children's zoo with goats, pigs, sheep and rabbits.

The Zoo's large self-service restaurant, the Regent Café, has a good range of hot and cold meals, and special meals for children. High chairs are available. The Raffles Restaurant and Bar are open during summer, and there are other seasonal food outlets around the zoo grounds.

Open: daily from 10am to 5.30pm in summer and 4pm in winter
(closed Christmas Day)
Charges: adults £6; OAPs £5; children £4; under 4s free (1993
rates)
Baby changing: facilities next to Regent Café
Ⓟ own car park

CENTRAL LONDON

Ⓛ NATIONAL GALLERY, Trafalgar Square, WC2
Tel: 071 839 3321.
Nearest Underground: Leicester Square, Charing Cross.

The National Gallery was opened in 1838 to house the nation's
vast collection of paintings. It is one of the great art museums of
the world with a comprehensive array of pictures from the 13th
century to the early 20th century, and with all the great masters
represented.

Exhibitions from the collection come and go throughout the year,
and there are lectures and films almost every day.

The Café in the main building has several high chairs; it is
licensed and serves cakes and pastries, hot meals and salads. The
prices range from £1 to £6. The Brasserie in the Sainsbury Wing
has a more sophisticated menu: a three course lunch can be had
for between £10 and £15 and there is an excellent range of interesting dishes (main courses from £6 to £10).

Open: 10am to 6pm, Monday to Saturday; 2pm to 6pm on
Sundays
Closed at Christmas, New Year and Good Friday
Charges: admission free (entry charges for special exhibitions only)
Baby changing: parent and baby rooms in main building and
Sainsbury Wing
Ⓟ public car parks nearby

CENTRAL LONDON
Ⓛ NATURAL HISTORY MUSEUM, Cromwell Road,
SW7
Tel: 071 938 9123.
Nearest Underground: South Kensington.

The museum is housed in a handsome, eye-catching building and
tries to encapsulate all the wonders of the natural world.

As you enter you will see a wonderful model of a diplodocus, one
of the largest land animals known to man; it weighed in at ten tons
and was 26 metres long. There are special exhibitions about the dinosaurs. Other permanent exhibitions include the 'Creepie-Crawlies',
Ecology, Darwin and His Theories, Human Biology, the Story of the
Earth, Britain's Offshore Oil and Gas, Mammals and many others.

Special exhibitions are mounted at regular intervals, and there
is a Discovery Centre, designed for children, who are encouraged
to explore the natural world by touch.

The Museum Restaurant has several high chairs and is on the
ground floor in a rather pleasant room. Hot meals, salads and snacks
are served. The Waterhouse Café serves snacks and drinks, but
does not have any high chairs, and there is a picnic area and snack
bar in the basement.

This is one of the great museums of the world with a superb
array of exhibits.

Open: 10am to 5.50pm, Monday to Saturday; from 11am on
Sundays
Charges: adults £4.50; children and OAPs £2.20; under 5s free
(1993 prices)
Baby changing: well-equipped mother & baby room
Ⓟ difficult

CENTRAL LONDON
Ⓛ TOWER OF LONDON, Tower Hill, EC3
Tel: 071 709 0765.
Nearest Underground: Tower Hill; British Rail to Fenchurch
Street; many buses.

This is one of the great tourist attractions of Britain, and can be crowded, but it is not a place to be excluded from anyone's tourist itinerary, and is full of interest on every level. The best way to see the Tower is on a free conducted tour in the care of a Yeoman Warder. It lasts just under an hour.

The heart of the fortress is the White Tower, which was mainly built by William the Conqueror and finished in the reign of his son, William Rufus. It had many functions over the centuries: Royal Palace, garrison, observatory, Royal Mint and even zoo. But it is most notorious as the prison where victims entered by the Traitors' Gate, some to face execution: Sir Thomas More, the Earl of Essex, Anne Boleyn, Catherine Howard and Lady Jane Grey among others. Sir Walter Raleigh was imprisoned in the Bloody Tower, where the 'little princes' were thought to be murdered.

Apart from these grim, but fascinating, aspects of the Tower's history there is much else to survey. The White Tower contains a magnificent collection of armour; the Chapel of St John is where Knights of the Bath kept vigil before their initiation; the Chapel of St Peter ad Vincula is the burial place of some of the most illustrious prisoners; and the Waterloo Block houses the Crown Jewels in the care of the Keeper of the Jewels.

There are various refreshment areas on the wharf providing snacks and drinks, and a high chair is available.

The Tower of London is a fascinating place to see, and is superbly organized. You should allow several hours in order to do it justice.

Open: 9am to 6pm (5pm in winter) and from 10am on Sundays
Closed at Christmas and New Year
Charges: adults £6.40; OAPs £4.80; children £3.90; under 5s free (1993 prices)
Baby changing: a shelf in the toilets in the Brick Tower
℗ public car parks nearby, but difficult

LOWER HARDRES, KENT
℗ THE THREE HORSESHOES, Lower Hardres
Tel: 0227 700 810.
Off the B2068 south of Canterbury.

This lovely old coaching inn with its flat-brick front was built some time around 1700. The friendly landlord has deeds which date back to that time. He displays his sense of tradition further in the wide range of beers he makes available straight from the barrel. He reckons to have served over 300 different brews in the last ten years.

It's a charming and relaxed 'pubby' pub; as the landlord stresses, a real pub – 'untrendy, with no space invader or cigarette machines'. Children, who must be supervised, are welcome in a pleasant room overlooking the garden which, in its turn, overlooks mile after mile of open country.

Bar food is served at lunchtimes only at markedly low prices, and mention must be made of the fine collection of English cheeses which is always available.

You should note that the pub is closed on Mondays, except for bank holidays.

✕ (12pm to 2pm, Tues to Sat) £2–4: ploughman's, Spanish omelette, smoked mackerel & salad, terrine, hot dish of the day
🍺 Ale: Young's, and guest beers. No music
Ⓟ small car park and street

LYMPNE, NR HYTHE, KENT
Ⓛ PORT LYMPNE WILD ANIMAL PARK, Lympne
Tel: 0891 800 605 (Infoline, 38p/45p per minute).
Close to junction 11 of the M20 and off the A20.

This was the second of John Aspinall's wild animal parks and includes a rather splendid mansion built in the Dutch colonial style. It houses a number of exhibitions, including a collection of wildlife paintings, and is well worth a look.

The gardens are beautifully laid out, and you have a wonderful view of the whole park from the top of the 125 steps that lead down to the mansion. It is hilly, so you need to be feeling fit if you have a child in a pushchair. The circular walk through the park measures nearly a mile, so wear flat shoes. During the summer, the Safari Trailer runs several times a day, but it is very popular and you should try to book your seats in advance.

Food, both hot and cold, is available in a café housed in a sizeable conservatory. There is a reasonable choice of food and high chairs are provided; there is a barbecue during summer. The parent and baby room has a changing table and paper towels.

Port Lympne is clean and tidy, with adequate signs, and helpful and friendly staff. A good day out, in very interesting surroundings, can be had here.

Open: every day except Christmas Day from 10am to 5pm or dusk
Charges: adults £6.50; children and OAPs £4.50; under 4s free
Baby changing: parent and baby room
ⓟ ample

MAIDSTONE, KENT
Ⓛ LEEDS CASTLE, Maidstone
Tel: 0622 765 400.
Four miles east of Maidstone at junction 8 of the M20/A20.

Leeds Castle is certainly one of the most romantic castles in England. It sits on two small islands in the middle of a lake and is surrounded by 500 acres of beautiful parkland, with lakes and streams, a woodland walk, a traditional English garden, and a vineyard which still produces wine.

The aviary houses a fine collection of rare birds and there are many ducks, swans, geese and peacocks wandering through the grounds. The maze, with its underground grotto, is a great attraction.

The Castle was originally built as a stronghold but Henry VIII converted it into a royal palace. It was much altered over the centuries and part of the main building was completely rebuilt in 1822. It was given to the nation in 1976.

As well as the glories of the building and the grounds, the Castle houses a superb collection of furniture, and it is of course very busy during the holiday season. The efficient staff seem to control everything well, but you must be prepared for some queueing.

The restaurant is housed in the Fairfax Hall, a 17th-century tithe barn with a self-service restaurant and a bar. You can choose from a range of snacks, salads and hot meals. Several high chairs are available.

The considerable programme of special events should be mentioned. The hot air balloon and Bentley car fiesta are always popular with children, as is the Easter egg hunt. Adults will enjoy the festival of English wines.

Open: March to October, 11am to 5.30pm; November to February, 10am to 3pm
Charges: adults £6.50; OAPs £5.50; children £4.50; under 5s free (1993 prices)
Baby changing: a purpose-built baby changing facility close to the Fairfax Hall
℗ ample

MILTON STREET, NR ALFRISTON, EAST SUSSEX

℗ SUSSEX OX, Milton Street
Tel: 0323 870 840.
Watch out as it's easy to miss: take the road to Alfriston off the A27, turn left on the road to Litlington and left again to Milton Street.

The Sussex Ox has been in the Guide since the first edition and is one of our favourites, a secluded and traditional country pub set in lovely Sussex countryside near the pretty village of Alfriston.

There are excellent facilities for families. The 'sty', at the back of the pub, is the family room and has a brick floor, nice pine tables and settles and doors on to the garden. It is a pleasant and airy room (and two high chairs are available) and an alternative for families is the spacious eating area, an appealing room on two levels with a beamed ceiling, a dresser and oak pillars.

There are some bench tables set out at the front of the pub, but the huge safely enclosed garden at the rear is an instant attraction on summery days. You can sit at your ease and enjoy the views of gentle Sussex hills, while the children play on the large wooden climbing frame, Wendy House, a slide and a seesaw. It is a delightful spot, maintained in pristine condition, and the landlord is planning to install an adventure playground for the spring of 1994.

A good range of freshly cooked food is available every day and the menu changes to suit the seasons; but there is always fresh fish and seafood available. Barbecues are held on summer weekends and during the winter there are special dining evenings (Thai, seafood, Indian etc).

This is an outstanding family pub where everyone, from the youngest to the oldest, will be welcome.

✖ (12pm to 2.15pm & 6.30pm to 9.30pm) £2–10; cheesy cottage pie, whole plaice, nut loaf, steak & ale pie, ham & eggs
Children: own menu, half portions
🍺 Ale: Greene King Abbot, Harvey's and guest. No music or machines
Ⓟ own car park

NEWPORT, ISLE OF WIGHT
Ⓡ GOD'S PROVIDENCE HOUSE, Newport
Tel: 0983 522 085.
In the middle of the town, by St Thomas's church.

The unusual name, so the story goes, refers to the luck of its inhabitants in escaping the ravages of the Plague. Some parts of the building date back before 1665, although it is a charming mixture of styles, with Georgian windows, for example.

Three rooms make up the restaurant, all nicely furnished with oak tables and wheelback chairs; one room looks out on to the pretty square, with its church and small shops.

The staff are friendly and welcoming and there are four high chairs available. You can change a baby in the Ladies, where there is a wide shelf and a chair can be put in there, too.

✖ £1–5: roast of the day, steak pie, wholemeal quiche, roast chicken
Children: half portions
Open 9am to 5pm (closed Sundays)
No credit cards. Licensed
Ⓟ on the street. No music

OVING, WEST SUSSEX
Ⓟ GRIBBLE INN, Oving
Tel: 0243 786 893.
Between the A27 and the A259 just east of Chichester.

This was the cottage in which Rosa Gribble lived for nearly a
hundred years. It became a pub as recently as 1980 and there have
been additions, for example a large eating area and a kitchen. The
whole pub maintains the same delightful style, with bare brick walls,
ancient exposed timbers, old church pews and wooden settles and
tables.

There is plenty of space in the bar and the eating area – just as
well because this is, deservedly, a very busy and popular place. The
family room is spacious and relaxing, with several cushioned settles,
stools and sturdy tables. Part of it is a no-smoking area. A smaller
room alongside leads out to a large and very pretty lawned garden,
with an abundance of trees, bushes and bright flowers.

The pub's own brewery is now in operation – yet another good
reason for a visit. You can sample such brews as Reg's Tipple and
Harvest Gold.

✕ (12pm to 2pm & 6.30pm to 9.30pm, not Sun pm) £1–7:
whitebait, turkey & ham pie, seafood special, sirloin steak,
vegeburger
Children: smaller portions
🍺 Ale: Hall & Woodhouse, Palmer's, Gribble
Ⓟ own car park. No music

OWER, NR ROMSEY, HANTS
Ⓛ PAULTONS PARK, Ower
Tel: 0703 814 455.
Just off junction 2 of the M27 north-west of Southampton. Well
signposted.

We were very impressed by the whole ambience of Paultons Park,
which offers a splendid day out for the whole family. It was opened
on the site of the Paultons Estate in 1983, although the house
burned down in 1963.

The beautiful gardens provide an excellent backdrop to the place and adults can find many a shady spot to relax on a warm day. Indeed, there is masses of space to picnic throughout the park.

Young children are particularly well catered for with dozens of rides and there are some little boats for children with gentler dispositions. They will also like the Magic Forest. There is a spacious playground with a full array of slides, swings and climbing frames; and Kids' Kingdom, which has a wonderful collection of things to slide, climb and ride on (and a safe surface for happy landings), is as good an adventure playground as we have seen. Other popular attractions include the six-lane Astroglide, bumper boats, go-karts (extra charge), pets corner, Land of the Dinosaurs and the clock maze. Two new children's rides, the Flying Saucer and the Pirate Ship, were opened last year.

Apart from the gardens and the attractive lake which surrounds the park, adults will certainly appreciate the Romany Museum, with its collection of every known type of Romany caravan bar one, and the Village Life Museum. Everyone will enjoy the collections of birds and animals: parrots and macaws, owls and peacocks, flamingoes, llamas, Shetland ponies, wallabies and numerous other breeds of wildfowl.

There are food kiosks in the park and two restaurants. The Waggoners is next door to the entrance and is a spacious and bright self-service restaurant, which offers sandwiches, snacks, salads and hot dishes of the day (vegetable curry, fish and tomato gratin for example) at prices from £1 to £4. There is a children's menu and a three-course lunch for around £6.

Next door is an excellent mother and baby room, brightly decorated, and with tables, chairs, lavatory, hand basin, paper towels, etc, and with nappies on sale. A trained nurse is on duty at all times.

Close to the miniature railway you will find the Station Tea Rooms, another bright and attractive café with a terrace.

Paultons Park is a very well-organized leisure park where the owners cater for families in an enterprising and caring way.

Please note that dogs (except guide dogs) are banned from the park.

Open: March to October, 10am to 6.30pm (last admission 4.30pm). Earlier closing in spring and autumn
Charges: please telephone 0703 814 455 (24 hours) for details

Baby changing: mother and baby room
Ⓟ unlimited

PADDOCK WOOD, KENT
ⓅⓇ BROOKERS OAST, The Hop Farm
Tel: 0622 872 818.
On the B2015 east of Tonbridge.

This large family pub and restaurant sits alongside the Whitbread
Hop Farm and offers a great amount of space and an array of
facilities for everyone in the family.

Some old oast houses form part of the pub and in one section
you can sit under the wooden rafters, with windows on three sides.
It's a very agreeable spot. There are many other areas in which to
settle, including little alcoves, a spacious no-smoking room and a
little dining room at one end of the pub which has a table for eight
people and a few smaller tables. The comfortable furniture, grass
screens, predominance of wood panelling and the cheerful prints
on the walls add up to an agreeable place for a meal or a drink.

Families have their own separate room and it has a little play
area at one end and a nappy changing facility nearby. Outside is a
very large enclosed garden with lots of bench tables on the grass.
There is an adventure playground and swings to keep the children
amused.

It is a delightful spot and a visit to see the splendid shire horses
at the Hop Farm is obligatory.

✖ (11.30am to 10pm; from noon on Sunday) £2–8: lamb bake,
fish dippers, chicken escalope, sole bearnaise, vegetable crumble
Children: own menu
🍺 Ale: Flower's, Fremlin's, Wadworth's
Ⓟ own car park

PLUCKLEY, NR ASHFORD, KENT
H SC ELVEY FARM, Pluckley

Tel: 0233 840 442.

Off the A20 west of Ashford.

At the end of a quiet country lane you will find the splendid Elvey farmhouse, which was built in 1430. The adjoining stables and an oast house have been converted with great skill and sympathy, the abiding aim being to preserve the existing features of the building.

The two communal rooms are delightful. The restaurant is housed in an old barn and the ancient black beams are decorated with old farm implements; long wooden tables complete the picture. Alongside, there is a very comfortable lounge with brick walls and a beamed ceiling, plenty of easy chairs, a good selection of books, a bar and french windows leading out to the garden.

The various rooms offer a great deal of flexibility for family accommodation, since most of them are equipped with kitchens and can therefore be rented as self-catering apartments. For example, the five units made from the stables fall into this category and another comprises a double bedroom and a twin-bedded room which could accommodate two children. All the rooms are furnished to the highest standards and the wood panelling ensures a warm and appealing ambience.

The oast house offers the same flexibility since it contains a sitting room, kitchen and three separate bedrooms, two of which are contained in the roundel. The house could be rented as a self-contained unit by a family and we have rarely seen a more interesting and attractive building.

Elvey Farm (and it is still a working farm, by the way) is an absolute delight and its setting amid rolling countryside ensures guests of peace and seclusion.

There is plenty of space for children to play, a sun terrace and a spacious lawn; and the stable apartments have their own little verandahs. Guests are welcome to explore the farm and in H E Bates country they should see plenty of darling buds. There are plenty of pubs and restaurants within reach and the nearest one, the Rose and Crown at the bottom of the lane, has an excellent reputation for its food.

Elvey Farm offers outstanding value, stylish accommodation, and the flexibility to suit the needs of any family, who can use the place either as an hotel or on a self-catering basis, or as a mixture of both.

Nearby: This is an excellent base from which to enjoy the many attractions of this part of the country. Wildlife enthusiasts will head for Port Lympne Zoo Park or Howletts, and railway buffs can enjoy both the Kent and East Sussex and the Romney, Hythe and Dymchurch railways. Sissinghurst Castle Gardens, Scotney Castle Gardens, Bedgebury Pinetum, Leeds Castle and the historic town of Canterbury are all within easy reach.

£ medium
Children: cot £5; £15 from 3 to 16 years
Facilities: 3 cots and 2 high chairs; baby listening by arrangement
10 rooms, 6 family Open all year
No music
ℙ ample
Self-catering: The rents vary from £50 per night (a minimum of three nights) to £150 a night for the three-bedroomed Oast House at the height of the season.

RICHMOND, SURREY
ℝ REFECTORY, 6 Church Walk
Tel: 081 940 6264.
Park either in the Paradise Road multi-storey or in Sheen Road. Street parking is easy on a Sunday.

The restaurant is in a quiet corner by the parish church and you can sit in the paved courtyard by the entrance if the weather is kind. Inside, the dining room is simply and agreeably furnished with good wooden furniture, and the atmosphere is friendly and welcoming.

We like this restaurant because it is one of the few in the London area which offers a genuine welcome to all the family: apart from the high chairs, the owners provide a changing table in the Ladies, and no one looks askance at breast-feeding mothers. But this is also a real restaurant with freshly cooked English food and splendid vegetables and puddings, generously served. Above all the prices are sensible: a rare thing in the London area. There is an unusual wine list, too, with English and Australian wines.

This is a popular restaurant and booking ahead is advisable; it is also open for coffee from 10am to noon and for afternoon teas from 2pm to 5pm, Tuesday to Saturday.

✗ LUNCH (12pm to 2pm Tue–Sun) £10: seafood flan, Exmoor lamb casserole, treacle tart
Children: smaller portions
Closed Mondays, Christmas & New Year and 2 weeks in August
Access/Visa Licensed
🍺 Ale: Young's
Ⓟ street or public car park. No music

ROMSEY, HANTS
Ⓡ COBWEB TEA ROOMS, 49 The Hundred
Tel: 0794 516 434.
Close to the centre of the town and opposite the entrance to Broadlands.

The Cobweb Tea Room is housed in a building which is 500 years old in parts, although it has an 18th-century front. The façade is freshly painted and is cheerfully decorated with an abundance of bright flowers which grow in tubs and hanging baskets. Inside you will find an archetypal English tea shop, immaculately laid out and in pristine order. The old wooden beams and pillars testify to the age of the building and are nicely offset by the cream-painted plaster walls, the brick fireplace and the wide window on to the street.

At the back there is a walled patio with a flagged floor; with its bright flowers and the cheerful sounds of birds it is a very pleasant place to sit.

The owner is happy to welcome families and makes her private accommodation available to mothers who need to attend to babies.

You can have snacks throughout the day, and light lunch dishes from noon; all the food is homemade.

✕ £1–4: soup, toasted sandwiches, chicken curry, goulash, beans on toast
Children: half portions
Open 10am to 5.30pm, Tue to Sat. No credit cards
No smoking. No music
Licensed
Ⓟ public parking 100 yards away

SELLING, NR FAVERSHAM, KENT
Ⓟ WHITE LION, Selling
Tel: 0227 752 211.
South of Exit 7 of the M2 and accessible from the A251 and A252.

This splendid 18th-century inn is made immediately appealing by the array of bright flowers which greet you at its front. The good impressions are enchanced as you enter the main bar, with its beamed ceiling, the two large open fires and the wooden tables and settles. A wooden dresser and a collection of teapots and plenty of plants and flowers add to the great charm of the place.

The family room is off the bar and also has its own entrance from the car park. It is a pleasant and comfortable room, with an open fire and a few tables and chairs. Pictures of jazz men decorate the walls – Louis, Dizzie, Miles, Humph, and many others – and the landlord runs jazz nights each week. The pretty lawned garden, with its rose trees and silver birches, is the place to be on a summer day, and it is enclosed by a small fence.

There is an excellent range of food here, generously served, on offer both in the restaurant and in the bar.

✕ (12pm to 2pm & 7pm to 9.30pm) £2–12: crab paté, plaice & chips, various curries, steaks, spicy samosas
Children: half portions
🍺 Ale: Shepherd Neame
🅿 own car park

NR SEVENOAKS, KENT
🅿 CROWN POINT, Seal
Tel: 0732 810 669.
On the A25 east of Sevenoaks at Seal.

One of the major virtues of this pub is its very large garden, with a good expanse of lawn and terrace with bench tables, an adventure playground, tyre swings and a bouncy castle.

The family room is close to the garden and there is a bright and cheerful family dining area at the other end of the pub.

Good amenities are provided for families, including many high chairs and a nappy changing unit. Food is available every day throughout opening hours and real ale fans are also well catered for since there are usually six varieties on offer.

✕ (11.30am to 10pm, from noon on Sunday) £2–8: chargrilled cajun chicken, vegetable crumble, fish dippers, sirloin steak, Spanish omelette
Children: own menu
🍺 Ale: Boddington's and guest beer
🅿 own car park

SINGLETON, NR CHICHESTER, WEST SUSSEX
🄻 WEALD AND DOWNLAND OPEN AIR MUSEUM, Singleton
Tel: 024363 348.
Just off the A286, near Singleton.

The museum has a most attractive setting, surrounded by gentle hills, and is devoted to the rescue of historic buildings, which are then re-erected at Singleton.

There are nearly forty buildings, and they include a village school, a medieval farmstead, 16th- and 17th-century houses, a market hall, a carpenter's shop, a watermill and so on. The buildings are in superb condition, and there is usually something new to see as additions are made to the museum. For example, a new 'hands-on' gallery which explores building techniques is now in operation.

You can walk in the woods where the charcoal is made or have a picnic by the pond. There is also a restaurant which is housed in an old farm building and by now this will have been extended. All the food is homemade and includes soup, cakes, jacket potatoes and other snacks.

It is a delightful place with much to interest both parents and older children.

Open: 11am to 6pm, 1 March to 31 October; 11am to 4pm, Wednesdays, Saturdays and Sundays from 1 November to 28 February
Charges: adults £4; OAPs £3.50; children £2
Baby changing: a table in the Ladies
P ample

STAINES, MIDDLESEX
P SWAN HOTEL, The Hythe
Tel: 0784 452 494.
Close to Staines Bridge where the A30 meets the A320.

This stately 18th-century inn stands in a wonderful location over-looking the river and was once a haunt of the bargemen who plied the Thames.

The lounge bar has superb views over the water, as does the very spacious conservatory, where families are welcome to settle down for a meal or some refreshment. The various bars are just as sizeable and are furnished in a relaxing way with padded seats and settles and wooden tables. Two large open fireplaces house roaring log fires during the winter months.

On warm days you can sit on the paved terrace which runs the length of the building. With its lovely river views and the abundance of bright flowers in pots and hanging baskets, it is a delightful spot.

It is an excellent inn for families since it is open all day from

Monday to Saturday and food is available most of that time.

✗ (12 to 10pm) £2–9: pork satay, seafood pancake, steaks, plaice & chips, beef curry
Children: own menu
🍺 Ale: Fuller's
Ⓟ some spaces in front and on street

STEYNING, WEST SUSSEX
Ⓟ STAR INN, 130 High Street
Tel: 0903 813 078.
In the centre of the village.

We were not surprised to learn that the Star was Sussex Pub of the Year a couple of years ago, since it is a most attractive and welcoming place, a flat-fronted, 18th-century, brick building which was once a home, run by the Quakers, for waifs and strays.

You enter a very smart lounge bar with a large wooden farmhouse table on one side, and two alcove rooms. The ceilings are unusually decorated with walking sticks.

Through the business-like public bar with its slate floor, you will come to the excellent family room, partitioned off by old beams and a little stable door. There are comfortable padded benches, a low brick fireplace and a beamed ceiling; adjoining this room is a playroom with a collection of toys and some teddy bears.

The pretty garden at the side of the pub has a high flint wall with climbing plants on one side and a little stream on the other. In between there is a paved area and some lawn with tables and chairs. Across the car park there is another enclosed, grassy area with more seating and a children's play area.

The pub is open throughout the day from 11am to 11pm on Saturdays.

✗ (12pm to 2pm & 7pm to 9.30pm) £2–10: cottage pie, sirloin steak, plaice & chips, salmon & broccoli pasta
Children: own menu
🍺 Ale: Boddington's, Flowers, Morland's, Wadworth's
Ⓟ own car park

WESTERHAM, KENT
Ⓛ CHARTWELL, Westerham
Tel: 0732 866 368.
Two miles south of Westerham, off the B2026.

Chartwell was the home of Sir Winston Churchill from 1924 until he died. The hub of the house, which is left much as it was during his life, is the study, where he did most of his writing.

The rooms are beautifully kept and packed with information. There are lots of Churchill's pictures in evidence, plus political cartoons and informal photographs, and the house still has an indefinable, lived-in atmosphere.

The house is perched on the side of a valley with superb views across the Kentish Weald. The gardens are delightful and you will be able to find the wall that Churchill built during his years in the political wilderness. His studio contains many of his paintings.

The restaurant has several high chairs, and is a spacious and airy spot. There are some tables on a terrace outside and you can enjoy the wooded gardens from there. The mother and baby room adjoins the restaurant.

Open: April to end October: Tuesday to Thursday noon to 5pm; Saturday and Sunday and bank holiday Monday 11am to 5.30pm. Closed Monday and Friday.
Charges: adults £4.50; children £2.25
Baby changing: mother and baby room with changing mat
Ⓟ ample

NR WESTERHAM, KENT
ⓅⓇ SPINNING WHEEL
Tel: 0959 72622.
On the A233 towards Biggin Hill.

This modern, low-slung brick pub sits just outside Westerham and offers a fine array of facilities for families. There is a very large family dining room which is a no smoking area and it has a play area with blackboards and toys and a Postman Pat van. The pub provides food throughout the day until 10 o'clock, has several high chairs and a nappy changing facility.

The family room leads out to an enclosed garden with many bench tables and a children's play unit, made of wood and placed on a safe bark surface.

There is a great feeling of space and light in the rest of the pub, where the emphasis is on comfort and a cheerful decor. Good wooden tables and comfortable padded benches and chairs, a richly patterned carpet, wood panelling and stained glass skylights, and mullioned windows all add up to a welcoming interior. The large scale of the pub is tempered by dividing it into different rooms, with alcoves set here and there.

✗ (11.30am to 10pm; from noon on Sunday) £2–8: hot mushrooms, gammon steak, roast chicken, fish pie, lasagne verde
Children: own menu
🍺 Ale: Boddington's, Flowers
🅿 own car park

WINCHESTER, HANTS
Ⓛ MARWELL ZOOLOGICAL PARK, Winchester
Tel: 0962 777 406.
Six miles south-east of Winchester at Colden Common. Follow the signs from the A33.

Marwell has one of the most interesting and comprehensive collections of wildlife in Britain and the park is organized and maintained with great skill and imagination.

It is a real pleasure to walk around the 150 acres; although you can take your car in, it is much more fun to do your tour on foot. If you want a rest there is a miniature train and a road-train also runs around the park in summer.

There are some wonderful animals to see and in general their enclosures are sizeable: camel, cheetah, buffalo, zebra, gazelle, giraffe, jaguar, lion, tiger, llama, lynx, meerhat, Przewalski's horse, antelope, snow leopard and many others.

The children can visit a farmyard where there are goats, calves, sheep and rabbits, and can also meet some of the tamer animals at close quarters.

The Treetops restaurant is close to the entrance and is a large cafeteria which serves both hot and cold food and snacks; salads, scampi and chips, chicken chasseur, for example. There are plenty of high chairs available. In addition, other refreshment kiosks are dotted about the park. Down below the restaurant there are play areas for the children.

This is a splendidly organized and appealing zoo where a family can enjoy a full day's entertainment.

Open: every day except Christmas Day. 10am to 6pm (or dusk)
Charges: adults £5.95; OAPs £5.45; children £4.50; under 3s free
Baby changing: two well-equipped mother and baby rooms
Ⓟ own car park

NR WINCHESTER, HANTS
⒫Ⓡ CAPTAIN BARNARD, Otterbourne
Tel: 0962 712 220.
On the A31 at Otterbourne.

This is a very large, purpose-built brick pub with wooden cladding on the upper storey of the façade. There are two gardens, one at the front of the pub which is aimed at the adult customers and a large enclosed area at the rear of the pub where there is a substantial children's playground and several rides.

There is loads of space inside the Captain Barnard, all carefully divided up into a series of rooms and areas by the skilful use of wooden and stained glass screens and by timber covered pillars. The wood panelling and many prints on the walls add to the fun and the pub is very nicely furnished with wooden tables and padded benches and chairs.

It is an excellent family pub with food on offer throughout the day, high chairs and a nappy changing facility, a family dining room where smoking is denied, and a little indoor play area for the children.

✕ (11.30am to 10pm; from noon on Sunday) £2–8: hot mushrooms, steak & kidney pie, fried scampi, fish pie, lamb rogan josh
Children: own menu
🍺 Ale: Flowers, Strong's
Ⓟ own car park

Thames and the Chilterns

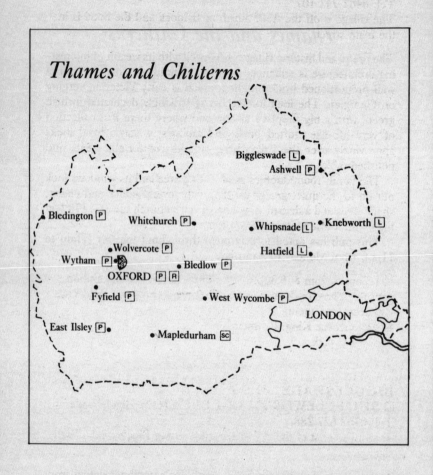

Thames and Chilterns

Bigglewade ⬛L

Ashwell P

Bledington P   Whitchurch P

Whipsnade L   Knebworth L

Wolvercote P   Hatfield L

Wytham P

Bledlow P

OXFORD P R

Fyfield P   West Wycombe P

LONDON

East Ilsley P

Mapledurham SC

ASHWELL, HERTS
P THREE TUNS HOTEL, 6 High Street
Tel: 0462 742 107.
The village is off the A505 north of Baldock and the hotel is in
the main street.

The pretty and historic village of Ashwell with its wealth of interesting architecture is enhanced by this splendid old coaching inn, a
well-proportioned brick building which is early Victorian verging
on Georgian. The long lounge bar is strikingly decorated in lush
green, with a big fireplace at one end where there is a collection
of very life-like stuffed birds and animals; a stag's head looks
approvingly over the smart bar, with its comfortable seats and
polished tables.

   The family room doubles as an eating area and its windows look
out on to the quiet grassy garden, with several tables and chairs,
shady trees and a distant view of Ashwell's church tower – 176 feet
high with a distinctive spike on top.

   This pub has opted to stay open throughout the day (11am to
11pm) from Monday to Saturday.

✗ (12pm to 2pm & 6.30pm to 9.30pm) £2–9: savoury Stilton
pancake, Scotch salmon, beef in Guinness, entrecote Bordelaise
Children: own menu
🍺 Ale: Greene King, Rayment's
P own car park

BIGGLESWADE, BEDS
L SHUTTLEWORTH COLLECTION, Biggleswade
Tel: 0767 627 288.
Two miles west of the A1 where it by-passes Biggleswade. Well
signposted.

This remarkable museum has examples of aeroplanes dating from
the earliest days of powered flight up to the machines of the Second
World War. Most of them can still be flown and the names them-
selves are redolent of the history and romance of flying: Bleriot,
Avro Triplane, Hawker Tomtit, Tiger Moth, Dragon Rapide,
Gloster Gladiator and the immortal Spitfire.

In the hangars, there is also an interesting collection of cars, motor cycles and bicycles.

There is loads of space here and if the interest of the children wanes, they can enjoy themselves in the large playground with its selection of swings, slides, roundabouts, etc.

The basic self-service cafeteria has one high chair and serves sandwiches and snacks, and such things as steak and kidney pie and chips. There are no baby changing facilities, although the toilet areas are clean and spacious.

If you and your family have any interest in aeroplanes this is a fascinating museum – especially when the flying displays take place, on the first Sunday of each month from May to October inclusive.

Open: 10am to 4pm (3pm in winter) every day except 2 weeks at Christmas and New Year
Charges: adults £4; children and OAPs £2.50; under 5s free (1993 prices)
Baby changing: no facilities
P ample

BLEDINGTON, OXON
P KINGS HEAD INN, The Green, Bledington
Tel: 0608 658 365.
Off the B4450, to the east of Stow-on-the-Wold.

Situated in a charming Cotswold village, the pub is in a marvellous position by the immaculate village green, with its stream and attendant ducks. There are even some swings and a slide on the green quite close to the pub and within easy shouting distance of a small garden at the front.

It's a superb 15th-century stone inn, with steep slate roofs; you enter directly into a delightful bar, with black beams and pillars, wooden settles and a big open fireplace at one end. As well as the bar menu, there is a full *à la carte* menu. It is worth a trip for the imaginative food alone, and everything is homemade.

Families are welcome in the garden room, which is furnished in the same style as the rest of the pub, with wooden tables and chairs, stone-flagged floors, a wooden screen and wooden beams. There is a pleasant atmosphere here, and smoking is forbidden. Doors lead out to the courtyard and the garden.

✕ (12pm to 2pm & 7pm to 9.45pm) £2–6: basil & mozzarella pancake, lasagne, smoked salmon & dill pasta, braised kidneys, casserole of the day
Children: own menu, smaller portions
🍺 Ale: Adnams, Hook Norton, Wadworth's and guests
🅿 own car park

BLEDLOW, BUCKS
🅿 LIONS OF BLEDLOW, Bledlow
Tel: 084 44 3345.
Off the B4009 near Chinnor. Look out for West Lane – the pub's at the top of the hill.

The pub is housed in a long and low-slung white painted 16th-century building, with dormer windows set in a steep roof, and is situated in lovely countryside at the foot of the Chilterns. When the sun shines you might sit on the patch of green which fronts the pub and be quite at peace with the world; and the pub also has a large garden at the rear.

The interior has all the delightful attributes of a classic English pub: low beamed ceilings, huge open fires, alcoves here and there with padded wooden settles and wooden tables. It's a busy and cheerful place, with a really pubby atmosphere. At one end of the pub there is a sizeable family room; it used to be the games room and is functional and comfortable enough.

At weekends families have the use of the restaurant.

✕ (12pm to 2pm & 7pm to 9.30pm, not Sun pm) £2–5: steak & kidney & mushroom, spicy chicken, spare ribs, salads, fresh mussels
🍺 Ale: Ruddles, Wadworth's, Courage, Morland's & guests
🅿 own car park. No music

EAST ILSLEY, BERKS
P CROWN & HORNS, East Ilsley
Tel: 0635 281 205.
Off the A34.

This agreeable 18th-century pub is well worth a short detour from the busy A34 not far north of Junction 13 of the M4. The village is in 'horsey' territory and the sport of kings motif is prevalent in the pub, with lots of prints of famous jockeys on the walls, horse brasses on the beams, and so on. Some of the customers arrive by horse and there are stables alongside the pub.

There are two rooms where children may go: a small one facing the main bar and a larger one to the side, and both are well provided with wooden tables and chairs. There is also a small dining room.

The old stable yard with its paved floor and chestnut trees has a colourful array of umbrellas over the tables and, during the summer, a cold table is set up and barbecues are prepared.

✗ (11am to 2pm & 6pm to 10pm) £1–10: cottage pie, lemon sole, sirloin steak, chicken Kiev, vegetable lasagne
Children: half portions
🍺 Ale: Wadworth's, Morland's, Fuller's, Bass, Theakston's
P own car park

FYFIELD, NR ABINGDON, OXON
P WHITE HART, Fyfield
Tel: 0865 390 585.
Off the A420, seven miles from Abingdon.

It would be difficult to nominate a better pub than the White Hart with its delightful atmosphere and wide choice of real ale and excellent food. It is impossible to name a better family pub.

There are no less than four rooms in which children are welcome with their adults: a pretty gallery, which overlooks the main bar; a spacious, well-furnished room down some stairs; and yet another room on the ground floor with tables, a large open fireplace and ancient wooden walls. On Sunday lunchtimes, a fourth area, a lovely room with wooden beams and pillars, which is normally the restaurant, is also pressed into service. What with the large grassy garden for summer days, you will always find somewhere to park yourselves and your children.

The pub, built in the 15th century as a charity house, is actually owned by St John's College, Oxford, and any academic would feel at home in the bar with its high, handsome, vaulted ceiling – and a handsome selection of real ales too.

You will find an imaginative and wide-ranging selection of food on tap as well. It's homemade, and even the bread is baked on the premises. There is a table and chair in the Ladies to help with changing or feeding of babies, and there are two high chairs on the premises.

The White Hart is an exceptional pub in every way, where the whole family is made welcome.

✗ (12pm to 2pm & 7pm to 10pm) £2–9: spinach & feta strudel, steaks, moussaka, chicken Strasbourg, local trout, venison casserole
Children: own menu, half portions
⊟ Ale: Boddington's, Hook Norton, Theakston's, Wadworth's & guest beers
Ⓟ own car park

HATFIELD, HERTS
Ⓛ HATFIELD HOUSE, Hatfield
Tel: 0707 262 823.
Two miles from junction 4 on the A1(M) – well signposted.

Robert Cecil, 1st Earl of Salisbury, built this house in the early years of the 17th century and it is one of the most impressive Jacobean mansions in England, with tall stone walls and mullioned windows.

There are some superb rooms including the Marble Hall, the King James Drawing Room, the Long Gallery and the Winter Dining Room. It is full of magnificent furniture and fine portraits, and the William IV kitchen, opened a couple of years ago, is also of great interest.

The children will no doubt be interested in the contents of the Armoury, much of which was armour captured from the Spanish Armada, and in the model soldiers exhibition which contains 3000 items. Please note that, except on Sundays and bank holidays, you can only see the house as part of a guided tour.

The grounds are lovely and great fun to explore. There is a small adventure play area and a nature trail and much of the park has been left in its natural state; there are delightful woodlands, a lake and a great variety of wildlife to see. The West Gardens were re-created in a formal 17th century style, with a privy garden, wilderness garden, scented garden and a palace knot garden. There is a picnic area under cover. Entertainments are staged on Sundays: jugglers, Punch and Judy shows etc.

The Old Palace Yard restaurant is a most attractive room with a mural of Hatfield House. There are pine tables and chairs and high chairs are provided.

Open: 25 March to the second Sunday in October: Park daily 10.30am to 8pm; Gardens daily 11am to 6pm except Good Friday and Easter Sunday; House (guided tours) 12 to 4pm, Tuesday to Saturday; 1.30 to 5pm, Sunday
Charges: adults £4.50; children £3 (1993 prices)
Baby changing: a table in the Ladies
Ⓟ ample

KNEBWORTH, HERTS
Ⓛ KNEBWORTH HOUSE, Knebworth
Tel: 0438 812 661.
On the A1(M) just south of Stevenage; direct access from junction 7.

The Lytton family have lived here since the late 15th century, and it was Edward Bulwer-Lytton who transformed the Tudor manor house into an extraordinary, Gothic extravaganza in the mid-19th century. It is an astonishing sight and reflects Bulwer-Lytton's character. Disraeli once described someone as 'the most conceited man I ever met, though I have read Cicero and known Bulwer-Lytton'.

The house is full of interest, especially the great banqueting hall with its 17th-century oak screen and the Queen Elizabeth Room with its massive four-poster bed. There is some magnificent furniture to be seen, and family relics including an exhibition of Lord Lytton's days as Viceroy of India.

The park would be the main attraction for children. There is loads of space in which to wander and many special events are put on at weekends: jousting, re-creations of famous battles, falconry displays and car rallies.

There is a miniature railway and an adventure playground, which is enormous fun for children, especially the giant slide, which is very popular.

The cafeteria has two high chairs available and offers a range of hot and cold meals and snacks.

Open: Easter to end of September, noon to 5pm. Closed on Monday except bank holidays
Charges: adults £4; children & OAPs £3.50 (1993 prices)
Baby changing: chairs in the spacious toilets (Barns cafeteria)
Ⓟ ample

MAPLEDURHAM, NR READING, BERKS
SC MAPLEDURHAM ESTATE, Mapledurham
Tel: 0734 723 350.
Off the A4074 north west of Reading. Well signposted on the Wallingford side of the village.

The estate is so quiet and secluded that it is difficult to realize that Reading is just a few miles away. The core of the estate is the magnificent Elizabethan mansion, Mapledurham House, with its splendid grounds and a lovely old watermill. The mansion and the mill and a riverside park are open to the public at weekends from Easter to the end of September.

The various cottages and houses are mostly of 17th- and 18th-century vintage and several of them are within walking distance of Mapledurham House. The two alms cottages, delightful low-built dwellings of brick and tile, are able each to accommodate six people, by dint of extensions at the rear of the original cottages. They both have large grassy gardens.

The size of the gardens is an excellent feature of all the properties and makes them highly suitable for family occupation. For example, when we visited the Mill House an impromptu family game of cricket was underway in the sizeable back garden. The Mill House is a delightful Queen Anne house of three storeys and made from brick and flint, and can accommodate seven people. Its rooms are well-proportioned and there are two sitting rooms.

Most of the other properties can sleep four to five people, but there are two superb thatched cottages – charming, archetypal English country cottages with pleasant gardens – on the edge of the estate which sleep two people. In contrast Bottom Farm House is a very spacious property which sleeps eight people and has a sofabed for a further two.

The owner, whose ancestors have owned Mapledurham for several hundred years, told us that the furniture is comfortable but deliberately functional because of the wear and tear it has to withstand. Nevertheless the manager, Jean Emary, confirmed that there is a constant process of refurbishment.

As well as having their large gardens, guests have access to the large area by the mill and the river, a pleasant place for a picnic and where the children can play. Coarse fishing is also available. Temporary membership of Mapledurham's 18-hole golf course is included for the length of a visit at no extra charge.

Nearby: Mapledurham is well-placed for visits to London, half an hour by rail and a comfortable enough journey outside the rush hours, and you have easy access to many other places of interest: Windsor, with its castle and museum; the Courage Shire Horse Centre and the Childe Beale Wildlife Trust; Cliveden; Basildon Park; and the Bekonscot Model Village; you can reach Oxford easily and the Cotswolds beyond.

Units: 11
Rent: £110 to £475 a week
Other costs: linen on hire for some cottages; heat and light
metered only in winter
Heating: central heating
6 cots & 3 high chairs
Open all year

OXFORD, OXON
Ⓡ BROWNS, 5–11 Woodstock Road
Tel: 0865 511 995.
On the A34 close to its junction with the A423 and just north of
the city centre (near St Giles).

This big, bustling restaurant has a simple and effective decor of
bentwood chairs and wooden tables, and lots of plants and mirrors.
The ambience is that of a cheerful and relaxed brasserie. A large
skylight gives a spacious effect to the place, as does the bar area
which, on warmer days, opens out on to the pavement.

The menu concentrates on salads, pasta and grills, and offers
plenty of things to appeal to a young palate. There are lots of high
chairs available; and there are even two mother and baby rooms
with changing tables and chairs. The staff make a real effort to
welcome parents with young children; indeed people of all ages
find a warm welcome.

You can eat breakfast until noon and the special lunchtime
dishes, posted on blackboards, are generally a little cheaper than
the usual menu; they generally sell out by 3 o'clock.

The restaurant has been extended and the extra space includes
a larger no-smoking area.

✕ £2–10: spaghetti with various sauces, fisherman's pie, roast
poussin, burgers, steak & mushroom & Guinness pie
Children: own menu, small portions
Open 11am to 11.30pm, every day (from noon on Sundays)
Closed at Christmas Access/Visa
No smoking in over half the restaurant
Ⓟ on street

OXFORD, OXON
P EAGLE AND CHILD, St Giles
Tel: 0865 58085.
Near the city centre.

This lovely old pub stretches back in a series of narrow wood panelled rooms with many old photographs on the walls. It has interesting literary associations, since it was the 'local' of C.S. Lewis and J.R. Tolkien. As you enter there are two or three cosy little alcoves, which can only accommodate half a dozen people in any comfort, and then two more rooms. The last of these is a conservatory with a few tables, and is the most suitable for families, especially because it is a no-smoking area. Through the glass doors there is a little patio with a few bench tables and it is safely enclosed.

   The Eagle & Child has a really pleasant atmosphere, offers a good choice of pub food at reasonable prices, plus a selection of real ales. A pretty good formula, especially since families are made thoroughly welcome by the licensees and staff.

✗ (12pm to 2pm every day, and 6pm to 8pm Mon-Sat) £1–4:
lasagne, vegetable pot, pizzas, chilli con carne,
Children: small portions
⌑ Ale: Ind Coope Burton, Tetley, Wadworth's
P on street or in nearby car parks

WEST WYCOMBE, BUCKS
P GEORGE & DRAGON, West Wycombe
Tel: 0494 464 414.
In the main street of the village.

The 18th-century brick front, with its splendid sign, gives no clue to the spacious lay-out of this well-known coaching inn. As you swing into the courtyard, where the London to Oxford coaches and horses have gone before you, you will find a very large car park and alongside it an equally spacious garden. There is masses of space on the lawn, which is enclosed on three sides and has a lovely display of shrubs and flowers. There are plenty of bench tables at which to perch on warmer days, and the children have a play area with a swing, climbing frame and slide, and a safe bark surface.

From the garden you can see that the back of the pub is much older than the front – it's a rambling black and white building which dates back to the 15th century.

Inside the large bar is comfortably laid out, and heavy wooden cross beams and pillars support the ceiling. Away from the bar there is a charming little room where families are welcome. It has a low ceiling, walls partly panelled in wood, and a few tables and chairs. In a small alcove an antique high chair is stored, alongside an old cash register.

Just along the road you can visit West Wycombe Park, which was the home of Sir Francis Dashwood, who founded the notorious Hell Fire Club in the 18th century.

✗ (12pm to 2pm & 6pm to 9.30pm) £2–5: potted Stilton, salmon fishcake, coronation chicken, herb mushrooms
🍺 Ale: Courage, Marston's. No music
Ⓟ own car park

WHIPSNADE, BEDS
Ⓛ WHIPSNADE WILD ANIMAL PARK, Whipsnade
Tel: 0582 872 171.
On the B4540 east of Luton. Signposted from the M1
(junction 9).

Whipsnade was founded in 1931 and has features common to both safari and wildlife parks. The park covers a very wide area and you have the option either to walk (the full circuit is two miles or so) or to take your car in and stop at intervals to view the animals. There are plenty of car parks, or you can use the free Trailbreaker road train.

There is a real impression of space and the animals, including the lions and tigers, have large open paddocks in which to roam. You can see elephants, bears, cheetahs, camels, penguins, Indian and White rhinos, various types of deer, chimps, yaks, giraffes, hippos, etc. You can see demonstrations by elephants, eagles and sealions every day. At the Children's Farm you can make friends with rare domestic breeds of sheep, goats and pigs and with the shire horse; there is also a Run Wild Playcentre and a Bear Maze. The Discovery Centre houses insects, mammals, fish and birds from different areas around the world. Special events are held throughout the year. The information boards are plentiful and clear.

The Coffee Shop is a large and functional place, with several high chairs; snacks, sandwiches and hot meals are served.

This is a well-organized wildlife park with a great deal to see. There are wonderful views of the countryside and plenty of places where you can have a picnic. It all adds up to an excellent day out for the family.

Open: every day, 10am to 6pm (or dusk)
Charges: adults £6.95; OAPs £5.95; children £5.45; under 3s free. A charge of £6 to take your car inside (1993 prices)
Baby changing: two mother and baby rooms
Ⓟ ample

TREVOR BEST
1982

WHITCHURCH, NR AYLESBURY, BUCKS
Ⓟ WHITE SWAN, 10 High Street
Tel: 0296 641 228.
On the A413 north of Aylesbury.

This attractive village has a pub to match: a charming flat fronted brick building, possibly built in the 16th century, with a partly thatched roof.

There are two bars, a small one at the front, and a larger and very pleasant one at the side. It has a lowish beamed ceiling, walls partly panelled in wood, a nice settle and good chairs, including some leather dining chairs, and a grandfather clock. It is a comfortable and friendly place, and you might meet Charlie, the pub's labrador, after whom the bar is named.

Along the corridor is the family room. It has wood panelled walls and several pine tables and is primarily intended for customers to eat their food, but families are welcome to use it to eat or to drink. There is an extensive and reasonably priced range of food on offer.

The large grassy garden at the back is delightful. Surrounded by trees and bushes, with bench tables scattered beween the trees, it looks out to open countryside. Next door is the village cricket ground and so, after a few draughts of ale, you might stroll through the trees and watch the local cricketing stars.

✗ (12pm to 2pm & 6pm to 9.45pm, not Sun pm or bank holiday pm) £1–8: chicken tikka, fish pie, vegetable lasagne, haddock & chips, rump steak
Children: half portions
🍺 Ale: Fuller's
🅿 own car park

WOLVERCOTE, NR OXFORD, OXON
🅿 TROUT INN, Godstow Road
Tel: 0865 54485.
Take the Godstow road off the roundabout north of Oxford city centre where the A40 and A43 cross. Wolvercote is signposted at the roundabout.

This ancient and celebrated inn has been a favourite of Oxford dons and undergraduates for hundreds of years. Its origins lie in the 12th century when it was a hospice for visitors to Godstow nunnery, the ruins of which lie across the river.

The lovely stone pub sits in an unrivalled position alongside the River Isis, and the extensive stone terrace provides ample room for customers to enjoy the scene. You may be accosted by one of the many peacocks which frequent the gardens; and we noticed that the garden was used in an episode of 'Inspector Morse' last year.

There is masses of space inside the pub, which has a series of fine rooms with paved floors and big open stone fireplaces. Families are welcome in the Stable Bar, a superb high-ceilinged room with good wooden tables and a huge open fireplace underneath a massive oak beam. An alternative is the snack bar at the other end of the pub: this is another spacious room with plenty of tables and chairs.

A bonus for families is that the pub is open throughout the day and food is available for most of the time on Friday and throughout the weekend.

✗ BAR SNACKS (12am to 3pm and 6pm to 10pm; 12pm to 10.30pm on Fridays and at weekends) £2–6: ploughman's, salads, game pie;
RESTAURANT (12pm to 3pm & 7pm to 10pm) £2–14: smoked salmon, jugged venison, steaks, baked trout
Children: half portions
⊞ Ale: Bass, Charrington
Ⓟ own car park

WYTHAM, NR OXFORD, OXON
Ⓟ WHITE HART, Wytham
Tel: 0865 244 372.
Off the A34 north-west of the city centre.

This pub is very close to the Trout Inn at Wolvercote (qv) and is yet another classic Cotswold pub, with steep stone roofs over its mellow stone walls. The front wall is bright with trailing plants and flowers.

Families are welcome to use the conservatory which has a paved floor, long scrubbed wooden tables, and plenty of greenery. An iron stove warms the room during the winter months. The main bar is a delight, with its low ceiling, wooden beams, a large dark wood settle and a large open fireplace. A lovely place to sit and chat over a beer or two. A barn should by now have been converted to provide a further eating area.

A pretty garden beckons on warmer days. It is part lawn and part terrace, bounded on one side by a stone wall, with several wooden tables and benches and a nice display of flowers.

✕ (12pm to 2pm & 7pm to 9.45pm) £2–8: cold buffet, pork in cider, chicken Kiev, mixed grill, steaks
Children: half portions
🍺 Ale: Ind Coope Burton, Tetley, Wadworth's & guests
ℙ own car park

Heart of England

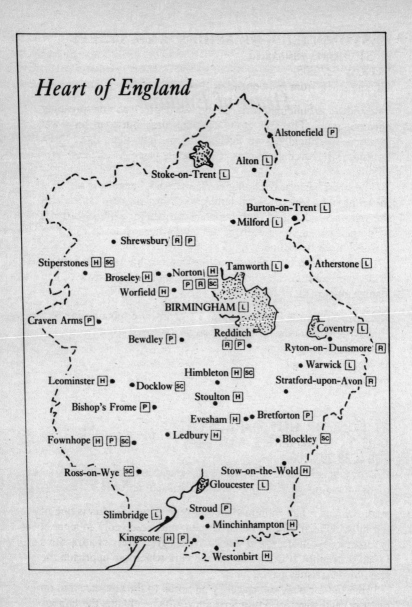

Heart of England

Alstonefield P

Alton L

Stoke-on-Trent L

Burton-on-Trent L
Milford L

Shrewsbury R P

Stiperstones H SC
Tamworth L   Atherstone L
Broseley H   Norton H
Worfield H   P R SC

BIRMINGHAM L

Craven Arms P

Coventry L

Bewdley P   Redditch
R P   Ryton-on-Dunsmore R

Himbleton H SC   Warwick L

Leominster H   Stratford-upon-Avon R
Docklow SC

Stoulton H

Bishop's Frome P

Evesham H   Bretforton P

Fownhope H P SC   Ledbury H   Blockley SC

Ross-on-Wye SC   Stow-on-the-Wold H

Gloucester L

Slimbridge L   Stroud P

Minchinhampton H

Kingscote H P

Westonbirt H

ALSTONEFIELD, NR ASHBOURNE, STAFFS

P GEORGE, Alstonfield
Tel: 033 527 205.
Off the A515 from Ashbourne to Buxton.

This old stone building overlooks the village green and its spreading chestnut trees. The grey stone can look drab but even on a wet evening Alstonfield has an ageless charm. It is high above Ashbourne and Dovedale and is a gathering place for walkers and climbers.

The main bar is a charming room with oak beams and an open fire. The long, low-ceilinged family room has six stout tables, and the walls are decorated with copper bric-a-brac. There is a large field enclosed by stone walls at the rear, where children can play; it is also used by campers.

If you are keen on walking and the outdoor life you can recover from your exertions here with a few draughts of Burtonwood, and a substantial plate of food.

✗ (12pm to 2pm & 7pm to 10pm) £2–7: meat & potato pie, chicken & chips, plaice & chips, lasagne, smoked trout
Children: small portions
⊞ Ale: Burtonwood
P own car park

ALTON, NR CHEADLE, STAFFS

L ALTON TOWERS, Alton
Tel: 0538 702 200.
East of Cheadle off the B5032. Well signposted from all main roads including the M6 (junctions 15 and 16) and M1.

With two and a half million visitors a year, Alton Towers is one of the most popular attractions in Britain, and deservedly so since it is run in a very professional way and has a great array of attractions for all the family. It is the only theme park which can approach the scale of the Disney parks.

From the car park you travel by monorail to the entrance and on the way catch sight of Thunder Valley, which contains the famous Thunderlooper, the New Beast and the Beastie; Gloomy Wood with the World's Most Haunted House; and Katanga Canyon with the Runaway Mine Train and the Congo River Rapids. Since we are of nervous dispositions, we looked the other way, just as we avoided the Corkscrew Rollercoaster and the Black Hole. The Log Fume was bad enough and you get soaking wet into the bargain.

But there are lots of gentle rides, too: the Swan Boats for example; the vintage cars; the canal boat ride located on the quieter farm site; and the miniature railway. Kiddies Kingdom is a marvellous adventure playground with a wonderful array of equipment; it is divided into two sections, one for toddlers and one for children under 14 years. A new attraction for this year is the Land of Make Believe, an area of magic and mystery with street entertainers and rides for all the family.

There are restaurants and snack bars in every sector of the park and they are all well-designed, clean and welcoming. The concentration is certainly on fast food, but if you want a relaxing lunch you should head for the Swiss Cottage, a very attractive place which looks out over the gardens and offers an excellent three course lunch (half portions for children). High chairs are generally available.

An alternative is to take your own food and use one of the many picnic areas. The gardens themselves are beautiful and a real oasis amongst the hurly-burly of the theme park.

There is a well-equipped mother and baby room in the Ingestre Centre. It is alongside the medical centre which is staffed by two nurses.

A family would not exhaust the many attractions of Alton Towers in one day, so parents should be reconciled to a marathon outing. The entrance fee entitles you to enjoy all the rides and the various shows but don't forget to budget for food and drink and other extras.

Open: every day, 9am to 5pm, 6pm, 7pm or 8pm, according to season
Charges: adults £13; OAPs £5.50; children under 14 £9.99; under 4s free
Baby changing: mother and baby room
P lots

ATHERSTONE, WARWICKS
Ⓛ TWYCROSS ZOO, Atherstone
Tel: 0827 880 250.
On the A444 north of Atherstone (at Twycross); and close to
Junction 11 of the M42.

This is a compact and well-kept zoo, set in fifty acres of parkland,
which is ideal for children of all ages, and pleasant for adults also,
since there are plenty of grassy areas where one can relax and have
a picnic.

There is a splendid play area for young children; it is enclosed
and has swings, an old tractor, a wooden train, a boat and so on.
Older children can let off steam on the climbing ropes, slides and
frames.

The zoo has a notable collection of monkeys and apes, and a
comprehensive display of other creatures: flamingoes, waterfowl,
sea lions, penguins, meerkats, giraffes, camels, cheetahs, lions and
reptiles.

The two self-service cafeterias have several high chairs and a
children's menu; there is also a snack bar.

This is an excellent zoo, where both children and parents can
have an enjoyable and interesting time. The official guide book is
notable for the high standard of its information and design.

Open: 10am to 6pm, March to October; until 4pm in winter
Charges: adults £4; OAPs £2.60; children £2; under 3s free (1993
prices)
Baby changing: a shelf and a chair in the Ladies
Ⓟ ample

BEWDLEY, HEREFORD & WORCS
Ⓟ LITTLE PACK HORSE, High Street
Tel: 0299 403 762.

This pub is tucked away off the High Street of this interesting
town. It does not have a car park so you are advised to park in the
main public car park and go on foot. It is a fascinating little pub,
which is determinedly traditional. You enter down a corridor with
an interesting mosaic on the walls, and then find a number of small

rooms with flagstone floors, ancient black beams, old photographs and advertisements on the walls.

The old stable room at one end of the pub is designed for families, a pleasant and cosy room with wooden tables and chairs, an old wooden desk complete with ink well, and a wood burning stove. There are more photographs, woodworking tools and horses' tack on the walls.

You will find an interesting choice of food, including Desperate Dan pie and jam suet roly poly – but, we are delighted to report, no chips.

✗ (12pm to 2.30pm & 6pm to 10pm) £1–5: grilled fresh sardines, filled jacket potatoes, vegetable samosa, chicken & ham pie, cauliflower cheese
Children: half portions
⊞ Ale: Ind Coope Burton, Lumphammer and guests
ℙ public car park

BIRMINGHAM, WEST MIDLANDS
Ⓛ BIRMINGHAM BOTANICAL GARDENS,
Westbourne Road, Edgbaston
Tel: 021 454 1860.
South of the A456 (Hagley Road). Well signposted.

Only about a mile from the centre of the city you will find this jewel of tranquillity with beautiful lawned gardens, hundreds of trees and delightful displays in the various glasshouses; rain forest vegetation in the Tropical House; orchids, tree ferns and cycads in the Palm House; citrus fruits in the Orangery; and a re-creation of an arid desert scene in the Cactus House.

The adventure playground is a great spot for children to let off steam, and younger children love the Rabbitry. There is also a collection of exotic birds in indoor and outdoor aviaries. On Sundays, in summer, a brass band plays.

It is a lovely place to spend an hour or two and the Pavilion self-service restaurant serves morning coffee, lunches and afternoon teas. It is fresh and bright and is a no-smoking area. Smokers can use the adjoining terrace. Two high chairs are available and there is a children's menu.

Open: 9am to dusk or 8pm, every day. From 10am on Sunday
Charges: adults £2.90; children and OAPs £1.60; under 5s free
Baby changing: mother and baby room
P own car park

BIRMINGHAM, WEST MIDLANDS
L BIRMINGHAM MUSEUM AND ART GALLERY,
Chamberlain Square
Tel: 021 235 2834.
In the centre of the city.

The building is splendid and evokes the self-confidence of
Birmingham before ugly concrete and glass took over. The
many rooms are large and the store of treasures is laid out in a
spacious way. There is comfortable seating for those who wish
to contemplate.

What treasures there are here! Of great importance is the collection of pre-Raphaelite paintings, including Ford Madox Brown's
masterpiece, *The Last of England*; Bellini's *Mother and Child*; and
works by Canaletto, Pissarro, Turner and Constable.

In addition, there are collections of coins and medals, ceramics
and glass, jewellery, rocks and gems, butterflies, wood carvings and
stuffed animals.

The Edwardian Tea Room serves light meals and snacks and
you will find a couple of high chairs here. There are occasional
piano recitals.

This is a fine museum with a lot to interest everyone.

Open: 9.30am to 5pm, Monday to Saturday; 2 to 5pm, Sunday
Charges: admission free
Baby changing: separate mother and baby room
P public car parks

BIRMINGHAM, WEST MIDLANDS
Ⓛ MUSEUM OF SCIENCE AND INDUSTRY, Newhall Street
Tel: 021 235 1661.
In the centre of the city.

There is so much to see and do here that people of any age will find something at which to marvel. For example, the Light on Science room will appeal to everyone as a hands-on display of everyday scientific phenomena: you explore light and sound, pendulums, gyroscopes and many other things to see how and why they work.

There are many machines on display, including some of the world's oldest steam engines; the Locomotive Hall is dominated by the City of Birmingham train, which moves once every hour. There are guns, bicycles, tramcars, machine tools, motor bikes, aircraft and cars, including John Cobb's Railton Special, in which he raised the world land speed record to 394 mph.

It is a fascinating place in which a family could spend many an interesting hour. The facilities are fairly basic; for example, the refreshment area comprises a few tables and some vending machines, but it is only a short walk from the museum in Chamberlain Square (qv).

Open: 9.30am to 5pm, Monday to Saturday; 2 to 5pm, Sunday
Charges: free admission
Baby changing: a fold-down shelf with a changing mat, and chairs in the Ladies
Ⓟ public car parks

BISHOP'S FROME, HEREFORD & WORCS
Ⓟ GREEN DRAGON INN, Bishop's Frome
Tel: 0885 490 607.
Just off the B4214 north of Ledbury.

This is an excellent pub with all the right basic ingredients – a good choice of food and of real ales, which are augmented by guest beers. There are two large bars with beamed ceilings, ancient stone floors, good wooden furniture and a huge open fire in one of them.

At one end, the pub has been extended and there is a very large pool room which doubles as a function room.

The family room is primarily an eating area with half a dozen tables and there are tables and chairs in a little lawned garden.

✕ (12pm to 2pm & 7pm to 9.30pm) £2–10: whitebait, plaice & chips, vegetable curry, cider chicken, venison pie
Children: own menu
🍺 Ale: Wadworth's, Tetley, Timothy Taylor's, Robinson's, Wood's & others
Ⓟ street parking

BLOCKLEY, NR MORETON-IN-MARSH, GLOS
SC LOWER FARM COTTAGES, Blockley
Tel: 0386 700 237.
In the village, which is off the A44 west of Moreton-in-Marsh.

Lower Farm Cottages are situated in a delightful Cotswold village, and the conversion, from a huge old barn with mellow stone walls, has been done with great style and charm. The main building, with two roof-to-floor pillared windows, resembles a small manor house.

The cottages can accommodate between four and six people,

with the exception of Ratty's Retreat, which is for two people only. It has a galleried bedroom with a Victorian half-tester bed.

We were very impressed with the excellent design of the cottages we saw and, in particular, the feeling of space. Some of the entrance halls go up to the rafters and most of the rooms have lovely vaulted ceilings. Clever use has been made of floor to ceiling windows, which give lovely views of the gardens; there is some splendid antique furniture, complemented by old wooden doors; and two of the cottages have spiral staircases.

The kitchens are extremely well equipped and have everything a cook would need. There is a laundry room and you will find comprehensive information here also about the surrounding area.

The three acres of garden comprise immaculately kept lawns, which are bounded by a cheerful brook. Swings, a commando net and a tree fort are provided for the children, plus footballs and toys. All the family can play croquet or table tennis and make friends with the ducks and chickens. Herons and kingfishers also visit the garden.

These are exceptional and well-organized properties in a delightful spot.

Nearby: Katie Batchelor, who runs Lower Farm, gave us a huge information pack (it is supplied to every cottage) and this tells you of the array of things to see and do in the locality. Batsford Arboretum is on the doorstep; and Sezincote, Snowshill Manor, Hidcote Manor Garden and Sudeley Castle are close. The children will want to see the waterfowl at Folly Farm and the Cotswold Farm Park; Bourton-on-the-Water has a model village, a motor museum and Birdland; and the Cotswold Wildlife Park and Blenheim Palace are a short drive away.

Units: 10
Rent: £170 to £500. Special breaks also available
Other costs: none
Central heating: provided
4 cots and 3 high chairs
Open all year

BRETFORTON, HEREFORD & WORCS
P THE FLEECE, Bretforton
Tel: 0386 831 173.
In the centre of the village off the B4035 east of Evesham.

This is one of our favourite pubs, a gem of a medieval building, which started life as a farmhouse, became an inn in 1848, and was left to the National Trust by Lola Taplin, who ran the pub for over thirty years. Her bequest stipulated that there should be no crisps, music, fruit machines, pool tables, or advertisements: a lady of great taste and perception! It is beautifully furnished throughout with old oak tables, high-backed settles, dressers, brass and copper pub measures and so on.

Families are welcome in a room next to the servery; this houses a superb collection of pewter, which dates from the Cromwellian period and may indeed have been left there by the infamous Oliver.

There is a very large garden with a swing, a climbing frame, and a log Wendy House. There are tables and benches to seat up to sixty people.

At weekends, if the weather is kind, a barbecue is set up in the garden; and this is supplemented by a salad bar in the restored barn. Prices range from £1 to £4. There is a beer festival in mid-July and morris dancers visit on most Sundays.

✗ (12pm to 2pm & 7pm to 9pm, not Mon pm) £1–6: gammon steak, plaice & chips, Gloucester sausages & chips, steak & kidney pie
Children: own menu
Ale: Hook Norton, Marston's and guest beers
P in village square. No music

BROSELEY, SHROPSHIRE
H CUMBERLAND HOTEL, Jackson Avenue
Tel: 0952 882 301.
On the B4373 – look for the sign to the hotel.

You would be hard pushed to find two more charming examples of 18th-century architecture than the two buildings which comprise the Cumberland Hotel. It is a pleasant shock to find them – just

off a main road through the town – and realize just how peaceful the hotel is.

The main building was extended in Victorian times and has a couple of bars on the ground floor, where you will always find a good choice of real ales. The dining room is attractively decorated and is notable for its collection of Coalport china. At the front there is a large lawned garden, a peaceful place with lots of flowers.

The annexe is another superb Georgian building which has a direct connection with the Industrial Revolution. It was at a meeting here in 1775 that the decision was taken to build the famous Iron Bridge. It also has a delightful and tranquil garden.

The bedrooms are comfortable and quiet and very nicely decorated, and most of them overlook the various gardens. This is a really excellent hotel which offers value for money to families.

Nearby: It is a good spot if you wish to visit Ironbridge, which has a marvellous museum. The exhibits are spread over six sites, including the Museum of Iron, the Coalport China Museum, the Jackfield Tile Museum, and so on. South Shropshire is a delightful area, and there are many other attractions including the Midland Motor Museum, the Severn Valley Railway, Carding Mill Valley and Wilderhope Manor.

✗ BAR MEALS (11.30am to 3pm & 6.30pm to 9.30pm)) £2–4:

fennel goulash, vegetable Stroganoff, mixed grill, smoked haddock pasta, chicken & ham crumble
DINNER (7pm to 9.30pm) £11: chilled melon, rump steak, pudding or cheese
Children: own menu, half portions
£ low ·
No Bargain Breaks
Children: £5 approx.
Facilities: 3 cots and 2 high chairs; baby listening system
14 rooms, 3 family. Diners/Visa
⊞ Ale: Ruddles, Webster's. Open all year
ℙ own car park. No smoking in dining room and bedrooms

BURTON-ON-TRENT, STAFFS
Ⓛ BASS MUSEUM, Horninglow Street
Tel: 0283 42031.
In the town centre.

It may seem curious to include a museum devoted to the history of a well-known beer in a guide to family leisure facilities, but this guide is for the whole family, and especially for the adults (all adult visitors get a free drink).

Any adult who likes the occasional glass of ale will be interested in the comprehensive account of the history of brewing in Burton. But the children can see one of the largest working railway models in Europe – set up exactly as it was on 10 October 1921. There are many vehicles on display, especially horse-drawn ones, and of particular interest is a 1916 steampowered delivery dray, which is driven some weekends. The Bass shire horses, which are stabled here, are, of course, great attractions, too.

The recently refurbished Wheelwrights restaurant is most attractive with its vaulted roof and gallery and it is decorated with many Bass mirrors, pictures and old pub signs. A good array of sandwiches and snacks is served at prices up to £8. The lunch menu (noon to 2.30pm) includes hot meals. There is a high chair and a children's menu available, and a changing shelf and a chair in the Ladies, if a baby has to be dealt with.

Open: 10am to 5pm, weekdays; from 10.30am at weekends

Charges: adults £2.95; children £1.50; OAPs £1.95
Baby changing: facilities in the Ladies
Ⓟ own car park

COVENTRY, WEST MIDLANDS
Ⓛ MUSEUM OF BRITISH ROAD TRANSPORT,
St Agnes Lane, Hales Street
Tel: 0203 832 425.
In the city centre.

The city is an appropriate place to boast such a museum, surrounded as it is by a large selection of the British automobile industry.

There are all types of vehicles to see including a collection of bicycles through the years, and a whole host of cars, many of them with famous but extinct names. There are cars used by the Royal Family, the latest Jaguar which will set the customers back several hundred thousand pounds, and Thrust II, Richard Noble's jet-powered car, in which he broke the world land speed record in 1983.

If you have an interest in cars this is the place to visit with its superb collection of vehicles, and a display of model cars from around the world has been added to the museum's attractions.

There is no cafeteria, just a few tables and some drinks machines.

Open: every day 10.30am to 4.30pm
Charges: adults £2.50; children and OAPs £1.50 (1993 prices)
Baby changing: well-equipped mother and baby room
Ⓟ public car park nearby

NR CRAVEN ARMS, SHROPSHIRE
Ⓟ SUN INN, Corfton
Tel: 058 473 239.
On the B4368 north of Ludlow.

The pub has been in business as a roadside tavern since the 17th century and is situated in the lovely Corvedale area of South Shropshire. The great age of the building is apparent when you see the exposed interior beams. The comfortable and appealing lounge bar includes a spacious eating area.

Families are welcome in this room which is nicely furnished with pine tables and padded chairs and settles. In addition, there is a charming dining room. On summer days, families can sit on the terrace alongside the pub or head for the garden above the pub, which is enclosed and has some bench tables and various amusements for the children including swings and a slide, and old tractor, a trampoline and ducks and chickens to befriend. The views here are a delight to the eye.

An excellent range of food is available here: it usually includes around ten daily specials and several vegetarian meals. It is all freshly cooked on the premises and the Sunday lunch at under £6 is great value. A high chair is provided.

Lovers of real ale should know that there is always an interesting choice here; the landlord reckons to serve well over a hundred different brands in a year and the Boddington Mild was proving very popular when we last visited.

✗ (12am 2.30pm & 6pm 9.30pm) £2–12: chicken Kiev, lamb & onion pie, game casserole, steaks, broccoli & cream cheese bake
Children: own menu, half portions
🍺 Ale: Boddington's and guests
🅿 own car park

DOCKLOW, NR LEOMINSTER, HEREFORD & WORCS
SC DOCKLOW MANOR, Docklow
Tel: 056 882 643.
On the A44 east of Leominster.

The ten acres of gardens around Docklow Manor make this a wonderful place for a family holiday. There is masses of space for everyone to enjoy and very little formality; the gardens ramble round the house with a delightful variety. There are smooth lawns on which to loll, or you can play croquet and make use of the giant chess board; there is a stretch of dense woodland to explore and a little garden playhouse on its boundary; magnificent mature trees enhance the appeal and they include ancient Wellingtonia or giant redwood trees, which were planted in the mid-19th century. All sorts of arbours and unexpected places await you and there are many animals with whom the children can make friends: rabbits, guinea pigs, a goat, cats, hens and a magnificent peacock.

Lovely views of the encircling countryside await you on every side and especially to the west where you can see the Black Mountains.

Apart from croquet and outdoor chess there is a grass tennis court and an excellent and sizeable outdoor swimming pool, which has its own enclosed and terraced area. Children must be supervized here. A table tennis table is provided in one of the barns.

The cottages are all grouped around the manor house and were once the stables and other ancillary buildings. They form a court-yard and we were struck by the easy informality of the layout. The cottages, like the manor house, were built of the local stone and the interior pine panelling has largely been retained. In the Coach House, you can still see the wooden pegs on the walls on which the harnesses were hung, and this cottage accommodates six people. The living room, simply and comfortably furnished, and with a wood-burning stove, also contains a well-equipped kitchen; there are three cosy bedrooms, one with a double bed and the others with twin beds.

The eleven cottages vary in size and can house from two to six people. Several of them have their own small gardens, enclosed by trees and shrubs; but the main gardens are only a step or two away, and all the cottages have delightful views.

We were very impressed by Docklow Manor, which offers peace and seclusion in relaxing surroundings and excellent facilities, including a laundrette.

Nearby: The surrounding countryside is a delight for walkers or you can see it from horseback; there are riding stables in the locality. Golfers and fishermen are also well provided for and there is a multitude of places to visit, including some fine towns and villages, such as Ludlow, Hereford, Hay-on-Wye, Leominster and Ledbury. You can quickly reach Berrington Hall, Croft Castle, Witley Court, Elgar's birthplace near Worcester, the West Midland Safari Park and the Falconry Centre at Newent. The Wye Valley lies to the south beyond Hereford.

Units: 11
Rent: £130 to £325 (short breaks available)
Other costs: none
Heating: night storage
4 cots and 2 high chairs
Open all year

EVESHAM, HEREFORD & WORCS
H EVESHAM HOTEL, Coopers Lane
Tel: 0386 765 566.
Just off the A44 by the river, and close to the town centre.

The building was modernized early in the 19th century but its origins lie back in the 16th century. A modern wing was added behind the original building a few years ago and as you approach the entrance it is difficult to believe that there are forty bedrooms here. We looked at several of them and were most impressed by the amount of space which is provided and at the high degree of comfort. Not only are the decorations and the furniture of a high quality but it is indicative of the concern for guests' comfort that easy chairs are provided in each room. There is ample space, too, for a cot or an extra bed.

In the original building we looked at a marvellous family suite under the rafters, which are still in place. There is a double bedroom with a bathroom and up a few steps is a little sitting area. On the other side, and up some steps there is a twin bedded room. It is an excellent, practical and most attractive set of rooms for a family.

Many of the bedrooms look out on to the gardens, over two acres of lawns with bright flowers and many mature trees, including several ancient mulberry trees and a venerable cedar. You can laze around on the terrace or try your hand at croquet or putting and there is play equipment for children, including a slide, a swing, a climbing frame and a trampoline. If the weather is unkind there is an indoor play area with toys, a slide and many board games. Above all, you can take some exercise in the indoor swimming pool, where the provision of toys, floating mats and water pistols ensures plenty of fun; table tennis and table football are also provided.

Great care is taken at this hotel to welcome guests of any age;

families are cared for in the same way as everyone else. It is an extremely comfortable and friendly place; any hotelier who leaves copies of the *Dandy* and *Beano* in the lavatories gets our vote every time.

Nearby: Beautiful countryside and all the interesting places in the Cotswolds lie close to hand: Sudeley Castle, Cotswold Farm Park, Sezincote, Snowshill Manor, Cotswold Wildlife Park, Ragley Hall and Coughton Court. The famous towns and villages are within easy reach: Stratford-upon-Avon, Broadway, Stow-on-the-Wold, Winchcombe, Bourton-on-the-Water and Chipping Campden.

✕ LUNCH (12.30pm to 2pm) £14: chicken liver paté, salmon, pudding or cheese (or a buffet lunch for under £7)
DINNER (7pm to 9.30pm) £18: Greek salad, roast rack of lamb, sticky toffee pudding
Children: own menu, half portions
£ high
Best Bargain Break: £78–102 per person, two nights – dinner, b&b
Children: £1.50 for each year (i.e. £1.50 for a one-year-old, £3 for a two-year-old, etc)
Facilities: 5 cots and 3 high chairs; baby listening system
40 rooms, 1 family. Access/AmEx/Diners/Visa
Ⓟ own car park. No music

FOWNHOPE, HEREFORD & WORCS
Ⓗ Ⓟ ⓈⒸ GREEN MAN INN, Fownhope
Tel: 0432 860 243.
In the centre of the village on the B4224.

We were delighted to find this handsome pub some years ago. It is situated in beautiful countryside, very close to the lovely River Wye. It is a classic 15th-century inn with most of the essential attributes: a black and white, part-timbered façade, a low-beamed bar, and above all a friendly atmosphere. One of its most celebrated landlords would not have had any trouble with drunken customers – he was Tom Spring, bare-knuckle heavyweight champion of England.

You will always find food on the go here, and the dining room,

housed in an old barn, is a lovely sight – very spacious, with black beams and pillars, and an outlook on one side to a very large grassy garden with lots of trees, and flowers. There are swings and a climbing frame for the children.

The bedrooms are well furnished and very comfortable: indeed, their style and ambience put many a three-star hotel to shame. Of the three family rooms, two have a double and single bed and the other a double and two singles. The pub has the great advantage, too, of having a separate room off the main bar where children can sit with their parents. It is the Buttery, a comfortable and spacious room with plenty of wooden settles and tables. The adults have a good selection of real ales to sample including Marston's.

Nearby: The pub is close to Hereford with its famous cathedral, and the delightful Wye Valley meanders in crazy loops south to Ross-on-Wye and beyond. Guests can fish the Wye since the landlord has fishing rights to a mile of river. There are many castles to see on the Borders including the famous triangle of the Skenfrith, Grosmont and White castles. The Falconry Centre at Newent will certainly be on the children's visiting list, as will the Wye Valley Centre with its maze, butterfly house and bird centre.

✕ BAR FOOD (12pm to 2pm & 6pm to 10pm) £1–7: plaice & chips, grilled trout, Tom Spring's steak sandwich, lasagne verdi, chicken curry

DINNER (7.15pm to 9pm) £15: seafood St Jacques, beef
Straganoff, pudding or cheese
Children: own menu, half portions
Ⓟ medium
Best Bargain Break: £69 per person, 2 nights – dinner, b&b
Children: £2.50 under 5 years; £10 from 5 to 12 years
Facilities: 4 cots and 3 high chairs; and 3 baby listening lines
20 rooms, 4 family. Open all year
Access/AmEx/Visa. No music
Ⓓ Ale: Hook Norton, Marston's, Sam Smith's
No smoking in guests' lounge
Ⓟ ample
Self-catering: Mr and Mrs Williams have one cottage for rent.
Fern Cottage is in Fownhope and has a double and a twin bedroom,
with a sofa bed also provided. There is a pleasant garden. Linen
is provided and the electricity is metered. The rent varies from
£110 to £250 a week.

GLOUCESTER, GLOS
Ⓛ NATIONAL WATERWAYS MUSEUM, Gloucester
Arcade
Tel: 0452 307 009.
Follow the signs for 'historic docks'.

The museum tells the story of Britain's canals and is housed in a
converted corn warehouse, seven storeys high. A variety of display
techniques are used: photographs, video film, prints and quotes
from those who lived through the 'canal age'.

There are several boats on display and they include a steam
dredger, narrowboats and a barge. It is great fun to board these
and a crew will show you around the dredger, which goes into
action at weekends. The children will also enjoy the 'hands on'
approach of the museum; there are many working exhibits with
which they can get to grips. Blacksmiths and carpenters show how
the boats and the canals were maintained.

The museum's horse bus gives tours of the docks and you can
also have a boat trip through the docks and along part of the
Gloucester and Sharpness canal.

The museum's café, The Waterside, overlooks the docks and serves snacks and light meals. One high chair is provided.

Open: 10am to 6pm, every day (until 5pm in winter)
  Charges: adults £4.25; children and OAPs £3.25
Baby changing: a surface in the Ladies
Ⓟ ample

HIMBLETON, NR DROITWICH, HEREFORD & WORCS
Ⓗ⌷SC⌷ PHEPSON FARM, Himbleton
Tel: 090 569 205.
South-east of Droitwich. Can be reached from the A422 or the B4090.

This handsome 17th-century farmhouse is at the centre of a working farm of 170 acres, on which beef and sheep are reared. Guests are welcome to walk the farm, as long as they observe the obvious rules of the country code, and there is no shortage of lovely walks in the surrounding area, plus fishing, horse riding, golf, etc. You can also relax in the lawned gardens, and there is a swing for the children, who have ample room to play: there are eight acres of woodland, for example.

The various rooms have their full quota of oak beams and include a charming and comfortable lounge, with a wood-burning stove in the inglenook fireplace. A selection of board games is provided. The dining room is in the same style and is just as appealing.

There are three bedrooms in the farmhouse and they share a bathroom. Two of these are spacious family rooms; each has a double and a single bed and the larger one also has a sofabed. The old granary alongside the farmhouse has been converted in the most attractive way to house a self-contained flat on the top floor (with a double bedroom and a sofabed) and two bedrooms on the ground floor. One is a double and the other a twin and both have their own bathrooms. A large family party could rent the whole building and enjoy peace and tranquillity for a very reasonable cost. The self-catering flat is rented out at between £135 and £200 a week, including linen, electricity and heating.

Nearby: There is much to do and see in this part of England:

Hanbury Hall, Spetchley Park, the Worcester Woods Country Park, Elgar's birthplace and the Jinney Ring Craft Centre are all on the doorstep; and a little further east are Stratford-upon-Avon, Ragley Hall, Charlecote Park and the city of Warwick with its famous castle.

P low
Children: various reductions according to age
Facilities: a cot and 2 high chairs
5 rooms, 1 family, 1 set interconnecting
Open all year except Christmas and New Year
No smoking in bedrooms. No music
P plenty

KINGSCOTE, GLOS
H P HUNTER'S HALL, Kingscote
Tel: 0453 860 393.
On the A4153 west of the junction with the A46.

This impressive old coaching inn, built of mellow stone, stands alone opposite the turning to Kingscote Village. It is very much a pub which welcomes families and has plenty of space to cope with the large number of people who gather to eat and drink here. There is a good-sized bar and a large dining room on the other side of the pub.

Upstairs, there is a lot more space including a room specifically designed for families. It is a pleasant spot, nicely decorated and well furnished with pine tables. At very busy times you can overflow into a beamed function room alongside.

The garden is really delightful: it is huge with an immaculate lawn and is beautifully laid out with bushes and small trees. There are lots of tables; and a play area with swings, a mini assault course, and a fort. Barbecues are held here at weekends.

The various bedrooms are in the converted stable block and blacksmith's shop alongside the inn and the one family room is ideal for a family of four, since it has two bedrooms, a small dining area and a small kitchen.

Nearby: This is a delightful part of the world with some interesting towns in which to browse – Tetbury and Malmesbury, for example. You can easily reach the Wildfowl Trust at Slimbridge and Berkeley Castle, with its remarkable history, is quite close, as is the famous Westonbirt Arboretum.

✕ BAR SNACKS (12pm to 2pm & 7pm to 9.45pm) £2–8: breast of pigeon, steak & kidney pie, cold buffet, vegetable pie, loin of pork
DINNER (7.30pm to 9.45pm) £15: seafood pancake, venison with barley wine sauce, pudding or cheese
Children: own menu
P medium
Best Bargain Break: £49 per person: 2 days, b&b
Children: cot free; extra bed £5
12 rooms, 1 family. Open all year
Access/AmEx/Diners/Visa
⊡ Ale: Bass, Hook Norton, Uley, Wadworth's
P own car park

LEDBURY, HEREFORD & WORCS
H WALL HILLS COUNTRY GUEST HOUSE,
Hereford Road
Tel: 0531 632 833.
Off the A438 west of Ledbury

This handsome and spacious red-brick Georgian house stands on the side of a hill which overlooks the pleasant town of Ledbury, and beyond you have superb views of the Malvern Hills. The front entrance is bright and welcoming with a porch full of pot plants and hanging baskets of flowers. The large walled garden is an ideal spot for guests to relax, and mostly consists of lawns, but with well-established shrubs and flower beds. The several acres of grounds includes a 15th-century cruck barn, and there is an Iron Age fort on a neighbour's land.

You will receive a very friendly and enthusiastic welcome from Mr and Mrs Slaughter, who have plenty of space for their guests: the sitting room is large and comfortable and has French windows looking out to the walled garden, and the dining room is similarly spacious and attractive. All the bedrooms are large and can take an extra bed or cot and have views of the surrounding countryside.

The family room has loads of room and includes a double bed, a single bed and a sofa bed, and has its own bathroom.

The cooking, in the hands of David Slaughter, has prompted much favourable comment from the guests. Most of the vegetables are home-grown and organic and some unusual varieties are often on the menu, which changes every day.

Nearby: Ledbury is excellently placed for holidaymakers to take advantage of the lovely countryside all around, and the many attractive towns such as Hereford, Gloucester, Malvern and Cheltenham. The Wye Valley is close by and there are many other attractions, such as the castles at Eastnor and Goodrich, the Falconry Centre at Newent, the Nature Reserve at Knapp, the Malvern Hills Animal and Bird Gardens, and the Birtsmorton Waterfowl Sanctuary.

✕ DINNER (7.30pm to 9pm) £14: baked avocado au gratin, breast of pheasant, fresh fruit tartlets
Children: high teas, small portions
Ⓟ low
Children: cots £3; £8 from 2 to 10; £12 from 11 to 15 years
(includes breakfast)
Facilities: 2 cots and 1 high chair; baby listening by arrangement
3 rooms, 1 family. Access/Visa
Open all year except Christmas and New Year
No smoking in dining room. No music
Ⓟ ample

LEOMINSTER, HEREFORD & WORCS
Ⓗ ROYAL OAK HOTEL, South Street
Tel: 0568 612 610.
In the middle of town on the A49/A44.

This friendly and welcoming hotel is situated in the town centre. It dates back to the early 18th century when it was a notable coaching inn, and has an excellent reputation for its food. You will find a good choice of real ales, too. The Royal Oak has been in the *Guide* every year since it began in 1984 and deserves its reputation as being 'family friendly'. The lounge bar, with its oak beams and open fires, is a pleasant spot to settle in for a drink and a snack; and the Cellar Bar, with its brick, arched alcoves, is an excellent alternative.

It is a good hotel to know about if you are in the area with your family not least because of the very competitive prices. There is an extensive bar menu with lots of daily specials and an interesting vegetarian menu with such homemade dishes as rice and bean burgers, potato and cheese and leek bake, vegetable lasagne and so on. All the food is freshly cooked.

As well as the two family rooms, several others are large enough to take an extra bed, and there are two sets of interconnecting rooms.

Nearby: Leominster is an interesting town with an array of antique shops, and all around there is delightful countryside. If you go north, perhaps via Croft Castle, you can enjoy the lovely expanses of South Shropshire, and perhaps see the fine town of Ludlow, Clun with its castle and the Carding Mill Valley at Church Stretton. The Severn Valley Railway is within reach, as is the Midland Motor Museum at Bridgnorth. To the south lies Hereford and the Wye Valley.

✖ BAR MEALS (12pm to 2pm & 6.30pm to 9pm) £2–8: omelettes, salads, steaks, trout;
LUNCH (12.30pm to 2pm) and DINNER (7pm to 9pm) £15: prawns with crudités, fillet steak, pudding
Children: own menu, half portions
Ⓟ medium
Best Bargain Break: £40 per person 2 nights – b&b only
Children: no charge up to 12 years
Facilities: 4 cots and 4 high chairs; a baby listening system

18 rooms, 2 sets interconnecting. Access/AmEx/Diners/Visa
Open all year
🍺 Ale: Hook Norton, Wood's, Wadworth's and guests
Ⓟ own car park

MILFORD, NR STAFFORD, STAFFS
Ⓛ SHUGBOROUGH HALL, Milford
Tel: 0889 881 388.
Off the A513 east of Stafford.

There are several aspects to the Shugborough Estate and between
them they add up to an enjoyable visit for the whole family, younger
and older.

The mansion itself was mostly built at the end of the 17th century
for the Anson family and enlarged over the next century or so. The
surrounding gardens and parkland are delightful and notable for
an extraordinary array of neo-classical monuments, financed in the
first half of the 18th century by George Anson, who was First Lord
of the Admiralty. The eight remaining include a Doric temple, a
triumphal arch and the Tower of the Winds. Great fun.

In addition, original servants' quarters, close to the mansion
house, illustrate life 'downstairs'. Demonstrations of Victorian cooking are given; there is a working laundry, brewhouse, coach house
and kitchen.

Finally, the Park Farm is a great favourite with children and
includes a working corn mill and various exhibits. The animals here
are all rare breeds such as Gloucester Old Spot pigs and Jacob
sheep. Special events are staged throughout the year: a gamekeeper's fair, candlelit evenings, donkey day, flower festivals, etc.

The smart tea rooms are self-service and have one high chair.
Snacks, hot luncheon meals and salads are on offer here and you
can sit outside in a pleasant picnic area with plenty of bench tables.

Open: March to end of October, 11am to 5pm; open all year to
booked parties
Charges: adults £7.50; children and OAPs £5; under 5s free (1993
prices)
Baby changing: a changing table, shelf and a chair in the Ladies
Ⓟ ample

MINCHINHAMPTON, NR STROUD, GLOS
Ⓗ BURLEIGH COURT HOTEL, Minchinhampton
Tel: 0453 883 804.
Off the A419 east of Stroud. The hotel brochure has a good map.

Burleigh Court is a handsome Cotswold-stone manor house, its façade covered in Virginia creeper. It sits in five acres of immaculate gardens on the side of Golden Valley and you have wonderful views of the surrounding countryside.

The emphasis at the hotel is placed firmly on comfort and style: from the attractive furnishings of the lounge areas and the dining room to the charming and spacious bedrooms, which have each been decorated and furnished in their own individual ways. Ten of the bedrooms can easily accommodate a cot or an extra bed for a child, and there are also two suites. We looked at the ground floor suite, an ideal design for a small family: there is a sitting room as you enter, with a double bed behind a screen and a separate bedroom with bunks for younger children. It has the great bonus of looking straight out to the garden and the swimming pool.

The gardens are a delight, the smooth lawns at the back divided here and there by stone walls, and the swimming pool is a genuine Victorian plunge pool – a fine sight. At the front, a huge expanse of lawn, ringed by mature trees, slopes away from the hotel. A little fountain plays in a corner and there is a play area for the children, with swings, a climbing frame, a rope ladder and a tree house. On the other side there is a large and very smooth putting green and a practice net.

This is a delightful hotel where all the family will receive a warm welcome.

Nearby: The hotel is on the fringe of Minchinhampton Common, where you can play golf, go riding or walking or just browse in the sun. Within a reasonable radius you can reach Berkeley Castle and Sudeley Castle, Westonbirt Arboretum, the Cotswold Water Park, the Wildfowl Trust at Slimbridge, the Cotswold Wildlife Park near Burford, and the various attractions at Bourton-on-the-Water. All the charms of the Cotswolds lie in one direction and of the lovely city of Bath in the other.

✗ BAR SNACKS (12pm to 2pm) £2–6: savoury cheese peach, sausage & mash, seafood pancakes, steak & kidney pie;

LUNCH (12pm to 2pm) £12: Stilton & pear mousse, piquant lamb, pudding or cheese;
DINNER (7pm to 8.45pm) £20: warm asparagus tartlets, sole au gratin, pudding or cheese
Children: high teas, flexible portions
P high
Best Bargain Break: £54 per night – dinner, b&b
Facilities: 3 cots and 2 chairs; baby listening to each room
17 rooms, 2 suites, 3 sets interconnecting
Open all year except Christmas to 7 January.
Access/AmEx/Diners/Visa
No smoking in dining room. No music
P own car park

NORTON, SHROPSHIRE
H P R SC HUNDRED HOUSE HOTEL, Norton
Tel: 095 271 353.
On the A442 between Bridgnorth and Wellington.

This hotel and pub has been renovated and adapted with great style by the Phillips family. You enter a bright and airy reception area, with a tiled floor, exposed brick walls, doors with stained glass panels, and bunches of dried flowers and herbs hanging from the ceiling.

The style is continued in the various rooms which make up the bar and restaurant areas. There is a lovely high-ceilinged room with a Colebrookdale cast-iron range and families can sit here together. There are windows on to the sizeable garden, shaded by trees. The two donkeys, Gerrard and Susan, are still on hand to crop the lawns.

The large bar has cast-iron cooking pots and other utensils hanging from the beamed ceilings – a suitable reminder of the old industries of this region, where nearby Ironbridge is regarded as one of the cradles of the Industrial Revolution. The museums there are well worth a visit.

The bar is on two levels, and families can relax at the tables in the eating area which is notable for a huge fireplace. There is a great emphasis on food here, and the menu certainly looks enticing.

Some of the produce will come from the hotel's own vegetable garden: mange-tout and asparagus perhaps, as well as the herbs.

It is good to report that food is available throughout the day here from Monday to Saturday, and during the usual Sunday pub opening hours, when there is also a three-course lunch for around £11.

The bedrooms are furnished and decorated with great style, and they include a high proportion of family rooms.

Nearby: There is no shortage of entertainment in this part of the world. The beautiful countryside of South Shropshire can easily be reached and a trip through Ludlow to Stokesay Castle and Clun and back through the Carding Mill Valley is recommended. The famous Ironbridge Gorge Museum is close at hand, as is the Midland Motor Museum and the Aerospace Museum at Cosford. The Severn Valley Railway runs from Bridgnorth.

✖ BAR SNACKS (11.30am to 2.30pm & 6pm to 10pm) £3–11: savoury pancakes, avocado & crab gratin, sirloin steak, salmon fishcakes, lasagne;
DINNER (6pm to 10pm) £15: salmon & sole terrine, roast rack of lamb, pudding or cheese
Children: own menu, half portions
Ⓟ high
Best Bargain Break: £90 per person, 2 nights – dinner, b&b
Children: free up to 16 years
Facilities: 4 cots and 4 high chairs, and a baby listening system
10 rooms, 4 family. Open all year
🍺 Ale: Brain's, Phillips, Flowers and guests
Access/Visa. No music
Ⓟ own car park
Self-catering: The hotel can also offer two cottages in Ironbridge, the Music Master's House and Timmins Cottage. They are close to the museum. The house has three bedrooms and a sofa bed and can accommodate a fairly large family. It has a pretty walled garden which overlooks Ironbridge Gorge. The cottage adjoins the house and can sleep two adults and two children. Timmins Cottage has a small, enclosed garden. The rents vary from £90 to £310 a week and include electricity, gas, linen and towels.

REDDITCH, HEREFORD & WORCS
P R NEVILL ARMS, Astwood Bank
Tel: 0527 892 603.
On the A441, south of Redditch, at the junction with the B4090.

This handsome brick-walled pub has been expanded to form a very large family pub and restaurant. Although there is loads of space, the interior has been skilfully divided into a series of smaller, interconnected rooms and alcoves, some on slightly different levels to others. The wide windows, cheerful decorations, wooden screens, coloured lights, and the prints on the walls combine to make it an attractive pub.

The facilities for families are outstanding and include a no smoking family dining room with a play area which has a ball swamp and other amusements. There are several high chairs, a nappy-changing facility and a children's menu; and food is available throughout the day. The garden includes an enclosed adventure playground for the children.

✕ (11.30am–10pm; from noon on Sunday) £2–8: prawn cocktail, sirloin steak, sole bearnaise, vegetable crumble, chicken masala
Children: own menu
🍺 Ale: Boddington, Castle Eden, Flowers
P own car park

NR ROSS-ON-WYE, HEREFORDSHIRE
SC WYE LEA, Bridstow
Tel: 0989 62880.
Off the A49, just west of Ross-on-Wye.

Immense care and considerable thought has been lavished on Wye Lea, a development of eleven cottages and two apartments within an estate of nearly twenty acres. It was completed a couple of years ago by Mr and Mrs Bateman who live in the attractive sandstone manor house, built in the mid-19th century, which forms the hub of the estate.

There are two apartments on the first floor of the house and the larger one, Wysteria, sleeps four people in its two bedrooms, each of which has its own bathroom. As one would expect in a Victorian house the rooms are spacious, and they have been decorated and furnished to a very high standard. The second apartment, Peartree, will house two people and both properties have views of the immaculately maintained gardens with their smooth lawns, mature trees and profusion of flowers and shrubs. Many young trees have been planted for the future.

Three cottages have been built from the old stables, a very appealing sandstone building like the main house. Each of the cottages has a double and a twin bedroom (and two bathrooms or shower rooms), a dining room and a sitting room and the exposed beams are offset by the smart decorations and excellent furniture. Nothing has been stinted either in terms of space, decoration or equipment. Each of the properties has plenty of garden in which to laze, and a terrace. Linhay has been designed on one level and is suitable for disabled guests. It has a lovely enclosed stone terrace, which faces south.

Close by there is a detached cottage, Squirrels, which can sleep up to eight people. There are particularly spacious living areas and a spiral staircase leads up to the three bedrooms and two bathrooms. A large and splendid garden completes the picture.

Bramble Court was built from scratch as holiday accommodation and comprises seven cottages of varying sizes to sleep from four to eight people. The building resembles a mews, the walls partly of brick and partly rendered, and the design is nicely completed by a small central clock tower. Each cottage has plenty of space and the beamed ceilings and stylish decorations are instantly appealing. The kitchens, as in all the properties, are superbly equipped and designed; everything a cook would need is provided. Everything is laid on to make a visitor feel cossetted and at home, including two bath or shower rooms per cottage. Guests can savour the superb views of the Wye countryside from their own terraces.

Above all, the extra facilities provided at Wye Lea are first class. There is an excellent indoor swimming pool, with very smart changing rooms; it adjoins a bar lounge and a restaurant which opens on Thursday, Friday and Saturday evenings and also for Sunday lunches; these times can vary according to demand. There are two hard tennis courts, which are floodlit, a croquet lawn and a 9 hole putting green. Mr Bateman, a keen fisherman, owns a stretch of the Wye River and guests can take advantage of this facility too.

Finally there is a children's play area with a climbing frame, swings, two swing ball games, table tennis and other play equipment.

We were greatly impressed by Wye Lea. The owners have expended considerable skill and imagination in developing their estate; the accommodation and the facilities are superb and the whole atmosphere is instantly and warmly welcoming.

Nearby: You need hardly leave Wye Lea, such are its attractions, but the beautiful Wye Valley also beckons. The Wye Valley Visitor Centre is a good starting point and the ruins of Goodrich Castle are also close to hand. In Gloucestershire, you can visit the Wildfowl Trust at Slimbridge, Berkeley Castle and the Dean Forest Railway; over the border in Gwent there is a ring of castles to see and the famous Tintern Abbey. Golf is easily available in the locality, as are horse riding, canoeing and clay pigeon shooting.

Units: 13
Rent: £257 to £822 (short breaks available)
Other costs: gas & electricity by meter reading; £3 per hour for tennis, £4 per hour for croquet, and £2 for putting
Heating: central heating
4 cots and 4 high chairs
Open all year

RYTON-ON-DUNSMORE, WARWICKS
Ⓡ RYTON ORGANIC GARDENS, Ryton-on-Dunsmore
Tel: 0203 303 517.
On the B4029 east of Coventry. It is signposted from the A45 and the A428.

A table on the lawn is a most agreeable place to have a meal, as we discovered at Ryton Gardens last summer. The restaurant has proved so popular that it has been expanded.

It is all part of the National Centre for Organic Gardening and all the food is freshly cooked from ingredients grown on the spot. No additives are ever used.

The restaurant has a terrace and a lawned garden with bench tables and from there you look over to the Centre's twenty acres of gardens, which include a rose garden, a herb garden, a wild flower meadow, a picnic area and a children's play area with a wooden climbing frame and some swings. There is a table and chair and paper towels in the Ladies, if a baby needs to be changed.

The menu changes on a daily basis and is reasonably priced. You can also sample a comprehensive choice of organic wines from France, Germany, Italy and England and organic beers and lagers.

✗ £1–3: salads, broccoli quiche, Hungarian pancakes, mushroom homity pie, celery & walnut casserole
Children: small portions
Open 9am to 5pm (till 4pm, Oct to March)
Open all year. Access/AmEx/Visa
Licensed. No smoking
No music. One high chair only
ℙ own car park

SHREWSBURY, SHROPSHIRE
ℝ GOOD LIFE, Barracks Passage, Wyle Cop
Tel: 0743 350 455.

This excellent vegetarian restaurant offers a warm welcome to families, and has no less than four high chairs available. You can also cope with changing a baby, since a pull-down shelf is provided in the Ladies.

The restaurant is housed in a fine 14th-century timbered building just around the corner from the Lion Hotel, in one of the most attractive parts of the old town where timber-framed Tudor houses alternate with stately Georgian buildings.

There are two very attractive rooms in which you can settle to enjoy the wholefood cooking. All the dishes are prepared on the spot, and there is always a hot dish of the day and a good range of salads from which to choose.

✗ £1–2: homemade soup, five-bean cheese pot, savoury flans and quiches
Children: smaller portions
Open 9.30am to 3.30pm Mon to Fri, 9.30am to 4.30pm Sat.
Closed Sun
No credit cards accepted. No music
No smoking downstairs
ℙ public car park nearby

NR SHREWSBURY, SHROPSHIRE
ⓟⓡ BRIDGEWATER ARMS, Harmer Hill
Tel: 0939 290 377.
On the A528 about six miles north of Shrewsbury.

This fine old sandstone pub stands four-square on the road north to the delightful little town of Ellesmere.

The Bridgewater Arms has been transformed into a very extensive family pub and restaurant with a good array of facilities which include a large family dining area (no smoking) and a little play area for tiny children, plenty of high chairs, a children's menu, and a nappy-changing unit. Outside there is a children's adventure playground, safely enclosed, and a bouncy castle.

One of the merits of the pub is the amount of space inside. It is a pleasant, open-plan interior with Laura Ashley style wallpaper, richly patterned carpets, comfortable furniture, and wood panelling, glass screens and cheerful prints on the walls.

✗ (11.30am–10pm; from noon on Sunday) £2–8: smoked trout, roast chicken, sirloin steak, lasagne verde, lamb rogan josh
Children: own menu
Ⓐ Ale: Boddington's, Marston's, Whitbread
Ⓟ lots

SLIMBRIDGE, GLOS
Ⓛ WILDFOWL AND WETLANDS CENTRE,
Slimbridge
Tel: 0453 890 333.
Off the A38 south of Gloucester. Signposted from the M5 (junctions 13 and 14).

Sir Peter Scott founded the Trust in 1946 with the aim of conserving wildfowl and nowhere in Britain can you see more waterfowl from around the world than on the 100 acres of Slimbridge. Berwick's swans from Siberia, Pochard, Greylag geese, pintail, white fronted geese and all six varieties of flamingo can be seen in their thousands. It is a heartening sight.

You can wander around for hours and watch these beautiful creatures and also enjoy the trees, under whose shade there are plenty of seats and benches, and the masses of wild flowers. There are plenty of picnic areas, too.

There is also a tropical house in which you can see humming birds, among other creatures.

The self-service cafeteria has a selection of snacks, salads and hot meals such as steak and kidney pie and chicken and chips. You can sit outside on the terrace or a grassy area at the rear and admire the flamingoes on the adjoining water.

Open: every day, except Christmas, 9.30am to 5pm (4pm in winter)
Charges: adults £4.50; OAPs £3.40; children £2.25; under 4s free (1993 prices)
Baby changing: a spacious mother and baby room with tables and chairs
Ⓟ plenty

STIPERSTONES, SHROPSHIRE
Ⓗ ⓈⒸ TANKERVILLE LODGE, Stiperstones
Tel: 0743 791 401.
Off the A488 south of Shrewsbury. The brochure has clear
directions.

This is a lovely and unspoilt part of Shropshire, made famous by
Mary Webb's novels, *The Golden Arrow* and *Gone to Earth*. It also
provided the setting for Malcolm Saville's adventure stories for
children.

Roy and Sylvia Anderson have a wonderful setting for their
accommodation which comprises four bedrooms in an extension to
their own house, the original part of which was an 18th-century
hunting lodge. Three of the bedrooms have twin beds and the
other a double and they are all bright and clean and comfortably
furnished. They are fairly compact in size but there is a good-sized
sitting room on the ground floor (with a colour television) and a
pleasant dining room with pine furniture. The charges are
extremely modest (approximately £14 per person for bed and
breakfast).

Across the lovely secluded garden, surrounded by flowers and
greenery, there is Ovenpipe Cottage, the self-catering accommodation. It was once a pottery and an art gallery and the living area is
on the first floor in order to take advantage of the many windows.
There is plenty of space, comfortable furniture and a well-equipped
kitchen. Down below is a cosy family bedroom, which contains a
double bed and two bunk beds built into one corner, with little
windows through the stone walls. It is a light and airy room, made
more so by the white-washed stone walls.

It is a delightful spot, on the site of the old Tankerville Mine and
with the Devil's Chair looming above. All around is the magnificent
Shropshire countryside and from the road above you can see for
miles across the rolling fields to the hills beyond. It is only a short
walk to the Stiperstones Inn which serves food all day and every
day, and the menu includes vegetarian and vegan dishes. There is
a shop and a post office attached to the inn.

Nearby: All of south Shropshire is at your feet: the Long Mynd,
much of which is owned by the National Trust, the Stiperstones
Nature Reserve (with the famous Devil's Chair) and Carding Mill

Valley are nearby, and golfers should know that Church Stretton golf course, designed by the incomparable James Braid, is a charming course on the hills. The children will be keen to see the Acton Scott Working Farm Museum near Church Stretton and Powis Castle. Lake Vyrnwy is also within easy reach.

Further south are the Clun villages – 'the quietest places under the sun' – Ludlow with its famous castle, and the Clee Hills. A round trip would then take you to Bridgnorth via the Severn Valley Railway Station and the Midland Motor Museum and on to Ironbridge with its fascinating museums. And don't forget Buildwas Abbey, the Roman City at Wroxeter and Wenlock Priory. Coarse fishing and horse riding can be arranged nearby.

✕ DINNER (7pm) £8: courgette & mint soup, Shropshire fidget pie, raspberry pavlova, cheese
£ low (Ovenpipe Cottage costs from £75 to £140 a week, electricity is extra)
Facilities: 1 cot
4 rooms. Open all year
No credit cards. No music
Ⓟ own car park

STOKE-ON-TRENT, STAFFS
Ⓛ CITY MUSEUM AND ART GALLERY, Bethesda Street, Banley
Tel: 0782 202 173.
In the centre of Hanley.

This purpose-built museum was opened in 1981 by the Prince of Wales, and we wonder what his opinion of the building, which resembles a DIY store, was.

The heart of the museum is the display of pottery and the history of pottery manufacture in Staffordshire. The various displays are laid out in an imaginative and interesting way and include a natural history gallery, archaeology and fine arts. There is also a tribute to Reginald Mitchell, the designer of the Spitfire and one of Stoke's famous sons.

The cafeteria, agreeably furnished with wooden furniture and with pine walls and pillars, is efficiently run and serves basic snacks and meals – pasties, lasagne, pizza, etc. There are a couple of high chairs.

Open: 10am to 5pm, Monday to Saturday; 2 to 5pm, Sunday
Charges: admission free
Baby changing: a mother and baby room with a changing table and chairs
℗ public car parks nearby

STOULTON, NR WORCESTER, HEREFORD & WORCS
Ⓗ CALDEWELL HOUSE, Pershore Road
Tel: 0905 840 894.
On the A44 south-east of Worcester.

The house is very well positioned for travellers and tourists since it is about three miles from junction 7 of the M5 south of Worcester. It is a handsome house, with a Georgian facade and some Victorian additions, with its history on display inside, and a little museum. There is loads of space surrounding the house: a huge and well-maintained front lawn where you can play tennis and there are swings for the children, and a lawn where you can play croquet in the lovely and secluded rear garden. There is a miniature steam railway in the grounds, and the owners arrange special railway weekends.

Any family will enjoy the surroundings, which include several acres of woodland and a small lake; and there are farm animals – a cow, sheep, donkey, goats and hens – to befriend.

The various rooms are generous in size and include two very large family rooms at the front of the house: one has a double and a single bed and the other a double and two singles and plenty of room for a couple of easy chairs as well. The two rooms at the back of the house are delightfully secluded and look out over the garden. One of them has its own en suite bathroom and has a connecting door to a twin-bedded room. They can be used as a self-contained family suite.

The public rooms include a sitting room and a stately and charming dining room with wide windows on to the gardens.

Caldewell House has a relaxed charm of its own, excellent facilities in tranquil surroundings and offers excellent value.

Nearby: For holiday makers there is a multitude of choices nearby: Bredon Hill on one side and the Malvern Hills on the other; further afield the Cotswolds and the Wye Valley; and quite close at hand Worcester Woods Country Park, Hanbury Hall, the Avoncraft Museum, Spetchley Park and Eastnor Castle. Music lovers might be interested in Elgar's birthplace (on the west side of Worcester).

✘ DINNER (by arrangement) £8
Children: half portions
£ low
Children: cot free; half price up to 12 years
Facilities: 1 cot and 1 high chair; baby listening by arrangement
4 rooms, 2 family, 1 set interconnecting. Open March to December
No credit cards. Unlicensed
℗ ample. No music

STOW-ON-THE-WOLD, GLOS
Ⓗ FOSSE MANOR HOTEL (Consort), Stow-on-the-Wold
Tel: 0451 830 354.
On the A429, just to the south of Stow-on-the-Wold.

This privately owned hotel is housed in a stately Victorian manor house, its walls covered in Virginia creeper. It has the great bonus for families of a large garden, which runs to about seven acres and provides loads of space for children to play and for adults to relax. A play area is laid out on the smooth lawn at the front of the hotel and has a sand pit, swings and a slide, and there is a croquet lawn. A pleasant terrace lies at the back of the hotel and overlooks a quiet, enclosed garden with lawns and a pond; giant chess is laid out here.

The public rooms, spacious and comfortable, include a very pleasant lounge with lots of easy chairs and sofas, a large bar and a bright and cheerful dining room with wide windows on to the garden. The family bedrooms offer plenty of space and lovely views over the countryside.

The Fosse Manor is an excellent family hotel in a superb location in the heart of the Cotswolds where there is much to enjoy.

Nearby: The Cotswold Farm Park, Birdland and the model village at Bourton on the Water, the Folly Farm waterfowl sanctuary and the Cotswold Wildlife Park are all within easy reach as are Sudeley Castle, Sezincote, and Chedworth Roman Villa. The hotel staff can arrange riding, fishing and clay pigeon shooting, and there are several golf courses in the vicinity.

✂ BAR SNACKS (12pm to 2pm & 6pm to 9.30pm) £2–10: ravioli, chicken tikka, venison steak, grilled salmon, pork & cider sausages; LUNCH (12.30pm to 2pm) £13: hot oriental prawns, grilled pork chop, pudding or cheese; DINNER (7.30pm to 9.30pm) £16: potted local trout, beef Stroganoff, pudding or cheese
Children: own menu, half portions
£ high
Best Bargain Break: £59 per person per night – dinner, b&b
Children: free
Facilities: 4 cots and 4 high chairs; and a baby listening system
20 rooms, 3 family, 2 sets interconnecting
Open all year excluding Christmas week. Access/AmEx/Diners/Visa
Ⓟ own car park. No smoking in restaurant

STRATFORD-UPON-AVON, WARWICKS
Ⓡ CAFE NATURAL, Greenhill Street
Tel: 0789 415 741.
Next to Safeways in the town centre.

This cheerful vegetarian café has a strategic position in the busy and tourist-laden town of Stratford only a few doors away from the Teddy Bear Museum. A must on any family itinerary – move over Will Shakespeare.

This is a pleasant place for a family to stop if they are hoofing it around the tourist spots of this famous town. There is a good choice of fresh food, and it is good to report that smoking is banned from the restaurant. The Café Natural has the distinction of being the only wholly vegetarian restaurant in the town.

If you need to change a baby the staff will find some space for you.

✗ £1–4: filled jacket potatoes, savoury roulade, salads, lasagne
Children: small portions
Open 9am to 5pm, Mon to Sat. Closed Sunday
Unlicensed. Access/Visa
One high chair only. No smoking
℗ public car parks

NR STROUD, GLOS
℗ OLD LODGE INN, Minchinhampton Common
Tel: 0453 832 047.
Well signposted in the middle of Minchinhampton Common.

This pleasant pub, which began life as one of Henry VIII's hunting lodges and, at one time, was a golf clubhouse, is situated in a wonderful position on the Common. It is surrounded by the golf course, and the clubhouse is now next door.

It is very popular with families out for some fresh air, and has a functional family room with doors on to the garden. This is a large area, with a well-kept lawn, tables and chairs, children's toys scattered about, and all enclosed by a stone wall.

There is a strong emphasis on food here, which is cooked by the owners' son. There is a huge selection of dishes, including over twenty vegetarian meals, and new meats such as bison and ostrich have been tried. The wild boar pie is especially popular. Food is available throughout most opening hours, while the restaurant is closed on Sunday and Monday evenings. Families will perhaps be interested in the Sunday lunch, which is good value at around £7. Real ale fans will also note the good selection available here.

✗ (12pm to 2.30pm & 6pm to 10pm) £1–13: smoked mussels, wild boar pie, poached halibut mornay, roast poussin, vegetable casserole

Children: own menu, half portions
🍺 Ale: Theakston's, Wadworth's and guests
Ⓟ own car park

NR TAMWORTH, STAFFS
Ⓛ **DRAYTON MANOR PARK & ZOO**
Tel: 0827 287 979.
Off the A4091 south of Tamworth and near junction 9 of the
M42. Well signposted.

There is a lot going on at this leisure park and the emphasis is on
the many rides which are available; there are some 'white knuckle'
ones amongst them. There are a ferris wheel, log flume, Splash
Canyon, flying Dutchman, a buffalo coaster, a pirate ship and many
others. The brave or the foolhardy should try the looping coaster,
the sky flyer or the new ride for 1994, the Shock Wave, a stand-up
roller coaster.

There are several gentler rides for younger children (and parents)
including rowing boats, dodgems, a carousel, the jungle cruise and
the Rio Grande railway: and there is a special children's corner.

The zoo covers 15 acres of parkland and has an interesting collection of reptiles, big cats, bears, primates and farm animals, plus
penguins and sea lions.

With a collection of dinosaur models, an animated show and
family adventure shows there is clearly plenty for the whole family
to enjoy here.

There are several eating areas, including take-away outlets. The
Hamilton Restaurant has high chairs and offers a good range of
meals including a cold buffet, steaks, plaice and chips, etc.

Open: Easter to end of October, every day, 9am to 7pm (closes
earlier in winter)
Charges: adults £2.50; children £1.50. Wristbands cost £6 (£4.50
for a child under 1m tall) (1993 prices)
Baby changing: three mother and baby rooms
Ⓟ ample

WARWICK, WARWICKS
Ⓛ WARWICK CASTLE, Warwick
Tel: 0926 495 421.
On the A41. Well signposted.

One of the most magnificent castles in Britain, the building has its origins in the 10th century, but the present buildings were mainly erected in the 14th and 15th centuries. Some of the most influential families in England were Earls of Warwick: the Dudleys, the Beauchamps and the Nevills and were at the centre of great events. Sir Walter Scott described the castle as 'the fairest monument of ancient and chivalrous splendour that yet remains uninjured by time'.

The rooms are superb, even daunting, and there is an award winning exhibition, 'A Royal Weekend Party, 1898', which illustrates a Victorian house party with guests including the then Prince of Wales (the future King Edward VII). The children will probably be more interested in the Armoury and the Great Hall, which has another display of weapons and armour; and, above all, in the dungeon and the torture chamber.

There are three places to eat and drink. The Stables Café is a pleasant room in the old stables and offers sandwiches and snacks. The Stables Restaurant is a delightful and spacious restaurant housed in the former hayloft with its brick walls and wooden crossbeams. Hot dishes, sandwiches and snacks are served at prices up to £4. Finally the Undercroft Restaurant is situated in a fine 14th-century vaulted chamber and hot meals and snacks are available. The various restaurants are open all day, with lunches served from noon to 2pm. High chairs are available in the two restaurants. There is a mother and baby room close to the Undercroft Restaurant.

The gardens of the Castle are beautiful and peaceful, with plenty of space for picnics. Bench tables are set up under the trees. If you are feeling really energetic, try the walk around the ramparts, with 200 steps up and 200 down.

Open: every day (except Christmas Day), 10am to 5.30pm from March to October (till 4.30pm otherwise)
Charges: adults £6.25; OAPS £4.25; children £3.80; under 4s free

Baby changing: mother and baby room by the Undercroft
Restaurant
P ample

WESTONBIRT, NR TETBURY, GLOS
Ⓗ HARE AND HOUNDS HOTEL (Best Western),
Westonbirt
Tel: 0666 880 233.
On the A433 south-west of Tetbury.

The gardens of this attractive Cotswold-stone building, part of which started off as a farmhouse in the early 19th century, are a major attraction: ten acres of delightful gardens, with wide and smooth lawns, beautifully kept flower beds and hedgerows, and grand, mature trees. There is also a shady, walled garden outside the bar, with several bench tables.

Other facilities include two hard tennis courts, a croquet lawn, a squash court, table tennis and snooker; and down the road is the famous Westonbirt Arboretum, which is open every day of the year.

A full range of meals can be found here, and there is a small area off the main bar where families can park themselves, as well as the lounge areas. The three course Sunday lunch offers pretty good value.

Nearby: The Arboretum is very close to the hotel and there is a variety of places to visit within a reasonable radius: Berkeley Castle, the Wildfowl Trust at Slimbridge, Lydeard Country Park, Corsham Court and Sheldon Manor. The Cotswold Water Park provides all sorts of water sports and has a nature reserve and an adventure playground.

✗ BAR SNACKS (12pm to 2.30pm & 7.30pm to 9.30pm) £2–10: smoked trout, sirloin steak, game pie, poached salmon
LUNCH (12.30pm to 2pm) £11: egg & prawn mayonnaise, supreme of chicken, pudding or cheese;
DINNER (7.30pm to 9pm) £17: fresh asparagus, soup, escalope of venison, pudding or cheese
Children: own menu, half portions
£ high

Best Bargain Break: £98 per person, 2 nights – dinner, b&b
Children: free to age 16
Facilities: 3 cots and 2 high chairs; 5 baby listening lines
30 rooms, 5 family, 3 sets interconnecting
Access/AmEx/Visa. Open all year
🍺 Ale: John Smith's, Wadworth's. No music
🅿 own car park

WORFIELD, NR BRIDGNORTH, SHROPSHIRE
Ⓗ OLD VICARAGE HOTEL, Worfield
Tel: 07464 497.
Off the A454 east of Bridgnorth.

This large red-brick house was built in 1905 and was bought from
the Church Commissioners by Mr and Mrs Iles over a decade ago.
It is a small and very comfortable hotel; there are some fine antique
pieces, and the walls display watercolours and engravings. The
lounge bar, with its wide windows, is a relaxing place to have a
drink, as is the splendid and spacious conservatory, full of plants
and with excellent views of the countryside. The main dining room
looks out to the gardens and there is also a small private dining
room.

Hotels often claim that their bedrooms are individually designed,
and this is certainly true at the Old Vicarage, where the rooms are
very smartly furnished and decorated in fine style. The four rooms
in the Coach House merit special mention since they have the extra
luxuries of jacuzzi baths and double shavers. They are spacious
and extremely comfortable and the ground floor rooms (one of
which is superbly equipped for disabled guests) have their own little
gardens. It is no surprise to learn that the hotel is one of the very
few in Britain to be placed in the de luxe category by the AA.

The hotel garden is safely enclosed and has spreading lawns and
several mature trees. There is plenty of space for children to play
and adults can try their skills on the croquet lawn.

Nearby: South Shropshire is a lovely part of the world with so
many attractive villages and towns: Church Stretton and the Carding Mill Valley, Clun with its castle, Ludlow and Bridgnorth, which
has a motor museum. Within an easy distance you can visit the

Ironbridge Gorge Museum, the Severn Valley Railway, Wilderhope Manor, the Safari Park at Bewdley, Wyre Forest and the Aerospace Museum at Cosford. You can play golf at Worfield at half price and Patshull Park is an alternative venue.

✗LUNCH (12pm to 2pm) £16: smoked salmon & avocado salad, entrecote of beef, pudding
DINNER (7pm to 9pm) £20: terrine of chicken & sweetbreads, fillet of brill, pudding or cheese
Children: own menu, half portions
£ high
Best Bargain Break: £111 per person, 2 nights – dinner, b&b
Children: babies free; up to £15 thereafter (includes meals)
Facilities: 1 cot and 1 high chair; baby listening system
14 rooms, 1 family. Open all year
Access/AmEx/Diners/Visa. No smoking in restaurant, bar and some bedrooms
Ⓟ own car park

East of England

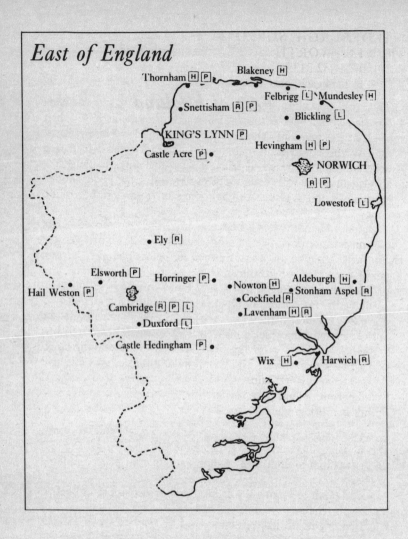

East of England

Thornham [H] [P]
Blakeney [H]
Felbrigg [L] Mundesley [H]
Snettisham [R] [P]
Blickling [L]
KING'S LYNN [P]
Hevingham [H] [P]
Castle Acre [P]
NORWICH
[R] [P]
Lowestoft [L]
Ely [R]
Elsworth [P]
Horringer [P]
Aldeburgh [H]
Hail Weston [P]
Nowton [H]
Stonham Aspel [R]
Cockfield
Cambridge [R] [P] [L]
Lavenham [H] [R]
Duxford [L]
Castle Hedingham [P]
Wix [H]
Harwich [R]

ALDEBURGH, SUFFOLK

Ⓗ WENTWORTH HOTEL, Wentworth Road

Tel: 0728 452 312.

Next to the beach, near the town centre.

This very appealing hotel has a splendid position overlooking the sea across a pebbled beach, where the fishermen still sell their catch in the morning. Many of the bedrooms have lovely views, as have the attractive restaurant and the sun room which is a delightful spot in which to relax. The main lounge is alongside, an elegant room with comfortable sofas and some good antique furniture. There is also a reading room cum library on the ground floor.

On one side of the hotel there is a sunken terrace and it is a sun trap on warmer days; on the other side is a small lawned garden. The wide expanses of sea and beach lie before you and you can walk for miles in either direction.

Although there are no permanent family rooms here, fourteen of the bedrooms can be set up to take two adults and a child.

Nearby: Although the beach is shingle, Aldeburgh lies on the Suffolk coastal path which runs from Felixstowe to Lowestoft. Just to the north you can visit Minsmere Nature Reserve and the interesting village of Dunwich with its museum. A music festival is held every June at Snape Maltings and there are castles at Orford and Framlingham. Adults with an interest in wine might try visits to Brandeston Priory and Bruisyard Wines.

✗ BAR LUNCH (12pm to 2pm) £2–8: rump steak, chicken curry, prawn aioli, fisherman's pie, grilled lamb's liver;

LUNCH (12pm to 2pm) £13: Stilton pate, fillet of plaice, pudding or cheese;

DINNER (7pm to 9pm) £17: dressed crab, roast sirloin of beef, pudding or cheese

Children: high teas, half portions

£ high

Best Bargain Break: £104 per person, 2 nights – dinner, b&b

Children: free to age 2, £7.50 thereafter

Facilities: 2 cots and 2 high chairs; baby listening system

31 rooms. Access/AmEx/Diners/Visa

Closed 2 weeks after Christmas. No music

P own car park & on street
⊈ Ale: Adnams

BLAKENEY, NORFOLK
Ⓗ BLAKENEY HOTEL, The Quay
Tel: 0263 740 797.
Just off the A149 between Cromer and Wells.

The fine old building, made of flint and brick, sits in a marvellous situation overlooking the harbour, which is owned by the National Trust. The rooms are spacious, many of them with lovely views, and the family rooms contain extra bunk beds.

There are excellent facilities for families, beginning with the splendid and sizeable garden, with its smooth lawns. It is beautifully maintained, safely enclosed, and has a children's play area at one end. The games room has a pool table, table tennis and darts, and there is a full-sized snooker table as well (for over 16s only). In addition there is a heated indoor swimming pool, a sauna, a jacuzzi and a fitness room.

The public rooms are comfortable and relaxing and the spacious bar area looks out over the harbour, as does the attractively decorated restaurant.

All in all, this is a very agreeable hotel in a lovely part of the country. One of our readers described it as 'superb all round' and we agree with that summary.

Nearby: Blakeney Point is an area of outstanding natural beauty, over 1000 acres of it, and has a great wealth of bird life. There are two observation hides and a nature trail for children. Holkham Hall, the Norfolk Shire Horse Centre, Felbrigg Hall and the North Norfolk Railway, Blickling Hall and the Norfolk Wildlife Park are all within easy reach. If the area is a paradise for naturalists, so it is for golfers with Hunstanton, Brancaster and Sheringham close by. Boat hire is easily arranged, as are horse riding and fishing.

✘ LIGHT LUNCH (12pm to 2pm) £2–7: seafood pancake, Norfolk trout, lasagne verdi, cold buffet;
DINNER (7pm to 9.30pm) £15: prawn cheesecake, pork escalope, pudding or cheese
Children: own menu, half portions

£ high
Best Bargain Break: £59 per person per night – dinner, b&b
Children: £5 up to 12 years
Facilities: 8 cots and 4 high chairs and a baby listening system
60 rooms, 6 family. Access/AmEx/Diners/Visa
Open all year
🍺 Ale: Greene King
Ⓟ own car park

BLICKLING, NORFOLK
Ⓛ BLICKLING HALL, Aylsham
Tel: 0263 733 084.
On the B1354 just west of Aylsham. Signposted from the A140
(Cromer road).

The original medieval manor house went through many changes
before Sir Henry Hobart, Chief Justice to James I, had it rebuilt
in the early 17th century. The house is a gorgeous sight as you
approach across the gardens.

The house contains some magnificent formal rooms, with fine
furniture and paintings. The Long Gallery is especially worthy of
note due to its ornate plaster ceiling and a very extensive library of
about 12000 volumes. The Peter the Great room is also remarkable
since it contains a tapestry of the Russian ruler, presented to the
2nd Earl of Buckinghamshire by Catherine the Great. There are
also portraits by Gainsborough of the Earl and his wife.

There are excellent walks in the parkland and along the lake,
and a picnic area. You can buy a permit to fish in the lake.

The self-service restaurant is alongside the main courtyard and
has several high chairs and a children's menu. As well as a range
of snacks, hot and cold dishes are available at lunchtimes; they
include soups, casseroles, vegetarian dishes and a good selection
of salads. The prices range from £2 to £5 and on Sundays a traditional roast is available for around £6.

Open: House from April to October 1pm to 5pm, closed Monday
and Thursday (shop open 12pm to 5pm); Park open all year from
dawn to dusk; Plant Centre open daily 10am to 5pm
Charges: adults £4.90; children £2.40 (1993 prices)

Baby changing: two facilities
Ⓟ ample

CAMBRIDGE, CAMBS
Ⓡ BROWNS, 23 Trumpington Street,
Tel: 0223 461 655.

Part of a small chain of restaurants (see the entries for Bristol, Oxford and Brighton), this is a huge building opposite the Fitzwilliam Museum. We were told that it was once the casualty department of the old Addenbrookes Hospital. It has the familiar and effective decor of cream walls, bentwood chairs, overhead fans, Edwardian mirrors and converted gas lights.

It is a cheerful place which offers an excellent range of food to suit most palates, including young ones. If you need to change a baby there is a mother and baby room with good facilities and there are plenty of high chairs.

We should warn you that parking is difficult in Cambridge, as it is, strangely, in Oxford. So it is best to park your car in a public car park and enjoy the sights on foot.

✕ £2–10: spaghetti, steak & mushroom & Guinness pie, toasted olive bread with sun-dried tomatoes, pasta with various sauces, roast pork ribs, fisherman's pie
Children: own menu, half portions
Open 11am to 11.30pm (from 12 on Sunday). Licensed
No smoking in part of restaurant. Access/AmEx/Visa
Ⓟ meters and own car park

CAMBRIDGE, CAMBS
Ⓡ HOBBS PAVILION RESTAURANT, Park Terrace
Tel: 0223 67480. Right on Parker's Piece, and alongside the
University Arms Hotel.

The restaurant is housed in a brick pavilion which was opened by
Jack Hobbs himself in 1930 and faces Parker's Piece where the
maestro learned his cricket. Its origins are clearly apparent inside
and, under its high ceiling, the restaurant is attractively furnished
with pine tables, a dresser and old advertising signs (Wills's Gold
Flake, Kops Crisps, Sunlight Soap etc.).

The back room is just as appealing, and especially so to cricket
lovers with its photographs of pre-war cricketers, cigarette cards of
cricketers and portraits of Ranjit Sinjhi and of Hobbs, whose career
is encapsulated on a wooden plaque.

Amid such sporting nostalgia one must remember that this is a
restaurant where you can eat salads and soup but the restaurant
concentrates on a very full range of pancakes, savoury and sweet.
The fixed price menu at just under £9 for three courses is excellent
value, or you can have two courses at lunchtime for under £6. All
the food is made, on site, by the owners, and includes a vegan
menu; even the ice cream is homemade and, as well as the ever-
popular vanilla, includes flavours such as white chocolate, and
honey and lavender.

There is a small terrace outside with a few tables and children
have the whole of Parker's Piece on which to romp – the perimeter
measures nearly a mile. The restaurant has some lavatories and a
baby might be attended to there.

✕ £2–7: pancakes – Dijon chicken, black pudding & mash &
apple, hot & sweet lamb, cyclists (steak, mash, spinach and egg),
maple syrup, etc
Children: half portions
Open Tue to Sat 12pm to 2.30pm & 7pm to 10pm (Thurs dinner
starts 8.30pm); closed mid-Aug to mid-Sept, Christmas and Easter,
Sun and Mon
No credit cards accepted. Licensed
No smoking in half the restaurant
Ⓟ not easy, street parking only

NR CAMBRIDGE, CAMBS
Ⓛ WIMPOLE HALL, PARK AND HOME FARM
Tel: 0223 207 257.
Off the A14 south-west of Cambridge and near junction 12 of
the M11.

Rudyard Kipling's daughter, Elsie Bambridge, bequeathed this fine
18th-century mansion, a dominant sight in the flat landscape. Mrs
Bambridge had spent much of her life restoring the house which
with its surroundings adds up to an interesting day out.

The focal points of the house are the famous library which was
built by Lord Harley to contain his huge collection of books and
prints, which were later given to the British Museum; and the
yellow drawing room designed by Sir John Soane. The house is
not suitable for prams and pushchairs, but baby slings are provided.

The grounds amount to about 3000 acres and have been remodelled many times, particularly by the ubiquitous Capability Brown
and by Humphrey Repton. There are splendid walks to be done,
while the children can enjoy an adventure playground. Waggon
rides are laid on every half hour and start from the Stable Courtyard, and there are many animals to be seen at the Home Farm,
including a children's corner.

Food and drinks are made available in the Stables Kitchen, at
the Home Farm and in the superbly decorated restaurant in the
Hall. Plenty of high chairs are provided and there is an excellent
range of meals and snacks on offer.

Open: 26 March to 30 October every day except Monday and
Friday, hall from 1pm to 5pm; farm from 10.30am to 5pm
Charges: adults £6; children £2.50
Baby changing: mother and baby room in the Stables
Ⓟ ample

NR CAMBRIDGE, CAMBS
ⓅⓇ THE PLOUGH, Fen Ditton
Tel: 02205 3264.
Off the B1047 by the river.

The Plough has an idyllic position by the River Cam and from the
terrace and the large, grassy garden you can enjoy the peace and

tranquillity of the scene. The occasional college boat will row by and you can glance up from your refreshments to check their style.

The pub is now a part of the Brewers Fayre chain, and a fine range of facilities is offered for the family. High chairs are made available, there is a splendid high-tech play unit in the garden, a little playpen with toys and a blackboard in the eating area and space to change babies in the toilet areas. A play leader is in attendance during several afternoons a week and will keep the children amused while the adults relax.

The open-plan bar and restaurant has been designed on two levels and there are good views of the river and the gardens from the wide windows. It is a comfortable and well-organized place, attractively furnished and decorated, and has the great merit of offering reasonably priced food and a good choice of real ales.

✗ (11.30am to 10pm, from noon on Sundays) £2–8: smoked trout, fish pie, sirloin steak, vegetable crumble, chicken masala
Children: own menu
⏥ Ale: Boddington's, Flowers and guest beer
Ⓟ lots

CASTLE ACRE, NR KINGS LYNN, NORFOLK
Ⓟ OSTRICH INN, Castle Acre
Tel: 0760 755 398.
Off the A1065 three miles north of Swaffham.

In a small and quiet village, you will find this splendid pub, built of brick and flint with a flat front. Its origins lie back in the 16th century. There's a lovely feel to the pub, with its large and unfussy bar, and a notable feature is the large brick-built open fireplace.

It is dwarfed, however, by the fireplace in the family room; it is in the same style and soars high into the vaulted roof. This is a most attractive and spacious room, with a wall at one end which is made of various types of stone and brick. It was once the kitchen, and opens on to the garden.

The garden is quite a large, grassy area, mostly enclosed with flint walls, and has a vegetable patch at the far end. There are bench tables on the lawn, and some caged birds and a few rabbits at the side.

There is an interesting selection of meals available every day – mostly cold food at lunchtimes, and hot in the evenings.

The village is well worth a visit to see the Norman castle and the medieval priory.

✖ (12pm to 2pm & 7.30pm to 10.30pm) £1–8: omelettes, burgers, salads, trout, seafood platter, steaks
Children: own menu, half portions
🍺 Ale: Greene King
ℙ own car park

CASTLE HEDINGHAM, ESSEX
ℙ BELL INN, 10 St James Street
Tel: 0787 60350.
On the B1058.

This splendid 16th-century pub is in the main street of an attractive village with a notably well-preserved Norman castle. The large bar has exposed brick walls, and a multitude of wooden beams and pillars. It is well furnished with easy chairs and wooden tables. Families are welcome in several rooms, including a little a room between the two bars, which looks on to a small terrace. There is also a very pleasant no smoking room where families can settle down for food and drink.

The large walled garden is more like an orchard with shady trees, bench tables, a couple of swings and a croquet pitch. A good place to relax on a summer day.

✖ (12pm to 2pm & 7pm to 10pm, not Mon evenings) £2–7: smoked prawns, mussels in garlic, steak & Guinness pie, sirloin steak, liver & bacon with apple
Children: half portions
🍺 Ale: Greene King
ℙ own car park

COCKFIELD, SUFFOLK
Ⓡ THATCHERS RESTAURANT, Cross Green
Tel: 0284 828 246.
On the A1141 north of Lavenham.

You will easily spot this restaurant by the road side. It is a lovely sight; as the name tells you it has a fine thatched roof over pink-washed walls, with windows and shutters smartly painted white. The front of the 16th-century building is a blaze of colour, with tubs of flowers and climbing plants on show.

There are a few tables and chairs by the entrance and a delightful garden at the back. A long lawn is fringed with trees, a very inviting spot on a warm summer's day.

The inside is just as appealing. A low-ceilinged lounge with a bar has a comfortable sofa and plush chairs, and this leads into the restaurant. This is on two levels, with oak pillars and beams, and brick fireplaces at either end. It all looks very smart.

The set lunches are excellent value, and this includes a traditional Sunday lunch at around £12 (£7 for children). There is a good range of bar snacks, too. Morning coffee and afternoon teas are also served.

At present there are no special facilities to change a baby, but the lavatories are spacious.

✕ BAR SNACKS £1–6: prawn salad, steak & kidney pie, plaice & chips, roast chicken & chips;
LUNCH two courses £10: pate, poached salmon;
DINNER £16: fresh asparagus, fillet of lamb, pudding or cheese
Children: half portions
Open 10am to 2pm & 7pm to 9pm; 10am to 5pm Sunday; closed Monday
Access/Visa. Licensed
No smoking at some tables
Ⓟ own car park

DUXFORD, CAMBS
Ⓛ IMPERIAL WAR MUSEUM, Duxford
Tel: 0223 835 000.
South of Cambridge on the A505 and close to junction 10 of the M11.

The museum lies fifty miles from London and was a key airfield in the defence of Britain. During the Battle of Britain, Spitfires and Hurricanes defended the skies under the leadership of the legendary Douglas Bader. Later, American Thunderbolts were based at Duxford.

These famous aircraft are well represented in the museum along with a whole range from the First World War onwards, including a Bristol fighter, Avro Anson, Lancaster, Gloster Meteor, Vampire, Hunter, Canberra, Dakota, Vulcan, the ill-fated TSR-2 and a prototype of the Concorde.

The museum also has a fine collection of tanks, trucks and guns. The museum undertakes an extensive programme of restoration and there are always a number of aircraft and other vehicles being worked on in full view of visitors.

There is everything here for the aircraft enthusiast, including a full programme of flying displays when the historic aircraft take to the skies again. Pleasure flights in a 1930s Dragon Rapide are available at summer weekends, weather permitting.

You can spend many an interesting hour here and you can sustain yourself with a meal or a snack in the beautifully decorated 1940s-style self-service restaurant. There are high chairs available and a picnic area.

Open: every day except Christmas and New Year, 10am to 6pm from mid-March to mid-October; until 4pm otherwise
Charges: adults £5.80; children £2.90; OAPs £4; under 5s free (1993 prices)
Baby changing: functional mother and baby room near Hangar 1
Ⓟ ample

ELSWORTH, CAMBS
Ⓟ GEORGE & DRAGON, Boxworth Road
Tel: 0954 267 236.
Off the B1040 south of St Ives.

In a small farming village, with medieval origins, this 17th-century pub shows a modest exterior to the world, but inside you will find a delightful inn of several rooms.

The large bar area has dark panelled walls and lovely oak settles gathered at one end around a fireplace with a long wooden mantle. The landlady's collection of copper kettles cluster on the ceiling beams and a blackboard shows the daily 'specials'.

The separate children's room is really splendid, spacious and light and well-furnished with cane furniture, so that the parents can relax as well – as the owners pointed out. The owners have quite rightly declared this a no-smoking area. This opens out to a stretch of grassy garden, with two patio areas, and there are swings, a slide, and a climbing frame.

A very enterprising range of bar food is always available; and there is now also a handsomely furnished restaurant which is open most lunchtimes and evenings.

All in all, a splendid pub for all the family.

✕ (12pm to 2pm & 7pm to 10pm) £2–10: trout & salad, coquilles St Jacques, chicken Normandy, steaks, Hungarian goulash
Children: own menu
⊕ Ale: Boddington's, Flowers, Greene King, Tetley's and guest beer
Ⓟ own car park

ELY, CAMBS
Ⓡ OLD FIRE ENGINE HOUSE, 25 St Mary's Street
Tel: 0353 662 582.
In the town centre – on the A10.

Hard by the superb cathedral, you will find this handsome 18th-century building which, at the turn of the century, really did house the town's fire engine, and was originally built as a farmhouse.

Its attractive rooms now house an art gallery on the upper floors as well as a restaurant, and the dining room, a pleasant, well-proportioned room with a tiled floor and good oak tables, looks out to a delightful walled garden, with a smooth lawn and several shady apple trees. On summery days, this is a delightful place to have a meal.

The cooking is English in emphasis and local ingredients are used whenever possible. If you need to change or feed a baby, there is a bathroom and a sitting room upstairs.

✗ LUNCH (12.30pm to 2pm) £15: salmon & mushroom au gratin, casserole of rabbit, apple pie & cream
DINNER (7.30pm to 9pm) £17: kipper paté, roast leg of lamb, syllabub
Children: half portions
Open 10.30am to 9pm
Closed public holidays, 2 weeks from 24 Dec, Sunday evenings
Access/Visa. No music
🍺 Ale: Adnams
Ⓟ at side and on street

FELBRIGG, NR CROMER, NORFOLK
Ⓛ FELBRIGG HALL, Felbrigg
Tel: 0263 837 444.
On the B1436 to the south-west of Cromer.

The original medieval manor house was replaced in the early 17th century by a new building and the Jacobean south front still survives. Over the next century or so extensions were made and the orangery was built in 1705; the last major additions were made in the 19th century. The house was left to the National Trust in 1969.

The original 18th-century furniture and pictures and a superb library are the notable features of the house and new rooms have been opened in the Servants' Hall, Estate Office and the Old Kitchen. It is surrounded by lovely parkland and woods with several miles of footpaths. The walled garden is worth a browse and contains a wonderful dovecote.

Both the Park Restaurant and the Turret Tearoom provide high chairs. The more informal Tearoom supplies a range of snacks (ploughman's, pasties, quiche) at prices up to £6; while the restaurant has more expensive lunch dishes, both hot and cold, from £5 upwards.

Open: 27 March to 31 October, on Monday, Wednesday, Thursday, Saturday and Sunday; House – 1pm to 5pm; Garden – 11am to 5pm
Charges: adults £4.40; children half price
Baby changing: well-equipped parent and baby room

HAIL WESTON, CAMBS
Ⓟ THE ROYAL OAK, Hail Weston
Tel: 0480 472 527.
Off the A45 north of St Neots.

This fine 17th-century pub is always in pristine order, inside and out. Situated in a small village, it is painted white, with dormer windows set in a steeply pitched thatched roof; and cheerful window boxes and baskets of flowers adorn the walls. The inside is very much in keeping with oak pillars and splendid beams and a huge inglenook fireplace – a smart and agreeable bar.

Families are welcome in their own room off the bar; it has several tables and bar billiards. Two high chairs are provided. There is also a restaurant which is open in the evenings and on Sunday lunchtimes.

The garden is safely enclosed and the large lawn has plenty of tables and chairs with sun umbrellas. Behind a row of firs, the play area has swings, a slide, a climbing frame and a seesaw. There is also a patio area with several tables. The sensible landlord prohibits dogs from the garden.

✕ (12pm to 2.30pm & 7pm to 10pm, not Sun pm and Mon pm)
£2–5: scampi, plaice & chips, vegetable curry & rice, turkey Kiev, burgers
Children: own menu
🍺 Ale: Adnams, Wells and guest beer
Ⓟ own car park

HARWICH, ESSEX
Ⓡ THE PIER AT HARWICH, The Quay
Tel: 0255 241 212.
On the quayside, in the town centre.

This stately listed building on the quayside dates from 1874, and contains a small hotel on the upper floors and two excellent restaurants. If you are catching a ferry, make sure that you have time to sample some fine and fresh fish at The Pier.

On the ground floor, you will find the bar with plenty of comfortable seats; the Ha'penny Pier restaurant is alongside and is very well suited to the family budget since a main course of fish and chips costs just over £5 and the children's menu of soup, fish and chips and ice-cream costs just over £4 and is splendid value for money.

Both these rooms have bold and cheerful murals and so has a part of the upstairs restaurant, which is divided into two areas; and the second room has smart pine tables and some wonderful original travel posters. Both rooms have wonderful views out to sea.

✗ *Ha'penny Pier* (12 to 2pm and 6pm to 9.30pm) £2–7: smoked mackeral paté, cod, haddock or plaice & chips, broccoli and cream cheese bake, supreme of chicken;
LUNCH £9, 2 courses: prawns mornay, Dover sole meuniere;
DINNER £16: Galia melon, baked Scottish salmon, fresh raspberries and cream
Children: own menu, half portions
Open all year. Access/Visa
⊞ Ale: Adnams
Ⓟ own car park

HEVINGHAM, NORFOLK
ⒽⓅ MARSHAM ARMS HOTEL, Holt Road
Tel: 0605 48268.
On the B1149 north of Norwich.

This appealing inn, smartly decorated under its tiled roof, stands in the countryside about seven miles from Norwich and was originally a hostel for farm labourers, built in the 19th century. The wooden beams and large, open fireplace survive from the original design.

The building has been extended over the years especially to provide better facilities for families who are welcome to use a spacious and nicely furnished room away from the bar. It is good to report that it is a no-smoking area. There is an excellent range of food on offer, and a good choice of real ales.

There is a terrace with tables and chairs and wooden benches – a pleasant place to sit in the sun with a meal or a drink. Alongside there is a children's play area, which is surrounded by trees.

Eight comfortable rooms are situated in a smart single storey block alongside the pub. These are spacious rooms, equipped with either twin or double beds and sofa beds. They can accommodate a family of four without any strain and offer very good value for money.

The Marsharm Arms, out in the countryside but so close to Norwich, provides excellent all-round facilities for families.

Nearby: The Broads are quite close and it is not too long a drive to reach the coast where two quiet and sandy beaches can be recommended – at Sea Palling and Happisburgh. This stretch of coast is, mercifully, undeveloped. There are many tourist attractions within reach: Norfolk Wildlife Park, Thrigby Hall wildlife gardens, Blickling Hall, and on the north Norfolk coast, Felbrigg Hall, the Norfolk Shire Horse Centre and the North Norfolk railway.

✕ BAR SNACKS (12pm to 2pm & 6pm to 10pm) £1–12: lasagne, fried scampi, steaks, whole lemon sole, smoked chicken;
DINNER (6pm to 10pm) £15: smoked mackerel, chicken supreme, pudding or cheese
Children: own menu, half portions
£ medium
Children: free up to 5 years; £8 from 5 to 14 years
Facilities: 2 cots and 3 high chairs; 2 lines for baby listening
8 rooms, all family. Open all year
Ale: Adnams, Bass, Greene King
Access/AmEx/Visa
P own car park

HORRINGER, SUFFOLK
ℙ BEEHIVE, Horringer
Tel: 0284 735 260.
On the A143, just south of Bury St Edmunds.

The simple flintstone front of this 18th-century pub gives no clue to the roominess of the interior. There are several rooms, well-proportioned and pleasantly intimate under the low ceilings, gathered around a central bar area; they include two delightful small rooms at one side, with wood panelling and excellent oak and pine furniture, and families with children are welcome there.

There is a wide range of interesting food at the Beehive, and new dishes appear on the menu (and on the blackboard of daily specials) at regular intervals. There is an enterprising wine list as well. If the weather is warm you might enjoy the food on the smartly furnished terrace, or in the immaculate garden. These areas are floodlit in the evenings. There is a small farm next door and children are welcome to visit the various animals: sheep, geese, horses, chickens and ducks.

✗ (12pm to 2pm & 7pm to 9.45pm, not Sun pm) £2–8: scrambled eggs with smoked salmon, taramasalata with pitta bread, Basque-style hot pot of pork, omelette Arnold Bennett, chicken mousse
Children: half portions
⌳ Ale: Greene King
ℙ own car park

KING'S LYNN, NORFOLK
ℙ FARMERS ARMS, King's Lynn
Tel: 0553 675 566.
At the intersection of the A148 and the A149 just east of King's Lynn.

The pub is part of the Knights Hill Village and is constructed from the old stables and a grain store; the original carrstone walls make an attractive frame for a very well-designed and roomy pub. There is a restaurant at one end, with brick and stone walls and a high vaulted roof. Adjoining this is another eating area, and then a long bar area with loads of wooden tables and chairs scattered about.

Families are, of course, welcome in the restaurant, and high chairs are available, but if you merely require a drink or a snack, there are a couple of delightful alcove rooms off the bar, and the hayloft on the first floor may also be used.

Outside, there is a big grassy area with a number of bench tables – a bit noisy because a main road is nearby, but pleasant enough on summer days.

We were most impressed with the care that has gone into this project – and it is a particularly useful place for families since the pub is open throughout the day (Monday to Saturday) and food is always available.

✕ (11am to 10pm) £2–10: chilli burgers, lemon sole, fisherman's bake, steaks, spaghetti Bolognese
Children: own menu
🍺 Ale: Adnams, Bass, Ruddles
Ⓟ own car park

LAVENHAM, SUFFOLK
🏨📖THE GREAT HOUSE, Market Place
Tel: 0787 247 431.
In the centre of town.

The town has so many beautifully preserved mediaeval buildings; over 300 are listed as being of historic significance. The Great House was built in the 14th and 15th centuries, and acquired a new front when it was renovated in the 18th century. Its other claim to fame is that it was the home of the writer Stephen Spender in the 1950s.

It is now a delightful hotel and restaurant, which has been decorated and furnished with great style and taste. As the manager told us, the rooms have 'cheerfully out of kilter floors and well-worn antiques'. The four rooms justify their description as suites, since they all have sitting areas. Two of them have separate and spacious sitting rooms, and the newest suite has two double bedrooms and a lounge.

You are offered excellent value for money here, and that goes for the food as well as the accommodation. The menu has an enterprising choice of dishes, and you can have a snack for as little as £2. The three course Sunday lunch costs around £15 (£9 for children). The whole family, from babies to grandmothers, are welcomed here, in the French tradition: which is not surprising since the management is French. We were not surprised to learn that the hotel won a 'value for money' award a couple of years ago.

At the back of the hotel there is a paved terrace, with plenty of space. It is surrounded by flowers and greenery and can be left open to the weather or completely covered, at the top and the sides, with canvas. This is a good solution to the problems of the English climate but plans are afoot to install a conservatory here.

Below the terrace there is a walled garden which has the merit of being a sun trap. It is in two sections, both lawned; at one end there is a barbecue, and at the other some swings for the children.

Nearby: The town is a splendid place in which to browse, as are the neighbouring ones of Long Melford and Sudbury. The children will enjoy Clare Castle Country Park and the adults will enjoy Cavendish Manor Vineyards. You can also reach Ickworth, Gainsborough's House in Sudbury, Blakenham Woodlands Garden and the Colne Valley Railway with ease.

✕ BAR SNACKS (12pm to 2pm) £2–8: roast rack of lamb, poached salmon, tagliatelle with salmon and basil, lamb cutlets, mixed grill brochette;
DINNER (7.30pm to 10.30pm, Tues to Sat) £15: cheese fondue, roast partridge, pudding or cheese
Children: half portions
£ high

Best Bargain Break: £48 per person per night – dinner, b&b
Children: free up to 3 years; £10 from 4 to 12 years; £15 thereafter
Facilities: 2 cots and 3 high chairs; baby listening system
4 rooms, 3 family. Access/Visa
Open all year, except January
Ⓟ at front

NR LOWESTOFT, SUFFOLK
Ⓛ PLEASUREWOOD HILLS AMERICAN THEME PARK
Tel: 0502 508 200.
Off the A12 just north of Lowestoft.

This theme park sets its cap at the family market and succeeds admirably in providing entertainment for young children, teenagers and even adults. There are several 'white knuckle' rides including the Waveswinger, the Star Ride Enterprise, the Tempest and the Rattlesnake Coaster. Younger children will enjoy the enchanted Parrot Show, the Fun Factory and the sealion show. There are plenty of gentler rides and playgrounds, too, in the junior playland and in the junior carousel. There is a boating lake and a miniature railway and a Western train, which gives you a good view of the whole park, as does the chair lift. The Superhuman Circus has clowns, jugglers and acrobats.

There is a wide choice of food available at Peppers Carriage Diner (burgers), Capone's Coffee Shop, the Hungry Bear Pavilion (burgers, fish and chips), plus pizzas, fried chicken, hot dogs and ice cream. An excellent facility is the barbecue area where you can buy steaks, chicken and sausages and grill them yourselves. It's a great way to have a picnic. High chairs are available in Peppers and Capone's, and there are lots of baby buggies at the front entrance.

Open: Easter and weekends in April and early May; then 15 May to 19 September, 10am to 5pm or 6pm, depending on the season
Charges: adults and children £8.75; OAPs £5; under 4s free
Baby changing: a separate mother and baby room near the entrance
Ⓟ ample

MUNDESLEY, NORFOLK
Ⓗ THORNLEA, 51 High Street
Tel: 0263 720 598.
In the centre of the village.

This is a semi-detached Edwardian house, which has been well modernized and is only minutes from the sandy beaches. It has the advantage of a large, grassy garden, which faces south and has several facilities to amuse families: a badminton set, a netball stand, boules which can be used on the lawn, and even a football or two is available.

The owners of this guest house offer unpretentious accommodation at a reasonable price. The family room has a double bed plus two bunk beds and there is another spacious double bedroom which can easily accommodate a cot. A bathroom is shared between the three bedrooms. The food is cooked on the spot with fresh ingredients; there are no microwaved dishes here.

Nearby: Mundesley is an unspoilt place, and that is one of the charms of this part of Norfolk, but there is plenty to do and see. The beach offers safe bathing, and good fishing can also be had locally. It's also a great area for walkers and nature lovers; and for golfers, too, with a course in the village and Cromer and Sheringham fairly close. There is a variety of things to do and see in the neighbourhood: Felbrigg Hall and its fine gardens; the Shire Horse Centre near Cromer; the North Norfolk Railway; Blickling Hall; and the Norfolk Wildlife Park north of East Dereham.

✗ DINNER (6pm to 7pm) £8
Children: half portions
£ low
Children: free up to 2 years; half price to 12 years
Facilities: 2 cots and 2 high chairs; and a baby alarm
3 rooms, 1 family Open all year (except Christmas)
No credit cards. Unlicensed
No smoking in bedrooms. No music
Ⓟ own car park

NR NORWICH, NORFOLK
PR VILLAGE INN, Little Melton
Tel: 0603 810 210
Off the B1108 west of Norwich.

This very large pub and restaurant is fully equipped to deal with families and one of its great advantages is that food is available all day and every day right through to 10 o'clock at night.

The huge bar and restaurant area does not overwhelm you with its size because it is broken up by alcoves and wooden screens; and the wooden tables, padded settles and the colourful carpet give a very smart and welcoming appearance to the interior.

The family room is also sizeable and has plenty of tables and chairs and a fine array of play equipment for the children; slides, a lego table, a rocking horse and a blackboard and balloons for very small children. Outside there is an excellent play unit and a changing table is provided in the Ladies toilet area.

When a fine selection of real ales, reasonably priced wines and an uncomplicated menu are added to the comprehensive facilities, this adds up to an excellent (and very popular) family pub.

✗ (11.30am to 10pm, from noon on Sundays) £2-£8: smoked trout, fish pie, sirloin steak, vegetable crumble, chicken masala
Children: own menu
⌘ Ale: Boddington, Flowers and guest beer (e.g. Wadworth's, Woodforde's, Marstons)
P lots

NOWTON, NR BURY ST EDMUNDS, SUFFOLK
H HIGH GREEN HOUSE, Nowton
Tel: 0284 386 293.
Off the A134 south of Bury St Edmunds; the brochure has a clear map.

The original part of this remarkably interesting house was built early in the 16th century and the spacious sitting room displays many of the characteristics of Tudor building: wood and plaster walls, a beamed ceiling and a huge brick fireplace. It is a delightful room and is well matched by the dining room alongside. The other half of the house was added in Victorian times.

All the bedrooms have their own bathrooms and the one on the ground floor has been redesigned to make a small family suite. There are two more attractive twin-bedded rooms on the upper floor, both with low ceilings and old wooden doors, and the views across the rolling Suffolk countryside will soothe the mind. Finally, there is a magnificent room with ancient wooden pillars and beams and a fine four-poster bed. You walk through a narrow corridor to a spacious bathroom which has the upper part of the Tudor chimney still in place.

The house is surrounded by a large, lawned garden. There is an old covered well in the front garden, and apple trees to one side. The lawns are walled or fenced, but there is a pond at the side, so the children must be careful. But there is masses of space to play, and the house is surrounded by open countryside, where there are pleasant walks.

If you want some peace and quiet in unusual surroundings you should head for High Green House; the prices are very reasonable too.

Nearby: This is good fishing country, and if you are in the mood for sightseeing, Ickworth Mansion is nearby; as is Norton Tropical Bird Gardens, and West Stow Anglo-Saxon Village. The delightful old towns of Lavenham and Long Melford, Cavendish Manor Vineyards and Clare Castle Country Park are a short drive away.

✗ DINNER (7.30pm to 9pm) £13
Children: high teas
£ low
Best Bargain Break: £80 per person 3 nights – dinner, b&b
Children: babies free; 20 per cent discount from 2 to 12 years
Facilities: 2 cots and 1 high chair, and baby listening
4 rooms, 2 family. No credit cards accepted
Open all year. No music
Ⓟ ample

SNETTISHAM, NORFOLK
Ⓟⓡ ROSE AND CROWN INN, Old Church Road
Tel: 0485 541 382.
Just off the A149 on the north side of the village.

This ancient pub, of 14th-century origin, presents a lively face to the world, with a wealth of bright flowers adorning its front. You wouldn't guess that there is so much space inside, but there are three excellent bars, an attractive restaurant and a very large family room.

The front bar is a delightful room with heavy black beams, which have an array of cooper's and carpenter's tools, a tiled floor and a huge open fireplace. Another smaller bar leads through to the pleasantly decorated restaurant; and there is a very comfortable back bar with a large brick fireplace.

Off the back bar is a really splendid family room. A lounge area leads up to a very spacious eating and drinking area which also contains a barbecue. The room is light and bright, with a wooden vaulted ceiling, tile floors and bentwood furniture. French windows open on to a spacious terrace with plenty of bench tables and an immaculately lawned garden, safely enclosed by a wall. To one side there is a large play area under a weeping willow. There are swings, a wooden hut and a wooden Wendy house, and a safe surface of wood chippings.

It is good to report that the Ladies has a surface on which a baby could be changed.

✗ (12pm to 2pm & 6.30pm to 10pm) £2–12: smoked salmon, steaks, savoury pancakes, leek & Stilton bake, mixed grill
Children: own menu, half portions
Open all year. Access/Visa
🍺 Ale: Adnams, Bass, Greene King, Woodforde's
Ⓟ own car park

STONHAM ASPEL, SUFFOLK
Ⓡ STONHAM BARNS, Pettaugh Road
Tel: 0449 711 755.
On the A1120 east of its junction with the A140.

What was originally a garden centre has expanded apace in the last few years and is now a crafts centre with shops selling farm products, flowers, clothing, pine furniture and antiques, picture frames and so on. There is even a golf range at one end of the centre, and a pets corner where children can, under supervision, feed the animals.

The restaurant has two eating areas; the smaller one, near the self-service counter, is nicely furnished with pine tables and there is a spacious conservatory alongside. All the food is freshly made on the premises and is offered at reasonable prices.

If a baby needs a change of nappy, facilities are provided in the Ladies.

✕ £1–5: curried egg mayonnaise, beans on toast, omelettes, all day breakfast, filled jacked potatoes
Children: own menu, half portions
Open 10am to 5.30pm (4.30pm in winter). Closed at Christmas
Access/Visa
Ⓟ lots

THORNHAM, NORFOLK
ⒽⓅ LIFEBOAT INN, Ship Lane
Tel: 048 526 236.
Turn off the A149 towards the church and take the first turning on the left.

This is one of our favourites, a cracking old pub in a lovely part of Norfolk, and across the flat landscape you can see the sea in the distance. The attractive interior has everything a rural English inn should have: low ceilings, sloping floors, wooden settles and gnarled pillars.

Several rooms cluster around the bar and families should head for the spacious conservatory, where an old vine covers the glass roof; it looks out to a walled patio with bench tables. There is also a small snug, which can take a dozen or so people, and there are tables outside the pub too.

It is good to report that some of the outbuildings have been converted to form a hotel and the atmosphere is just as appealing as in the pub itself. There is an open fire in the high-ceilinged entrance hall and alongside there is a stylish and spacious dining room. We looked at several of the bedrooms which are spacious and decorated and furnished to very high standards. Several of them have splendid views out to sea.

An interesting choice of homemade food, which changes seasonally, is served both in the bar and the restaurant. This is an excellent place for families since it is open all day every day during the summer.

✗ BAR SNACKS (12pm to 2.15pm & 6.30pm to 10pm) £2–10: fish pie, chargrilled darne of salmon, chicken & ham pie, sirloin steak, grilled sole
DINNER (7pm to 10pm) £18: gravadlax, rosette of lamb, pudding and cheese
Children: own menu, half portions
£ high
Best Bargain Break: £90 per person, 2 nights – dinner, b&b
Children: free
Facilities: cots and high chairs provided; baby listening service
13 rooms, 3 family
🍺 Ale: Adnams, Greene King, and guest beers
Open all year. No music
Ⓟ own car park

WIX, NR MANNINGTREE, ESSEX
Ⓗ NEW FARM HOUSE, Spinnels Lane
Tel: 0255 870 365.
The village is off the A120 west of Harwich. In Wix take the road to Mistley and Bradfield and there is a sign to New Farm House.

This large modern farmhouse, at the hub of the fifty acres of arable farm, is very well equipped to welcome families, especially if they are using the nearby Harwich ferries. Of the twelve rooms, five are family sized; we looked at several of them and they were spacious and comfortable. The six bedrooms in the annexe all have their own bathrooms and the family room there has a double bed and two bunk beds. As well as a large and comfortable lounge with a television, there is a quiet lounge where guests can read or write. There are facilities to make tea and coffee in all the rooms, and a small kitchen which guests can use.

The garden is not only large but immaculately maintained, with smooth lawns, a pond and a rockery. There is plenty of space to enjoy and, even better for youngsters, there is a large grassy paddock with swings and a slide, goalposts and masses of room for other games.

Nearby: Wix is surrounded by open farming country and there are delightful walks to be done, perhaps to the lovely Mistley, which has the largest population of mute swans in Britain. Castle House, the home of Alfred Munnings whose paintings are on show there, is at nearby Dedham, while Flatford was the home of John Constable, and children can feed the ducks at Flatford Mills. Other local attractions include Beth Chatto Gardens, St. Osyth's Priory, the wildlife sanctuary at Fingringhoe Wick, Abberton reservoir which is a great haven for birds of all varieties, and the zoo near Colchester.

✕ DINNER (6.30pm to 7.30pm) £9: soup, roast beef & Yorkshire pudding, fruit flan, cheese
Children: half portions
£ low
Children: free up to 2 years; from £4 to £15 according to age
Facilities: 3 cots and 3 high chairs; baby listening system
12 rooms, 5 family. Open all year
Access/Visa. Unlicensed
P own car park

East Midlands

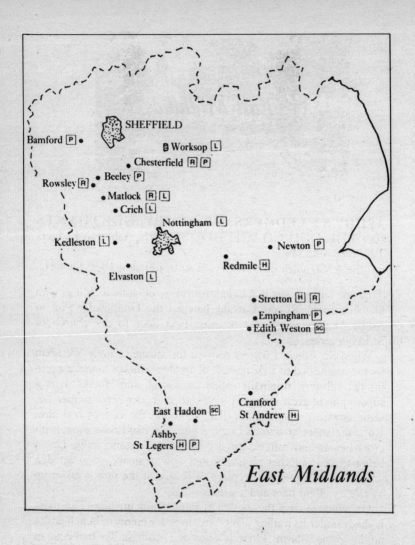

Bamford P •

SHEFFIELD

B Worksop L

• Chesterfield R P

Rowsley R • • Beeley P

• Matlock R L

• Crich L

Nottingham L

Kedleston L •

• Newton P

Redmile H

• Elvaston L

• Stretton H R

• Empingham P

• Edith Weston SC

East Haddon SC

Cranford
St Andrew H

Ashby
St Legers H P

East Midlands

ASHBY ST LEDGERS, NR RUGBY, NORTHANTS
H P THE OLD COACH HOUSE INN, Ashby St Ledgers
Tel: 0788 890 349.
Off the A361 north of Daventry, close to Junction 18 of the M1.

This fine old pub sits in a delightful village of stone buildings with
thatched roofs. Robert Catesby hatched the Gunpowder Plot in
Ashby Manor, an elegant mansion next door to the church of
St Leodegarius.

When Sir Edwin Lutyens restyled the village, a stone Victorian
facade was added to a farmhouse of an older vintage to make a pub
for the villagers, originally called the Coach and Horses. It is a
superb pub of great character with several areas where families can
settle down to enjoy the excellent food and the various real ales.
Up some stairs at one end of the pub is a handsome room with
cross beams and rafters, wood panelling and stone walls. Down
below there is another pleasant room with an alcove, good wooden
tables and a large open fireplace. The rest of the pub is taken up
by two excellent bars and a games room.

On summer days the garden is wonderfully inviting. The patio
is shady under its trailing plants and there are plenty of bench tables
on the spacious lawn. There is a new and business-like barbecue in
the garden and people with young children can use the newly
installed parents and baby room. By the coming spring a children's
garden, safely enclosed, will be ready for action, and the village
playground is next door.

We looked at all six bedrooms and were impressed by the high

standards of decoration and the excellent furniture (pine in general).
All the bedrooms have their own bathrooms and there is a very
spacious family room with a double and two single beds; two other
rooms have sofabeds and could therefore accommodate a family of
four. A bonus is the lovely views of the surrounding countryside.

✗ SNACKS (12pm to 2pm and 6pm to 9.30pm) £2–12: smoked
trout, cold buffet, lasagne, steaks, range of vegetarian dishes
DINNER (6pm to 9.30pm) £14: Whitby scampi, rack of lamb,
pudding or cheese
Children: own menu, half portions
£ medium
Children: free up to 5 years; £7.50 thereafter
Facilities: 1 cot, 1 high chairs and booster seats; baby listening
6 rooms, 1 family. Open all year
🍺 Ale: Bateman's, Boddington's, Everard, Flowers, Jennings,
Thwaites
Access/Visa
℗ own car park

BAMFORD, DERBYSHIRE
℗ DERWENT HOTEL, Bamford
Tel: 0433 51395.
In the centre of the village, just off the A57.

This imposing country hotel, with a half-timbered façade, dates
from the late 19th century. There are several rooms off the central
bar area and the staff are clearly used to dealing with families and
welcome them.

The spacious and bright family room is adorned with bric-a-brac
and has plenty of tables, comfortable padded benches and a bay
window at one end. It is a pleasant and relaxing room, and families
are also welcome in the pleasant dining room with its pine panelling.

There is a large garden with tables and umbrellas that is walled
off from the road so the children can play in safety, and a little
terrace in front of the pub.

The pub is open throughout the day from Monday to Saturday.

✗ (12pm to 2.30pm & 7pm to 9.30pm) £2–9: cauliflower cheese,

fillet steak, halibut mornay, plaice & chips, turkey cordon bleu
Children: own menu, half portions
🍺 Ale: Boddington's, Ward's, Stone's and guests
🅿 own car park

BEELEY, DERBYSHIRE
🅿 DEVONSHIRE ARMS, Beeley
Tel: 0629 733 259.
On the B6012, north of Matlock.

An absolute beauty of a pub which nestles in a charming village
only a couple of miles from Chatsworth House and close to Haddon
Hall. Three cottages were converted in 1741 and the original thick
stone walls and mullioned windows remain; with the river meander-
ing by it is a perfect spot.

Neither will you be disappointed inside since the low ceilings
and blackened beams, flagstones and open fires confirm the age of
this splendid hostelry. The family room has a few wooden tables
and the unusual feature of a stone wishing well; beyond it there is
a food and coffee bar, where there is ample space for families since
they can also use another room upstairs away from the bar.

✖ BAR MEALS (12pm to 2.15pm & 7pm to 10pm) £2–9: devilled
whitebait, garlic chicken, haddock & chips, Barnsley chop, steak
& ale pie
Children: half portions
🍺 Ale: Black Sheep, Boddington's, Theakston's, Marston's
🅿 own car park

NR CHESTERFIELD, DERBYSHIRE
🅿🆁 HIGHWAYMAN, Baslow Road, Eastmoor
Tel: 0246 566 330.
On the A619 west of Chesterfield.

Up on the moors, four miles outside Chesterfield, this large,
recently modernized pub is a useful stopping off point for families
heading for Chatsworth House, particularly since the pub is open
throughout the day.

Great care has been taken to provide the facilities which any family would welcome. The family room itself is on two levels and has plenty of comfortable seating. There are plenty of high chairs, a baby-changing facility, a little indoor play area with toys and lego sets, and a very spacious Fun Factory with a ball pool and all sorts of diversions for the children.

There is a sizeable garden at the back of the pub which overlooks lovely countryside. Partly paved and partly lawned, the garden has a children's play area and a barbecue. An extra facility during the summer months is a bouncy castle. There is another lawned area at the front of the pub where you can sit and have a drink and a meal.

The spacious interior can cope with large numbers of families and is an agreeable place with its comfortable furniture, wood and stained glass screens, pot plants and coloured lights.

The stone pub dates back to 1620 and is mentioned as the New Inn in a Sherlock Holmes mystery. It has unrivalled views of some beautiful countryside through large picture windows.

✗ (11.30am to 10pm; from noon on Sunday) £2–8: fish dippers, roast chicken, sirloin steak, plaice & chips, vegetable crumble
Children: own menu, half portions
🍺 Ale: Boddington's, Marston's, Whitbread
Ⓟ: own car park

CRANFORD ST ANDREW, NORTHANTS
Ⓗ DAIRY FARM, Cranford
Tel: 0536 78273.
Off the A14 (A604) just east of Kettering. The farm is off the High Street of the village.

This thatched manor house, which was built in the early 17th century, is full of character. Underneath its steeply pitched roof, with its dormer windows and tall Northamptonshire chimneys, you will find charmingly furnished rooms. The comfortable lounge has a large ceiling beam and a recessed window which overlooks the garden and the dining room is just as agreeable with its inglenook fireplace. The family room has a double bed and its own bathroom, and either a cot or a single bed can be set up as well.

The bedrooms all have lovely views of the gardens and the countryside and include a very spacious room with a four-poster bed and its own en suite bathroom. There is plenty of room here for a cot or an extra bed. The stable block also houses a suite with a double room, an interconnecting twin room and a bathroom. It is a functional, no frills unit which is only rented out during the summer.

There is half an acre or so of delightful garden, with some fine mature trees, smooth lawns and a notable medieval stone dovecote; you can see the village church through the trees. The grounds are mostly enclosed and children can play in safety, and there is also a swing and a croquet lawn. Guests are welcome to wander around the farm, as long as they stay well clear of any machinery.

Nearby: This is an interesting part of the country and, apart from the pleasant walks which you can enjoy, there are many other diversions. The children will no doubt be keen to see the nearby Wicksteed Leisure Park, while Guilsborough Grange is a bit further away and has a wildlife park. Boughton House, Lamport Hall, Lilford Park, and Rockingham Castle are all within easy reach, as are Burleigh House and Rutland Water.

✗ (7.30pm) £10: celery soup, chicken casserole, trifle
Children: half portions
£ low
Children: half price under 10 years
Facilities: 1 cot and 1 high chair; baby patrol by arrangement
3 rooms, 1 family. Open all year except Christmas
No credit cards. No music
Ⓟ own car park. Unlicensed

CRICH, NR MATLOCK, DERBYSHIRE
Ⓛ NATIONAL TRAMWAY MUSEUM, Crich
Tel: 0773 852 565.
Just outside Crich village off the B5035, and about six miles south of Matlock.

Take a trip back in time and discover how they got around in pre-motor car days at this excellent tramway museum which is done in period style right down to the last detail.

There are about 50 restored electric, horse drawn and steam trams of all colours, shapes and sizes and the beauty is that you can actually travel on many of them along the museum's tramway which includes tram halts with all the authentic fittings of yesteryear.

You must even use an old penny (provided by the museum) as your fare for the ride, part of which runs along the track bed of an old narrow gauge mineral line once used to link the adjacent limestone quarries to the main railway line a couple of miles away.

The focal point of the museum, which also includes indoor static exhibitions, is a reconstructed period street complete with cobbles, Edwardian pavements and shops, all faithfully constructed to match the age when the tram reigned supreme. A spacious new exhibition hall has now been added, as has an interpretative gallery.

There is a pleasant cafeteria which serves a variety of food, including hot meals such as plaice and chips and turkey and ham pie plus the usual snacks, cakes and sandwiches. There is one high chair and baby changing facilities, including nappy vending machine, are available on request. There is no smoking in the cafeteria.

Apart from the cafeteria, you will also find a refreshment kiosk outside plus a souvenir and gift shop and there are two attractive landscaped areas with bench tables for picnics.

The whole enterprise is owned and run by the volunteer Tramway Museum Society with only limited help from outside bodies and it is a marvellous example of enterprise, and a thoroughly good place to visit.

Open: 10am to 5.30pm, early April (on certain days) to end October (until 6.30pm at weekends and bank holidays)
Charges: adults £4.20; OAPS £3.50; children £2.40; under 5s free (1993 prices)
Baby changing: facilities available in the museum's offices
P extensive

EAST HADDON, NORTHANTS
[SC] RYE HILL FARM COTTAGES, Holdenby Road
Tel: 0604 770 990.
Off the A428 north-west of Northampton.

The farm sits in delightful rolling countryside; you really can see for miles and miles and the views from the windows of the cottages give you a great sense of peace and relaxation.

The five cottages are grouped around a gravelled courtyard and were made from old barns and stables. The conversions have been done with imagination and style; the original features have been retained wherever possible and used to good effect. There are some fine old wooden beams holding up the ceilings, whose slopes and angles are particularly attractive. The use of spiral staircases in three of the cottages is a very successful feature.

Two of the cottages can sleep up to six people and two can sleep four. There is also one small single storey cottage for two people and it is suitable for disabled guests.

The cottages are very comfortably furnished and some of them contain bunk beds for children. We were impressed by the high standard of the decorations and furnishings; guests are made to feel at home, and all the equipment any cook might need is present in the kitchens, including microwave ovens and dishwashers. Boxes of toys and games are put in cottages when children are expected.

There is plenty of space for children to play in the two and a half acres which surround the smallholding and they can make friends with the many animals: goats, a pig, sheep, ducks, chickens and geese. There is a badminton net on one of the lawns, boule, a playground with swings and a climbing frame, a duck pond, a sand-pit and bicycles to borrow.

In addition, there is a playroom with plenty of toys and games, a mini snooker table, Subbuteo and a rebounder (a small version of a trampoline). On a practical note there is a very well-equipped laundry room, with four washing machines, tumble driers and iron-ing facilities.

Mrs Widdowson provides really excellent self-catering accommo-dation, where familes are very well cared for; the rental costs are very reasonable.

Nearby: The charming village has an excellent pub, and it is a delightful part of the world in which to browse. There are good facilities for fishermen and golfers, and plenty of stables from where you can ride out. Althorp, the house owned by Princess Diana's family, is just up the road, as is Holdenby House and Coton Manor Gardens. Billing Aquadrome has a whole host of water sports, and a little further afield you can visit the Stoke Bruerne Waterways Museum, Sulgrave Manor, Canons Ashby and Draycote Water Country Park. Stratford-upon-Avon, Oxford and Warwick are within easy driving distance and there are excellent antique shops at Weedon.

Units: 5
Rent: £120 to £340 a week
Other costs: electricity is on a meter and read at the end of the visit
Heating: storage heating, open fires and stoves
2 cots and 2 high chairs are available
Open all year

EDITH WESTON, NR STAMFORD, LEICS
[SC] RUTLAND WATER COTTAGES, Edith Weston
Contact: Mrs K Walmesley, Dormer Cottage, Ryhall
Tel: 0780 64001.
Off the A47 and the A6121 west of Stamford.

The charming village of Edith Weston, full of attractive stone cottages, is actually in Rutland and very close to Rutland Water with its many attractions. Mr and Mrs Walmsley have four delightful cottages in the village and it was no surprise that they won the East Midlands Tourist Board's Best of Tourism Award in the self-catering category in 1992.

Number 3 Well Cross is an archetypal English cottage, built of stone and with a collyweston slate roof. It is part of a terrace which was built in the mid-19th century and the interior is clean and bright and very comfortably furnished. The sitting room is a particularly appealing room with windows not only on to the little patch of front garden but also with a glass door to the enclosed lawned garden. It is a secluded spot and also has a small terrace. The kitchen has a dining area and upstairs there are two twin bedrooms and a bathroom.

Down the street past the local shop you will come to Barn Cottage which is only a few minutes' walk from Rutland Water. All the accommodation is on the ground floor and you enter from a paved courtyard, a sunny place to sit. The good-sized lounge has windows on to the paved garden and, down the corridor, there is a separate kitchen and two twin-bedded rooms and a bathroom. Barn Cottage can accommodate disabled guests and their families.

A little further through the village there are two small cottages which can accommodate two adults and children on Z-beds or cots. Both Corner Cottage and Middle Cottage are built on two storeys and have wooden porches, made all the more cheerful by the encircling roses and hollyhocks. The front doors of both cottages take you straight into the comfortable living rooms with their stone walls and nice wooden doors. Beyond there are kitchens with little dining areas; upstairs there is a spacious L-shaped bedroom with a bathroom. Corner Cottage is surrounded by a lawned garden, and Middle Cottage has an enclosed garden at the back. The cottages share a private drive.

Great care has been expended on the four cottages and the interiors are all in pristine condition. The furniture is smart and comfortable and there are many charming touches, such as the good wooden doors, the solid wood dining tables and the variety of antique pine chests which are scattered through the cottages. All have open fires with logs provided, washing machines and freezers, and showers as well as baths.

Nearby: You can stroll down to Rutland Water, a huge man-made lake of over 3000 acres. Sailing, windsurfing and fishing are the main activities and there is a nature reserve around the shore, with a nature trail. You can walk or cycle around the perimeter of the lake. There is a castle to see at Oakham and a railway museum to the north of the town. Belvoir Castle is within easy reach, as is Kirby Hall, Burghley House, Southwick Hall, Lilford Park, Rockingham Castle and Boughton House. Just over the border in Lincolnshire, you can visit Grimsthorpe Castle, Woolsthorpe Manor and Belton House.

Units: 4
Rent: £150 to £325
Other costs: none
Heating: night storage

2 cots and 2 high chairs
Open all year

ELVASTON, DERBYSHIRE
Ⓛ ELVASTON CASTLE COUNTRY PARK, Elvaston
Tel: 0332 573 144.
Situated about three miles south-east of Derby, on the B5010.

The 200 acres of park woodland belonging to the castle were described at the turn of the century as one of the most remarkable regal gardens in England. Today you can still see why they were held in such high regard and although the house itself is boarded up and not open to visitors, the surrounding courtyard and buildings are well maintained.

Much remedial work has been carried out recently to bring the gardens up to their pristine state after some years of neglect, and the formal gardens are particularly attractive. Primarily this is a place for nature lovers as there are scores of glades and dells to explore where the wildlife, including the squirrels, seem remarkably tame.

Around the forecourt you will find a number of facilities including the cafeteria which serves light refreshments such as toasties and sandwiches and the prices are very reasonable. There is one high chair available.

There is also a museum which tries to re-create the life of the estate just after the turn of the century. You can wander through the cottages and workshops and see the blacksmith, the cobbler and the wheelwright at work.

Open: grounds – daily from 10am to dusk
Museum – 11am to 4.30pm, Easter to 31 October
Charges: admission to grounds free
Baby changing: a table and a changing mat in the Ladies
Ⓟ ample

EMPINGHAM, NR OAKHAM, LEICS
ⓟ WHITE HORSE INN, Main street, Empingham
Tel: 078 086 221.
On the A606.

Very close to Rutland Water with its many facilities, this pub began life as a courthouse in the 17th century, and is a long, well-proportioned stone building, with white shutters.

Families are welcome to use a nicely decorated room (the Orange Room) up some stairs from the bar; there are several tables and comfortable seating, and it is good to report that this is a no smoking area.

At the side there is a small enclosed lawned garden; and a terrace at the front with plenty of rustic tables and chairs, and enlivened by the climbing plants and bright flowers. The main bar is spacious and comfortable, and broken up into sections by stone pillars and a central fireplace.

Morning snacks and afternoon teas are also served, and this is a useful pub for families since it is open all day.

✖ (12pm to 2.15pm & 7pm to 10pm) £2–8: seafood stir fry, beef & vegetable pie, sirloin steak, lasagne, red bean & pepper pie
Children: half portions
🍺 Ale: Adnams, Courage, John Smith's
ⓟ own car park

KEDLESTON, NR DERBY, DERBYSHIRE
Ⓛ KEDLESTON HALL, Derby
Tel: 0332 842 191.
Three miles north of Derby, near Duffield, just off the A6. Also signposted from the A38 bypass, east of Derby.

Stately homes do not come much grander than this masterpiece which is immaculately maintained and has a spectacular setting amongst some breathtaking parkland. Described officially by its owners, the National Trust, as a classical palace, it has been the home of the Curzon family since the 12th century but was largely rebuilt after 1759 by Robert Adam.

Many of the visitors arrive simply to enjoy the beautiful grounds and rolling parkland where there are any number of different walks to enjoy. Others head for the house itself and particularly the Indian Museum which houses the collections of Lord Curzon of Kedleston who was Viceroy of India at the turn of the century.

There is a spacious restaurant which was probably once the hall's main kitchen, which offers some excellent home-made food. The lunch menu includes soup, ploughman's, salads, a daily special and vegetarian dishes. Later in the day, afternoon teas are on the go, but whatever time of day you eat here, the food is good value. There are two high chairs and half portions are available. The restaurant is licensed and is a no smoking area.

Open: Hall – 30 March to 31 October, Saturday to Wednesday 1pm to 5.30pm; Park – 11am to 6pm but also on Thursdays and Fridays
Restaurant open same days as hall.
Charges: adults £4.20; children £2.10
Baby changing: a small table in the Ladies
P own car park

MATLOCK, DERBYSHIRE
R STRAND RESTAURANT, 43 Dale Road
Tel: 0629 584 444.
Near the town centre, and on the A6.

This nicely decorated restaurant has echoes both of a teashop and a brasserie, with its tiled floor, pot plants and wooden tables and chairs. It is on two levels, with a gallery running round the edges of the high-ceilinged room.

All the food here is freshly-cooked by the owners who offer an enterprising choice of dishes which change on a daily basis according to the produce available at the markets. Youngsters are very welcome at lunchtimes, and also during the early evening, but must not outstay that welcome at night.

You could just about manage to change a baby in the Ladies.

Live music is played at times during the week, on Friday night for example; there is jazz on Thursday evenings and a piano on Tuesdays.

✗ LUNCH £1–9: broccoli & mushroom crumble, homity pie, sirloin steak, Brooklyn tuna bake, stuffed vine leaves;
DINNER £14: gravadlax & prawns, rack of lamb, pudding or cheese
Children: half portions
Open 10pm to 2pm & 7pm to 10pm, Tues to Sat; open on Mon during summer
Access/Visa. Licensed
🍺 Ale: Marston's
Ⓟ own car park

MATLOCK, DERBYSHIRE
Ⓛ RIBER CASTLE WILDLIFE PARK, Matlock
Tel: 0629 582 073.
One mile off the 615, east of Matlock.

Riber Castle itself is set high on Riber Hill with commanding views over Matlock. The twenty acres of grounds which make up the wildlife park are well maintained. If you enjoy watching the sort of wild animals which are not always found in a standard zoo then this is the place for you.

The park houses a host of rare and endangered species but is probably best known for its magnificent collection of lynx; the park is said to have the most comprehensive collection in the world. You can also see arctic foxes, wild boar, reindeer and otters and there is a surprise around every corner. All the animals are housed in spacious pens which allow visitors to get some marvellous close-up views. The 'Rabbit Patch' building is a great favourite with children.

You will find a children's playground and souvenir shop in the grounds and some pleasant picnic areas.

The spacious cafeteria and bar area provides inexpensive snacks such as scampi and chips, soup and sandwiches plus daily specials advertised on a blackboard. There are two high chairs in the cafeteria.

Open: Daily except Christmas Day, 10am to 5pm (or dusk)
Charges: adults £3.80; OAPs £3; children £2 (1993 prices)
Baby changing: a changing table and a chair in the Ladies
Ⓟ ample

NEWTON, LINCS
P RED LION, Newton
Tel: 052 97 256.
In the village, off the A52 east of Grantham.

This delightful pub, long and low and built of stone, is a real find in a county which is very short of places we can recommend.

Children are welcome in three rooms in the pub: in the food bar, notable for its penny farthing in one corner; in a very smartly furnished family room with a nautical theme and big open fireplace; and in another lovely room at the garden end of the pub. It is furnished with padded wooden settles, a little dresser and plenty of wooden tables.

The garden itself is enclosed and immaculate with a long smooth lawn, a swing and a slide, a small paved patio with white furniture, and bags of bright flowers.

The food is based on a comprehensive cold buffet: lots of fresh salads, prawns, pies and an array of meats. The landlord serves small, normal or large portions and to tackle the large plate you would have to be in the gargantuan class. At Sunday lunchtime a carvery of hot roasts is also available.

An unusual feature of the pub is the presence of a squash club with two courts, and visitors can play here if they book in advance.

✗ (12pm to 2pm & 7pm to 10pm) £1–9: soup, paté, cold buffet
Children: own menu, half portions
🍺 Ale: Bass, Bateman's
P own car park

NOTTINGHAM, NOTTS
L NOTTINGHAM CASTLE MUSEUM, Nottingham
Tel: 0602 483 504.
Signposted from the city centre.

The 'castle' was built as a grand palace for the first Duke of Newcastle between 1674 and 1679 and stands on the site chosen by William the Conqueror in 1068. It was damaged by fire in 1831 and was acquired by the Council in 1875 for conversion to a museum. It became the first municipal museum outside London.

The museum houses both permanent and temporary exhibitions. There is an audio-visual show depicting the history of Nottingham in the basement – this lasts for about 20 minutes. There are many things to see including the picture collection in the beautiful Long Gallery, a varied programme of temporary exhibitions and the glass, ceramic and silver galleries.

Visitors may take guided tours of 'Mortimer's Hole', a 321 foot tunnel cut in the Middle Ages from the 'upper bailey' of the castle to the foot of the cliff on which the castle stands. (Adults £1, children 50p).

There are panoramic views of the city from the castle and visitors can stroll in the gardens.

The Castle buttery has large arched windows, olive green walls and lace tablecloths, and offers sandwiches, soup, salads, ploughman's, and cream teas. You might try the home-made Bramley apple pie. There are two high chairs and the staff are extremely helpful. There is also a Buttery Bar.

Open: 10am to 5.45pm, April to September; 10am to 4.45pm, October to March. Closed on Christmas Day
Charges: admission free (small charge on certain days; please telephone for details)
Baby changing: changing table in the Ladies and Gents
Ⓟ public car park nearby

REDMILE, NOTTS
Ⓗ PEACOCK FARM, Redmile
Tel: 0949 42475.
Off the A52 west of Grantham. Follow the signs to Belvoir Castle.

This farmhouse was built early in the 18th century, and is no longer part of a working farm. Instead it offers most of the facilities necessary for an enjoyable family break or holiday. As you enter the property you will see a lovely lawned garden, with several apple trees, swings, a climbing frame and a seesaw. There is a small covered swimming pool, a summer house, a play room with table tennis and a pool table, and ten bikes for guests to use.

A bar area sits alongside the partly wood-panelled dining room, and there is a small patio where you can enjoy a drink on summer days. The guests' sitting room, with windows on two sides, is bright and comfortably furnished with sofas and easy chairs.

A great advantage of Peacock Farm is the presence of five family-sized rooms, and the rooms on the top floor, with sloping ceilings under the rafters, are especially attractive. A family room on the first floor (with a double and a single bed) shares a bathroom with a small single room and could be used as a family suite. The ground floor rooms, with french windows on to the lawn, are sizeable and include a family room. The Coach House, which has two single beds and two bunk beds and a bathroom, is a self-contained family suite and there is another separate family room by the patio.

The cooking is based on fresh local produce, and the fruit, vegetables and herbs will mostly come from the garden. Real ale fans will be pleased to hear that the bar serves Ruddles bitter.

Nearby: The famous Belvoir Castle is just up the road, and indeed can be seen from several of the rooms in the farmhouse. The interesting town of Grantham is just a short drive away, with Belton House and Woolsthorpe Manor, where Sir Isaac Newton was born, not very far away. Grimsthorpe Castle is a short drive away and west towards Nottingham you will find Colwick Country Park, with its water sports, fishing and a nature reserve, Green's Mill, and the Holme Pierrepoint water sports centre.

✘ BAR SNACKS (12pm to 9pm) £2–6: mussels marinière, raj curry, Austrian farmhouse fry, cheese provençale en croute
DINNER (7pm to 9pm) £12: sweet pickled herring, turkey schnitzel, tipsy bread and butter pudding, local Stilton cheese
Children: own menu, half portions
£ low
Children: cot £5; two thirds of the adult rate from 3 to 10 years
Facilities: 3 cots and 3 high chairs; baby listening and a patrol
10 rooms, 3 family suites. Open all year
Access/AmEx/Visa
⊟ Ale: Ruddles. No smoking in restaurant
Ⓟ own car park

ROWSLEY, NR MATLOCK, DERBYS
Ⓡ CAUDWELL'S COUNTRY PARLOUR, Rowsley
Tel: 0629 733 185.
Signposted off the A6 between Matlock and Buxton.

This is a wonderful place to bring the family for an afternoon out with a difference. The small but immaculate café is part of the Caudwell's Mill Craft Centre complex. This features a working 19th century flour mill, driven by a water wheel and five craft workshops open to the public where glassblowers, wood turners and potters keep alive dying traditions.

The food is almost entirely vegetarian with all the flour used having been ground at the mill and everything is prepared freshly every day. No additives are used in the food and every effort is made to use environmentally friendly products: recycled paper, etc. Their policies are to be applauded and encouraged.

The complex is surrounded by lawns and a mill stream idles its way past. It is a peaceful haven away from the commercialism that has blighted so much of beautiful Derbyshire.

You can change a baby in the disabled toilet where there is a pull-down shelf.

✕ £2–4: tuna & anchovy tart, crofters pie, spinach & mushroom bake, lasagne
Children: half portions, own menu on request
Open 10pm 6pm, winter until 4.30pm. Closed Christmas Day, Boxing Day & weekends in Jan/Feb
No credit cards. No smoking
Unlicensed
Ⓟ own car park

STRETTON, NR OAKHAM, LEICS
Ⓗ Ⓡ RAM JAM INN, Stretton
Tel: 0780 410 776.
On the A1, about 9 miles north of Stamford.

This old pub, familiar to anyone who has travelled up the A1, maintains the best traditions of the English inn. The stone front of the inn remains but behind it is a restaurant which offers food from

7am onwards. The various menus offer a really enterprising choice of food at competitive prices; ignore all those ghastly fast food places on the Great North Road and have some real food and good coffee at the Ram Jam Inn.

As you enter there is a snack bar, where for example breakfasts are served; down the stairs is a large bar area with a tiled floor, some sofas in one corner, and a glass dome over the centre; and at the far end are two dining rooms, smartly turned out with coral coloured walls, polished wood floors and moulded ceilings.

Off the bar area there is a patio with a few tables and chairs, a stretch of lawn, and the open countryside of Rutland beyond.

There are seven comfortable and well-furnished bedrooms, including a family room. All but one of them overlook the orchard and the garden; despite the proximity of the A1 you will be assured of peace and quiet.

✗ BAR SNACKS (7am to 11pm) £2–7: falafel with salad, corned beef hash, rabbit stew, grilled Rutland sausage, fresh pasta of the day;
DINNER (7pm onwards) £17: fresh linguini, noisettes of lamb, warm treacle tart with ice cream
Children: own menu
£ medium
Children: cot free, £10 for an extra bed
Facilities: 1 cot and 2 high chairs
7 rooms, 1 family. Access/AmEx/Diners/Visa
Open all year
🍺 Ale: Ruddles
🅿 own car park

WORKSOP, NOTTS
Ⓛ CLUMBER PARK, Worksop
Tel: 0909 476 592.
Off the A614 south of Worksop.

This is an enormous park of 3800 acres of parkland and forest which once belonged to the Dukes of Newcastle and is on the edge of Sherwood Forest. The house was demolished in 1938, and only the Duke's study survives.

The pleasure grounds, a series of grassy glades networked with paths among the trees and rhododendrons, are still in place, as are the Vineries and the Palm House, a group of spectacular 19th century glasshouses. There is an avenue of lime trees which stretches for three miles; and a Roman temple faces a Greek temple across a huge man-made lake, spanned at one point by a classical 18th century bridge.

There is plenty of space in which visitors can wander, and the park is a wonderful haven for birds and small mammals. You can hire cycles, see the park on horseback, or, of course, on foot.

The restaurant facilities are in two parts – the self-service area is brightly lit with a sloping pine ceiling and large windows over-looking a patio with tables and chairs. There are daily specials such as turkey and ham pie, steak and kidney pie, baked potatoes, Cornish pasties, and salads. The restaurant has a small bar and two high chairs are available. Booking for the restaurant is advised at weekends as it is very popular.

Open: during daylight hours
Charges: £2.50 for car park
Baby changing: shelves in the Ladies
Ⓟ ample

North-West England

North–West England

Talkin [P]

CARLISLE

Bassenthwaite [H]

Melmerby [R]

Mungrisdale [H] [SC]

Penrith [H]

Braithwaite [H] [P]

Keswick [H]

Loweswater [H] [P]

Helton [H]

Appleby [H] [P]

Borrowdale [H]

Grasmere [P]

Ambleside [H]

Far Sawrey [H]

Kendal [L]

Corney [H]

Newby Bridge [H]

Ulverston [SC]

Cark-in-Cartmel [L]

Whitewell [P]

Blackpool [L]

Ormskirk [L]

MANCHESTER [L]

LIVERPOOL [L]

Chisworth [R]

Rowarth [P]

Knutsford [R] [L]

Langley [P]

Higher Burwardsley [P]

Cholmondeley [H] [P]

AMBLESIDE, CUMBRIA
Ⓗ ROTHAY MANOR HOTEL, Ambleside
Tel: 05394 33605.
A few hundred yards out of the town on the Coniston Road.

This elegant Regency-style hotel was once the home of a prosperous Liverpool merchant and has a distinct colonial look. The wide windows and terrace on the ground floor overlook the immaculate garden with a fine variety of trees and a rockery; on the first floor there is a veranda with iron railings. Climbing plants and hanging baskets of flowers add to the attractions.

The hotel has been in the care of the same family since 1967 and many antiques have been collected during that time to adorn the main rooms. The restaurant is non-smoking and so is one of the lounges.

The bedrooms are all individually furnished to a very high standard. Three suites are available in the grounds of the hotel, two of which are ideal for families. They are spacious and beautifully furnished and each has one double and one twin bedroom. An adjoining single room can be used by either suite and they have little terraces and enclosed gardens of their own.

Residents have free use of a nearby leisure club (one mile away) with swimming pool, sauna, steam room and jacuzzi. Squash is also available. During the winter the hotel offers music, bridge, art and antiques, painting and gardening courses.

The hotel has an excellent reputation for its food which is freshly cooked from local produce. It is a delightful place to stay in a splendid part of the Lake District.

Nearby: The hotel is situated in the heart of the Lake District with all its attractions. Fishing, golf, riding and watersports are readily available. Brockhole Visitor Centre, the Steam Boat Museum, Sizergh Castle, Levens Hall, Brantwood, the Beatrix Potter Exhibition, Fell Foot Park, Grizedale Forest Centre and the Ravenglass and Eskdale Railway (the 'Ratty') are all within easy reach.

✗ LUNCH (12.30pm 2.pm) £7: cold buffet
DINNER (8pm to 9pm), £24: smoked duck breast, soup, brised wood pigeon, fresh fruit salad
Children: high teas, half portions

£ high
Best Bargain Break: £65 per person, per night – dinner, b&b
Children: cot free; extra bed £10
Facilities: 3 cots and 2 high chairs; baby listening
18 rooms, 5 family rooms, 2 suites. Open February to December
Access/AmEx/Diners/Visa. No music
No smoking in dining room and one lounge
P own car park

APPLEBY, CUMBRIA
H APPLEBY MANOR HOTEL (Best Western), Appleby
Tel: 07683 51571.
Off the A66. Follow the signs to the hotel.

This imposing manor house, made of rose coloured Westmorland
stone, overlooks the village of Appleby and the castle. The hotel
was extended a few years back and is an excellent mix of old and
new, and there is a notable pitch-pine staircase in the hall. The
attractive public rooms include a stately and elegant sitting room,
a pleasant bar and a light and airy dining room with wonderful
views over the gardens to Appleby and the distant hills.

The same views will delight the eye from the splendid gardens
which are shaded by some fine old trees. Other facilities include
the games room, which has pool and table tennis, and the leisure
club, which has a plunge pool, sauna, jacuzzi, solarium and some
exercise machines.

The family bedrooms are well-designed and offer plenty of space;
four of them have either double or twin beds and bunk beds, and
the others have various combinations of double and single beds.

With the eight family rooms, the interconnected rooms, a good
supply of cots and high chairs and the excellent all-round facilties,
this is a first-class family hotel and a good base for exploring this
part of England.

Nearby: there is superb countryside all around, a great area for
walking, fishing and riding. Golf is available in the vicinity. Appleby
is a delightful town and the children will enjoy a visit to the conservation centre based at the castle. Lowther Park, with its nature
trails, adventure playground and miniature railway, is close and it

is easy to reach all the attractions of the Lakes and of the Yorkshire Dales.

✗ DINNER (7pm to 9pm) £16: smoked mackerel paté, escalope of chicken, pudding or cheese
Children: own menu, half portions
£ high
Best Bargain Break: £124 per person, 2 nights – dinner, b&b
Children – free to age 15
Facilities: 5 cots and 4 high chairs; and a baby listening system
30 rooms, 8 family, 4 sets interconnecting. Access/AmEx/Diners/Visa
Open all year. No smoking in restaurant
Ⓟ own car park

APPLEBY, CUMBRIA
Ⓟ ROYAL OAK INN, Bongate
Tel: 07683 51463.
Half a mile off the A66.

This delightful old coaching inn, long and low, is an attractive sight with its colourful hanging baskets and window boxes. It enhances an already appealing town, which used to be the county town of

Westmoreland. Parts of the building may date back to the 12th century, and the River Eden is nearby.

You will not be disappointed with the inside, with its wealth of brasses, old furniture, and low dark beams. Families can use a spacious room just inside the front door and it is comfortably furnished. There is an equally agreeable dining room alongside.

The long and varied menu doubles up for both bar meals and dinner, and also includes vegetarian dishes and daily specials. A high chair is provided.

There is always a very good choice of real ales here; as many as nine are on the go at any one time.

✕ (12pm to 2pm & 6.30pm to 9pm) £1–8: savoury green pancakes, savoury crumble, seafood Mornay, Cheddar chicken, steaks
Children: half portions
🍺 Ale – Yates, Theakston's, Younger's and guests
ℙ on forecourt. No music

BASSENTHWAITE, NR KESWICK, CUMBRIA
Ⓗ ARMATHWAITE HALL HOTEL, Bassenthwaite Lake
Tel: 07687 76551.
Off the A591 – don't go to Bassenthwaite village but follow the signs for the Lake. Turn off at the Castle Inn.

This is a splendid 18th-century stone building very much in the 'baronial' style, and set in 400 acres of parkland; its lawns flow down to Bassenthwaite Lake, where guests can fish, and Skiddaw Mountain looms dramatically in the background.

Sir Hugh Walpole wrote of it: 'Speaking of Romance, is there anything more romantic than Armathwaite Hall. With the trees that guard it and the history that inhabits it, it is a house of perfect and irresistible atmosphere.'

There are some wonderful rooms here including a huge lounge with a grand marble fireplace, wood-panelled ceiling and walls and leaded windows – all glassily surveyed by the stags' heads on the walls.

In addition to its beautiful situation, there are splendid facilities within the hotel: a leisure centre with indoor heated swimming pool, gymnasium, a hard tennis court, a pitch and putt course, and a croquet lawn. A snooker table (for over-16s) is in a remarkable panelled room with walls covered with scores of original Punch cartoons. The hotel also has an Equestrian Centre with fully quali-fied instructors and over twenty horses and ponies.

The hotel makes a considerable effort to look after and entertain all members of the family and, in addition to the excellent facilities mentioned above, there are special treats for the children. 'Trotters & Friends' is an animal farm park (open from April to October) with many animals to make friends with and feed; there is a Farm Trail Quiz every day; and Family Treasure Hunts are held several times a week.

The Armathwaite Hall Hotel is an outstanding hotel in delightful surroundings where families will find all they need for an enjoyable stay.

Nearby: From this base you can reach any part of the Lakes with ease, including Grasmere, Hardknott Roman fort, Brantwood, the Lake District headquarters at Brockhole. The children will no doubt vote for Fell Foot Park which has facilities for all types of water sports, or the Grizedale Forest Visitor Centre. Railway buffs have several choices including the famous Ravenglass and Eskdale, known as 'Ratty', and all the family will love a trip on it.

✖ LEISURE CLUB (12pm to 5.30pm & 6.30pm to 10pm) £2–9: garlic mushrooms, spaghetti Napoli, chicken curry, sirloin steak;
LUNCH (12.30pm to 1.45pm) £14: mushrooms with garlic mayonnaise, roast beef with Yorkshire pudding, lemon cheese cake;
DINNER (7.30pm to 9.30pm) £27: avocado salad, soup, grilled Dover sole, pudding or cheese
Children – own menu, half portions
£ high
Best Bargain Break: £120–160 per person, 2 nights – dinner, b&b
Children: free
Facilities: 6 cots and 6 high chairs, and a baby listening system for each room
42 rooms, 4 family, 2 sets interconnecting
Access/AmEx/Diners/Visa
Ⓟ own car park

BLACKPOOL, LANCS
Ⓛ BLACKPOOL ZOO PARK, Stanley Park
Tel: 0253 765 027.
Well signposted off the A583, M6 and M55.

The zoo is sited on the outskirts of Blackpool, just off the main road into the centre. It is spread out over about thirty acres and is pleasantly landscaped with plenty of seating at regular intervals should you get leg weary. Both push chairs and wheelchairs are available at the main entrance.

The zoo seldom becomes overcrowded, even in the peak holiday season, because of its spacious and well-organized lay-out. You will find most of the usual zoo animals here but the most popular attractions are clearly the apehouse, the giraffes, the sealion pool and the lions and tigers. Man-made lakes house quite a collection of wildfowl and you can also see emu, penguins, flamingoes, storks, cranes, parrots and cockatoos.

The zoo not only has good facilities for visitors but the animals are housed in modern buildings with good viewing arrangements, which means there is seldom a crush for spectators.

Apart from the main attraction of the animals, there is also a miniature railway and a small playground for younger visitors.

There is a large cafeteria, which is functional, clean and brightly decorated with an outside seating area for warm weather. Here you can obtain a good range of hot and cold meals, drinks and ice creams for reasonable prices. High chairs are available and children's meals at under £3 are on offer.

You will find ice cream kiosks at various sites and there is a large picnic area where you can relax, plus a gift shop on site.

Open: daily 10am to 6.30pm (4pm in winter)
Charges: adults £3.65; children and OAPs £1.80 (1993 prices)
Baby changing: mother and baby room close to the main gate
Ⓟ ample

BORROWDALE, CUMBRIA
Ⓗ STAKIS LODORE SWISS, Borrowdale
Tel: 07687 77285.
On the B5289, south of Keswick.

Many of our readers have praised this hotel, which 'nestles close to the shores of Derwentwater and is shadowed by beautiful waterfalls'. These are the words of the manager, and we endorse his excellent description.

It is indeed a splendid hotel: a traditional-looking Cumbrian slate facade gives way to an interior which is modern and very comfortable. The list of facilities on offer for families would be hard to surpass – even by the grandest hotel.

There are both indoor and outdoor swimming pools, a gym and a sauna; the priceless bonus of a supervised nursery with trained nannies from 8am to 6pm each day (and where children's meals are served); a games room; an outdoor play area; and tennis and squash courts.

The hotel actually stands in forty acres of grounds, which include the famous falls, and there are a couple of acres of lawned garden, where several thousand geraniums are planted each year.

The fine, and difficult, balance is struck here between the needs of children, and the comfort and relaxation of adults. One of the compromises is that children under six have their evening meals in the nursery and this leaves the adults and the older children free to enjoy their dinner together at a later hour in the dining room.

To quote one of our readers: 'extremely comfortable, wonderful food, and very friendly staff'. It is a marvellous place to stay.

Nearby: A short drive will take you to the heart of the Lake District – to Grasmere, the Hardknott Roman Fort and the Ravenglass and Eskdale Railway; to Windermere and the Lake District headquarters at Brockhole, where the children can see, amongst many other things, a Beatrix Potter exhibition. Fell Foot Park has all sorts of water sports (as have the other lakes) and the Grizedale Forest Centre is the starting point for many interesting walks.

✗ BAR SNACKS (12.30pm to 5.30pm) £4–6: hors d'oeuvres, beef curry, spaghetti Bolognese, vegetable stir fry;
DINNER (7.30pm to 9.30pm) £13: potted shrimps, soup, roast leg of lamb, pudding or cheese

Children: own menu
£ high
Best Bargain Break: £38 per person per night – dinner, b&b
Children: from £13 to £43 depending on age (includes meals)
Facilities: 10 cots and 5 high chairs; and baby listening to every room
70 rooms, 10 family. Access/AmEx/Diners/Visa
P own car park

BRAITHWAITE, NR KESWICK, CUMBRIA
H COLEDALE INN, Braithwaite
Tel: 07687 78272.
Just off the A66 at the top of Braithwaite village.

Set snugly up a small hill, towards the top of this picturesque village, you will find the Coledale Inn which is a small country hotel and pub. It was built in the early 19th century as a woollen mill, became a pencil mill and was then converted to an inn. The building commands superb views of Skiddaw at the front while to the rear, the panoramic Grisdale Pike rises steeply into the sky.

It is a particularly welcoming pub with two roomy bars and an attractive dining room, nicely decorated, and with a bay window which overlooks the garden. Families are made very welcome and the adults will find an excellent choice of real ales.

The bedrooms are all very well furnished indeed with the sort of facilities you would normally associate with more pretentious establishments. The family rooms, three of them with a double and a single bed, and one with a double bed and bunk beds for children, are spacious aand well-organized. Upstairs, there is also a very smart residents' lounge with a splendid Victorian fireplace. Scattered through the hotel you will find plenty of Victorian prints, furnishings and antiques.

Apart from the other normal hotel facilities, guests also have the bonus of two convivial bars at their disposal which serve real ale and a good range of meals and bar snacks. There is also a children's menu.

There is an attractive garden with colourful shrubberies and lawns and bench seats and tables where you can take your ease in fine weather. If you fancy more active pursuits, the proprietor can offer membership of the nearby tennis and bowls club.

Nearby: The wonderful Lakes scenery is all around you and Keswick is well worth a visit for its interesting shops and other attractions. The birthplace of William Wordsworth is very close and the many sights of the Lake District lie to the south: Grasmere and Windermere, the Grizedale Forest, Fell Foot Park, Brantwood and so on.

✗ BAR SNACKS (12pm to 2pm & 6.30pm to 9pm) £1–7: filled baked potatoes, Cumberland sausage, scampi, chilli con carne; DINNER (6.30pm to 9pm) £10: smoked mackerel, sirloin steak, pudding or cheese
Children: own menu
£ medium
Best Bargain Break: £46 per person per night – b&b
Children: under 4s £5; half price thereafter
Facilities: 2 cots and 1 high chair
12 rooms, 4 family. Open all year
No smoking in residents' dining room. Access/Visa
Ⓟ own car park
🍺 Ale: Coledale XXPS, Jennings, Yates, Younger's

CARK-IN-CARTMEL, CUMBRIA
Ⓛ HOLKER HALL AND GARDENS, Cark-in-Cartmel
Tel: 05395 58328.
On the B5278, just outside the village, and near J36 of the M6

You can spend an entire day here exploring the wonderful stately mansion, its magnificent gardens and the 120 acre deer park – to say nothing of all the other attractions which are on offer.

The house was originally built in the 17th century and has both Georgian and Victorian additions. There was a calamitous fire in 1871 after which the Duke of Devonshire commissioned a new wing and this is the part which is open to the general public.

The Hall contains some wonderful features, notably its carved cantilever central staircase and its splendid library. Its collection of more than 3,000 books is said to be one of the biggest in the north of England.

Outside the Hall, there is a string of attractions for both young and old including 25 acres of meticulously maintained gardens, a motor museum with a superb collection of vehicles, a patchwork and quilting display and shop, a photographic exhibition, adventure playground, colour mazes, gift shop and cafeteria.

Many visitors are content however to laze or stroll around the vast expanse of parkland which is an excellent place for a picnic.

The cafeteria is sited just off one of the courtyards near the clock tower and offers well-prepared, home-made snacks such as sandwiches, toasties and salads. Two high chairs are provided. In good weather the outside seating area is a popular spot to enjoy a coffee or a bite to eat in splendid surroundings.

The whole place is excellently signposted and kept spotlessly clean. The staff, too, are notable for their helpful and cheerful attitude.

There are no ropes or barriers confining any part of the hall or grounds and visitors are encouraged to explore at will and take their time doing so. On the first weekend in June the Great Garden and Countryside Festival is held at Holker; and there is an MG Rally on August bank holiday Sunday.

Open: 1 April to the end of October, 10.30am to 6pm; closed on Saturday
Charges: adults £5.50; children £3.10; free up to 6 years (1993 prices)
Baby changing: mother and baby room
P ample

CHISWORTH, CHESHIRE
R WOODHEYS FARM RESTAURANT, Glossop Road
Tel: 0457 852 704.
On the A626 between Marple and Glossop.

It would be difficult to find a restaurant with a more enchanting outlook than Woodheys. From the wide picture windows which run along two sides of the smart restaurant you can look over a remarkable panorama which includes Etherow Country Park and Werneth Low. The Peak National Park is also very close. From the comfortable and welcoming lounge bar you also have commanding views over the countryside.

A beautiful garden surrounds the restaurant: twenty acres of sloping lawns, rockeries and woodland. It is a delightful place, especially on a fine day.

The food is based on a cold buffet and hot carvery and children under 12 are charged half price. The weekend family buffet lunch is very good value and deservedly popular. Throughout the week the restaurant is available for party bookings. The Ladies has plenty of room in which a baby can be changed.

✗ LUNCH AND DINNER £12: 3 course carvery menu (price includes coffee)
DINNER £17: salmon & asparagus mousse, beef & oxtail goulash, pudding or cheese
Children: half portions
Open 12pm to 2.30pm Sat & Sun, & 7pm to 9.30pm Tues to Sat. Closed Monday
Access/Visa. Licensed
Ⓟ own car park

CHOLMONDELEY, NR MALPAS, CHESHIRE
ⒽⓅ CHOLMONDELEY ARMS, Cholmondeley
Tel: 0829 720 300.
On the A49 five miles north of Whitchurch.

The Harrison family used to own the excellent Crown at Hopton Wafers, which has been listed by us for many years. Together with Guy and Carolyn Ross-Lowe they have now converted this Victorian school (it was the local school until 1982) and have made a really splendid job of it.

The original building has not been altered, but the interior has been opened into three sections; in the centre is a bar and there are two areas, away from the bar, which are intended mainly for food and where families can settle.

The high schoolhouse windows are curtained from top to bottom, and there is a mixture of oak and pine furniture: oblong and round tables, settles, bucket and cane chairs, standard lamps in the corners, and china plates and prints scattered on the walls. It all hangs together very well.

There is a huge lawned garden with plenty of bench tables, and a children's play area with swings and a large wooden climbing frame.

Nearby: You are close both to the Shropshire and the Welsh borders, with lovely countryside within reach. There are many interesting castles on the borders: Erddig and Chirk for example; and you can see the lovely Dee Valley by taking the Llangollen steam railway. The fascinating town of Chester is not too far away, while Bridgemere Wildlife Park and Stapeley Water Gardens are close at hand.

✗ (12pm to 2.15pm & 7pm to 10pm) £1–10: saffron prawns, blinis with smoked salmon, chicken piri piri, Madras beef curry, salmon fishcake
Children: own menu, half portions
£ low
Children: £5 for cot or extra bed
Facilities: 1 cot and 4 high chairs, 2 baby listening lines
4 rooms, 1 family. Open all year
🍺 Ale: Boddington's, Flowers, Marston's and guests
Access/Visa
Ⓟ own car park

CORNEY, NR BOOTLE VILLAGE, MILLOM, CUMBRIA
Ⓗ FOLDGATE FARM, Corney
Tel: 0229 718 660.
Off the A595 north of Bootle.

The farm covers ninety acres and is situated in delightful countryside and is within relatively easy distance of most of the Lake District amenities.

The farmhouse is built of Lakeland stone and is partly 19th century, and partly of an earlier vintage. It is a comfortable place, with traditional furniture such as an old dresser with china mugs hanging on it, and meat hooks in the ceiling. The friendly owners have a long experience of looking after holiday makers, and you will get good country cooking, including the farm's own fruit, vegetables and lamb, and free range eggs.

A small garden sits at the back of the farmhouse and you can fish for brown trout in a nearby beck.

Nearby: The Ravenglass and Eskdale railway is close, as is Muncaster Castle with its wonderful rhododendron garden; and it is not too long a drive across to Coniston and Windermere Lakes, to Grasmere and all the other attractions of the Lake District: Brantwood, Belle Isle, the Steamboat Museum at Windermere, Holker Hall and the Lakeside and Haverthwaite Railway. The children will particularly enjoy a visit to Fell Foot Park and the Grizedale Visitor Centre.

✗ DINNER (6pm) £8
Children: half portions
£ low
Children: reductions by age
Facilities: 1 cot and baby sitting by arrangement
2 rooms, 1 family. Open January to November
No credit cards. Unlicensed
Ⓟ ample

FAR SAWREY, CUMBRIA
Ⓗ THE SAWREY HOTEL, Far Sawrey
Tel: 05394 43425.
On the B5285, one mile from the west side of the Windermere car ferry.

The hotel is situated close to the famous lake and the ferry runs every twenty minutes during the summer and is always busy. The core of the building is of 18th century origin, and various additions have been made over the years; for example the stables were made into a bar, called the Claife Crier, and for parents who fancy a sustaining glass of Theakston's it is useful to know that there are various alcoves, away from the bar, where they and their children can settle down. There is a good range of bar snacks available here at lunchtimes.

There is another bar in the main part of the hotel and a large lounge with plenty of easy chairs. The family rooms, functional and comfortable, provide adequate space. One of the hotel's bonuses is its lovely lawned garden, partly enclosed by hedges; it's a fine place to sit in the sun.

This hotel offers excellent value to families, especially if you take advantage of their four-day or weekly terms in the off-peak periods.

Nearby: The village of Near Sawrey is famous as the home of Beatrix Potter, and a pilgrimage to her house, Hill Top, at Near Sawrey will no doubt be on the programme. In the heart of the Lakes, you will hardly be short of holiday diversions, even on the simplest level of walking through the lovely countryside, or enjoying the watersports which are available on the lakes. Within easy reach are Fell Foot Park; Grizedale Forest with its wildlife centre and various nature trails; the Steamboat Museum at Windermere; John Ruskin's house, Brantwood which you can also see from the deck of the steam yacht 'Gondola', which cruises on Coniston Water; the Lakeside and Haverthwaite Railway; and so on.

✕ BAR SNACKS (11.30am to 2.30pm) £1–7: roll mop herring, Cumberland sausage, local smoked trout, sirloin steak;
DINNER (7pm to 8.45pm) £13: 5 courses, changed each day (eg, Stilton vol au vents, poached salmon, fresh fruit salad, cheese)
Children: own menu, half portions
£ medium
Best Bargain Break: £55 per person, 2 nights – dinner, b&b
Children: cots £5; half price to age 13
Facilities: 4 cots and 2 high chairs; and baby listening to each room
17 rooms, 3 family, 1 set interconnecting. No credit cards
Open all year except second half of Dec. No music
⊞ Ale: Black Sheep, Theakston's, Jennings
℗ own car park

GRASMERE, CUMBRIA
℗ TRAVELLER'S REST, Grasmere
Tel: 05394 35604.
On the A591 north of the village.

This long white pub is reputed to be the oldest building in Grasmere. Flanked by spectacular views of the Langdale Pikes,

Helvellyn and the Fairfield Horseshoe it provides a handy resting place for walkers and tourists.

There is lots of space to eat outside either in the beer garden or on the tables at the front of the pub. The smart and traditional interior has a very agreeable lounge with padded benches ranged along the plastered stone walls and families have their own room up a few stairs at one end of the pub. There is plenty of space here and there is a pool table. An alternative for families is the large dining room at the other end of the building.

Two high chairs are available and there are baby changing facilities: just ask the helpful staff. It is a useful pub for families to know since it is open throughout the day (Monday to Saturday) and has a limited menu during the afternoon period.

✕ (12pm to 3pm & 6pm to 10pm) £2–11: chicken Kiev, vegetable lasagne, lamb brochette, sirloin steak, Cumberland sausage
Children: half portions
⏃ Ale: Jennings

HELTON, NR PENRITH, CUMBRIA
Ⓗ BECKFOOT HOUSE HOTEL, Helton
Tel: 0931 713 241.
Off the A6 south of Penrith.

The house is actually about a mile south of the village of Helton, which has a pub and is itself six miles or so from Penrith. It is quite a stately house, built of stone in the late-19th century, with a large and immaculate lawn at the front with a charming sundial and a great fir-tree. It is surrounded by a variety of fine trees and at the back of the house the ground slopes up to a small paddock which is also encircled by trees. There is plenty of room for children to play, and they have an adventure playground. There is easy access to the fells with many delightful walks and masses of wildlife to spot.

The rooms are beautifully proportioned and contain several fine marble and oak fireplaces; the spacious sitting room is furnished with a variety of comfortable easy chairs. You have splendid views of the gardens and the countryside beyond, and an open fire for cooler evenings. Board games and children's toys are available. Like

the lounge, the dining room has nice wood panelling and wide windows overlooking the garden.

This is very much a house where families are made welcome and there are cots and high chairs as well as three family rooms. As you would expect of this handsome and spacious place, they are of a generous size and very well furnished and decorated: one has a double and two single beds, and the others each have a double and a single bed. All the bedrooms here have their own en suite facilities and television sets.

Nearby: There is much to do and see in this part of Cumbria, especially if you like walking, riding or water sports. Ullswater is a few miles away, as is Haweswater Nature Reserve. Up the road is the pretty village of Askham which lies next to the huge Lowther Park with its deer park and nature trails. It also has an adventure playground and a miniature railway. A sprint down the motorway will take you close to all the other tourist attractions of the Lakes – Grasmere, Ambleside, Coniston, Windermere and so on.

✗ DINNER (7pm)
Children: half portions
£ medium

Best Bargain Break: £90 per person, 3 days – dinner, b&b
Children: free up to 5 years; half price up to 12 years
Facilities: 1 cot and 1 high chair
6 rooms, 3 family. Open March to November
No credit cards. No music
No smoking in dining room
Ⓟ ample

HIGHER BURWARDSLEY, CHESHIRE
Ⓟ PHEASANT INN, Higher Burwardsley
Tel: 0829 70434.
Off the A534 or A41 west of Nantwich.

This lovely old pub, built in the 17th century, has a marvellous location about ten miles from Chester in the Peckforton Hills and you have splendid views across Cheshire to Wales. The pheasant has outstanding facilities for all its customers and especially for families who are welcome to use the spacious conservatory, a most agreeable room with its smart furniture and wonderful views.

In addition there is a sizeable lounge bar where the beamed ceiling is complemented by wooden pews and tables, and plush benches and chairs. It is also notable for the huge fireplace, open on two sides and believed to be one of the biggest in the country. There is also a very pleasant restaurant, the Highland Room.

On summer days you can sit on the stone terrace at the front of the pub and enjoy the view, and families can enjoy the grassy garden where there is a play area with swings, a slide and a climbing frame, and plenty of bench tables for the adults.

This is an excellent family pub in delightful surroundings.

✗ (12pm to 2pm & 7pm to 9.30pm) £2–10: liver & onions, Lancashire hotpot, smoked salmon, sirloin steak, rack of lamb
Children: half portions
🍺 Ale: Bass
Ⓟ own car park

NR KENDAL, CUMBRIA
Ⓛ LEVENS HALL, Sedgwick
Tel: 05395 60321.
Just off the A6, south of Kendal.

This beautiful Elizabethan house, which was developed around a 12th-century pele tower, offers many treasures to the visitor. The fine collection of Jacobean furniture, elaborate panelling and plasterwork, paintings by Rubens and Lely, Cordova leather wall coverings and the earliest English patchwork are the main features of the house.

The gardens are famous in their own right and contain wonderful examples of topiary and date back to 1694. Castles, top hats and birds have been lovingly sculpted from yew and beech.

An adventure playground in a woodland setting at the bottom of the garden is thoughtfully set into safety bark so that falling adventurers will probably bounce. There are several picnic tables in this area.

The house also has a fine display of steam engines which date from 1820 to 1920. A half size traction engine gives rides around the grounds.

The tea room is situated in the old servants' dining room and features oak panels, mullion leaded windows and floral prints on the walls. It is open from 10am to 5pm. There is a high chair or you may wish to park your buggy in the courtyard and eat at one of the tables outside. Ploughman's, baked potatoes with fillings, salads, rolls and cakes are served.

Open: 11am to 5pm, Easter to the end of September, Sunday to Thursday
Charges: adults £3.80; OAPs £3.30; children £2.20
Baby changing: mother and baby room
Ⓟ ample

NR KESWICK, CUMBRIA
Ⓗ MARY MOUNT HOTEL
Tel: 07687 77223.
On the B5289 south of Keswick.

The hotel has a wonderful location on the shores of Lake Derwent-water amid the relaxing surroundings of water, mountains and woodland. It is an excellent base for exploring this part of the Lake District.

The Mary Mount is housed in an imposing 1930s slate-fronted building with dormer windows, and the public rooms are spacious and bright. They include a comfortable lounge, a very welcoming wood-panelled bar and a sizeable dining room with wide windows which overlook the gardens. They are extensive, with sloping lawns, lots of fine trees and a stream. It is a delightful place in which to sit and enjoy the peace and quiet.

We looked at several of the bedrooms and were impressed by the amount of space provided and by the excellent standards of the furnishings and decorations. This was especially so in a very large family room which has four single beds and plenty of room for some easy chairs; with three windows looking out to the lovely surroundings, it is a very bright and welcoming room. Six rooms are contained in an adjoining bungalow and these rooms are very quiet and secluded; two large double rooms can easily accommodate an extra bed or a cot.

The Mary Mount is a very congenial family hotel in a beautiful location and the rooms are reasonably priced.

Nearby: All the outdoor pursuits of the Lakes are here to be enjoyed – walking and climbing, water sports, fishing, horse riding and golf. The many attractions of the Lakes are all within reach, including Lowther Park, Grasmere, Townend, Belle Isle, Brant-wood, the Grizedale Forest Centre, Fell Foot Park and the Raveng-lass and Eskdale Railway.

✗ BAR SNACKS (12pm to 2pm) £1–6: paté, smoked trout, beef in red wine, plaice & chips, Cumberland sausage
DINNER (6.30pm to 9pm) £11: prawn platter, chicken supreme, pudding or cheese
Children: own menu, half portions
£ medium

Children: £5 up to 4 years; half price thereafter
Facilities: 2 cots and a high chair
14 rooms 5 family. Access/Visa
Open all year
Ⓟ own car park

KNUTSFORD, CHESHIRE
Ⓡ DAVID'S PLACE, 44 King Street
Tel: 0565 633 356.
In the centre of the town.

This restaurant has been in the *Guide* since its first edition over ten years ago and its standards have never wavered. It is located in a smart and interesting street and those words apply also to David's Place. Reports have commended the quality of the food ('excellent') and its presentation ('superb') and the welcoming staff.

Beyond the agreeable bar area there is a very attractive dining room, spacious and bright, and alongside there is another connecting room. A little balcony holds two tables. The furniture includes some nice wicker chairs and large pots contain trailing plants.

Children can have smaller portions of the various dishes, and the lunch menu offers excellent value. A series of regional menus are offered in addition to other choices; when we visited, tarte Alsacienne and poulet au Riesling caught the eye. A glass of wine is included in the price of £13.50 for two courses.

✗ LUNCH (12pm to 2pm) £14: spinach & salmon pancakes, braised spring lamb, pudding or cheese;
DINNER (7pm to 10pm) £24: prawn & mushroom parcel, veal Romanoff, pudding or cheese
Closed Sun & bank holidays. Access/AmEx/Diners/Visa
Licensed
Ⓟ public car park or street parking

KNUTSFORD, CHESHIRE
Ⓛ TATTON PARK, Knutsford
Tel: 0565 654 822. (Infoline 0565 750 250).
Off the A5034 north of Knutsford; signposted from the M6 and
M56.

There is an enormous amount to see and enjoy at Tatton Park and
it is highlighted as a 'story for every age'. The house that was
originally on the site was owned by the powerful Egerton family in
the 17th century, but the present mansion was built in the neo-
classical style at the end of the 18th century. The interior is rich
and elaborate, filled with splendid furnitures, silken drapes and fine
paintings. Some of the rooms were used in the television version
of *Brideshead Revisited*.

Amid parkland of about two thousand acres, the beautiful gardens
cover about fifty acres and one feature after another commands your
attention: the Orangery, the fernery, the Edwardian rose garden, the
tower garden, the arboretum, the Japanese garden with its thatched
tea house, and the Italian garden.

In addition the Home Farm is run as it was in the thirties, and
this is a great favourite with the children, who can see the various
animals and poultry. You can even try your hand at threshing in
the Old Hall barn and see how a Tatton gamekeeper lived in the
1900s, or discover where man camped nearby at the end of the last
Ice Age. The objective at Tatton Park is to encapsulate several
thousand years of history; in the story of this estate you can see the
natural progression whereby the existing land and buildings provided the wealth to build the mansion and then to create the
gardens.

The huge park has various trails to help you to explore it, either
on foot or by bicycle, and you can fish and swim in one of the two
meres. There is also an adventure playground which covers over
two acres.

The large self-service restaurant is part of the stable block and
there is a reasonable range of hot and cold food (£2 to £5). There
are several high chairs available. Mothers who need to care for
their babies must head for the emergency rest room which contains
a large table, a bed, a chair and a wash basin.

Tatton Park is full of interest for the whole family and you could comfortably spend a whole day here. There are plenty of special events throughout the year: concerts, craft displays, classic car rallies, carriage driving, a children's week, etc.

Open: complex variations in times, but the park and gardens are open every day except Mondays and Christmas Day. The mansion and the Old Hall and farm are open from Easter to the end of October. Farm also open Sundays in winter.
Charges: all-in ticket – adults £6: children £4.20; under 5s free
Baby changing: facilities in the emergency rest room
ℙ ample

LANGLEY, NR MACCLESFIELD, CHESHIRE
ℙ HANGING GATE INN, Langley
Tel: 0260 252 238
Off the A54 Congleton/Buxton road at signpost for Langley.

This comfortable and traditional pub, smartly painted white, stands on a hillside and parts of it date back to the 16th century. It was once a farm, and there are now small terraces, one with a small lawn, on three sides of the pub and you have superb views of the Cheshire plains and the Pennines. On a clear day you can see past the Jodrell Bank telescopes to the Wirral.

The same views can also be seen from the family room, which is down some stairs from the bar and has an open fireplace and pine tables and stags' horns on the wall. In addition there is a charming, little room where families are welcome. This is the Blue Room with a couple of wooden tables, a beamed ceiling and horse brasses on the wall. You can book this for small parties, but not at weekends.

Food is served every day and includes a good selection of daily specials.

✗ (12pm to 2.30pm & 7pm to 9.30pm) £2–7: local trout, plaice, lasagne, cottage pie, sirloin steak
Children: own menu, small portions
⊕ Ale: Courage, Ruddles, John Smith's
ℙ own car park

LIVERPOOL, MERSEYSIDE
Ⓛ ALBERT DOCK, Wapping Pier Head
Tel: 051 708 8853.
On inner city ring road (A5036).

The transformation of Liverpool's Albert Dock into a brilliantly conceived complex of shops, bars, museums and exhibitions is without doubt one of Britain's tourist success stories.

The rebirth of the dock as a waterfront leisure park came about as part of the Government's attempts to regenerate large parts of the north west's industrial heartland early in the last decade. Today it is one of Britain's five biggest tourist attractions, with several million visitors each year.

The complex has been fashioned out of a number of huge warehouse blocks around the quayfront in attractive and imaginative style, and comprises pubs, wine bars, food outlets, coffee shops, restaurants, a variety of shops, displays and exhibitions. The food outlets include Italian, French, American and Tex-Mex plus a whole array of fast food. There are plenty of high chairs available, and excellent facilities for changing and feeding babies.

Also housed in the complex is the Merseyside Maritime Museum and Liverpool's own Tate Gallery which offers a number of permanent and changing exhibitions. One of the newest attractions is the Beatles Story, where you can re-live the days of the Mersey Beat and the Swinging Sixties.

Whatever the weather you have the ingredients for a perfect day out at Albert Dock because all the walkways and attractions are under cover but should the sun shine, there are plenty of outdoor areas available too.

The Albert Dock company has been most careful to see that every shop, bar and attraction blends in carefully with the maritime atmosphere. The whole family can have an enjoyable day out here.

Open: 10am to 5.30pm daily except Christmas Day
Charges: admission free to the Albert Dock; charges for some of the attractions
Baby changing: excellent facilities
Ⓟ ample and free

LIVERPOOL, MERSEYSIDE
Ⓛ LIVERPOOL CATHEDRAL, St James' Road
Tel: 051 709 6271.

If you are interested in magnificent buildings, you should visit Liverpool's Anglican cathedral, which is just a short walk from the city centre.

It is the largest cathedral in Britain and fifth biggest in the world – a truly awesome monument from the outside and a place which seems just as daunting when you walk inside. Work began on the cathedral in 1901 to the design of Sir Giles Gilbert Scott and its foundation stone was laid by King Edward VII three years later. It was finally dedicated in 1978.

The whole building is a great testimony to fine craftsmanship in stone, wood, stained glass, ornate plasterwork and bronze. To see the cathedral properly will take you at least half a day but the building has some good facilities, not least its impressive spacious refectory and its visitors' centre.

The refectory has some smart pine tables and chairs, and also a terrace and offers full meals at lunchtime and snacks during the rest of the day. There are two high chairs and plans are afoot to include children's portions on the menu.

Elsewhere children are given a special welcome. They have a children's officer who gives tours of the features most likely to interest youngsters.

There is a small charge to visit the cathedral tower where you will get some panoramic views of the city; otherwise there is a box for donations from appreciative customers.

Open: daily 9am to 6pm; refectory open 10am to 4.30pm (Sunday 12pm to 5pm)
Charges: admission free
Baby changing: basic facilities only in the lavatories
Ⓟ on street

LIVERPOOL, MERSEYSIDE
Ⓛ LIVERPOOL MUSEUM AND PLANETARIUM,
William Brown Street
Tel: 051 207 0081.
Situated just off the city centre, close to Lime Street Station.

Housed in a superb and archetypal Victorian building, this is one of Britain's most comprehensive museums where you can study collections from all over the world ranging from the wonders of the Amazonian rain forest to the mysteries of outer space, see Egyptian mummies, classical sculptures, and Anglo-Saxon jewellery, and study plants and geological specimens from all corners of the world.

The museum also contains a planetarium and natural history centre for which a small charge is made, although admission to the main museum building is free. Early this year a new exhibition will come on stream, a Space and Time gallery.

There is a cafeteria on the third floor, close to the Planetarium, and it can be reached in a lift. It is a long and functional room, designed to cope with large numbers of visitors, and its great bonus is the wide expanse of windows at one end which look out over the city. It is a magnificent view and you can enjoy a range of snacks and hot meals (baked potatoes, lasagne, chicken casserole, etc) at prices from £1 to £3. There are two high chairs and a children's menu is available during the school holidays.

Open: Monday to Saturday 10am to 5pm; Sunday 12pm to 5pm
Charges: admission free; small charge for the planetarium
Baby changing: facilities by Ladies on first floor
Ⓟ plenty nearby

LIVERPOOL, MERSEYSIDE
Ⓛ MERSEYSIDE MARITIME MUSEUM
Tel: 051 207 0001.
Housed in part of the Albert Dock.

The museum is made up of a number of different exhibitions which in turn tell something of the history of Liverpool as one of Britain's greatest seaports.

'Emigrants to a New World' tells the story of the nine million people who emigrated through Liverpool between 1830 and 1930. There is a full-scale reconstruction of a Liverpool street and the interior of an emigrant ship, complete with sound effects.

Another display charts the evolution of the port between 1207 and 1857, and the story is also told of some of the city's great shipbuilders with the help of a nine-screen video wall.

You can also see the work of artists who have captured the sea on canvas over the years and enjoy the display of over 200 models of ships from all over the world.

Other attractions include the Maritime Record Centre, the Piermaster's House and the Maritime Park, which features historic vessels and wooden boat displays.

Facilities here include a smorgasbord restaurant, a coffee shop (high chairs available in both) and a museum shop. It is an excellent day's outing for the whole family.

Open: daily from 10.30am to 5.30pm (last entry 4.30pm). Closed Christmas, New Year and Good Friday. (Maritime Park closed November to April).
Charges: adults £2.50; children & OAPs £1.30 (children under 16 must be accompanied by an adult)
Baby changing: excellent facilities
P ample

LOWESWATER, CUMBRIA
H P KIRKSTILE INN, Loweswater
Tel: 0900 85219.
Off the B5289 south of Cockermouth.

This 16th-century inn has an idyllic situation close to Crummock Water and from the bar you can see the brooding outline of Melbreak Fell in the background. It is very peaceful here, made more so by the splendid old church which is opposite the pub – these two focal points of village society, preaching and pints, are often found to be close neighbours.

The accommodation includes three family rooms and guests have the bonus of peace and quiet and the idyllic views.

As a pub this is a very useful place for families, since food is available (including breakfast from 8am and afternoon teas) during most of the day, and they can use either a small lounge at the side of the bar, or a room in an adjacent barn, which has a pool table, jukebox, etc. On warmer days you can enjoy a drink and a meal on the terrace or the lawn which runs along the front of the pub.

Nearby: This is a wonderful area for walkers, climbers and fishermen, and many other sports can be organized including golf, water sports, tennis and squash. The attractions of the Lakes are easily reached: Grasmere, Hardknott Roman Fort, Townend, Brockhole, Belle Isle, Fell Foot Park and Grizedale Forest.

✕ (12pm to 2.30pm & 6pm to 9pm) £1–9: omelettes, Cumberland sausage, haddock & chips, sirloin steak, bean & tomato casserole
Children: own menu
£ medium
Children: £11 for an extra bed
Facilities: cots and high chairs available
10 rooms, 3 family. Access/Visa
🍺 Ale: Jennings. No music
ℙ own car park

MANCHESTER
Ⓛ MUSEUM OF SCIENCE AND INDUSTRY,
Liverpool Road
Tel: 061 832 2244.
In the centre of the city, not far from Deansgate railway station.

You could easily spend a day at this huge museum, which offers fun for the whole family and a splendid insight into the industrial history of the region.

The various galleries are housed in a fine collection of renovated industrial buildings and there is something to interest everyone. For example, the Lower Byrom Street Warehouse includes 'Xperiment', a hands-on science centre very much aimed at youngsters who can try out the various exhibits designed to illustrate many basic scientific principles. Great fun.

There is a café in this building which offers snacks and salads at very reasonable prices and it was extended last year. High chairs

are available and there is a separate baby changing room on the
ground floor (unisex, by the way).

The other exhibits include the history of power generation, the
story of electricity, an 1830's railway station and Underground
Manchester, which tells you all about the Victorian sewerage
system. The Air and Space gallery has a fascinating collection of
machines from the earliest bi-planes to a space shuttle. One of its
attractions is a simulator and we fought the Red Baron again across
First World War skies – and we won, of course. There is an extra
charge of £1 for adults and 50p for children. Another café, Kites,
has been opened here.

This is a really splendid place and we were particularly impressed
by the knowledgeable and helpful staff; their enthusiasm shone
through in this busy and bustling, very active museum.

Open: every day, 10am to 5pm, except 23, 24 and 25 December
Charges: adults £3.50; children, OAPs and students £1.50; under
5s free
Baby changing: separate room in Lower Byrom Street Warehouse
Ⓟ ample (£1.50 charge)

MELMERBY, CUMBRIA
Ⓡ VILLAGE BAKERY, Melmerby
Tel: 0768 881 515.
On the A686.

This is a most enterprising and picturesque restaurant. Housed in
an 18th century converted barn, it is set in some spectacular Cumbrian countryside where you will find some marvellous views.

The restaurant has stone walls, a stone-flagged floor, good
wooden tables and chairs, and a Welsh dresser against one wall.
There is a small and elegant conservatory on the front of the building. Upstairs under the wooden rafters the craft gallery has an
excellent range of products and there are several tables here too.

The food is baked in the restaurant's own wood-fired brick oven
and the bread, pie and pizzas use wholemeal flour ground at a
local water mill. Many of the vegetables are grown organically on
a smallholding at the back of the restaurant. The menu is comprehensive: you can enjoy breakfasts (the full breakfast, traditional or

vegetarian, will set up for the day), lunches, savoury snacks, and cream teas, all at very reasonable prices. The restaurant has won many awards, including a *Sunday Times* one for organic food at the Royal Show.

Mothers with babies can feed and change them in the Ladies, where there is a pull-down shelf and a changing mat.

The Village Bakery is in a lovely location right by the village green, which stretches away from the front door.

✗ £1–6: Inverawe kippers, leek & tomato bake, Lakeland char, Chester pie, baker's lunch
Children: half portions
Open 8.30am to 5pm (Tue to Sat) 9.30am to 5pm (Sun) Closes at 2.30pm in Jan and Feb. Closed at Christmas
Access/Diners/Visa. No music
No smoking
Ⓟ own car park

MUNGRISDALE, NR PENRITH, CUMBRIA
Ⓗ ⓈⒸ NEAR HOWE FARM HOTEL, Mungrisdale
Tel: 0768 779 678.
Off the A66 between Penrith and Keswick

Idyllic is the only word which adequately describes Near Howe, a lovely double-fronted farmhouse built of the traditional dark-hued stone of this part of the country. After you have driven up a long and bumpy road you can look back at the moorland which dips and rolls beneath. This is the Mungrisdale Valley over which John Peel and his companions used to hunt.

You will certainly find peace and tranquillity here, not least in the garden which fronts the house. It has an immaculate lawn, is safely enclosed and ringed with trees, and all around is the glorious countryside. It is a wonderful base for a holiday in an area which has so much to offer: fishing, golf, water sports, walking, or just plain relaxing.

There is a spacious and comfortable residents' lounge and a games room with a pool table, toys and records. The attractive dining room was built in the old dairy and through an arch is the bar. The views from the well-furnished bedrooms are wonderful and there is an excellent family room, with a double and single bed, at one end of the building.

Nearby: If you fancy seeing the sights you are only a short drive away from the popular parts of the Lakes: Grasmere, Windermere, Coniston Water and so on. Much nearer to hand is Ullswater and Derwent Water, and Lowther Park with its nature trails, adventure playground and miniature railway.

✕ DINNER (7pm) £9
Children: half portions
£ low
Children: half price under 12 years
Facilities: 2 cots and 2 high chairs
7 rooms, 1 family. Open March to November
No smoking in dining room. No credit cards
Ale: Mitchell's
[P] loads

Self-catering: There are three cottages to let which have been converted from an old slate and stone barn and you will have the same enticing views over the fells. Each has two bedrooms, a double and a twin-bedded room, and a very well-equipped kitchen. Guests have the use of the garden and terrace and of the other hotel facilities and there is a laundry room. The rents vary from £150 to £200 per week and include electricity, heating and linen.

NEWBY BRIDGE, NR ULVERSTON, CUMBRIA

[H] SWAN HOTEL (Exec Hotels), Newby Bridge
Tel: 05395 31681.

The core of this hotel is a 17th-century coaching inn. It has a wonderful position by the River Leven at the end of Lake Windermere and its 300 yards of lake frontage has moorings for boats. You can fish here or, even better, sit quietly on the terrace behind a screen of roses.

There is loads of space in the garden which runs at the rear of the hotel and there is a croquet lawn and a golf practice net. An adjoining field is often the take-off point for hot air balloons and there is a helipad here too. The indoor facilities include table tennis, darts, a small snooker table and a good selection of board games.

The various public rooms are very agreeable and include a stately, high-ceilinged cocktail bar and another spacious bar; the Tithe Barn, with its stone walls and wooden rafters; and, below, the Mail-coach Wine Bar, which offers a good range of bar meals in an informal atmosphere. It is good to report that there is a nappy changing facility nearby.

The bedrooms are furnished and decorated to a very high standard and the family rooms are light and bright and have plenty of space. Two of the family suites have separate bunk bedrooms for children, one of which includes a low-profile washbasin.

The Swan is a top-class family hotel in a delightful location.

Nearby: You are in the heart of the Lake District and an active holiday can start with all the water sports which are easily available, plus walking, fishing, golf and riding. The Lakeside and Haverthwaite Railway is on the doorstep, as is Fell Foot Park, with its own water sport facilities, picnic areas and adventure playground. Holker Hall, Sizergh Castle, Levens Hall, the Grizedale Forest Centre, Brantwood, Belle Isle and the Steamboat Museum at Windermere are all within easy reach.

✕ WINE BAR (11.45am to 2.45pm & 6.30pm to 9.45pm) £2–7: smoked salmon, Mailcoach pie, sirloin steak, fillets of plaice, vegetable lasagne
DINNER (7pm to 9pm) £18: smoked trout, tenderloin of pork, pudding or cheese
Children: own menu, half portions
£ high
Best Bargain Break: £55 per person per night – dinner, b&b
Children: cots £4; £18 extra bed (inc. breakfast)
Facilities: 3 cots and 3 high chairs; baby listening system
36 rooms, 3 family. Access/AmEx/Diners/Visa
Open all year
🍺 Ale: Boddington's, Theakston's
No smoking in restaurant and wine bar
🅿 own car park

NR ORMSKIRK, LANCS
Ⓛ THE WILDFOWL AND WETLANDS TRUST,
Martin Mere
Tel: 0704 895 181.
Off the A59 or A565 north of Ormskirk. Well signposted from
all points.

Martin Mere is a 350-acre haven for birds from all over the world
with visiting birds that change with the seasons. Some of the birds
are residents: these include Chilean flamingos, the Falkland Islands
flightless steamer duck, and the rare Recherche Island cereopsis
goose of which there are only five in captivity. In winter there are
thousands of pink footed geese, whooper swans from Iceland and
Berwick's swans from Siberia.

A nature trail links nine bird watching hides and you can enjoy
the wild flowers. The waterfowl garden has plenty of seating if you
fancy a picnic.

There is a children's adventure playground; facilities for brass
rubbing; and special events arranged throughout the year, which
include children's activities every Sunday, holiday weekends and
on bank holidays.

The Scandinavian-style visitor centre with its turfed roof provides
views through a huge window of Swan Lake and there is a gift shop
and an art gallery. Light meals are available in the licensed Pinkfoot
Pantry and there are four high chairs.

Open: 9.30am to 5.30pm in summer. Until dusk in winter. Closed
at Christmas
Charges: adults £3.75; OAPs £2.80; children £1.90; under 4s free
(1993 prices)
Baby changing: a changing mat in the Ladies
Ⓟ ample

PENRITH, CUMBRIA
Ⓗ NORTH LAKES GATEWAY HOTEL (Shire Inns)
Penrith
Tel: 0768 68111.
Just off exit 40 of the M6.

This hotel was built only a few years ago, and presents a fairly functional face to the multitude of traffic which passes its location close to junction 40 of the M6. But the interior belies these first impressions, and the high vaulted ceilings, with wooden beams, stone fireplaces and excellent furnishings give a smart and spacious tone to the hotel. There is quite a large garden at the back of the hotel.

The leisure club, unlike many others which lay claim to the description, offers proper facilities and has plenty of space. The pool is sizeable and superbly done under a vaulted pine roof and includes a children's pool; there are two excellent glass-backed squash courts; and an exercise room well-equipped with bikes and other good quality equipment. There is also a snooker room.

The hotel has six family rooms. Apart from two parents, they can accommodate up to three children with bunk beds and a convertible sofa. Since children under 16 stay free, these rooms, charged at the standard rate, represent very good value if you are on the move with several youngsters.

Unusually for a hotel of this size, proper draught ale is served – a perfect way to round off a busy day in the Lake District or after a couple of hours in the leisure club.

Nearby: Penrith itself is an interesting town, as is Appleby just down the A66. Beautiful Ullswater is on the doorstep while the southern Lakes with all their attractions are not far away: Grasmere, Belle Isle, Lake Windermere. The children will enjoy a visit to Hill Top, the home of Beatrix Potter. Nearer to hand for the hotel is Lowther Park with its nature trails and adventure playground.

✗ BAR MEALS (12pm to 2pm) £2–5: chicken curry, beef & mushroom pie, vegetable stir fry, filled jacket potatoes;
LUNCH (12.30pm to 2pm, not Saturdays) £10: salmon mousse, roast leg of pork, pudding or cheese;
DINNER (7pm to 9.30pm) £18: savoury mushrooms, honey baked ham, pudding or cheese

Children: own menu, half portions
£ high
Best Bargain Break: £27.50 per person per night – b&b
Children: free up to 16 years
Facilities: 6 cots and 5 high chairs; baby listening system for every room
85 rooms, 6 family, 6 sets interconnecting
Access/AmEx/Diners/Visa. Open all year
⊕ Ale: Thwaites
℗ own car park

ROWARTH, CHESHIRE
℗ LITTLE MILL INN, Rowarth
Tel: 0663 743 178.
Off the A626 Marple-Glossop road. There is a turning on the south west side of the village of Charleworth and then you will find signs to Rowarth and the Little Inn.

The pub is situated in marvellous rolling countryside – the drive to it across the hills is a delight, and we were lucky enough to do it on a sunny Autumn day. The original building was an 18th century mill and photographs inside show how the mill wheel was swept away by a flood in 1930. Chris Barnes, the licensee, has recently installed a new wheel, 36 feet in diameter, and it is in full working order.

The family room is off the bar and is charmingly furnished with seats and tables from a railway dining car and has a good collection of train pictures, including the Flying Scotsman. The carriage itself is at the back of the pub and now houses three bedrooms and it's called the Derbyshire Belle Motel. The bar is most attractive with its stone pillars, wooden beams and padded settles, and there is a lovely old fireplace too. There is a small pool room off the bar.

The children will be delighted with the garden because it has four swings, a climbing frame and a tree house with a slide which takes you right across the mill stream to the other side. Great fun. The adults can watch from the terrace at the front of the pub.

The pub is open all day and you will find food on offer throughout opening hours. There is a high chair on the premises.

✗ (11am to 11pm) £1–5: Bury black pudding, grilled trout, curries, salads, plaice & chips
Children: small portions
🍺 Ale: Banks, Marstons's, Robinson's and guests
Ⓟ own car park

TALKIN, NR BRAMPTON, CUMBRIA
Ⓟ HARE AND HOUNDS, Talkin
Tel: 06977 3456.
In the centre of the village. Three miles off the A69.

This traditional black and white village inn is set high in the Cumbrian countryside and close to the picturesque Talkin Tarn. It is a truly unspoiled pub with an interior which has probably not changed much over the years. The monks who once used it as a stopping place on their journeys from Armathwaite to Lanercost Priory would recognize it.

The main bar is a cosy affair with black beams, rustic furniture, and the renowned stained glass coats of arms. In winter, you will find a log fire in the stone fireplace. The family room, at the back of the pub, is very much in character, its walls scattered with various curios, and there is a pool table.

There is a small walled garden at the side of the pub, with some tables and chairs, sun umbrellas and many flowers.

✗ (12pm to 2pm & 7pm to 9.30pm) £1–7: paté, whitebait, fillet
steak, rainbow trout, venison in red wine, chilli con carne
Children: own menu
🍺 Ale: Jenning's, Theakston's and guests. No music
🅿 across the road

NR ULVERSTON, CUMBRIA
SC THE FALLS, Mansrigs
Tel: 0229 583 781.
Off the A590 north of Ulverston. The brochure has clear
directions.

This group of stone cottages, built in the 18th century, has an
idyllic location amid rolling Cumbrian countryside. If you want
some peace and quiet in beautiful surroundings, you should take
yourself off to the Falls; not that you are very far away from the
local amenities, since Ulverston is only a mile away and contains
the usual shops, as well as over thirty pubs.

The stone buildings, set round the farmyard, are a delight to the
eye. They will accommodate four or six people, with the exception
of Far Applethwaite. This is intended for two, although there is a
sofa-bed if required. The bright living room is upstairs under a
beamed roof, with a kitchen alongside down a few stairs. The bedroom is on the ground floor.

Isaacs Cottage can sleep six people and is also an 'upside down'
building with a delightful living room on the top floor. This very
large room has splendid old wooden beams and contains a sitting
room, dining room and kitchen, and the views are wonderful. There
are three bedrooms on the ground floor: a twin, a double and a
bunk bedroom.

Low Rigg and High Rigg occupy the same building and each
accommodates four people. Once again the views of the countryside
are splendid. Mill Yeat has plenty of space for a family and also
has its living room under oak beams at the top in order to take full
advantage of the lovely views. A gallery overlooks the room and it
can sleep two people; downstairs there is a double, a twin and a
bunk bedroom. The sixth property, Wick End, was probably once
the dairy and adjoins the main house. It has two bedrooms and a
sofa-bed can also be used, if required.

All the cottages have great character and the original features have been used to good effect: the stone walls and old wooden beams are complemented by slate sills, nice wooden doors, oak shelves and log fires. The decorations and equipment are first class. If you want a break from shopping and cooking, the owners will also provide that service for you – an extra touch of luxury on your self-catering holiday.

You cannot but relax in such delectable surroundings, and all the attractions of the Lake District are on your doorstep. The children have plenty of space in which to play, in the gardens and the surrounding fields, and dogs are welcome.

Nearby: You can reach most of the well-known tourist spots with ease including Holker Hall, the Lakeside and Haverthwaite Railway, Fell Foot Park, Levens Hall, Brantwood and the various lakes. This is wonderful walking territory and such pastimes as fishing, horse riding, golf, tennis and swimming are all readily available.

Units: 6
Rent: £120 to £400 a week
Other costs: none
Heating: central heating
Cots and high chairs available
Open all year

WHITEWELL, NR CLITHEROE, LANCS
P INN AT WHITEWELL, Whitwell
Tel: 0200 448 222.
Off the B6478. Six miles north-west of Clitheroe.

Down the winding lanes of the forest of Bowland you will find this classic country inn alongside the village church. It is a solid stone manor house, parts of which date back to the 14th century, and was once the house of the Keeper of the Forest.

The interior is a mixture of dark antique and country pine furniture, and the east wing of the house is an art gallery, with a studio on the top floor. The enterprising landlord sells high quality shirts, sweaters and shoes; and he is also a wine merchant, which ensures a very comprehensive list. An interesting choice of bar food is always offered here, and is all cooked on the spot; it's jolly good value, too.

There is a comfortable and attractive public bar and families just calling in for a drink or a snack can use a spacious room just in from the main door which has lots of tables and easy chairs and is attractively kitted out with antiques and hunting prints on the walls.

From the rooms at the back of the building and from the garden you have delightful views of wooded hills and the river Hodder below, where the landlord has several miles of fishing.

✗ (12pm to 2pm & 7.30pm to 9.30pm) £1–13: savoury pancakes, Coniston smoked trout, fisherman's pie, Cumberland sausage, rack of lamb
Children: half portions
🍺 Ale: Moorhouse, Boddington's, Marston's. No music

North-East England

North-East England

Branton [SC]

Rothbury [L]

Longhorsley [SC]

Cambo [H]

Bellingham [H]

Chollerford [H]

Hexham [H] [SC]

NEWCASTLE

Washington [L]

Durham [R] [L]

MIDDLESBROUGH

Eaglescliffe [P]

Whitby [R]

Northallerton [R]

Rosedale Abbey [SC]

Sedbusk [H]

Thirsk [H]

Helmsley [L]

Gargrave [P] [R]

Ripon [L]

Malton [L]

Malham [P]

Burnsall [P]

Harrogate [R] [P]

Bolton Abbey [R] [L]

YORK [H] [R]

Ilkley [R]

Wighill [P]

Bradford [L]

Newthorpe [P] [R]

Sowerby Bridge [P]

Airmyn [P]

AIRMYN, NR GOOLE, HUMBERSIDE
P PERCY ARMS, 89 High Street
Tel: 0405 764 408.
Half a mile from the M62. Take exit 36.

This is an excellent pub in a small village just a stone's throw from the motorway and a good spot to know if you want to break a journey. It's built in rustic red brick with a cream frontage and is an attractive sight after the monotony of motorway travel.

Inside there's a smart tap room area with a well restored black range fire and an attractively furnished lounge bar.

Families can use a delightful, centrally heated conservatory with white garden tables and chairs and a profusion of indoor plants and other greenery. The conservatory leads out to a lawned garden with lots of children's play equipment including an excellent playhouse.

This is a well-run pub where families can be sure of a warm welcome. There is a good selection of food, a high chair is made available, and the staff will warm up baby food, if so asked. The landlord has the praiseworthy attitude that families make up an important part of the life of a traditional village pub.

✗ BAR MEALS (12pm to 2pm & 6pm to 9.45pm, not Sun pm)
£1–7: vegetable lasagne, chicken Kiev, moussaka, chicken & chips, steak pie
Children: own menu, half portions
🍺 Ale: John Smith's, Courage
P own car park

BELLINGHAM, NR HEXHAM, NORTHUMBERLAND
H RIVERDALE HALL HOTEL, Bellingham
Tel: 0434 220 254.
On a minor road just west of Bellingham on the north bank of the River Tyne. Bellingham is on the B6320, 16 miles north of Hexham.

The core of the hotel is a Victorian country house which overlooks the North Tyne River. It is the nearest hotel to Kielder Water and has recently undergone a major programme of refurbishment. It is excellent facilities which include an indoor swimming pool and a games room with a pool table.

The owner is a cricket enthusiast and has his own cricket field which also doubles for other sports. There is a putting green; you can fish in the adjoining river for salmon and trout and the golf course lies opposite. So sports fans are well catered for. Alternatively you can simply relax in the five acres of garden; from the terrace you have splendid views over the cricket ground to the hills beyond. The same views will also please you from the stately bar, the lounge and the pleasant dining room. The bedrooms are very well turned out and we were impressed by a spacious family room which has a four-poster bed and a single bed.

Nearby: Kielder Water, with its wide variety of water sports, can be enjoyed by the whole family; and the castle is the starting point for many walks and nature trails through the Kielder Forest. To the south you can follow the line of Hadrian's Wall with its chain of forts. Within easy reach you will find Belsay Hall, Wallington House, Cragside House and the ruins of Brinkburn Priory.

✗ BAR SNACKS (12pm to 2pm & 6.45pm to 9.30pm) £2–11: garlic mushrooms, steaks, stir fried dishes, tuna & brie bake, mixed grill;
DINNER (6.45pm to 9.30pm) £17: devilled whitebait, soup, roast Northumberland lamb, pudding or cheese
Children: own menu, half portions
£ high
Best Bargain Break: £84 per person, 2 nights – dinner, b&b
Children: free up to 4 years; one third of adult rate from 4 to 8; two thirds from 9 to 14 years
Facilities: 3 cots and 2 high chairs; baby listening system
20 rooms, 5 family. Access/AmEx/Diners/Visa
⊕ Ale: Ind Coope Burton, Tetley. Open all year
ℙ own car park

BOLTON ABBEY, NORTH YORKS
Ⓡ CAVENDISH PAVILION AND TEA ROOMS,
Bolton Abbey
Tel: 0756 710 245.
Look for the stone archway in the village and then for the tea
rooms sign. You will find the Cavendish Pavilion at the centre of
the Bolton Abbey Estate picnic area.

In its setting of unrivalled beauty within the bounds of the Bolton
Abbey Estate and by the River Wharfe, the Cavendish Pavilion has
excellent facilities for the whole family.

It has recently been completely rebuilt but still maintains its
general appearance as a pavilion with a terrace under its awnings
and plenty of colourful flowers. The interior is designed on a generous scale with plenty of good wooden tables and wicker chairs, a
tiled floor, lots of pot plants and a collection of china plates on the
walls. There are plenty of high chairs, a children's menu and a new
mother and baby room.

On a summer's day it is an idyllic place to have a meal and you
can enjoy all the natural beauty of the estate.

As we went to press, we learned that the Cavendish Pavilion may
also open on three evenings a week during the summer months.

✕ £2–10: filled Yorkshire pudding, burger with salad & chips,
grilled haddock, savoury pie, fillet steak
Children: own menu, half portions

Open 10am to 7pm March to Oct, weekends only in winter to
6pm
Closed Mon to Fri Nov to Mar. Access/Visa
Licensed. No music
Ⓟ £2.50 at nearby car park refunded if taking full meal

BOLTON ABBEY, NORTH YORKS
Ⓛ BOLTON ABBEY ESTATE
Tel: 0756 710 533.
Five miles east of Skipton. Just off the A59.

This spectacular country park is a haven for walkers, nature lovers
and general devotees of the great outdoors. Whether you are a
dedicated twenty miles per day trekker or just out for a quiet stroll
with the family, you will find plenty here for a day out in the fresh
air.

The estate, owned by the Duke of Devonshire, is part of the
Yorkshire Dales National Park, and is a beautiful spot.

The estate is dominated by the Priory Church of St Mary and
St Cuthbert which incorporates the ruins of the 12th-century
Augustine Priory which many tourists visit, completely unaware of
all the other facilities on offer nearby.

The River Wharfe runs along the valley and among the gentle
fields and fells you will find plenty of car park space and picnic
areas.

There is also an excellent cafeteria and restaurant, the Cavendish
Pavilion, which sells good quality meals and snacks, ice cream and
other refreshments. This has recently been rebuilt in splendid style,
has lots of high chairs, a mother and baby room and has been
recommended in *The Family Welcome Guide* since the first edition
(see the entry above). There is also a visitor centre and shop there.

Dotted in other parts of the estate are other tea rooms, a coffee
shop, crafts shop, a well-hidden camping and caravan site, and on
the main road itself, the Devonshire Arms Hotel and pub. There
is even a model railway.

But walking is one of the main reasons why visitors descend on
the place and you will find detailed maps and information to help
you on your way. There are also shorter, more gentle walks and
nature trails for the less ambitious.

Open: daily
Charges: £2.50 per car
Baby changing: possible in the Cavendish Pavilion
Ⓟ various car parks

BRADFORD, WEST YORKS
Ⓛ BRADFORD INDUSTRIAL MUSEUM, Moorside
Mills, Moorside Road
Tel: 0274 631 756.
Just off the A658, east of the city. Follow the signs for Harrogate
and the museum is signposted off the ring road.

The museum gives a fascinating glimpse of the days when wool
production provided the bulk of Bradford's Victorian wealth. It has
been painstakingly re-created in this former spinning mill, dating
from the days when the city was a huge producer of 'wools and
worsteds', worn by every self-respecting Briton.

The various galleries show all the processes of the woollen industry; the Motive Power Gallery has a flyer and spindle makers workshop, as well as steam and gas engines, water turbines and a huge
waterwheel; on the first floor you will find the Weaving and Spinning Galleries, with their combers, spinners, universal ring twisters
and looms.

The machinery harks back to the days when Britian was the
workshop of the world and their manufacturers' names are redolent
of the long-gone days of Industrial supremacy: Crossley Bros,
Thornley's Patent and Platt Bros of Oldham.

The Transport Gallery has an interesting collection of locally
made vehicles, many of them by Jowett Cars, including the famous
Javelin and the Kestrel. Nearby there are the only surviving Bradford Tramcar and Bradford Trolley Bus.

Across the cobbles opposite the main entrance, the stables house
three shire horses and a working cob and they are on show twice
a day (11am and 2.15pm). In addition there are tram and horse bus
rides three times a day, and the Horse Power Emporium tells you
all about horses at work.

Nearby you can see Moorside House and Gaythorne Row,
furnished houses which show how the mill workers lived in their

back-to-backs and how, in contrast, the mill manager lived. Guided tours are available several times a day.

There is a restaurant in the main building. Bobbins Bistro has a pleasant teashop ambience and offers a selection of snacks at very reasonable prices (Yorkshire pudding, burgers, jacket potatoes, etc). There is a high chair. The Mill Shop sells a good range of souvenirs, woollen goods, books and puzzles.

This is an excellent museum which is full of interest for all members of the family.

Open: Tuesdays to Sundays plus bank holiday Mondays, 10am to 5pm
Charges: admission free
Baby changing: in the toilets at the rear of Bobbins
P ample free car parking

BRADFORD, WEST YORKS
L NATIONAL MUSEUM OF PHOTOGRAPHY, FILM AND TELEVISION, Pictureville
Tel: 0274 727 488.
Overlooking the city centre.

Step into the world of the cinema as you've never experienced it before. Here you will find the largest frame ever used in the history of the cinema which brings a new startling dimension to the pictures with a soundtrack to match.

The Imax screen brings pictures and images dramatically to life whether it is a frighteningly real window seat aboard America's space shuttle, or a dramatic speed trip down the rapids of the Grand Canyon. With its five-storey-high screen and six sound channels you can really believe you are at the heart of the action. Although this is probably most people's highlight of the museum, there's lots more to see and enjoy on the five floors of the building, including a new gallery called TV Heaven, where you can wallow among all the famous old series: The Army Game, University Challenge, Edward and Mrs Simpson, Stars on Sunday, etc. Each day is dedicated to a particular year and, apart from the extensive library, you can take your pick of four television terminals.

You can experience the earliest television pictures from a completely new angle, experience the latest in satellite technology and visit many other working models, displays and reconstructions. You can also get involved with many of the exhibitions and try your hand at being a TV camerman, vision mixer and even a TV newscaster and see the results!

There are a restaurant and a coffee bar and they serve homemade cakes and meals. High chairs are available.

Special effects shows are put on at regular intervals each day but it is best to check by phone to determine just what is being screened at which time.

Open: Tuesday to Sunday, 10.30am to 6pm. Closed Mondays except bank holidays
Charges: museum free. Single show price adults £3.65; OAPs and children £2.50 (1993 prices)
No smoking in any part of the museum
Baby changing: in the Ladies on the ground floor
℗ in nearby pay and display park

BRANTON, NORTHUMBERLAND
SC BREAMISH VALLEY COTTAGES
Tel: 066 578 263.
Off the A697 near Powburn.

Located in a quiet and charming village, Breamish Valley Cottages were built from stone farm buildings which date back to 1817. They form a courtyard and there is a delightful lawned garden, fringed with shady trees and bushes, at the rear. There is also a slide for the children and a little football pitch in the adjoining field.

It all adds up to a tranquil setting for these holiday cottages, which can accommodate two, four or six people. Pottery Cottage has its two bedrooms (a double and a twin) on the lower floor and the sitting room, with its wooden rafters and wood burning stove, has splendid views to the Breamish Valley. The Old Granary runs along the upper storey and has a pleasant sitting room, a separate kitchen and three bedrooms (a double, a twin and a bunk bedroom for children). The other four cottages include two, Swallow Cottage and the Studio Flat, which are for two people only.

Great care has gone into the decoration and equipping of the cottages, with stripped pine and fitted carpets in the bedrooms, nice wooden furniture, wood burning stoves and very well-equipped kitchens. In short, the appropriate country cottage atmosphere has been maintained.

In the courtyard there is a games room with a table tennis table and a pool table and a well-equipped communal laundry. When we visited, a grass tennis court was about to be made ready for play and it is possible that a heated outdoor pool will be installed for the spring of 1994.

If you are looking for a family holiday in the tranquil surroundings of beautiful countryside, you should head for Breamish Valley Cottages.

Nearby: This is wonderful walking and cycling territory and all manner of country pursuits are available, including pony trekking, fishing, golf and swimming. There are excellent sandy beaches within reach: Embleton Bay, Beadnell Bay and Bamburgh for example. there are castles to see at Bamburgh, Dunstanburgh and Alnwick; you can visit Holy Island and the Farne Islands; and Chillingham Park, Cragside House, Wallington House and Brinkburn Priory are easily accessible.

Units: 7
Rent: £129 to £500 a week (short winter breaks also)
Other costs: none
2 cots and 2 high chairs
Heating: storage heating and wood burning stoves
Open all year

BURNSALL, NR SKIPTON, NORTH YORKS
P RED LION HOTEL, Burnsall
Tel: 0756 720 204.
On the B6160, in the centre of the village.

A wonderfully traditional old inn set in one of the classic Yorkshire Dales villages. Dating from the mid-17th century, this old building enjoys a perfect setting only a stone's throw from the attractive village green which goes down to the River Wharfe. With the magnificent Burnsall Fell and the rolling Dales countryside as a backdrop, it's a perfect spot in which to spend a few hours.

The pub is geared up to cater for its many tourists and you will find a comprehensive bar snack menu plus lunch and dinner menus; and several high chairs are made available.

There are two rooms where families may sit; a small room just across from the main bar or up some stairs a larger room which is furnished in attractive style. It was originally an old barn and some of the stonework has been retained. It has plenty of tables with comfortable chairs to match, and overlooks the garden, which comprises a terrace, a rockery and a patch of lawn. There are other stretches of lawn alongside the peaceful river, and you can also sit on the cobbled forecourt at the front of the pub.

✗ (12pm to 2.30pm & 6.30pm to 9.30pm onwards) £2–8: smoked chicken and avocado salad, steak and kidney pie, Cumberland sausage with red cabbage, poached salmon, sirloin steak
Children: half portions
🍺 Ale: Ind Coope Burton, Theakston's, Tetley's. No music
🅿 own car park

CAMBO, NORTHUMBERLAND
Ⓗ WALLINGTON HOUSE, Cambo
Tel: 067 074 283.
On the B6342 west of Morpeth.

The house was built in the late 17th century but remodelled about fifty years later and stands, classical and rather austere, in 100 acres of lawns, lakes and woodland. There is a delightful walled garden, where a Shakespeare play is performed each summer, and a fine conservatory with some marvellous fuchsias.

Eighteen rooms of the house are open to the public and the interior is notable for the Italian plasterwork, a collection of porcelain and of doll's houses. The central hall has an extraordinary array of paintings put on to panels by William Bell Scott.

The Clock Tower restaurant is an agreeable place and there are several high chairs and half portions for children. The food has a touch of imagination with sardine tart and Northumbrian casserole available on the menu when we visited.

The Ladies in the restaurant contains a table on which a baby could be changed.

Open: House – April to 31 October, every day except Tuesday, 1pm to 5.30pm; Grounds: all year during daylight
Charges: adults £4; children £2
Baby changing: a table in the Ladies
℗ ample

CHOLLERFORD, NR HEXHAM, NORTHUMBERLAND
Ⓗ GEORGE HOTEL (Swallow), Chollerford
Tel: 0434 681 611.
On the B6318.

If you follow the magnificent Roman road, arrow-like alongside Hadrian's Wall, you will find this charming old stone hotel parts of which date back to the 17th century. It has a peaceful location on the bank of the North Tyne, where guests can fish. The gardens running along the river are a mass of flowers in summer, and you can sit on the terraces in the summer.

There are some excellent facilities at the George, including a sizeable indoor swimming pool with a sauna and a whirlpool bath; It has a large conservatory where you can play table tennis and a terrace area where you can sit in the sun. Alongside there is plenty of space which includes a children's play area, a golf driving net and a pitch and putt course. Mountain bikes can also be hired.

The views over the river from the very comfortable and well-furnished lounges and especially from the attractive dining room with its wide windows are a great bonus. Many of the bedrooms have the same vistas and they are furnished and decorated to a very high standard; the family rooms are notably spacious and many of the rooms are big enough to accommodate an extra bed or a cot.

This is a very pleasant hotel with excellent facilities, and it is deservedly popular with families.

Nearby: The B6318 follows the line of Hadrian's Wall and you can visit several of the forts, the Roman Army Museum and the Roman site near Corbridge. There are many other attractions within reach including Belsay Hall, Wallington House and the Beamish Open Air Museum. Kielder Water has an array of water sports and Kielder Castle is the starting point for walks through the surrounding forest.

✗ LUNCH (12pm to 2pm) £13: seafood salad, cold buffet, pudding or cheese;
DINNER (7pm to 9.45pm) £20: poached trout, soup, sirloin steak, pudding or cheese
Children: own menu, half portions
£ high
Best Bargain Break: £85 per person 2 nights – dinner, b&b and one lunch
Children: free up to 14 years
Facilities: 6 cots and 6 high chairs; and a baby listening system
50 rooms, 2 family, 3 sets interconnecting
Open all year. Access/AmEx/Diners/Visa
Ⓟ own car park

DURHAM, CO. DURHAM
Ⓡ Ⓛ DURHAM CATHEDRAL, Durham
Tel: 091 386 4266.
In the centre of the city.

Situated high above the River Wear the great Cathedral dominates the city. It was begun in 1093 and completed forty years later. Huge marble columns support the vaulted roof, and the Galilee Chapel, built at the end of the 12th century, contains the tomb of the Venerable Bede.

The great central tower was rebuilt in the later 15th century and rises to nearly 200 feet. If you are feeling fit you can climb to the top and have superb views of the city.

Take a look at the 12th-century bronze knocker which used to be on the North door. Criminals who grasped it could claim the right of sanctuary, i.e. freedom from arrest. Not surprisingly this right was abolished in 1540. The Cathedral also has a museum which contains the remains of St Cuthbert's coffin.

Close to the treasury and the bookshop, you will find the restaurant, an attractive spot with light pine furniture and fine stone walls. There are several high chairs and a good range of food at fair prices.

Open: every day
Charges: admission free
Baby changing: a shelf in the Ladies
✕ £1–£4: soup, quiche, daily specials, cold buffet
Children: half portions
Open 10am to 5pm Mon to Sat (11am to 5pm Sun) Closed Christmas and Good Friday
No credit cards accepted
No smoking. No music
Ⓟ nearby public car parks

EAGLESCLIFFE VILLAGE, CLEVELAND
Ⓟ POT AND GLASS, Eaglescliffe
Tel: 0642 780 145.
Just off the A135, north of Yarm.

You may have a bit of fun trying to find this odd little pub set right at the back of this pretty village with its fine 11th-century parish church. Your best bet is to follow the boundary wall of the church round by the village green and you will locate the Pot and Glass in a dead end which is in fact opposite the back gate to the churchyard!

Your perseverance will be well rewarded for this is an establishment which is gloriously different, not least for its unlikely situation hidden away on the end of a smart avenue of houses.

It's deceptively spacious inside with the main bar serving a cosy tap room at one end and a larger lounge bar at the other. Drinks are also dispensed through a glass hatch to a central area with some wonderful red and black Victorian-style floor tiles. The family room is on the right hand side of the main corridor just in from the front door. It has some very comfortable powder blue upholstered bench seats which blend in well with the old black-stained beams and panelling.

Through the back of the pub, you will find a small patio with some bench tables and a climbing frame. It's a well-maintained little spot with plenty of greenery and flora.

As befits a 200-year-old building, there are plenty of relics from the past adorning the walls, including horse brasses and local items of interest.

The Sunday lunch is a bargain at under £5 (half portions depending on age).

✘ BAR MEALS (12pm to 2pm) £1–3: lasagne, quiche, steak pie, ploughman's
Children: half portions
⊟ Ale: Bass
℗ own car park (but very limited)

GARGRAVE, NR SKIPTON, NORTH YORKS
℗ ANCHOR INN
Tel: 0756 749 666.
On the A65 just west of Gargrave.

When we listed this pub a decade ago in the first edition of the *Guide* we called it 'a handsome stone roadside pub, which dates back to the 16th century'.

It still has its handsome stone facade but the interior has been totally changed and the pub is very much devoted to the family market. It is open all day and dispenses food for most of its opening hours, has plenty of high chairs, a children's menu and a nappy changing facility. In addition, there is a little play area indoors for the under 5s and two substantial playgrounds in the large garden at the rear.

The very spacious interior has been made into a series of inter-locking rooms and alcoves, on various levels and divided by wood and glass screens. There is wood panelling here and there, low ceilings, padded benches, the occasional sofa and sizeable no smoking areas (in particular the family dining room). It all adds up to an agreeable atmosphere with food at reasonable prices and a good selection of real ales.

✗ (11.30am to 10pm; from noon on Sunday) £2–8: vegetable parcels, steak & kidney pie, plaice & chips, lasagne verde, sirloin steak
Children: own menu
🍺 Ale: Boddington's, Jennings, Whitbread
Ⓟ lots

HARROGATE, NORTH YORKS
Ⓡ BETTYS CAFE TEAROOMS, 1 Parliament Street
Tel: 0423 502 746.
Off the A61 near the town centre and opposite Montpellier Gardens.

This is certainly not a place to be missed if you have children and are visiting this attractive town. It is a rare opportunity for parents of young children to relax in a stylish, high quality eating establishment. You can enjoy one of the café's delicious savoury snacks, including the well-known rarebits, or take your pick from one of the many freshly made cakes.

The Harrogate Bettys gives a terrific welcome to families; it provides excellent service and an interesting children's menu, including double decker sandwiches, Bettys clown or Bettys banana boat.

Like the other cafés in the Bettys chain (York, Ilkley and Northallerton), the Harrogate Bettys offers unbeatable facilities for mothers and babies; changing mats, playpen, potties, bibs and beakers are all made available, plus a great number of high chairs.

The kitchens will also supply a range of baby foods. It is also worth noting that Bettys has no objection to discreet breastfeeding in the restaurant – a policy which all breastfeeding mums will surely welcome.

✗ £2–8: scrambled eggs with smoked salmon, cheese & herb paté, Masham sausages with red cabbage, rarebits, rosti with bacon

Children: own menu, half portions
Open 9am to 9pm all week
Live piano music in the evening. Access/Visa
Most of the restaurant is no smoking. Licensed
Ⓟ street parking

NR HARROGATE, NORTH YORKS
Ⓟ NELSON INN
Tel: 0423 500 340.
Two miles west of Harrogate on the A59 to Skipton.

This old stone pub has long been a familiar sight to motorists on the
Skipton road and has now been greatly extended to accommodate a
wealth of facilities for families. Food is available throughout the
day, high chairs are provided in generous quantity and there is a
nappy changing facility. If you add to that a large indoor amusement
area for children (Treasure Island with a ball pool and many other
items) and a play unit in the enclosed garden, you can see that this
is very much a family orientated operation.

   Not that the adults will feel unloved because the interior is
designed in an agreeable way with Laura Ashley style wallpaper
amongst the stone walls, wooden panelling, glass screens and
painted skylights. It is comfortable and welcoming, the food is
reasonably priced and there is a choice of real ales.

✗ (11.30am to 10pm; from noon on Sunday) £2–8: smoked trout,
chicken escalopes, steak & kidney pie, vegetable crumble, lamb
rogan josh
Children: own menu
⌺ Ale: Boddington's, Castle Eden
Ⓟ own car park

NR HELMSLEY, NORTH YORKS
Ⓛ NUNNINGTON HALL, Nunnington
Tel: 04395 283.
Off the B1257 south-east of Helmsley.

This 17th-century manor house stands in several acres of grounds
on the bank of the river Rye near the packhorse bridge. It is an

interesting mix of Elizabethan and Stuart architecture and has been in the care of the National Trust since 1952.

There are three floors of period rooms on view including the panelled dining room, oak hall, great staircase, oak bedroom and drawing room. On the attic floor the famous Carlisle Collection is on display: sixteen miniature rooms decorated in the style of different periods, each room one-eighth of life size. There are also various exhibitions of dolls' houses and toys.

Fine tables, chintzy cloths and old dressers adorn the three tea rooms, which are all non-smoking areas. Picnic tables are set out on the lawn at the rear of the house. There are three high chairs available and the menu offers a range of snacks and salads, and afternoon teas and light lunches on Sundays.

Open: 26 March to 30 October, 2pm to 6pm (Tues, Wed, Thurs, Sat); Sun & bank holidays 12pm to 6pm; Friday in July & August, 2pm to 6pm
Charges: adults £3.50; children £1.50
Baby changing: well-equipped mother and baby room on the first floor
P ample

NR HEXHAM, NORTHUMBERLAND
H SC RYE HILL FARM, Slaley
Tel: 0434 673 259.
Off the B6306 south of Hexham.

This is a delightful 17th-century stone farmhouse which has been converted with taste and provides excellent facilities for visitors. The building forms an open courtyard with the farmhouse at one end and the guests' bedrooms situated in the central wing.

The agreeable dining room has some pine panelling and pine tables and the adjoining comfortable lounge includes a toys and games cupboard. We looked at several bedrooms, all of which have their own bathrooms, and were most impressed by the high standards of the furniture and decorations. There is a very spacious family room (with a double bed and two bunk beds for children) at one end of the building and it as superb views of the countryside from one of its windows (another window looks into a large barn).

There are thirty acres of grounds including a good stretch of garden and a patio, and there are fine views of Slaley Forest and of the undulating farmland. There is loads of room for children to play and they will find a swing, a slide and a climbing frame in the grounds. Indoors, there is an excellent games room with a pool table, and plenty of games and easy chairs.

Nearby: Northumberland has sometimes been called the 'forgotten county', and if you want glorious, unspoiled countryside, and an area crammed with history – in short a place to enjoy without hustle and bustle – this is the place to be. Hadrian's Wall runs just to the north of Hexham and you can follow the line of forts from the Roman Army Museum near Haltwhistle east to the Roman site of Corbridge. A bit further afield is Kielder Forest and Kielder Water, and the interesting city of Durham.

✗ DINNER (7.30pm) £10
Children: half portions
£ low
Children: free up to 2 years; half price up to 12
Facilities: 1 cot and 1 high chair
6 rooms, 2 family. Open all year
No credit cards. No smoking in bedrooms
Ⓟ ample. No music
Self-catering: The Old Byre can accommodate up to nine people and will therefore suit a large family. The lounge, dining area and kitchen are integrated in one attractive and spacious room with a

wood-burning stove and the kitchen has everything a cook might
need, a dishwasher, microwave oven and fridge freezer. There is
a twin-bedded room (plus a folding bed), a double room, both
with their own bathrooms, and a bunk bedroom for children. All
linen and central heating is included and the rent varies from £250
to £550 a week.

ILKLEY, WEST YORKS
🅁 BETTYS CAFE TEAROOMS, 34 The Grove
Tel: 0943 608 029.
In the town centre.

This busy and cheerful tea room, like the other Bettys (qv Harrogate, Northallerton and York), is immediately appealing with its
marble-topped tables, basket-weave chairs, the pot plants and its
delightful collection of teapots on shelves around the walls. There
are real flowers on the tables and the tea is also made from real
tea leaves; there is a wide selection, as there is of coffee.

The long room has windows down one side which makes it a
bright and airy place; and those adjectives might also apply to the
staff, who cope with the demands of a busy café with great charm.

Above all, the Ilkley tea rooms welcome families, provides an
interesting children's menu and superb mother and baby facilities,
with a playpen, changing mat and chair in the Ladies and eight
high chairs in the restaurant.

✗ £1–7: rarebits, raclette and ham florentine, cheese & herb paté,
haddock & chips, bacon muffins
Children: own menu, half portions
Open 9am to 6pm Mon to Thurs, 9am to 6.30pm Fri to Sun
Access/Visa. Licensed
No smoking in most of café
🅿 public car park at rear

LONGHORSLEY, NORTHUMBERLAND
SC BEACON HILL FARM
Tel: 0670 788 372.
Off the A697 just south of Longhorsley.

Beacon Hill Farm has a wonderful location high above the North-umbrian countryside, which rolls expansively away to the Cheviots in one direction and to the sea in the other. As the name suggests it was once a place where advance warnings could be given of raids by the marauding Scots: now the commanding views will delight your eye.

The fine array of facilities make it an ideal place for a family holiday. Above all there is plenty of space in which to relax, 350 acres which include large stretches of woodland around the cottages. It makes a splendid and safe playground for children and is of great interest to walkers and anyone interested in wildlife.

The other amenities, all of high quality, include a hard tennis court; a very well-designed indoor swimming pool with a terrace outside where you can sit and enjoy the view, a sauna and a solarium; a cricket net; and a very comfortable and spacious children's common room with easy chairs, a television, table tennis, a pool table and table football. This is a place where children can enjoy each other's company without supervision.

Horse-mad children will adore Beacon Hill since there are around 20 horses and ponies which can be ridden from Whitsun to mid-September (under supervision) at no extra cost.

Seven of the cottages are grouped together around a quiet grassy courtyard on one side and another open courtyard on the other. The majority of them will sleep six people; two of them will sleep four and Wood Cottage accommodates two people.

All of the cottages differ in design but have in common high-quality furniture, decorations and equipment. The kitchens, for example, contain everything a cook might need including microwave and conventional cookers and plenty of gadgets. They all have stretches of garden or terrace and the great bonus of the idyllic scenery. A nice touch is the provision of a wide range of books in every property.

We looked at several properties including Beech Cottage, which has its sitting room on the upper storey and a large arched window looks south, with windows on the other two sides. Beacon Hill

Cottage has masses of space by dint of a very large conservatory which takes full advantage of the wonderful views and there is a large sitting room alongside. Stable Cottage has a large arched window at one end of its high-ceilinged living room (there are two bedrooms, one with bunk beds). Finally we saw the detached Quarry House which sits in its own grounds and has panoramic views over the countryside. It is a very spacious house with a large sitting room with a terrace beyond the french windows, a splendid country kitchen with attractive wooden furniture and a utility room.

We were tremendously impressed with Beacon Hill Farm, where nothing has been stinted in the effort to provide first class accommodation and facilities for family holidays in a wonderful location. It was no surprise that it won an England for Excellence Award a couple of years ago.

Nearby: There are sandy beaches on the nearby coast, at Druridge Bay and Warkworth for example, and nature reserves and coastal walks. In addition to the sports available at Beacon Hill, golf and fishing and all the watersports can be arranged. Northumberland is a great place for castles: at Alnwick, Bamburgh, Dunstanburgh and Warkworth; and you can visit Holy Island, Cragside House, Chillingham Park, Wallington Hall and Brinkburn Priory.

Units: 8
Rent: £175 to £800 a week
Other costs: none
Heating: central heating and wood burners
Plenty of cots and high chairs
Open all year

MALHAM, NR SKIPTON, NORTH YORKS
P BUCK INN, Malham
Tel: 0729 830 317.
In the centre of the village.

This large stone inn, built in 1874, nestles in the centre of an attractive village which is a good base for exploring the dramatic limestone scenery in this area of the dales; Malham Cove and Malham Tarn are hikers' favourites.

The two bars both serve traditional Theakston's ale; the Hikers

Bar is designed for the walking fraternity and the Lounge Bar for those of a less robust nature. Both bars are open for food at lunchtime and in the evenings and families are welcome in both. (High chairs are available.) The dining room offers reasonably priced food every evening in cosy surroundings.

There are tables at the front of the pub and a terrace at the back. Accommodation is available; ten bedrooms, all with en-suite bathrooms.

✗ (12am to 2pm & 7pm to 9pm) £1–5: Malham & Masham pie, garlic & prawn pasta, Cumberland sausage & mash, chilli con carne, scampi
Children: own menu, half portions
Ⓟ own car park

MALTON, NORTH YORKS
Ⓛ EDEN CAMP, Malton
Tel: 0653 697 777.
Off the A64 north-east of Malton.

The camp was built from 1942 to house prisoners of war captured in North Africa. Both Germans and Italians were imprisoned here and built Eden Camp themselves.

Several years ago the whole place was re-vamped to tell the story of the British people during the Second World War. There are over twenty huts with a series of displays and moving tableaux, which include the sounds and smells of war, and these convey many of the key stories of that time: the Blitz, prisoners of war, a bomber operations room, the rise of Hitler and the Nazis, the Home Guard, the Bevin Boys and so on.

Hut 3 will certainly appeal to youngsters since it is the interior of a German U-boat and you experience the effects of being torpedoed and being set adrift on a life raft. They can also tackle the assault course which concludes with an escape route through a tunnel. On a lighter note you can see a twenty minute puppet show which shows some of the great entertainers of the time: Max Miller, Vera Lynn, Gracie Fields, Flanagan and Allen, Stanley Holloway. Pass me a handkerchief, mother!

It is a fascinating place which should appeal to anyone with an interest in modern history.

The 'Prisoners' Canteen' serves a range of hot and cold dishes, including a Nazi pasty and Rommel's pie (cottage pie). High chairs are provided. You can also have a drink in the Garrison Cinema Bar.

Open: 10am to 5pm, 14 February to 23 December
Charges: adults £3; children and OAPs £2 (1993 prices)
Baby changing: a baby changing and feeding room
℗ ample

NR MALTON, NORTH YORKS
Ⓛ CASTLE HOWARD, Coneysthorpe
Tel: 065 384 333.
Off the A64 south west of Malton.

Castle Howard is one of the most flamboyant stately homes in Britain. It waas designed for Charles Howard, the third Earl of Carlisle, by John Vanbrugh in 1700 and was his first commission as an architect. Not a bad start! His assistant was Nicholas Hawksmoor, who worked for Wren, and his influence is seen in the Great Hall with its vast domed ceiling.

The house is packed with treasures: paintings by Reynolds, Gainsborough and Van Dyck, and including a famous portrait of Henry VIII by Holbein; frescoes by Pellegrini; magnificent furniture; and one of the largest collections of costumes in Britain.

The grounds have huge expanses of lawn, woods, nature walks, and the Great Lake, where you can fish. You should also take a look at Hawksmoor's Mausoleum and Vanbrugh's Temple of the Four Winds. There are acres of space in which to wander, or have a picnic, and the children can enjoy the excellent adventure playground.

The bright and spacious self-service cafeteria overlooks a garden, and there are tables and chairs set out on the lawn. There are two high chairs and a children's menu. Smokers are confined to an adjoining room.

You can have a wonderful day out at this spectacular stately home, where there is so much to see and enjoy. Parents of small children should note, however, that pushchairs are not allowed in the house.

Open: Easter to November, from 10am (grounds), 11am (house and gallery)

   Charges: adults £5.50; OAPs £5; children £3; under 4s free (1993 prices)

Baby changing: a chair in the Ladies and a hard surface

P ample

NEWTHORPE, NR LEEDS, NORTH YORKS
P NEW INN, Newthorpe
Tel: 0977 682 325.
On the B1222 and close to the A1 at South Milford.

This is a gigantic family pub which has the added attraction for children of a Fun Factory housed in a separate building at the back of the pub. This has all sorts of amusements – a ball pool, slides, tunnels, toys and games – and is always supervised by a member of staff. In addition, there are children's rides on the terrace, a playground on a safe bark surface and a bouncy castle.

   If the children are catered for, so is everyone else, since the pub serves food throughout the day and for most of the evening. There is a children's menu, high chairs and a nappy changing facility.

   The interior of the New Inn may be large but it is not overwhelming since it is designed on various levels; for example one of the two large bars is downstairs and the pub is divided into manageable eating areas (several of which are no smoking) by the use of wooden pillars and glass screens. It is comfortable and welcoming and has food on offer at decent prices.

✗ (11.30am to 10pm; from noon on Sunday) £2–8: fish dippers, sirloin steak, sole bearnaise, chicken masala, Spanish omelette
Children: own menu
⊕ Ale: Boddington's, Whitbread
P own car park

NORTHALLERTON, NORTH YORKS
Ⓡ BETTYS CAFE TEAROOMS, 188 High Street
Tel: 0609 775 154.
On the main street.

You will find a civilized and charming atmosphere at this café, the smallest of the celebrated chain of Bettys. The standards are extremely high and the welcome for families is whole-hearted.

There are changing facilities in the Ladies (and a playpen) upstairs and, as well as several high chairs, nappies, bibs and beakers will be provided. The infants' and children's menu shows real flair and imagination.

If you find it hard to resist homemade cakes, this is the place and there is also a wide range of savouries, grills and sandwiches. There is also an excellent range of tea and unusual blends of coffee.

✗ £2–7: rarebits, haddock & prawns croustades, omelettes, cheese & herb paté, scrambled egg with smoked salmon
Open 9am to 5.30pm, from 10am Sundays. Access/Visa
No music. Licensed
No smoking in café
Ⓟ on street and car park nearby

RIPON, NORTH YORKS
Ⓛ LIGHTWATER VALLEY THEME PARK, Ripon
Tel: 0765 635 321.
Three miles north of Ripon, on the A6108.

The park is set in over a hundred acres of splendid North Yorkshire countryside and lakeland and the designers have succeeded admirably in maintaining the natural environment of the surroundings, and in providing a theme park which will appeal to people of all ages.

A large boating lake forms the focal point of the park and all around it can be found a diverse range of amusements for all the family: white knuckle rides including the Ultimate, the world's biggest roller-coaster; the Rat, the world's only subterranean roller-coaster; and the Soopa Loopa, a double looped roller-coaster. For younger children there is an adventure playground plus swings, roundabouts and sandpits. They will also enjoy Old MacDonald's

Farm with its goats, calves and lambs. Older children can test their skills with some Grand Prix go-karting or canoeing.

New attractions which arrived in 1993 included a 1000-seat big top circus, a family rollercoaster (the ladybird) and a futuristic games alley.

The different attractions are all well spread out and you must expect to do a considerable amount of walking to see everything there is on offer. If you do tire however, there is a miniature railway which takes visitors around the circumference of the grounds at regular intervals.

Most of the restaurants and cafés are located in one central area, built out of attractive rustic brick. Here you will find a pub, carvery, snack bars and a self-service restaurant, and high chairs are available.

The whole park is kept meticulously clean with plenty of litter bins and there are also good facilities for mothers and babies, first aid and facilities for the disabled.

We feel this theme park has a lot going for it. There are amusements galore for youngsters but also plenty of attractions for older children and adults. More importantly you do not feel engulfed by noise or merry-go-rounds and there is some gorgeous scenery for those who just want to sit and watch the world go by.

Open: Easter fortnight; weekends in May; 22 May to 30 May; daily in June, July and August; weekends only to end of October; 10am onwards
Charges: admission £8.50; OAPs £5.95; children under 1.3m in height £6.95; under 4s free (1993 prices)
Baby changing: a mother and baby room close to the adventure playground
P free car park

NR RIPON, NORTH YORKS
Ⓛ FOUNTAINS ABBEY, Sawley
Tel: 0765 608 888.
Off the B6265 west of Ripon.

Fountains Abbey was built in the 12th century by Cistercian monks and was once the most prosperous religious foundation in Britain.

Its fortunes were founded on the wool trade. It is now the largest monastic ruin in Europe and the scale of the buildings is remarkable: kitchens and guest houses, dormitories, an infirmary, workshops and cellars. It resembles a small village.

The roofless chapel of Nine Altars still shows its beautiful design, with fine pillars and graceful arches. A line of cloisters, over a hundred yards in length, makes a magnificent sight.

The Abbey stands on the banks of the River Skell and Studley Royal is the Abbey's garden, laid out in the 18th century with water gardens, temples and follies, statues and waterfalls. There is a lake and a large deer park.

The main tea room is at Studley Royal and overlooks the lake. It is a lovely spot and you can choose from a selection of snacks and hot meals, with a choice of country wines such as gooseberry and elderberry. High chairs are provided.

Open: every day except Christmas and Fridays from November to January. From 10am to between 5pm and 6pm
Charges: adults £3.80; children £1.90 (1993 prices)
Baby changing: a table in a bathroom in Fountains Hall
ℙ ample

NR RIPON, NORTH YORKS
Ⓛ NEWBY HALL AND GARDENS, Boroughbridge
Tel: 0423 322 583.
Off the A61 and the B6265 south-east of Ripon.

Newby Hall is a distinguished Queen Anne mansion with many additions and alterations made by Robert Adam in 1770.

The interior has recently been restored to its former splendour and includes some fine Chippendale furniture and tapestries by Gobelin. There is also a gallery of classical statuary, and a wonderful collection of chamber pots.

The beautiful gardens have a large variety of rare plants and are especially notable for the display of laburnums and for the herbaceous borders. A miniature train, the Royal Scot, runs through the grounds and will delight the children, as will the adventure playground, which is a great place to expend some energy.

The woodland discovery walk takes you on a circular route

through woodlands that have long been closed to visitors. There is a special picnic area close to the car park.

The restaurant has high chairs available and serves half portions for children.

Open: 11am to 5.30pm, 28 March to 29 September. Closed on Mondays (except bank holidays)
Charges: adults £5; OAPs £4; children £2.90 (1993 prices)
Baby changing: changing mat in the Ladies
P ample

ROSEDALE ABBEY, NORTH YORKS
SC BELL END FARM, Rosedale Abbey
Tel: 0751 417 431.
North-west of Pickering. The owners provide detailed directions.

Bell End Farm opened its doors to visitors in 1988 and is a triumph for Richard Castle's enterprise and imagination. A series of dilapidated barns and other farm buildings have been transformed into eight splendid holiday homes which have won many awards. The cottages form an L-shape and are built of stone under mellow red pantile roofs. Excellent use has been made of stone interior walls and exposed wooden beams, and the cottages have been furnished and equipped to a very high standard. It is pleasing to report, for example, that electricity and heating, linen and towels are all provided within the cost.

The cottages vary in size and can sleep from two to six people, and they are all (with the one exception of Park's Delight) suitable for family occupation. High chairs and cots are provided and the stairs have safety gates at top and bottom. The homes have marvellous views of the beautiful countryside, and several of them are designed with the living areas on the top storey to take full advantage of this.

The facilities at Bell End are exceptional. There are two acres of grounds in which the adults can relax and the children can play. The spreading trees and the views of the hills add to one's pleasure. The play area includes a climbing frame, sand pit and swing. Indoors, you will find a heated swimming pool and the thoughtful owner provides a playpen here. Mountain bikes can be hired, along with trailers which can carry two young children. Great fun. On a practical note, a washing machine and a drier are available in the utilities area.

Bell End Farm has been constructed with great flair, and with a grasp of detail which is essential if a family holiday is to be a success. It is no surprise that Bell End Farm was put in the Highly Commended category by the English Tourist Board. It is a splendid place in a beautiful part of England where everyone, especially families, is made welcome.

Nearby: You are in the heart of the North York Moors with wonderful walks all around you, and there are excellent facilities for horse riding, fishing on the Esk, Derwent, Dove and Rye, and golf. Racing fans have a choice of six well-known venues. It is a very good base if you wish to see the sights: Flamingo Land, Eden Camp, Nunnington Hall, Castle Howard, Shandy Hall, Rievaulx Abbey and Mount Grace Priory are all within easy reach, as are the coastal resorts between Whitby and Scarborough.

Units: 8
Rent: £300 to £813 a week (winter breaks available)
Other costs: none
Heating: night storage
Plenty of cots and high chairs
Open all year

ROTHBURY, NORTHUMBERLAND
L CRAGSIDE HOUSE AND COUNTRY PARK,
Rothbury
Tel: 0669 20333.
Off the B6341 north of Rothbury.

Lord Armstrong chose a magnificent setting for his house, which sits in bowl surrounded by wooded hills. The trees owe their existence to Lord Armstrong, who planted millions of them, plus rhododendrons, azaleas and a multiplicity of other plants and shrubs on the hillsides and in the 1000 acres of grounds.

He employed the Victorian architect, Norman Shaw, to design the house and it is a rare mix of styles including black and white timbering in the Tudor style, the Victorian chimneys and Gothic arches. The thirty or so rooms are furnished much as Lord Armstrong left them and a typical touch of Victorian panache is an Italian marble chimneypiece which weighs ten tons and is done in the Renaissance style.

This was the first house in the world to be lit by hydro-electricity from the series of man-made lakes in the grounds and you can see how it all worked on the 'power circuit' walk. There are walks galore, forty miles of them, through the beautiful gardens or you can do it the easy way – by car on the six mile scenic drive.

The visitor centre contains a video display, the Armstrong energy centre and a cafeteria with many photos of Vickers Armstrong ships and aircraft on the walls. There are a couple of high chairs. The mother and baby room is also located in the visitor centre, and has a changing table and a chair. It is spacious enough but rather chilly.

Open: House – 1 April to 31 October, 1pm to 5.30pm. Closed on Mondays; Park – every day, 10.30m to 7pm from 1 April to 31 October. Weekends only in winter, 10.30am to 4pm
Charges: adults £5.40; children £2.70 (1993 prices)
Baby changing: mother and baby room
P plenty

SEDBUSK, NR HAWES, NORTH YORKS
Ⓗ THE STONE HOUSE HOTEL, Sedbusk
Tel: 0969 667 571.
Off the A684 near Hawes.

This delightful country hotel is situated amid glorious scenery on the edge of the Yorkshire Dales. It has been highly recommended

for many years in *The Family Welcome Guide*, not only for the outstanding value it represents but also for the warm and friendly welcome which Mr and Mrs Taplin offer.

The house, a listed building, was converted less than a decade ago, and enormous care was taken to preserve its character. An old broom cupboard houses the serving hatch to the tiny bar, and the old library has been retained. There are plenty of books there, and a snooker table and an interesting collection of vintage slot machines. The hotel is encircled by a lawned garden, which includes a grass tennis court.

The food is cooked from fresh produce, and even the sausages are made on the spot. Children can have high teas, and although lunches are not served, the owners will supply packed lunches, if requested.

The hotel also has a niche in literary history. That wonderful writer, P.G. Wodehouse, found a name for his famous butler after meeting the original owner of Stone House, Hugh Crallan, whose own butler was called Jeeves.

Nearby: You may fancy a packed lunch because this is wonderful walking country, or you can vary this with some horse riding and fishing. It's a marvellous part of the world for touring around to see the sights: the Dales Folk Museum, Bolton Castle, Jervaulx Abbey and Richmond Castle are all within easy reach; and further away to the south you can visit Malham Cove, Stump Cross Caverns, and Bolton Abbey. Fishing, golf and sailing are all readily available in the locality.

✗ DINNER (7pm to 8pm) £15: bacon & mushroom savoury, beef bourguignon, fresh fruit salad, cheese
Children: half portions, high teas
£ medium
Best Bargain Break: £39 per person per night – dinner, b&b
Children: £6 (including breakfast)
Facilities: 2 cots and 2 high chairs; and a baby listening system
15 rooms, 1 family. Access/Visa
Closed Jan & midweek Nov to Mar. No smoking in dining room
ℙ own car park

SOWERBY BRIDGE, WEST YORKS
ℙ THE MOORINGS, Canal Basin
Tel: 0422 833 940.
Just off the A58.
On the canal!

You find pubs in some interesting places and this one, in a converted canal warehouse, is an ingenious piece of enterprise. The buildings date from 1790 and form part of the once major interchange moorings between the Rochdale canal and the Calder and Hebble Navigation. Today it is a marine leisure centre in its own right with several shops and is a base for a fleet of narrow boats which are available for hire.

The big picture windows in the pub offer fine views over the canal and if the weather is fine you can sit on the terrace and watch the array of colourful barges which populate the waterway.

The interior is decked out with scrubbed pine settles and tile-topped tables and children can use a special room off the main bar lounge with the same super views.

The landlord is rightly proud of his beer and various rosettes and certificates for real ale line the walls. He does not confine himself to British products – there are some interesting Belgian fruit beers and other powerful potions. We visited the pub on a Sunday lunchtime when it was packed and we were struck by the cheerful and friendly atmosphere. The customers included plenty of families and people of all ages and the staff coped with them all in splendid and efficient style. The food we had was excellent and families should note that the restaurant is open all day on Sunday.

✕ BAR MEALS (12pm to 2pm & 6.30pm to 9.30pm) £1–5: Bargee plates with salads, haddock & prawn crumble, Murphy's pie, baked potatoes, spinach & mushroom lasagne.
Children: own menu, half portions
🍺 Ale: McEwan's, Moorhouses, Theakston's & guest beers
Ⓟ on the wharf

NR THIRSK, NORTH YORKS
Ⓗ DOXFORD HOUSE, 73 Front St, Sowerby
Tel: 0845 523 238.
Off the A19 just south of Thirsk.

This Georgian house sits in a lovely tree-lined street in the attractive village of Sowerby on the outskirts of Thirsk. The rooms, with their good proportions and high ceilings, have a spacious look to them, especially the dining room and the comfortable lounge, with its piano. These are both at the front of the house with large bay windows and up above are the two family rooms. These are both sizeable and cheerfully furnished and have double beds and bunk beds for the children.

A large walled garden stretches away at the back of the house. There is plenty of lawn where the adults can relax and the children can play and there is also a paddock.

Nearby: You are in the heart of the Dales, with marvellous countryside to tour, either by car, on foot, on horseback or by bicycle. Thirsk itself was 'Darrowby' in James Herriot's novels and there are many other interesting sights to see; Rievaulx Abbey, Sutton Bank with its white horse, Nunnington Hall, Flamingo Land, Eden Camp, Castle Howard, Fountains Abbey and Aldborough Roman Town.

✗ DINNER (6.30pm) £7: soup, lamb steaks, sherry trifle
Children: small portions
£ low
Children: £1 per year of age to a maximum of £7
Facilities: 2 cots and a high chair; baby sitting by arrangement
4 rooms, 2 family. Open all year except Christmas
No smoking in bedrooms and dining room. Unlicensed
Ⓟ at front. No music

WASHINGTON, TYNE & WEAR
Ⓛ WILDFOWL AND WETLANDS CENTRE,
Washington
Tel: 091 416 5454.
East of Washington in District 15 and one mile from the A19. Signposted off the A195 and A1231.

This centre is one of eight run by the Wildfowl and Wetlands Trust, which was founded by Peter Scott.

In the 100 acres of the centre you can see an array of rare and interesting birds: Hawaiian geese, Great Spotted woodpeckers, Treecreepers, Chilean flamingoes, Trumpeter swans, King eiders, Mandarin, Shoveller and Carolina ducks. There are 27 species of wader and herons.

Special hides and a series of walkways give the visitor superb views across the countryside. You can wander through the woods, take a picnic and the children will enjoy the play area. The main visitor building has a coffee shop with a good choice of meals and snacks, and high chairs are provided.

Open: summer 9.30am to 5pm. Closes one hour before dusk in winter.
Charges: adults £3.20; OAPs £2.60; children £1.60; under 4s free (1993 prices)
Baby changing: mother and baby room
Ⓟ own car park

WHITBY, NORTH YORKS
Ⓡ TRENCHERS, New Quay Road
Tel: 0947 603 212.
In the town centre, opposite the tourist information office.

This family-owned restaurant looks so neat and clean with its white-tiled floor and green bench seats. The fresh flowers enhance the modern decor, and it is a very popular spot with locals and tourists alike. This area of the town is being redeveloped.

The menu is extensive and includes many different fresh fish dishes. The premises were recently extended and the restaurant can now seat nearly 200 people.

The facilities for families include high chairs, breastfeeding facilities, and a changing mat and child seat in the Ladies. The children's menu offers a good choice including chunky cod, cold roast ham, cottage pie and fisherman's casserole.

✗ £1-6: prawn salad, cottage pie, cod, haddock, plaice, sole, etc
Children: own menu, half portions
Open 11am to 9pm, mid-Mar to Nov
Ⓟ on street

WIGHILL, NORTH YORKS
Ⓟ WHITE SWAN INN, Wighill
Tel: 0937 832 217.
Off the A684. Look for the Wighill sign two and a half miles east of Tadcaster.

Located in a charming village, it is well worth straying off the main roads to stop off at this ivy-clad pub, with its terraces at front and rear.

It is a delightful pubby place which is made up from five small low ceilinged rooms, all of which are well-furnished, partly with antique pieces. There are log fires in all of them. Two of these rooms can be used by families: one is a most attractive room with a beamed ceiling and plenty of space; the other is a pretty little snug with padded benches around a wooden table. In addition there is a pleasant restaurant.

There is an enterprising choice of food here, available at all times except Sunday evening, a good selection of wines, much wider than most pubs, and of real ales.

It all adds up to a welcoming pub with good facilities for families.

✗ (12pm to 2pm & 6.30pm to 9pm Fri & Sat) £2–11: game pie, haddock and chips, fresh salmon, wild boar pie, sirloin steak
Children: small portions
🍺 Ale: Theakston's, Stone's, Tetley, Younger's
Ⓟ own car park

YORK, NORTH YORKS
Ⓗ CARLTON HOTEL AND RESTAURANT, 140
Acomb Road
Tel: 0904 781 181.
On the B1224, one and a half miles from the city centre.

A Victorian building which stands in its own substantial grounds with a wide expanse of lawn at the front and the back of the hotel, and there is plenty of space for children to play and for adults to relax. It is a quiet hotel with welcoming and hospitable owners and staff and has the advantage of being quite close to the centre of the city. There are several cots and high chairs and, apart from the two permanent family rooms, at least three others can be made up to accommodate a family.

We had a very complimentary report about the hotel from Jane Green, over from New Zealand with her family. She commented on the 'helpful, friendly staff . . . good food and service' and thought the hotel good value for money. We stayed there for a weekend a couple of years ago and entirely agree with her assessment.

Nearby: York is a fascinating and very attractive city with many places to see; the Minster as a start, the Treasurer's House, the Railway Museum, the City Art Gallery and the Jorvik Viking Centre. There is a great deal more within an easy drive including Beningborough Hall, Aldborough Roman Town, Newby Hall, Fountains Abbey, Ripley Castle, Shandy Hall, Castle Howard, Eden Camp and Flamingo Land.

✖ DINNER (6.30pm to 10pm) £15: seafood mornay, noisettes of lamb, pudding or cheese
Children: own menu, half portions
£ high
Best Bargain Break: £29 per person, per night – dinner, b&b
Children: free up to 3 years, £9 from 4 to 15 years
Facilities: 2 cots and 2 high chairs; baby listening system on 3 lines
12 rooms, 3 family, 1 set interconnecting. Access/AmEx/Visa
Ⓟ own car park

YORK, NORTH YORKS
Ⓡ BETTYS CAFÉ TEAROOMS, 6–8 St Helen's Square
Tel: 0904 659 142.

The famous Bettys chain of North Yorkshire tea rooms and restaurants are firm favourites of ours and has set out to cater with style for all their customers, including families.

Mothers with babies or small children can dine here with the knowledge that the Ladies offers changing facilities, a play pen and disposable nappies. There are also bibs, beakers, plates and spoons for young children plus both a toddler's and children's menu. They'll even heat up your own baby food if you ask them. There are no less than six high chairs on the premises.

The main menu is long and varied and offers anything from a piece of granary toast to gammon and eggs, with cakes and confectionery and a host of different blends of tea and coffee.

On Sundays the various breakfasts are very popular and you can eat at leisure, browse through the Sunday papers, and listen to the piano.

✗ £2–8: Swiss winter bake, haddock & prawn croustade, rarebits, haddock & chips, rosti with bacon
Children: own menu, half portions
Open 9am to 9pm every day. Access/Visa
Licensed. Pianist most evenings
No smoking in half the café
Ⓟ public car parks nearby

YORK, NORTH YORKS
Ⓡ BLAKE HEAD VEGETARIAN CAFÉ, 104 Micklegate
Tel: 0904 623 767.
In one of the city's main streets.

At the back of an excellent bookshop housed in a 17th-century listed building, you will find this delightful coffee shop and restaurant, which has been designed with some flair to make the maximum use of the available space. Brick pillars, plain wooden beams and a tiled floor set the style, and all down one side there is a glass canopy which gives a light and airy aspect to the place. Attractively plain wooden chairs and tables and interesting prints on the walls complete the picture.

It's a great place to buy books – including *The Family Welcome Guide* and Malcolm Hamer's thrillers! – and you can follow up with some excellent salads and vegetarian dishes. Wherever possible organically grown fruit and vegetables are used, and the cheeses are made with non-animal rennet. The wine and beers are also organic.

There are excellent facilities for mothers with babies, including a chair and a pull-down shelf in the spacious toilet area. Bibs, beakers and plastic plates are also provided.

✗ £2–5: salads, homemade soup, leek & cheese quiche, creamy lemon & mushroom pasta, cheese & spinach layer
Children: half portions
Open 9.30am to 5.30pm, every day, from 6.30pm Fri and Sat
Access/AmEx/Visa. Licensed
No smoking
Ⓟ public car parks nearby

YORKS, NORTH YORKS
Ⓡ TAYLOR'S TEA ROOMS, 46 Stonegate
Tel: 0904 622 865.

The wonderful aroma of freshly ground coffee greets you as you enter this homely tea room and coffee shop. You'll find the restaurant on the first floor and the first thing which confronts you is an array of different teas and coffees, and an interesting display of unusual and ancient teapots. If you fancy some Vintage Darjeeling, or some Formosa Oolong, this is the place.

The bright airy restaurant serves beverages, snacks and light meals all day; sandwiches rub shoulders with an extensive array of salads through to savouries, cakes and desserts.

Mothers with babies can relax here since there is a separate changing room, with a shelf and changing mat and a chair. Nappies, bibs and beakers, and baby foods are also provided.

The only music to reach your ears is the occasional strains of a busker from the pedestrian precinct below.

✖ £1–7: scrambled eggs on toast, rarebits, omelettes, breakfast grill, Swiss winter bake
Children: half portions
Open 9am to 5.30pm every day
Closed Christmas, Boxing Day & New Year. Access/Visa
No smoking in half the restaurant. Unlicensed
Ⓟ public car parks nearby. No music

Scotland

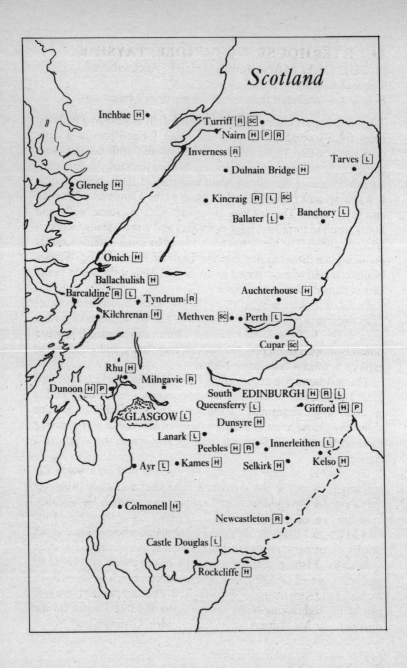

Scotland

Inchbae [H] •
Turriff [R] [SC] •
Nairn [H] [P] [R]
Inverness [R]
Tarves [L]
• Dulnain Bridge [H]
Glenelg [H]
• Kincraig [R] [L] [SC]
Ballater [L] • Banchory [L]
Onich [H]
Ballachulish [H]
Barcaldine [R] [L] • Tyndrum [R]
Auchterhouse [H]
• Kilchrenan [H]   Methven [SC] • Perth [L]
Cupar [SC]
Rhu [H]
Milngavie [R]
Dunoon [H] [P]
South ● EDINBURGH [H] [R] [L]
Queensferry [L]   • Gifford [H] [P]
GLASGOW [L]   Dunsyre [H]
Lanark [L]
Peebles [H] [R] •
Innerleithen [L]
Ayr [L]   • Kames [H]   Selkirk [H] •   Kelso [H]
• Colmonell [H]
Newcastleton [R] •
Castle Douglas [L]
• Rockcliffe [H]

AUCHTERHOUSE, NR DUNDEE, TAYSIDE
Ⓗ THE OLD MANSION HOUSE, Auchterhouse
Tel: 082 626 366.
Follow the hotel sign from the B954 north of Muirhead.

The original part of this stylish and beautifully maintained building
dates from around 1450, when the tower formed part of a large
courtyard castle. Additions were made in the 16th century and,
amongst the interior decorations, there is an unusual pendant ceiling which graces the dining room and part of the reception area.
It was a present from the Earl of Marr to the Countess of Buchan
and is a rarity. The interior is superb with its stone walls and
floors, antique furniture, huge open fires and a marvellous Jacobean
vaulted ceiling. The house has been owned by some notable families
including the Strathmores and the Earls of Buchan, and William
Wallace is said to have stayed in the house. Hence the tower to the
east is named 'Wallace's Tower'.

Facilities include a squash court, grass tennis court, heated outdoor swimming pool and a croquet lawn. The eleven acres of garden
are a delight to the eye and comprise a series of secluded lawns and
flower beds with sheltering yew hedges, huge trees, and woodland to
explore beyond a fast-running burn.

The bedrooms are decorated and furnished in excellent style and
there is a sizeable family suite which contains a four-poster bed, a
separate single room and a bathroom. Another family room runs
above the dining room and has a bathroom at one end and a shower
room at the other; it is very large, probably about the length of a
cricket pitch.

Bar food is available morning and evening and on a warm day
you might sit out in the courtyard. The chef will cook 'whatever
they want' for the children. The food is of an extremely high quality.

In the first edition of *The Family Welcome Guide* we wrote of the
Old Mansion House as 'an exceptional place, whether for a quick
drink or a longer stay' and that judgement is as appropriate as ever.

Nearby: Fishing and shooting can be arranged via the hotel
and there are some great golf courses within reach – Carnoustie,
St Andrews, Rosemount and Gleneagles for example. You are well
placed for sightseeing with Camperdown Wildlife Centre on the
doorstep; the McManus Galleries in Dundee, Glamis Castle, Scone

Palace, and J.M. Barrie's birthplace are within a reasonable distance.

✗ BAR SNACKS (12pm to 2pm & 7pm to 9.30pm) £2–11: smoked salmon canapé, cold buffet, steaks, fried fillets of sole;
LUNCH (12pm to 2pm) £15: curried chicken & melon cocktail, coquille of mixed seafood, rhubarb & ginger fool;
DINNER (7pm to 9.15pm) £24: smoked Tay salmon, medallions of venison, sticky toffee pudding
Children: half portions
£ high
No bargain breaks
Children: free to age 12
Facilities: 2 cots and 2 high chairs; 2 baby listening lines
6 rooms, 1 family, 1 suite. Access/AmEx/Diners/Visa
Open all year except Christmas. No music
No smoking in restaurant
Ⓟ own car park

NR AYR, STRATHCLYDE
Ⓛ CULZEAN CASTLE AND COUNTRY PARK,
Kirkoswald
Tel: 065 56 274.
Off the A719 north-west of Ayr.

The castle stands in its dominating position on a cliff top and was created by Robert Adam in the 1770s. It is one of his masterpieces and one of the notable rooms is the circular drawing room on the first floor, from the windows of which you can gaze out over the Firth of Clyde towards Ailsa Craig. The armoury is a great draw, especially for children, with its hundreds of swords, pistols and mini-cannons.

The visitor centre is housed in buildings contemporary to the castle. There is a licensed self-service restaurant here with a good selection of meals which are reasonably priced. High chairs are provided, as are half portions for children.

The centre also houses exhibitions and audio-visual shows which trace the history of the castle, and is the base for the Ranger service.

The park covers 550 acres and there is a whole host of things to see and do: apart from the two formal gardens, miles of paths meander through the woodlands and along the cliffs. At the Swan Pond there is an exhibition, aviary and adventure playground as well as lots of wildlife. There is a very informative series of leaflets about various aspects of the estate.

There are picnic areas, an adventure playground, a forestry exhibition, a deer park and a full programme of organized walks and events.

It all adds up to a superbly organized and entertaining enterprise. No wonder that Culzean Castle is one of the most popular places to visit in Scotland.

Open: Easter to 31 October, 10.30am to 5.30pm
Charges: car £6; adults £3.30; children & OAPs £1.70
Baby changing: mother and baby room
P ample

BALLACHULISH, HIGHLAND
H BALLACHULISH HOTEL, Ballachulish
Tel: 08552 606.
On the A828 on the south side of Ballachulish Bridge.

The hotel has a superb position alongside Loch Linnhe and is overlooked by the hills of Ben a' Bheithir. It is a grand building in the Scottish baronial style with curved Gothic windows and pointed gables. The public rooms are just as interesting. The cocktail bar is decorated in blue and its windows look out over a terrace and the loch; children can have their meals in here if they wish. The restaurant sits alongside, elegant with its deep blue and gold furnishings. It has the same enchanting views over the loch to the hills; in the evenings you can watch the slow setting of the sun. Finally the lounge is a spacious and comfortable room, with plenty of easy chairs and sofas, a grand piano, oil paintings, and log fires in winter.

We looked at several bedrooms and were impressed by the high standards which have been set. The rooms are spacious and very comfortable, with furniture and decorations which are easy on the eye; and many of the rooms have the benefit of loch views.

There is a garden with a lawn and it contains a little slide for younger children. You can enjoy the magnificent views and plan your next walk. All guests can take advantage of the excellent leisure facilities at the nearly Isles of Glencoe Hotel.

There is a relaxed atmosphere at this excellent hotel, where all members of the family are made very welcome.

✖ BAR MEALS (12pm to 10pm) £2–13: smoked Loch Leven salmon, haricot bean goulash, Scotch sirloin steak, venison & mushroom casserole;
DINNER (7pm to 10pm) £22: smoked Glenuig trout & spinach terrine, roast saddle of lamb, Drambuie trifle, cheese
Children: own menu, half portions
£ high
Best Bargain Break: £85 per person, 2 nights – dinner, b&b
Children: free up to 16 years
Facilities: 2 cots and 2 high chairs; and 3 lines for baby listening
30 rooms, 3 family. Open all year
Access/Visa
Ⓟ own car park

BALLACHULISH, HIGHLAND
Ⓗ ISLES OF GLENCOE HOTEL, Ballachulish
Tel: 08552 602.
Close to the A82, about a mile west of the village of Glencoe.

This splendid new hotel opened last year and is under the same ownership as the Ballachulish. It has its own distinctive style, built with a definite Scandinavian look, and has an unrivalled situation, right on the shore of Loch Leven with the dramatic pass of Glencoe behind. It gives the impression of almost being afloat. There are two lochside harbours and nearly two miles of water frontage, with an abundance of water sports available.

The bright and airy, and very comfortable bedrooms are notably spacious and many have spectacular views of the loch. The family rooms have bunk beds in addition to doubles or singles; and most of the other bedrooms can accommodate an extra bed or a cot without strain.

The dining room, with its metal rafters and rattan ceiling awnings and views over the water, reflects the relaxed style of this excellent hotel, a style which is aided in no small part by the youthful and cheerful staff.

A great bonus for guests is the leisure centre with its compact pool (with a wave machine and a jacuzzi), paddling pool and sauna. There is a little play area off the reception area for young children, and the hotel is located in several acres of parkland.

This is an exceptionally appealing family hotel.

Nearby: This is an unrivalled area for walking, and the hotel can advise you on the various routes. Fishermen have a choice of loch, sea or river, and all sorts of water sports can be arranged. Hill climbing, pony trekking and golf are all available and the leisure centre at Fort William has a swimming pool, squash and tennis. Glencoe and Ben Nevis are close, and the children will enjoy a visit to the Sea Life Centre north of Oban. In the winter the area is a popular ski centre.

✗ BAR MEALS (12pm to 9.30pm) £2–13: mussels Portugaise, garlic chicken scollops, steak and stout pie, sirloin steak, sweet & sour King prawns;
DINNER (7pm to 10pm) £17: seafood platter, supreme of chicken, pudding or cheese
Children: own menu, half portions
£ high
Best Bargain Break: £99 per person, 3 nights: dinner, b&b
Children: free up to 16 years
Facilities: 2 cots and 2 high chairs; 3 baby listening lines
39 rooms, 6 family. Open all year
Access/Visa
Ⓟ own car park

NR BALLATER, GRAMPIAN
Ⓛ BALMORAL CASTLE, Crathie
Tel: 033 97 42334.
On the A93 between Ballater and Braemar.

This has been the home of the Royal Family since Prince Albert bought the estate and rebuilt the castle between 1853 and 1856 for himself and Queen Victoria. It is a wonderful example of the Victorian style, with pepper-pot towers and mullioned windows.

The ballroom is the only room which visitors can enter and there is always an exhibition of paintings owned by the Queen. In the old stables you can see a model of the castle and a collection of the various horse-drawn vehicles which have been used on the estate.

The gardens are magnificent, with huge areas of lawn, wonderful displays of flowers and massive trees. There are commemorative statues and memorials to members of the Royal Family scattered about, and even some of the dogs are commemorated.

Visitors are free to picnic in the grounds and there are various walks laid out where you can enjoy the grounds and the views. You can stroll along the River Dee aand see the Highland cattle and the red deer. Pony trekking can also be arranged.

The café and restaurant was purpose-built a few years back and is a spacious and efficiently organized place. It is functional, with tiled floors, formica tables and pine chairs, and serves up a good range of reasonably priced food. Several high chairs are provided.

Everything possible is done to ensure the comfort and enjoyment of the visitors, and a family can have a delightful and very interesting day out here.

Open: 10am to 5pm, Monday to Saturday, 1 May to 31 July only
Charges: adults £2; OAPs £1.50; children free
Baby changing: top-class facilities in the Ladies
P ample

BANCHORY, GRAMPIAN
Ⓛ CRATHES CASTLE, Crathes
Tel: 033 044 525.
Just off the A93 east of Banchory.

Crathes Castle was the home of the Burnett family for over 350 years and is a fine example of the 16th-century Scottish castle, with high walls crowned by turrets and pepper-pot towers.

Among the many chambers there is the Room of the Nine Nobles with ceiling paintings of such notables as Julius Caesar, Alexander the Great and Charlemagne. The Green Lady's Room is named after a legendary ghost, who is said to carry a baby in her arms.

The gardens and grounds are delightful. The walled garden is divided into eight separate areas and has a remarkable collection of rare plants, and the yew hedges are cut into amazing shapes. Beyond there are 600 acres of grounds with various walks laid out; they vary in length from one to six miles and the rangers can offer all the necessary information on the flora and fauna.

There is a picnic area and an adventure playground close to the main car park.

The restaurant is attractively decorated and is situated in an old mill. High chairs are available and there is an excellent and varied menu: smoked haddock mousse, beef olives, baked potatoes and salads at prices up to £5.

You can have a most enjoyable day out here with all the family.

Open: Castle – 11am to 6pm, 1 April to end of October; Grounds – 9.30am to sunset, all year
Charges: adults £4; children and OAPs £2
Baby changing: mother and baby room
Ⓟ ample

BARCALDINE, OBAN, STRATHCLYDE
Ⓡ Ⓛ SEA LIFE CENTRE, Barcaldine
Tel: 063 173 386.
On the A828 north of Oban.

The Centre is in a glorious position on the shore of Loch Creran and is surrounded by woodland. The children will be enchanted by the seals, which can be seen close up from the under water observatory and also from the seal pool gallery. They will also enjoy the shudders induced by face to face encounters with conger eels, cat fish, octopus and lobsters.

There is a great variety of fish to see – flatfish, rays and herrings, plus a rock pool and a fish farm. Among the pine trees there is an excellent adventure playground.

The restaurant is attractively laid out under a high vaulted wooden ceiling, and you have lovely views of the woods and the loch. You can sit outside at various wooden tables and sample the food from a reasonably comprehensive menu (salmon pie, pizzas, baked potatoes, etc). There is also an oyster bar here. There are a couple of high chairs provided and baby changing can be done in the disabled toilets.

This is a splendid place, with much of interest for all the family, in a beautiful setting.

Open: mid-February to November, every day, 9am to 6pm
Charges: adults £4.25; children £2.95; OAPs £3.25 (1993 prices)
Baby changing: space in the disabled toilets
Ⓟ plenty
✕ £1–5: salmon, fisherman's pie, pizzas, baked potatoes
Children: half portions
Access/Visa. Licensed
No smoking in part of the restaurant

CASTLE DOUGLAS, DUMFRIES & GALLOWAY
Ⓛ THREAVE GARDEN, Castle Douglas
Tel: 0556 2575.
Off the A75 just west of the town.

The National Trust created the Garden when they were left the Threave estate; it covers sixty acres and includes rose, woodland, small heath, heather and rock gardens, a daffodil bank, a secret garden, an arboretum and an orchard. You can take a circular walk through all these.

In addition there is a wildfowl refuge along the banks of the Dee with five hides from which you can observe a wide variety of birds: ducks, geese, heron, kingfisher, cormorant and so on.

Finally you can take a ferry to the ruins of Threave Castle, which was built by one of the nastiest members of the Douglas family, Archibald the Grim.

There is nothing grim about the visitor centre at the Garden and it contains a very pleasant café, with a nice little terrace which looks out over the garden. There are two high chairs and a good selection of hot meals, salads and snacks.

Babies can be attended to in the disabled toilet area, where there is a small shelf – not ideal, but better than nothing.

Open: 1 April to 31 October, 9am to 5.30pm
Charges: adults £2.80; children and OAPs £1.40 (1993 prices)

Baby changing: small shelf in the disabled toilet
P plenty

COLMONELL, GIRVAN, AYRSHIRE, STRATHCLYDE
H BURNFOOT FARM, Colmonell
Tel: 046 588 220.
Off the A765 and close to the village of Colmonell.

This traditional Scottish farmhouse, long and low and built of stone which is now painted white, has a lovely situation on the south side of the Stinchar valley. The house is ringed by gentle hills and the green acres of the farm itself.

You will receive a warm and friendly welcome from the owner and the accommodation is especially suitable for families. One bedroom has a double and a single bed; and the family suite comprises two adjoining rooms, one with a double and the other with two single beds – ideal for a large family. Colour televisions and tea and coffee making facilities are provided.

There is a very comfortable and warm sitting room with several easy chairs and a dining room of pleasant proportions. It is good to report that many of the vegetables and fruit are grown in the large garden alongside the farmhouse.

Nearby: Whatever your interests you will find plenty to do and see in this part of Scotland. Visitors are welcome to join in the activities of the farm, which has 150-odd acres for sheep and cattle, and the children will no doubt make friends with the farm's Highland pony. There are sandy beaches nearby at Ballantrae, Girvan, Lendalfoot and Ayr, while the golfer has a multitude of fine courses to play. The river Stinchar offers excellent salmon fishing, and the locality offers lovely walks; Culzean Castle and Country Park is close, as is the Burns Museum and the bird sanctuary on Ailsa Craig.

✗ DINNER (6.30pm) £8
Children: half portions
£ low
Children: £6 up to 6 years; £8 from 6 to 12 years
Facilities: 1 cot and 1 high chair

2 rooms both family. Open 1 March to October
No credit cards. Unlicensed
No smoking in dining room and bedrooms. No music
ℙ ample

CUPAR, FIFE
Ⓢⓒ MOUNTQUHANIE HOLIDAY HOMES, Cupar
Tel: 082 624 252.
Just north of Cupar, off the A914. The owners provide clear maps
for all their properties.

The estate has been in the hands of the family of the present
owners, Mr and Mrs Andrew Wedderburn, for over 400 years and
one of their ancestors was lady-in-waiting to Mary Queen of Scots.
   The ruins of both Creich Castle and Mountquhanie Castle
remain on the estate, but the core of it is Mountquhanie House,
an elegant stone mansion which was built in 1820.
   Many of the twenty-one properties are scattered throughout the
estate and offer peace and seclusion in the wooded grounds. Three
of them, which sleep four, six and eight people, are part of the main
house. Gillespy House has three bedrooms, including a family-sized
room for three people, and a sitting room of lovely proportions.
The Garden House has a small conservatory and a sizeable and
comfortable sitting room. From the double bedroom above there
are views of the ruined castle. The kitchens are equipped with
everything a cook might need and there is a communal laundry
room.
   The others, stone farmhouses and cottages in a variety of interesting styles, can accommodate from four to twelve occupants. Most
of them have spacious and well-maintained enclosed gardens (some
with sandpits and play areas) and are highly suitable for family
holidays. Creich Farmhouse, which sleeps eleven people, stands
alongside Creich Castle. We also looked at the Lodge, Mountquhanie Farm, Forester's Cottage, Cedar Cottage and Drumond
Cottages and were impressed by their secluded character and excellent condition. You are assured of peace and quiet and superb
countryside at which to gaze.
   Some of the houses are in, or in the vicinity of, St Andrews and

are ideal properties for groups of golfers. The Nydie houses and cottages have superb views over the Eden Valley towards the Tay and the foothills of the Grampians. Knockhill of Nydie House accommodates up to ten people and has a pleasant enclosed garden.

We were very impressed with the quality of all the properties. They are decorated and equipped to an exceptionally high standard, with excellent kitchen and bathroom facilities and attractive furniture and decorations. Each kitchen includes a microwave oven, and there are dishwashers and freezers in the larger properties.

Guest are welcome to wander about the estate. There is a nature trail, a children's play area, burn fishing, a hard tennis court and mown grass areas where golfers can hone their chip and pitch shots.

This is a splendid place for a family holiday in the beautiful kingdom of Fife in the care of the friendly and well-organized Wedderburn family.

Nearby: Golfers have some of the best courses in Scotland to sample (St Andrews, Carnoustie and Gleneagles for a start) and fishermen, apart from the burns on the estate, can buy permits to fish on the estate's stretch of the River Eden at Nydie. Sightseers might start with a browse around St Andrews and there are many other spots within an easy drive: Earlshall Castle, the Hill of Tarvitt, Kellie Castle, Falkland Palace, the gardens at Aberdour Castle, the burgh of Culross and Scone Palace. If you pop south across the Firth of Forth you can visit Hopetoun House and the country parks of Beecraigs and Almondell, while Edinburgh with all its attractions is easily accessible.

Unit: 3 apartments, 11 cottages and 7 houses
Rent: £165 to £595 a week (golf packages can be arranged)
Other costs: electricity is metered; linen £8 a head
Heating: central heating
A dozen cots and high chairs available
Open all year

DULNAIN BRIDGE, GRANTOWN-ON-SPEY, HIGHLAND
Ⓗ MUCKRACH LODGE HOTEL, Dulnain Bridge
Tel: 047 985 257.
On the A938 half a mile west of Dulnain Bridge.

The hotel has a commanding position on a knoll on the outskirts of the town; it is a splendid stone house with attractive gable windows, built as a shooting lodge early in the 19th century, and sits in ten acres of delightful lawned gardens.

The various public rooms are spacious and decorated and furnished in fine style. There is a very agreeable lounge with bay windows which overlook the gardens and a splendid dining room, elegantly decorated in pink with patterned wall panels; it opens out into a large conservatory. It is a lovely spot to have a meal.

The bedrooms meet the same high standards and the two family rooms have ample space. In addition to these there are two self-contained suites in the old coach house; both have large sitting rooms on the ground floor (one has a sofa bed and one has a pull-down double bed) and twin-bedded rooms above with en-suite bathrooms.

The Muchrach Lodge is an exceptionally pleasant hotel where the owners and staff do their utmost to make their guests feel relaxed and at home. For example there is real flexibility about children's food; within reason it can be arranged to suit a child's likes and dislikes.

Nearby: This is a marvellous spot for fishermen with excellent salmon and trout fishing on the Dulnain, Findhorn (the hotel has its own private stretch of water) and Spey rivers; and for golfers, too, with four courses within ten minutes of the hotel. Walking, skating, swimming and pony trekking can all be arranged, and wild-life enthusiasts should head for the well-known osprey look-out at Boat of Garten. There are many attractions within easy reach: Culloden battlefield, the castles of Cawdor and Urquhart, the Loch Ness Monster Exhibition, Landmark Visitor Centre, Highland Wildlife Park, the Glenmore Forest Park and the Rothiemurchus Estate.

✕ BAR LUNCHES (12pm to 2pm) £1–10: smoked venison salad,

grilled lemon sole, roast gigot of pork, smoked Spey salmon, lobster mayonnaise;
DINNER (7.30pm to 9pm) £21: smoked gosling and orange salad, sirloin steak, pudding or cheese.
Children: half portions, and high teas
£ high
Best Bargain Break: £89 per person, 2 nights – dinner, b&b
Children: free in cots, then £5 up to the age of 12
Facilities: 1 cot and 2 high chairs; a baby listening system
12 rooms, 2 family and 2 suites. Access/AmEx/Diners/Visa
Open all year. No music
⊞ Ale: Federation
Ⓟ own car park

DUNOON, STRATHCLYDE
Ⓗ ENMORE HOTEL, Marine Parade
Tel: 0369 2230.
On the A815 just north of Dunoon.

The Enmore hotel is a most attractive building, long and low and white-painted; it stands on the Clyde Estuary where it has a small beach. There are two squash courts at the hotel and many other activities can be arranged in and around the local lochs and mountains – sailing, fishing, walking and island-hopping as well as tennis, golf, swimming, etc. The hotel has attractive terraced gardens and a games room with a pool table and darts.

Not surprisingly the five-course dinner menu includes Loch Fyne fish and another speciality is the children's cocktails. Children are, however, discouraged from the dining room in the evenings, since high teas are provided.

Nearby: Dunoon is an attractive resort with the advantage of the many water sports which can be done locally. If you are in the mood for sightseeing you can reach Inveraray Castle, the Younger Botanic Garden and the Kilmun Arboretum with ease. If you cross the ferry to Gourock you can reach the many fine museums and other attractions of Glasgow with ease.

✗ BAR SNACKS (12pm to 3pm & 5.30pm to 9.30pm) £2–10:

whole prawns in garlic butter, Loch Fyne herring, vegetable casserole, sirloin steak;
DINNER (7.30pm to 9pm) £20: smoked goose breast, soup, pork fillet en croute, pudding and cheese
Children: own menu
£ high
Best Bargain Break: £135 per person, 3 nights – dinner, b&b
Children: babies free; £5 from 1 to 7 years; half price from 7 to 15 years
Facilities: 1 cot and 1 high chair; 2 baby listening lines
12 rooms, 2 family. Access/AmEx/Visa
Open all year. No smoking in dining room
P own car park

NR DUNOON, STRATHCLYDE
P COYLET INN, Loch Eck
Tel: 036 984 426.
On the A815.

A friendly welcome awaits you at this 17th-century coaching inn. There is a small lounge where you may take the children and, on busy days, the dining room with dark oak tables and chairs is also put to use for families. You have a good view of the loch from this room, which is decorated with old china pieces and copper pans, and has a dresser.

Alongside the road is an attractive grassy garden surrounded by trees and across the road the splendid Loch Eck with towering hills behind.

✕ (12am to 2pm & 5.30pm to 10pm) £1–6: chicken liver paté, ploughman's, langoustine prawns, trout
Children: half portions
🍺 Ale: Deuchars, Younger's, McEwan's
P own car park

DUNSYRE, STRATHCLYDE
Ⓗ DUNSYRE MAINS, Dunsyre
Tel: 089 981 251.
Off the A702 north of Biggar.

When you leave the main road at Dolphinton follow the B&B signs to the farmhouse. As you drive along the tree lined road, past the sheep, horses and cattle beware of the occasional pheasant or sheep dog.

This is a working farm which rears a large flock of Scottish black face sheep and a big herd of beef cows. It has a lovely position on the edge of the Pentland Hills and is bordered by the Medwin River. The house itself was built in the 17th century, and the attached farm buildings form a courtyard, where there are masses of colourful geraniums, lobelia and begonias on show in pots and painted barrows.

The walled gardens, with stretches of lawn and flower beds, are spacious, and you will find the house comfortable and inviting. The family room has a double and a single bed. The lounge has a television and various board games for families, and there are some toys for the children.

Nearby: Although Dunsyre is in the Strathclyde region it is close to the Borders and is only twenty or so miles from Edinburgh which has so many places of interest. It is a most attractive area, with much to interest the holiday maker: the John Buchan centre at Broughton, Neidpath Castle and Kailzie Gardens at Peebles, Dawyck Botanic Garden and Traquair Castle are all in the near vicinity.

✗ DINNER (7pm) £9
Children: half portions
£ low
Children: various reductions according to age
Facilities: a cot and a high chair; baby listening by arrangement
3 rooms, 1 family. Open all year
No credit cards. Unlicensed
No smoking in dining room and bedrooms. No music
Ⓟ ample

EDINBURGH, LOTHIAN
Ⓗ THRUMS HOTEL, 14 Minto Street
Tel: 031 667 5545.
Not far from the city centre, on the south side, off the A7.

The hotel is very convenient for the centre of Edinburgh and is in an area with many small hotels and guest houses. It has been constructed from two large Georgian buildings, in which many of the original features have been retained. The comfortable and well-decorated lounge has plenty of sofas and easy chairs and the large bay window gives it a bright appearance. The six family rooms have plenty of space and are attractively decorated.

An agreeable aspect of this hotel is its dining room, since part of it is housed in a conservatory, which in its turn looks out to the sizeable lawned garden with its pretty borders of flowers. It is a peaceful retreat away from the city bustle. There is also a stretch of lawned garden at the front.

Nearby: Edinburgh is a fine city with so much to see and do: the famous Castle, the Palace of Holyroodhouse, the National Gallery, Huntly House Museum, the Museum of Childhood, the Royal Botanic Garden, and so on. Within easy reach are many other attractions: the Almondell and Calderwood Country Park and Beecraigs Country Park; and the city is surrounded by castles – at Dirleton, Hailes, Tantallon and Lauriston for example.

✗ LUNCH (12pm to 1.30pm) £7: soup, fish of the day, pudding; DINNER (5.30pm to 8pm) £12: prawn cocktail, sirloin steak, pudding
Children: own menu, half portions
£ medium
Children: cots free; half price up to 12 years
Facilities: 3 cots and a high chair
15 rooms, 5 family, 1 set interconnecting. No credit cards
Open all year except Christmas & New Year
Ⓟ own car park

EDINBURGH, LOTHIAN
Ⓡ HENDERSONS SALAD TABLE, 94 Hanover Street
Tel: 031 225 2131.
Off Princes Street and on the corner of Thistle Street and
Hanover Street.

A shop, wine bar, bistro and restaurant are encompassed in Henderson's, which is much more spacious than you would guess from outside, and is a real warren of rooms and alcoves. On the ground floor, fruit and veg and wholemeal bread from their own bakery is sold; and down the stairs you will find an attractive self-service vegetarian restaurant with pine tables. The choice of food is comprehensive with a very large range of salads. The emphasis is very much on wholefoods, fresh salads and crunchy vegetables, complemented by some toothsome deserts.

There is also a very pleasant, spacious, low-ceilinged wine bar (with live music throughout the week, including jazz, and classical), a separate no-smoking room, and two very snug alcoves with arched roofs (the old pavement cellars).

If you need to change or feed a baby, there is a pull-down shelf, a chair and paper towels in both the Ladies and Gents toilets.

✘ £1–4: vegetable curry, lentil stew, ratatouille, mushroom savoury, stuffed aubergine
Children: half portions
Open 8am to 10.45pm Mon to Sat. Bistro open Sunday lunch.
Closed Sundays, Christmas and New Year
Access/AmEx/Visa
🍺 Ale: Belhaven
No smoking in wine bar and restaurant
Ⓟ difficult, meters only

EDINBURGH, LOTHIAN
Ⓛ CITY ART CENTRE, Market Street
Tel: 031 225 2424.
In the centre of the city.

The Art Centre covers four floors and houses a wide collection of paintings, drawings and sculptures mainly by Scottish artists of the last three centuries.

There are apparently over 3000 works of art here, but the Centre is also notable for its temporary exhibitions, and there are usually a couple of these on the go at any one time.

There can be long queues for the popular exhibitions, but if you have a small child in tow you have the comfort of knowing that lifts travel to each of the four floors.

The café is a light and airy place with a jazzy mural depicting life in Edinburgh, by William Crosby. There is a high chair and a good choice of salads and home-baked cakes.

Open: 10am to 6pm, Monday to Saturday; until 5pm during winter
Charges: free entry
Baby changing: no facilities
Ⓟ on street (meters)

EDINBURGH, LOTHIAN
Ⓛ EDINBURGH ZOO, Corstorphine Road
Tel: 031 334 9171.
On the A8 Edinburgh to Glasgow road.

The zoo houses Scotland's largest collection of animals, around 2000 in eighty acres of parkland. It is set on a hill which, while this gives visitors superb views, makes it a hard push if you are in charge of a child in a buggy.

The zoo opened in 1913 and you can see a vast range of animal and bird life: gorillas, hippos, lions and tigers, wolves, bears, pandas, rhinos, zebras, giraffes, camels, and so on. The penguin parade and the sealion displays are special favourites with the children.

Children will also enjoy the play area which has a good array of equipment on which to swing, climb and slide. There is a picnic area and plenty of kiosks selling ice creams and soft drinks.

If you need a drink or a meal head for the Penguin's Pantry, a self-service cafeteria where there are high chairs and a children's menu. The Den is a covered area where you can take your own picnic and you can buy drinks here.

This is an excellent place for a day out with the family and you could indeed spend a whole day here, since it is a large zoo. The facilities for families are excellent, with a good range of refreshments on offer, loads of high chairs available (and a children's menu), and good facilities for baby changing.

Open: every day from 9am to 6pm (4.30pm in winter)
Charges: adults £4.80; children £2.50; under 3s free (1993 prices)
Baby changing: a mother's room by the main shop; tables and chairs in the various Ladies
Ⓟ own car park

EDINBURGH, LOTHIAN
Ⓛ MUSEUM OF CHILDHOOD, 42 High Street
Tel: 031 225 2424.
In the city centre.

The museum was doubled in size in 1986 and is jam-packed with toys of all kinds, set out in five galleries. The doll gallery has an extraordinarily comprehensive collection; there is a nickelodeon which can be played for 20p; a time tunnel which has tableaux of school, street, nursery and fancy dress party scenes; video presentations of Edinburgh street scenes; and an activity room with a rocking horse, dolls' houses, etc.

There is enough material here to fill another museum, and the information is well displayed and comprehensive.

Baby changing can be done in the disabled toilet area, where there is a large pull-down shelf; and there is an unofficial buggy park in a corner of the museum. Refreshments are not served here, but the museum is in the middle of the city and there are plenty of cafés and restaurants nearby, including an ice cream shop a few doors away.

It is a fascinating museum which can be enjoyed by adults and children alike.

Open: Monday to Saturday, 10am to 6pm; October to May, until 5pm. Sundays 2 to 5pm during the Festival
Charges: admission free
Baby changing: in the disabled toilet area
Ⓟ public car parks nearby

EDINBURGH, LOTHIAN
Ⓛ ROYAL BOTANIC GARDEN, Inverleith Row
Tel: 031 552 7171.
About a mile north of the city centre. Well signposted.

The Royal Botanic Garden was first established near Holyrood Abbey in 1670 and is thus the second oldest in Britain (after the Garden at Oxford). It moved to its present site in 1820 and has a magnificent collection of plants and trees.

Children love the rock garden because of the little paths that run hither and thither among the waterfalls. Please note that push-chairs are banned from here (too dangerous). There is also a duck pond – so remember to take some bread with you.

Other fascinating things to see include the plant houses, the 400 species of rhododendron, the herb garden and the woodland garden. The tropical aquatic house contains a viewing chamber from where visitors can see the fish and the plants from below.

The Garden is run with great attention to order and one of the stipulations is that children must be accompanied by adults.

Picnicking is not allowed in the grounds and you should head for the Terrace Café in Inverleith House, which is in the middle of the Garden aand also houses various exhibitions. You can buy hot meals such as beef and mushroom casserole, sole, and coronation chicken at prices up to £4, and snacks and salads. Several high chairs are provided, as are half portions for youngsters. An alternative is the tea room by the East gate.

Open: 10am to 4pm, 6pm or 8pm, depending on the season
Charges: entry free
Baby changing: a changing surface in the Ladies at the Terrce Café
Ⓟ on street

EDINBURGH, LOTHIAN
Ⓛ ROYAL MUSEUM OF SCOTLAND, Chambers Street
Tel: 031 225 7534.
South of the Royal Mile.

The staid exterior hides a remarkable Victorian design of cast-iron pillars and balustrades beneath a glass roof and this museum covers an amazing amount of ground: the decorative arts, geology, Ancient Egypt, European Art, natural history, and science and technology. It is a fascinating place and the two latter subjects are usually the most appealing to children. These exhibitions are both housed on the ground floor and were refurbished a couple of years back. Two of the favourite exhibits are a large whale and a dodo. Note that push-chairs are only allowed on the ground floor.

The Science and Technology section has many working models including the world's oldest steam locomotive and a giant water wheel. 'Hands on' is the current trend in museums and the Discovery Room offers you the chance to test out animal teeth, x-ray an axehead, taste tea and so on.

The café is spacious and its black and white furniture gives it a suitably high-tech look. Several high chairs are provided and the menu concentrates on inexpensive snacks such as pizzas, baked potatoes and salads.

Open: 10am to 5pm, Monday to Saturday; 2pm to 4pm Sundays
Charges: admission free
Baby changing: mother and baby room by the Ladies
P on street (meters)

EDINBURGH, LOTHIAN
R L SCOTTISH NATIONAL GALLERY OF MODERN ART, Belford Road
Tel: 031 556 8921.
North-west of the city centre – well signposted. The No. 13 bus goes to the door.

A formidable collection of 20th-century paintings and sculptures has been built up in this neo-classical building, which once housed John Watson's school.

The great names are well represented: Epstein, Nash, Moore, Hepworth, Sutherland, Dubuffet, Leger, Picasso, Giacometti, Magritte, Matisse, Braque, Miro, Dada, Paolozzi, Schulze and so on.

Most children will have fun looking at the amazing shapes and colours – and so will the adults; anyone with imagination will enjoy trying to interpret the remarkable paintings and sculptures.

The National Gallery of Scotland and the Scottish National Portrait Gallery are both in the centre of Edinburgh and are also well worth a visit (entry is free).

The café has been in *The Family Welcome Guide* for many years and offers an interesting choice of salads, snacks and hot meals. It is a bright and attractive place and has a terrace for summer days. Baby chairs which clip on to tables are provided.

✕ £1–4: quiche & salad, chicken & steak pie, filled baked potatoes, cheesy egg croissant
Children: half portions
Open: 10am to 5pm, Monday to Saturday; 2pm to 5pm on Sundays
Charges: entry free
Baby changing: pull-down shelves in the Ladies
Ⓟ own car park

GIFFORD, LOTHIAN
ⒽⓅ TWEEDDALE ARMS HOTEL, High Street
Tel: 062 081 240.
Six miles or so south of Haddington, on the B6355.

We have long been fans of this very attractive 17th-century coaching inn, situated in a smart village to the south-east of Edinburgh. It is a long, white-painted building, smartly furnished and the baskets of dried flowers hanging on the walls and ceilings add a cheerful touch.

In the last few years it has expanded to become a medium-sized hotel without losing its character as an inn. The long and spacious bar area is a most agreeable and welcoming place, nicely furnished with padded chairs and benches. When we visited last May, it was fun to see a family gathered there for lunch, complete with small child in a high chair. Across the corridor there is a very smart lounge, scattered with sofas and easy chairs; an open fire adds to its charm, as do some interesting oil paintings. The attractive dining room has French windows on to an enclosed garden.

We looked at several rooms, including an excellent family room, and found the standards of comfort and decoration to be of a high standard.

Families are welcome anywhere in the inn to eat and drink, and on summer days you might head for one of the two pretty walled gardens, where there is plenty of space and the added bonus of a climbing frame, a swing and a trampoline for the children. There is also a huge stretch of village green at the front of the pub.

There is an excellent choice of food on the bar menu, as well as a full restaurant menu in the evenings and at Sunday lunchtimes. In common with many of the pubs and hotels in Scotland, the bar is open throughout the day.

✗ BAR MEALS (12pm to 2pm & 7pm to 9pm) £2–8: spaghetti Bolognese, smoked salmon, escalope of turkey, sirloin steak, lamb Madras;
DINNER (7pm to 9pm) £19: smoked trout fillet wrapped in smoked salmon, soup, breast of duck, pudding or cheese
Children: own menu, half portions
£ medium
Best Bargain Break: £80 per person, 2 nights – dinner, b&b
Facilities: 3 cots and 3 high chairs; plug-in baby alarm
18 rooms, 3 family. Access/AmEx/Diners/Visa
Ale: Inde Coope Burton, Tetley
P on the street

GLASGOW, STRATHCLYDE

L ART GALLERY AND MUSEUM

Tel: 041 357 3929.
In Kelvingrove Park.

This impressive sandstone building, done in the Renaissance style, sits in the lovely surroundings of the Kelvingrove and you can quickly forget that you are in the middle of this busy and noisy city.

A huge range of paintings through the ages is on display: Rembrandt, Botticelli, Turner, Lowry, Monet, Renoir, Cezanne, Van Gogh, Dali and scores of other great artists.

The children will perhaps be more interested in the natural history collections, the geology section, the models of dinosaurs and elephants, and the armour.

There is an attractive restaurant with two high chairs, and it is a no-smoking area. Toasted sandwiches, baked potatoes and cream teas are served, and the three-course lunch at around £4 is marvellous value. There is also a self-service cafeteria.

Open: 10am to 5pm, Monday to Saturday; 12pm to 6pm, Sunday
Charges: admission free
Baby changing: baby changing area in the Ladies with a shelf, a bin and a paper towel dispenser
Ⓟ on street and in front of the museum

GLASGOW, STRATHCLYDE
Ⓛ BURRELL COLLECTION, Pollock Country Park
Tel: 041 649 7151.
On the Pollockshaws Road. Follow the signs.

This unrivalled collection of paintings, 15th and 16th century tapestries, stained glass, furniture, silver and ceramics was given to the city by Sir William Burrell in 1944. But it was not until 1983 that this beautiful gallery was created in the Pollock park, which in its turn had been given (along with Pollock House) to the city in 1966. Exhibitions are put on at regular intervals.

The restaurant is just as stylish as the rest of the gallery. It is conservatory room made of sandstone, timber and glass and has attractive wooden furniture. There is an excellent range of food and you look out on the park which contains many sculptures, including some by Henry Moore. Two high chairs are provided.

This is clearly a museum mainly for adults and older children with an interest in the fine arts.

Open: 10am to 5pm, Monday to Saturday. From 2pm on Sundays
Charges: admission free
Baby changing: no facilities
Ⓟ plenty

GLASGOW, STRATHCLYDE
Ⓛ MUSEUM OF TRANSPORT, Kelvinhall
Tel: 041 357 3929.
Off Argyle Street, beside Kelvin Hall sports centre.

The museum was moved to this site in 1988 and is like a splendid great warehouse. As you enter you see the first of many large vehicles on display and it is a marvellous sight. There are steam engines, gypsy caravans, carriages, trams, bicycles and motor bikes, fire engines and all sorts of cars from vintage to modern.

In addition there is a model of a 1938 Glasgow street; a reconstruction of a subway station of the Glasgow Underground; models of ships which were built on the Clyde; and a display of railway locomotives.

It is a fascinating museum which can provide hours of entertainment.

The spacious self-service cafeteria is housed in a gallery which overlooks many of the exhibits. There are hot and cold meals and snacks on the menu: soup, haddock and chips, and spaghetti Bolognese for example. Smaller portions can be ordered for children, but there is only one high chair.

Open: 10am to 5pm, Monday to Saturday. From 2pm on Sunday
Charges: admission free
P on the street

GLASGOW, STRATHCLYDE
L THE PEOPLE'S PALACE MUSEUM
Tel: 041 554 0223.
On Glasgow Green.

The People's Palace was opened in 1898 at Glasgow Green, the city's oldest public park. The museum is intended to record the history and development of the city and the major part of the collection concentrates on the 19th century and particularly the industries of that time.

There is a fine collection of Glasgow stained glass, and extensive material on the theatre (including one of Billy Connolly's costumes), the cinema and football. There is quite a concentration on political and social history and especially on the trade union movement, women's suffrage and the Co-operative movement.

The museum is housed in a three-storey sandstone building and alongside is the Winter Gardens, made of glass and cast iron. The self-service cafeteria is in the latter building and serves a good range of wholemeal snacks – quiche, pizza, pastie, chicken and ham pie, with salads. There are two high chairs.

Open: every day 10am to 5pm (from 2pm on Sunday)
Charges: admission free
Baby changing: a large tiled bench in the Ladies
Ⓟ plenty of space in the grounds

GLENELG, HIGHLAND
Ⓗ GLENELG INN, Glenelg
Tel: 059 982 273.
Off the A87 and west of Loch Duich.

If you crave some peace and quiet, if you have the urge to forget
the travails of everyday life, this is the place to visit. The Glenelg
Inn is situated in a beautiful part of Scotland, close to the short
crossing to the Isle of Skye.

The inn was made from an old coaching mews right by the shores
of Glenelg Bay. It has been refurbished in relaxed style, and the
interior is notable for the low ceilings and huge wooden beams.
The occasional stag's head will regard you balefully from a wall.
The dining room is an attractive spot with pine furniture and warm
red rugs and curtains, and you will eat the best of local produce
here, especially seafood and wild salmon, local lamb and venison.

The bedrooms are bright and simply furnished and have a charm
of their own. Residents can use a pleasant sitting room, with very
comfortable sofas, a huge and ornate grandfather clock and a fine
array of family portraits. The bar is a busy and lively place. There
is a pool table and board games are available for guests.

The Glenelg has an expanse of lawns which lead down to the
sea and picnic tables are set out on a patio. It's a lovely spot to sit
on a summer's day.

Nearby: This is a place to enjoy the countryside – walking, horse
riding, fishing (the Inn has its own boat) or just lazing about. The
scenery is wonderful, whatever you do. There is also plenty to see
including the Lochalsh Woodland Garden and the Eilean Donan
Castle. You can drive north to the Torridon Mountains Centre and
the Beinn Eighe Nature Reserve. Across on Skye there are two
museums and Dunvegan Castle to see.

✕ BAR SNACKS (12.30pm to 2.30pm & 7pm to 9pm) £2–5:

humous & pitta bread, local smoked salmon, tarragon chicken,
Hungarian goulash, seafood pilau;
DINNER (7pm to 9pm) £19: smoked salmon, pork fillet, chocolate
mousse, cheese
Children: half portions
£ medium
Best Bargain Break: £90 per person, 2 nights – dinner, b&b
Children: free up to 5 years; half to three quarters from 5 to 14
Facilities: 1 cot
6 rooms, 2 family. Open Easter to October
No credit cards. No smoking in dining room
P own car park

INCHBAE, NR GARVE, HIGHLAND
H INCHBAE LODGE HOTEL, Inchbae
Tel: 09975 269.
On the A835 north-west of Garve.

The journey to Inchbae Lodge is a joy in itself, through some of
the loveliest glens in the Highlands and passing Loch Garve and
Rogie Falls. Six miles from the nearest village, Inchbae is a remote
former Victorian hunting lodge, now a charming and informal hotel
with a reputation for good food.

The hotel sits alongside the River Blackwater and there are magnificent views of the heathered hills in every direction, with Ben
Wyvis towering over the scene. If you value peace and tranquillity,
Inchabae is the place for you, and it is an ideal base for a country
loving family who want to tour the Highlands.

The seven acres of grounds are not 'gardened'; they are mowed
by tractor and provide a lovely setting for the hotel. The children
will love the freedom and all the space. Younger children should
be supervised, however, since there is an unfenced pond, but there
are safe play areas in an enclosed area of the grounds.

Guests can fish in the river at the bottom of the garden, and the
children can make friends with the various animals: pet rabbits,
chickens, sheep, dogs, cats and cattle. If the weather is inclement
all sorts of games and puzzles are available in the hotel.

Nearby: All sorts of outdoor pursuits can be arranged – fishing, clay pigeon shooting, hill walking, golf and riding – and the area is a prolific one for wildlife. From Garve station you can take a trip by train to the Kyle of Lochalsh and then over the sea (a short ferry trip) to Skye for the day. If you fancy some sightseeing in other directions you can visit the Corrieshalloch Gorge, the Beinn Eighe Nature Reserve, and the Torridon Mountains Centre; near Inverness you can see the Loch Ness Monster Exhibition, Urquhart Castle, Cawdor Castle and the battlefield of Culloden.

✖ BAR SNACKS (12pm to 2.30pm & 5pm to 8.30pm) £2–10: sweet pickled herring, sirloin steak, fillet of haddock, haggis, casserole of the day;
DINNER (7.30pm to 8.30pm) £19: summer salad, spiced parsnip soup, roast grouse, pudding
Children: half portions
£ medium
Best Bargain Break: £110 per person, 3 nights – dinner, b&b
Children: free of charge
Facilities: 2 cots & 2 high chairs; baby listening system
12 rooms, 3 family. Open all year except Christmas
No credit cards. No music
Ⓟ own car park

INNERLEITHEN, BORDERS
Ⓛ TRAQUAIR HOUSE, Innerleithen
Tel: 0896 830 323.
Off the B709 just south of the town.

This remarkable house has been the Stuart family home since the 15th century and began life as a hunting lodge. As you see it now it is the epitome of an historic Scottish manor house – romantic to modern eyes but also designed to be defended.

The famous Bear Gates stand at the end of a long drive and were locked in 1745 after Bonnie Prince Charlie passed through them. The Earl swore that they would remain locked until a Stuart sat on the throne of Scotland.

The rooms are full of furniture, paintings, tapestries and mementoes of the house's long history, and especially memorabilia of Mary, Queen of Scots and of the Jacobite rising.

In the grounds there are woodland and river walks or you can get lost in the maze. The stables and other outbuildings contain workshops for leather working, jewellery making, silk-screen printing and carpentry, and Traquair Ale is brewed in the 18th century brewhouse. Try some . . . it's strong stuff.

The tea room is contained in an old cottage and is an attractive spot with its wooden rafters and ceiling and tiled floor. There is a very pleasant terrace at the rear and high chairs are provided.

Open: Easter week and 1 May to 30 September, 1.30pm to 5pm; from 10.30am in July and August
Charges: adults £3.50; OAPs £3; children £1.50; under 6s free (1993 prices)
Baby changing: no special facilities, but the toilets are spacious
P ample

INVERNESS, HIGHLAND
R THEATRE RESTAURANT, Eden Court Theatre, Bishop's Road
Tel: 0463 221 723.
Follow signs to 'town centre and castle' and then to 'Eden Court'.

We were alerted to this restaurant by one of our readers, and it is an ideal place for families in this famous city. It has several high chairs, a well-equipped mother and baby room, and excellent freshly cooked food.

It is a bright, airy and spacious restaurant and through the huge windows you have splendid views of the River Ness. It is in the grounds of the Old Bishop's Palace and the theatre complex also houses an excellent shop which sells Scottish arts and crafts.

The garden is delightful with large and immaculate lawns, rose beds and mature trees. You can sit here and look over the river to the castle.

The restaurant offers excellent value in a lovely setting. There is always a good vegetarian option and a fine choice of herbal teas and the local fish soup, cullen skink, is a meal in itself.

✗ £1–7: cullen skink, smoked salmon, roast chicken, fish & chips, vegetarian dish of the day
Children: half portions
Open 10.15am to 7.45pm. Closed on Sunday, Christmas Day & New Year
Access/Visa. Licensed
No smoking in half the restaurant. No music
Ⓟ car park behind theatre

KAMES, NR TIGHNABRUAICH, STRATHCLYDE
Ⓗ KAMES HOTEL, Kames
Tel: 0700 811 489.
South-west of Kames off the B8000.

This appealing, black-and-white building has been a hotel since the 19th century and was once an inn for the drovers who brought cattle across the Kyles of Bute. It is in a delightful spot on the Cowal Peninsula, with Loch Fyne on one side and the Kyles of Bute on the other. The hotel has its own free moorings off Kames Pier and has a safe beach just across the road.

The hotel has recently been refurbished in a most attractive style, with lots of wood panelling in the lounge and the bars; and the elegant and spacious dining room has a high ceiling and a huge carved wooden fireplace. Among the two family rooms, one can accommodate a family of five since it includes a double and a single bed and bunk beds.

In the lawned garden you can sit and admire the splendid views across to the Isle of Bute and watch the world and the yachts go by. There is a children's play area with swings, a slide and a climbing frame.

Nearby: This is a great spot for fishing, since the hotel has access to three hill lochs and two rivers, the Kilfinan and the Glendaruel, and can also arrange sea fishing. You can play golf on a course which is only half a mile from the hotel, and sailing can be organized. If you fancy some sightseeing you can head for the Younger Botanic Garden, the Kilmun Arboretum and Inveraray Castle. The scenery through which you will travel is magnificent.

✕ BAR MEALS (12pm to 9.30pm) £1–7: haddock, rump steak, shepherds pie, ham & mushroom crunchie;
DINNER (7pm to 9pm) £17: Waldorf salad, pork marsala, pudding or cheese
Children; own menu, half portions
£ medium
Children: cot free; £2 from 2 to 5 years; £5 from 5 to 14 years
Facilities: 2 cots and 1 high chair; plug-in baby alarm
10 rooms, 2 family. Open all year
Access/AmEx/Diners/Visa
🍺 Ale: Inde Coope Burton, McEwan's
🅿 own car park

KELSO, BORDERS
🅗 EDNAM HOUSE HOTEL, Bridge Street
Tel: 0573 224 168.
Go to the centre of town and look for the hotel sign.

This splendid and stately hotel offers real value to families at a time when many hotels overcharge disgracefully for mediocre service and facilities. Although none of the rooms are specifically designated as family rooms, most of them have ample space for a cot or an extra bed.

It's a grand Georgian mansion, built of sandstone in 1761 – a noted fishing hotel which was once owned by the Duke of Roxburghe. The beautiful interior retains its 'ducal' air with lots of carved wood and ornate plasterwork (in the main lounge there is a relief of Zeus chasing Aurora). The three acres of gardens have a croquet lawn and a long balustrade overlooking a lovely stretch of the Tweed. Handy for the town (once described by Sir Walter Scott as the most beautiful in Scotland) and many places of historic interest – and the staff will arrange other activities for you and your children: riding, golf, fishing etc.

Nearby: There are numerous interesting places to see in the locality including the remarkable Floors Castle and the ruins of Kelso Abbey. There are abbeys at Dryburgh and Jedburgh also and Sir Walter Scott's house, Abbotsford, is not far away. Bowhill, Traquair House, Dawyck Botanic Garden, Kailzie Gardens and Neidpath Castle are all within easy reach.

✗ BAR LUNCHES (12.30pm to 2pm, not Sun) £2–5: smoked trout, fried hake, mushroom & steak pie, vegetable & pasta stir fry; DINNER (7pm to 9pm) £17: haggis & stovies, soup, pot roasted duck, pudding or cheese
Children: high teas, half portions
£ medium
Best Bargain Break: £79 per person, 2 nights – dinner, b&b
Children: free up to 6 years, half price thereafter
Facilities: 4 cots and 2 high chairs; and a baby listening system
32 rooms. Closed Christmas & New Year
Access/Visa. No music
Ⓟ own car park

KILCHRENAN, BY LOCH AWE, STRATHCLYDE
Ⓗ CUIL-NA-SITHE HOTEL, Kilchrenan
Tel: 086 63 234.
On the B845 at Kilchrenan.

This hotel, housed in a tall Victorian building, has a secluded situation on the northern shore of Loch Awe, and you look across the waters to the hills beyond. The hotel has its own jetty and guests can take full advantage of the fishing on the loch, or merely have a quiet day's boating with a picnic on one of the many islands.

It is an hotel to visit if you have an active, outdoor family holiday in mind. The accommodation is comfortable enough, but functional and without frills; the two family rooms are spacious, have their own bathrooms and superb views of the loch. The attractive dining room has the same view through its large bay window and the bar looks back to the hills.

The beautiful gardens slope down to the edge of the loch and there is plenty of room in the three acres of grounds for children to play and for parents to relax. The smooth lawns have a wide variety of trees and flowers, including laburnum, cherry and Japanese maple trees, azaleas and rhododendrons.

Nearby: In addition to the delights of Loch Awe, the area has magnificent scenery and is a sheer delight for the nature lover. A little further south is Inveraray with its famous castle, and Oban is to the north west, with a Sea Life Centre close by. Oban is of course a thriving resort and is indeed the 'gateway to the islands and Highlands'. You can reach Glencoe, scene of the infamous massacre in 1692, quite easily and it is wonderful walking country, and has a great variety of wildlife.

✘ BAR SNACKS (12.30pm to 2.30pm) £2–8: lasagne, steak pie, trout, salmon;
DINNER (7pm to 9.30pm) £11: whitebait, grilled salmon, pudding or cheese
Children: own menu
£ medium
Best Bargain Break: £75 per person, 3 nights – dinner, b&b
Children: cot £3; half price thereafter up to 10 years
Facilities: 1 cot and 1 high chair, and a baby listening system
6 rooms, 2 family. Open all year
Access/Visa
Ⓟ own car park

KINCRAIG, HIGHLAND
SC Ⓡ LOCH INSH BOAT HOUSE, Kincraig
Tel: 0540 651 272.
Off the B9152 (it's parallel to the A9 north of Kingussie). Follow the signs to Loch Insh Watersports.

This restaurant, built from natural stone and old telegraph poles, has a superb position on the shore. Loch Insh is a great centre for watersports including canoeing, sailing, windsurfing, raft-building and salmon and trout fishing. You can also hire mountain bikes and there is an artificial ski slope as well.

There's a grassy and sandy area by the water's edge or you can seek the shade in the woods behind where tables are also set up. The picnic area is banned to dogs – another very sensible idea.

There's a good choice of fresh salads on the various menus (snacks, bar meals and à la carte) and the children's menu includes a drink and ice cream. Barbecue stands are available and you can use them in the woods or on the shore. Beach barbecues are held throughout July and August.

Self-catering: There are six log cabins for hire, very well-equipped and spacious and with the bonus of the beautiful surroundings. Four of them can sleep four or five people, one can sleep six and the largest can accommodate up to seven. The weekly rentals vary from £277 to £668 and short breaks are available at most times of the year.

✗ £1–11: filled jacket potatoes, hamburger, sirloin steak, venison casserole, lasagne
Children: own menu, half portions
Open 10am to 10pm, Jan to end Oct and New Year week
Closed end Oct to end Dec. Access/Visa
Licensed. No smoking in dining area
Ⓟ own car park.

KINCRAIG, HIGHLAND
Ⓛ HIGHLAND WILDLIFE PARK, Kincraig
Tel: 0540 651 270.
On the B9152 south of Kincraig.

The park is contained within nearly 300 acres of beautiful parkland and concentrates primarily on animals which are and were native to Scotland: wolves, bison, bears, lynx and wild boar. There are also others, such as red fox, wildcats, badgers, pinemarten and polecat, plus a great variety of birds. Binoculars are a useful accessory.

You can see most of the inhabitants from your car, but a walk-around area also contains animals and birds in large enclosures which are made as similar as possible to their natural environments.

The exhibitions in the visitor centre tell the story of Scottish wildlife through the ages.

The café overlooks a small loch and has a couple of high chairs. Basic snacks and sandwiches are available.

Open: April to October, 10am to 5pm (earlier in spring and autumn)
Charges: £4–9 per car, according to passenger numbers
Baby changing: facilities in the toilet block
P ample

LANARK, STRATHCLYDE
Ⓛ NEW LANARK VISITOR CENTRE, Lanark
Tel: 0555 665 876.
Off the A73 just south of Lanark.

The waters of the Falls of Clyde supplied the power for one of the largest cotton spinning centres in Britain. It was set up by David Dale and Richard Arkwright, who invented the spinning frame. But it is most famous as the model village where Robert Owen developed his social theories. The workers were properly housed and their children educated. The mill closed in 1968 and the Visitor Centre re-creates the life of the mill in the 19th century. The displays opened last year and includes the engine house and an audio-visual ride under the guidance of Annie McLeod, who is really a hologram.

You can take a walk by the Falls of Clyde and through the nature reserve, and there is an adventure playground and a picnic area. There is plenty for any member of the family to enjoy, including a display of classic cars.

There is a spacious self-service cafeteria, with the original stone walls and iron pillars in place. It is pleasantly furnished with pine tables and chairs and includes several high chairs.

Open: 11am to 5pm, every day
Charges: adults £2.60; children £1.60 (1993 prices)
Baby changing: a wide tiled window shelf in the Ladies
P in the village

METHVEN, PERTHSHIRE, TAYSIDE
SC STRATHEARN HOLIDAYS
Tel: 0738 33322 (office hours) or 0738 840 263 (evenings only).
West of Perth, off the A85.

The informative brochure of Strathearn Holidays has a centre
spread with a panoramic view of all the attractions and facilities
which lie within easy reach of the three cottages and the large house
which lie on the estate of around a thousand acres.

A group of three cottages (Cairnies, Dovecote and Ninetrees)
sits within half a mile of the main farm buildings or steadings.
Located on a slight rise, the cottages have fine views of the surrounding countryside and all have enclosed lawned gardens and
little terraces; safe for children and agreeable places to have an al
fresco meal or a drink. The recently renovated cottages each contain
a master bedroom with a king size double bed and a second bedroom which can accommodate two (Dovecote), three (Cairnies) or
four others (Ninetrees). The cottages are comfortable and we were
impressed by the high standard of the kitchen equipment, which
includes a microwave and dishwasher as well as everything else a
cook would need. There is also a small communal laundry.

A larger group should rent Bachilton House, a delightful and
imposing stone mansion, surrounded by six acres of beautiful gardens with smooth lawns and mature trees. There is plenty of space
here in the many handsome rooms, which include an excellent
farmhouse kitchen, a splendid sitting room with windows overlooking the garden, a second large lounge (with a television) and
an elegant oak-panelled room. There are three large bedrooms
upstairs and they include one with furniture and panels which were
hand-painted in 1936 and the decorations are still in fine condition.
There is a further bedroom, with bunk beds, downstairs.

Guests are welcome to roam around the estate and there are
many delightful walks. If you are interested in horses you will have
much in common with your hosts, the England family, who are
much involved in three day eventing and have around forty horses
on the estate. There is extensive stabling, a full BSJA show jumping
course and an all-weather riding school. You can arrange to
bring your own horse on holiday with you.

Nearby: Golfers will drool at the facilities available here, over sixty courses within an hour's drive and they include St Andrews, Gleneagles, Carnoustie and Blairgowrie. Fishing (on the Tay or on Loch Leven, for example) and shooting are easily arranged and there are ample opportunities for tennis, badminton, squash, swimming and other water sports, and skiing. If you fancy some sightseeing you can head for Perth, Blair Castle, Scone Palace, Huntingtower Castle or the Wildlife Centre at Loch of the Lowes. Beleaguered parents can take solace with a visit to the Glenturret Distillery.

Units: 4
Rent: £230 to £774 a week
Other costs: none
Cots and high chairs available
Heating: central heating
Open all year

MILNGAVIE, STRATHCLYDE
® THE FAMOUS COFFEE HOUSE, Findlay Clark
Garden Centre, Boclair Road
Tel: 0360 20700.
On the B8049 just south of junction with A807; look for the
Findlay Clark Garden Centre.

The largest garden centre in Scotland houses an excellent coffee shop in a conservatory, which is smartly decorated with trellis and curtains on the walls, pictures (for sale), basket weave chairs, and naturally lots of potted plants. The place has been extended and retains its agreeable atmosphere.

The whole place, with vast gift and garden accessory area indoors, is laid out in a spacious and attractive way, and there is a very wide range of food available: snacks, salads, hot dishes and pastries.

There are plenty of high chairs here, and nappies can be changed in the disabled toilet.

✗ £1–5: cheese & bacon quiche, cannelloni, open sandwiches, chicken tikka masala, spaghetti carbonara
Children: half portions
Open 10am to 5pm. Closed Christmas and New Year

No credit cards. Unlicensed
No smoking in most of the restaurant
ℙ own car park

NAIRN, HIGHLAND
ℍ INVERNAIRNE HOTEL, Thurlow Road
Tel: 0667 52039.
Off the A96. Turn into Albert Street towards the sea.

The large cream-painted hotel has a wonderful location overlooking the Moray Firth and many of the bedrooms have the same fine views. It was built over a century ago and the interior is notable for its wood panelling and fine fireplaces. The bar is a rather grand room with a vast inglenook fireplace, high ceilings and lovely views over the gardens to the sea beyond. The sun lounge is a particularly pleasant place to sit, and there is also a pool room in the hotel, and a small and attractive television lounge.

There are two cots on the premises, along with the three family rooms, plus a couple of high chairs, and all the bedrooms (with one exception) have their own bathrooms. The bedrooms are comfortable enough, functional and without frills. The garden is about an acre in size with a lawned area and a little wood, and a putting green. It has the bonus of overlooking the sandy beach, to which there is a private path.

Nearby: This area of Scotland has long stretches of beach, and Burghead Bay, just along the coast, is a sailing centre where you can hire boats. Sea fishing trips can also be taken from the harbour, or you can fish in nearby lochs and rivers. If you play golf you need look no farther than the Nairn links, a superb championship course, which is a few minutes walk from the hotel. There is an excellent swimming pool near the hotel. If sight seeing is on your agenda, there are many fine castles within reach: Cawdor, Urquhart, Brodie and Fort George, for example. The Culloden Battlefield is not far way and you can also visit the Loch Ness Monster exhibition at Drumnadrochit.

✕ BAR MEALS (12pm to 2.30pm & 6pm to 9pm) £4–8: chicken curry, chilli con carne, haddock, sirloin steak, salmon

DINNER (7pm to 8pm) £14: prawn & apple cocktail, grilled lamb
cutlets, pudding
Children: own menu, half portions
£ medium
Best Bargain Break: £108 per person, 3 nights – dinner, b&b
Children: free up to 10 years
Facilities: 2 cots and 2 high chairs; baby listening system
9 rooms, 3 family. Access/Visa
Open all year except Christmas and New Year
🍺 Ale: Theakston's. No smoking in dining room
Ⓟ own car park

NR NAIRN, HIGHLAND
ⒽⓅ COVENANTERS INN, High Street, Auldearn
Tel: 0667 52456.
Two miles east of Nairn, just off the A96, on the edge of the
hamlet of Auldearn.

The inn has quite a history since the rebel Covenanters fought the
battle of Auldearn with the Duke of Montrose in 1645 in what is
now the car park. The building began life as a mill and a brewhouse
in the 17th century and it is good to report that the original character
of the place is still apparent.

The lounge bar and restaurant are housed in what was the old
mill, an attractive room with its high beamed ceiling; the original
kiln is still in place at the far end. You can eat from a wide-ranging
menu and high teas are also available (good value at around £6).

The attractively decorated bedrooms are all on the ground floor,
and the two family rooms are spacious enough for two single beds
and two bunk beds. The residents' lounge comprises a conservatory
on one side of the building.

On sunny days you can sit on the paved terrace where there are
several bench tables. There is a small children's play area with a
wooden fort, climbing frame, a slide and swings.

Nearby: There are some fine sandy beaches in the area including
Burghhead, Nairn and Findhorn, which is a good surfing centre.
There are some fascinating places to visit within an easy drive:
Cawdor Castle, the Highland Wildlife Park, the battlefield of
Culloden, Urquart Castle, the Loch Ness Monster Exhibition and

Brodie Castle. Golfers have a good choice of courses, including the championship links at Nairn, and fishing, horse riding, and water sports are all readily available.

✕ BAR SNACKS (12pm to 2.30pm & 5pm to 9.30pm) £1–11: smoked venison, pickled herring, langoustines, roast pheasant, fillet steak
£ medium
Best Bargain Break: £25 per person, per night – dinner, b&b
Children: free up to 14 years
Facilities: 1 cot and 2 high chairs; baby listening to all rooms
8 rooms, 2 family. Open all year
Access/Visa
Ⓟ own car park

NEWCASTLETON, BORDERS
Ⓡ THE COPSHAW KITCHEN, 4 North Hermitage Street
Tel: 03873 75250.
On the east side of the main street, the B6357.

This restaurant used to be a grocer's shop and is now divided into two parts: the plain and simple tea room and the restaurant, which is also an antique shop. There is a huge old dresser on one side and shelves on the other, all inundated with antique china and bric-a-brac. The menu is the same in each although you pay a bit more in the restaurant – but the prices are very reasonable.

At the front is a shop where there are further antiques and second-hand goods for sale and more antiques up the stairs. The snack menu and children's menu serve as one and the same; quite right – why should the children always get the fish fingers.

The proprietor will provide a chair in the small Ladies for a mother wishing to breastfeed a baby.

✕ £1–9: egg mayonnaise, haddock & chips, steaks, lasagne, game pie
Children: own menu, half portions
Open 9.30am to 5.30pm every day; 7pm to 9pm Wed to Sat
(weekends only January to March)
    Access/Visa. Licensed
Ⓟ own car park

ONICH, NR FORT WILLIAM, HIGHLAND
Ⓗ ALLT-NAN-ROS HOTEL, Onich
Tel: 08553 210.
Just east of Onich village on the A82.

Beautifully situated by Loch Linnhe this hotel was once a Victorian manor house, and it has lovely views of the mountains and towards the Isle of Mull. You can take particular pleasure in these from the lounge and nicely decorated dining room. The bedrooms offer plenty of space, especially those with bay windows overlooking the loch.

There is a large, rambling garden at the front and the side of the hotel and you have superb views of the loch. It has terraced lawns and trees, a stream and pond, benches and picnic tables and a shady lawn at one side.

Nearby: Any form of water sport can be arranged and some tuition to accompany them. The area is a fisherman's paradise: for salmon or trout, sea fishing or coarse. Walking, climbing, golf and pony trekking can all be arranged and there is a leisure centre in Fort William. If you fancy some sightseeing, Glencoe and Ben Nevis are close, and the West Highland Museum is in Fort William. The children will certainly enjoy a visit to the Sea Life Centre near Oban.

✗ DINNER (7pm to 8.30pm) £20: smoked sturgeon with salad, venison with braised lentils, pudding or cheese
Children: own menu, half portions
£ high
Best Bargain Break: £135 per person, 3 nights – dinner, b&b

Children: £5 to age 3; £8 from age 4–12; £16 from age 13–16
Facilities: 2 cots and 3 high chairs; baby listening through the phones
21 rooms, 3 family. Access/AmEx/Diners/Visa
Open all year except November. No smoking in dining room
Ⓟ own car park

ONICH, NR FORT WILLIAM, HIGHLAND
Ⓗ ONICH HOTEL (Consort), Onich
Tel: 08553 214.
On the A82 in the village.

This white-painted hotel, with its various modern additions, stands in an exceptional position on the shores of Loch Linnhe and there is a multitude of activities to pursue on land and water.

The facilities at the hotel are excellent and include a games room with a pool table; on a practical level for families there is a laundry room and a drying room. The hotel garden is most attractive; the lawns with their trees and flower beds go down to the shore of the loch and there are swings and a climbing frame for children.

The various public rooms include an elegant dining room with cane furniture and a very comfortable residents' lounge, both of which have the benefit of panoramic views of the loch and the mountains beyond. A sun lounge overlooks the terrace and the gardens, and there is a residents' cocktail bar as well as a main bar which serves real ale.

We looked at several bedrooms, light and bright and very comfortable, and many with those wonderful views of water and hills. We were particularly impressed by a very spacious family room, with a double and a single bed, and the bonus of a balcony which looks out to the gardens and the loch.

Nearby: Fishing on sea, loch and river and all sorts of water sports can be arranged, as can pony trekking, golf and cruises from Oban. The leisure centre in Fort William has swimming, squash and tennis. The children will relish a visit to the Sea Life Centre near Oban, and Glencoe and Ben Nevis are near at hand. There are many routes for hill walkers and an excellent leaflet maps them out.

✕ BAR MEALS (12pm to 9pm) £1–11: herring & salad, sirloin steak, haddock & chips, cold buffet, lasagne;

DINNER (7pm to 9pm) £17: devilled whitebait, soup, roast rib of beef, pudding or cheese

Children: half portions

£ high

Best Bargain Break: £45 per person per day – dinner, b&b

Children: cot £2.50; 75 per cent reduction from 2 to 5; 50 per cent reduction from 6 to 12; 25 per cent reduction from 13 to 16 years

Facilities: 4 cots and 3 high chairs; and baby listening on 3 lines

27 rooms, 6 family. Access/AmEx/Diners/Visa

⊟ Ale: Alloa, Tetley. Open all year

℗ own car park. No smoking in coffee lounge and restaurant

PEEBLES, BORDERS
ⒽⓇCRINGLETIE HOUSE HOTEL, Peebles
Tel: 0721 730 233.
Two and a half miles north of Peebles on the A703.

This delightful hotel has been recommended in *The Family Welcome Guide* from its first edition onwards and has always been a favourite of ours. The house was built in 1861 for the Wolfe Murray family and one of those ancestors, Colonel Alexander Murray, had accepted the surrender of Quebec on the death of General Wolfe in 1759.

Cringletie is a most appealing and distinguished sandstone mansion and shows all the exuberance of the Victorian age with its high windows, pointed towers and tall chimneys. It is set in nearly thirty acres of beautiful gardens set against a background of gentle hills. You can certainly relax in such a setting, and the children can make use of the play area. There is also a new all-weather tennis court, croquet lawn and putting green.

The public rooms are elegantly furnished and well-proportioned, and there is an interesting choice of food; it is not surprising that the hotel has been recommended in the *Good Food Guide* for twenty years. A couple of acres of kitchen garden ensures that the ingredients for your meals are fresh.

Nearby: You are only about twenty miles from Edinburgh with its many attractions. Almost on the doorstep you can visit Neidpath Castle, Kailzie Gardens, Traquair House, Dawyyck Botanic Garden and the John Buchan Centre. You are surrounded by lovely countryside if you like walking; and horse riding, fishing and golf are all readily available.

✕ LUNCH (1pm to 1.45pm) £10: prawn & tomato cheesecake, escalope of pork Italienne, toffee cheesecake, selection of Scottish cheese;
DINNER (7.30pm to 8.30pm) £23: devilled crab, soup, roast sirloin of beef, toffee cheesecake, selection of Scottish chese
Children: half portions
£ high
Best Bargain Break: £57 per person, per night – dinner, b&b
Children: cot £2.50; extra bed £12.50
Facilities: 3 cots and 2 high chairs; and baby listening
12 rooms, 2 family. Open early March to 1 Jan
Access/Visa. No music
No smoking in dining room and one lounge
Ⓟ own car park

PEEBLES, BORDERS
Ⓗ PEEBLES HOTEL HYDRO, Peebles
Tel: 0721 720 602.
Off the A72 (Peebles to Galashiels).

A gigantic Victorian spa hotel, in thirty acres of grounds, whose portals you need never leave because everything you want is on site. The huge chandeliers, glass domed roofs, and miles of corridor hark back to a more expansive age.

The many and varied facilities include an excellent fenced-in children's playground, a 'commando course' for older children, two squash courts, badminton, three hard tennis courts, a volleyball court, a pitch and putt course, a putting green and an indoor heated pool in the leisure centre, which has been named 'Bubbles'. Sensibly there is a playpen in the Ladies changing room.

There is a vast games room with three table tennis tables, two snooker tables (for over 18s only), table football and space invaders, and in addition a playroom which is supervised and has toys, a slide, a rocking horse and a video. During the summer season the hotel has a number of full-time children's supervisors; and there are masses of events organized right through the day for children and for adults; plus dances and discotheques almost every night.

Nearby: There are dozens of golf courses and excellent places to walk, ride and fish. Within easy reach you will find Kailzie Gardens, Traquair House, Neidpath Castle, the John Buchan Centre, Dawyck Botanic Garden, Bowhill and Sir Walter Scott's house at Abbotsford.

✕ *Bubbles* (12.30pm to 10pm) £1–5: quiche, salads, beef Stroganoff, dish of the day, grilled salmon;
LUNCH (12.45pm to 2pm) £12: cold buffet, pudding or cheese;
DINNER (7.30pm to 9pm) £17: cheese & avocado mousse, roast guinea fowl, pudding or cheese
Children: high teas, half portions
£ high
Best Bargain Break: £118 per person 2 nights – dinner, b&b
Children: from £5 to £17 (includes breakfast & high tea)
Facilities: plenty of cots and high chairs; and baby listening via the telephones. Open all year
137 rooms, 26 family. Access/AmEx/Diners/Visa
⌘ Ale: Greenmantle
Ⓟ own car park

PERTH, TAYSIDE
Ⓛ SCONE PALACE, Perth
Tel: 0738 52300.
On the A93 just north of Perth.

The Scottish kings were crowned at Scone until the 16th century, but they would not recognize the present building which was erected in 1803. The famous Stone of Scone was looted by Edward I in 1296 and still reposes in Westminster Abbey.

The palace, built of pinkish-hued stone, houses a remarkable collection of French furniture, clocks and porcelain.

The grounds are delightful and immaculately maintained and contain a notable pinetum, with some rare trees including giant sequoia redwoods and Douglas firs. There are delightful walks through the 100 acres of gaardens where there is a picnic area and an excellent adventure playground.

The Old Kitchen restaurant is full of character, with its range and its copper pots and pans, and has an interesting menu: venison, game pie, salads and soda bread at prices up to £4. There is also a coffee shop where you can buy sandwiches and cakes. A high chair is provided.

Scone Palace is full of interest and a family could spend an interesting and amusing few hours here.

Open: Easter to mid-October, 9.30am to 5pm; from 1.30pm on Sundays, except in July and August (10am)
Charges: adults £4.20; OAPs £3.40; children £2.30; family ticket £12.50
Baby changing: a shelf in the Ladies
Ⓟ ample

RHU, STRATHCLYDE
Ⓗ ROSSLEA HALL HOTEL (Best Western) Ferry Road
Tel: 0436 820 684.
On the A814.

Built in the familiar mid-19th century baronial style and extended in the early 1970s, this hotel stands in quiet wooded surroundings on the shores of Gareloch, and a little away from the village. Its connections with the whisky trade are kept up, since each bedroom is named after a distillery.

The gardens are extensive, and indeed elegant with the lawns sheltered by high hedges and mature trees, with fine displays of flowers and shrubs.

Nearby: This is a splendid base from which to explore this part of Scotland. Apart from the various water sports which are available it is a great spot for walking, golf, riding and other activities. It is well placed for sight seeing too. The Kilmun Arboretum is close, as is the Younger Botanic Garden. You can quickly reach Inveraray Castle, and a number of country parks – at Ballock Castle and Culcreuch Castle for example. The Brian Marshall Lodge visitor centre and Loch Katrine are a bit further away, and finally Glasgow, with its many attractions, can easily be reached.

✕ BAR SNACKS (12.30pm to 2.30pm & 5.30pm to 9pm) £2–7: smoked salmon, paprika beef goulash, fried haddock, Irish stew; DINNER (7pm to 9.30pm) £18: seafood mousseline, sirloin steak, pudding or cheese
Children: own menu, half portions
£ high
Best Bargain Break: £104 per person, 2 nights – dinner, b&b
Children: £10 for a cot or an extra bed (inc. breakfast)
Facilities: a cot and 2 high chairs; and a baby listening line
39 rooms. Access/AmEx/Diners/Visa
Ⓟ own large car park

ROCKCLIFFE, DUMFRIES & GALLOWAY
Ⓗ BARON'S CRAIG HOTEL, Rockcliffe
Tel: 055 663 225.
Follow the sign to Rockcliffe from the A710.

This delightful granite-built hotel, with its unobtrusive modern additions, stands in lovely grounds overlooking the Solway and Rough Firth. From the elegant dining room and the airy, high-ceilinged lounges you have splendid views of the water and the wooded hills.

The hotel is set in a dozen acres of woodland, with immaculate lawns and colourful displays of flowers, especially when the massed ranks of rhododendrons are in full bloom. You can sit here at peace or perhaps take some gentle exercise on the putting green.

Nearby: This is a most attractive and unspoiled part of Scotland and there are miles of sandy beach around Southerness. In the vicinity of the hotel there is plenty to do in the way of sailing, fishing, golf (at Southerness, for example), wind surfing, horse riding and walking. If sightseeing is on the agenda there is plenty of scope: Threave Garden, Caerlaverock Castle and the nearby nature reserve, Broughton House and the Gem Rock Museum at Creetown.

✕ BAR LUNCHES (12.30pm to 2.30pm) £2–10: chicken liver

paté, goujon of chicken, haddock and french fries, smoked salmon, sirloin steak;
DINNER (7pm to 9pm) £20: smoked salmon, braised duck breast, pudding or cheese
Children: own menu, half portions
£ high
Best Bargain Break: £50–60 per person, per night – dinner, b&b
Children: free
Facilities: 4 cots and 4 high chairs; 3 baby listening lines
26 rooms, 2 family. Access/Visa
Closed end Oct to Easter. No music
ℙ own car park

SELKIRK, BORDERS
Ⓗ PHILIPBURN HOUSE HOTEL, Selkirk
Tel: 0750 20747.
Where the A707 and the A708 meet, just out of the town.

The house dates back to 1751, and not long before that date the Covenanters and the Royalists did battle at Philipbaugh which lies in the fields only a short distance away. It became a hotel in 1972 and specializes in family holidays.

In the rambling but well-kept grounds (for which the hotel won an award a couple of years ago) you will find a heated swimming pool, a pets corner, a trampoline, badminton court, adventure playground and a Wendy House. Inside there are two games rooms, with table tennis and snooker.

Adults who prefer a less active outdoor existence will find plenty of peace and quiet on the spacious back lawn, which has a number of bench tables and garden chairs.

There is a very flexible system of eating arrangements here. A quick bite menu served from 6pm is a favourite with older children while the comprehensive children's menu is served from 5.30pm at prices ranging from under £1 up to £5.

The management and staff make a big effort to keep their guests happy and the hotel will arrange a nanny for the odd morning or afternoon given reasonable notice.

Nearby: If you are the active type you can go walking, fishing or pony trekking and there is a fine selection of golf courses. There are many attractions within reach – Abbotsford (Sir Walter Scott's home), Bowhill, Traquair House, Floors Castle, the abbeys at Dryburgh and Melrose, and Kailzie Gardens.

✘ BAR SNACKS (12pm to 3pm & 7pm to 10pm) £2–13: croute Bengal, salmon fishcakes, Tiroler grostle, croque monsieur, roasted quail;
DINNER (7.30pm to 10pm) £23: haggis, gazpacho, roast loin of lamb, Italian trifle or cheese
Children: own menu, half portions
£ high
Best Bargain Break: £100–135 per person, 2 nights – dinner, b&b
Children: free up to 15 years
Facilities: 6 cots and 6 high chairs, and baby listening system
17 rooms, 11 family. Access/Visa
Open all year. No smoking in restaurant
Ⓟ own car park

SOUTH QUEENSFERRY, LOTHIAN
Ⓛ HOPETOUN HOUSE, South Queensferry
Tel: 031 331 2451.
Off the A904 just west of South Queensferry.

The original house was built for the 1st Earl of Hopetoun at the end of the 17th century and was enlarged by William Adam in 1721. Twenty-odd years later his sons carried on the work; much of the original furniture and wall coverings remain from that time and are a delight to the eye, as are the paintings by Rubens, Canaletto and Gainsborough and the Meissen ceramics.

There are various exhibitions including one on wildlife which should interest the children. The house has an observatory, which gives marvellous views over the Firth of Forth.

The gardens are extensive and include two nature trails and picnic areas.

If you fancy a snack or a meal there is a café in the Tapestry Room, which is indeed still hung with 17th-century tapestries depicting the seasons of the year. A high chair is made available.

Open: 10am to 5.30pm, every day from Easter to 3 October
Charges: adults £3.50; OAPs £2.90; children £1.80 (1993 prices)
Baby changing: changing surfaces in the Ladies
P ample

TARVES, NR ELLON, GRAMPIAN
L HADDO HOUSE, Tarves
Tel: 0651 851 440.
Off the B9005 north-west of Ellon.

The house was designed by William Adam for William Gordon, the Earl of Aberdeen, and was completed in 1735. It is a very handsome stone building but, despite its grand appearance, has a 'lived-in' feel. There is a wealth of paintings, ceramics and fine furniture to see, a magnificent library, and the 19th century chapel has a stained glass window designed by Edward Burne-Jones.

The grounds are superb. The serenely beautiful lakes, the landscaped gardens, the formal tree-lined avenues and the commemorative statues contrast to the woodland ways – trails and walks which abound with wildlife. A room in the grounds is set aside for children to learn more about the flora and fauna on the estate; and there are quizzes aand question boards. There is also an adventure playground.

A hall, quite close to the house, is the home of the Haddo House Choral Society and of the Arts Trust, and a varied programme of music and drama is put on through the year.

The Stables tea room is a bright and spacious place, with fresh wild flowers on the pine tables. There are high chairs here and an enterprising choice of food. There is also a large picnic area beside the car park with plenty of bench tables.

Haddo House is a splendid place where the whole family can have an enjoyable day.

Open: 1.30pm to 5.30pm over Easter and in May, June and September. From 11am in July and August.
Charges: adults £3.30; children £1.70 (1993 prices)
Baby changing: table and chair in the Ladies
P ample

TURRIFF, NR ELGIN, GRAMPIAN
SC DELGATIE CASTLE, Turriff
Tel: 0888 62750.
Just north of Turriff, off the A947. Follow the signs to the castle.

Delgatie is one of the most ancient castles in Scotland; its origins lie back in the 11th century and it became the home of the Hay clan in the 14th century. It was rebuilt in the 16th century and some of the rooms still have the fine painted ceilings from that time. It is a wonderful building, of great historic interest and imbued with a romantic ambience that only such great age can bring.

It is a rare opportunity to stay in such a place but the Symbister Suite, an apartment in the north wing of the castle, allows one to do so. It accommodates six people in splendid style and the apartment has its own entrance and a garden. The master bedroom is particularly spacious and has a four-poster bed; it even has a full suit of armour to make you feel at home. There is a twin-bedded room and another bedroom with bunk beds.

The other properties are scattered through the five hundred acres of the castle's grounds, and all have their own gardens. Oakwood stands near one of the main gates to the estate and can sleep eight people in its five bedrooms; East Lodge, also with its own garden, can accommodate four people and has the bonus of a lovely conservatory on one side of the house. The remaining four properties are contained within the Coach House. They are designed on two floors and whereas Beechwood can sleep six people, Ashwood and Cedarwood are intended for four. Elmwood has a ground floor which is suitable for disabled people and in total can accommodate seven people in its four bedrooms.

All the properties have been equipped to a very high standard (4 crowns commended by the Scottish Tourist Board), with fitted carpets, excellent decorations, comfortable furniture, well-appointed kitchens with everything that a cook might need, automatic washing machines and tumble dryers, and colour televisions. Every property has a cot and a high chair and stair gates are also fitted.

The extensive grounds are a delight and guests are free to explore them. It is a great spot for children with all that space in which to roam and there are many lovely walks. An outdoor play area has now been built for children. Guests can also fish in the lake. Please note that pets are not allowed at Delgatie, since it is a working estate with many animals.

Nearby: The coast is only a short drive away and has many lovely and unspoilt bays and splendid walks. Golfers and fishermen, as always in Scotland, are very well catered for and there are many famous distilleries to visit. Many attractions are within reach including other notable properties such as Fyvie Castle, Haddo House, Leith Hall, Pitmedden Garden and Castle Fraser. Balmoral Castle is about an hour's drive away, as is the battlefield of Culloden and the neighbouring Cawdor Castle. Nature lovers should visit the Forvie Nature Reserve and the Bennachie Forest.

Units: 7
Rent: £150 to £450 per week (short breaks available)
    Other costs: none
Heating: central heating
Cots and high chairs for each property
Open all year

NR TURRIFF, GRAMPIAN
Ⓡ TOWIE TAVERN, Auchterless
Tel: 08884 201.
On the A947 at Auchterless, a few miles south of Turriff.

The restaurant has been gradually refurbished over the past several years by the owners, Mr and Mrs Pearson, and has several rooms where families can settle down for a meal.

If you pass through the rather functional bar area you will find two very comfortable lounges and a choice of two dining rooms, both handsomely decorated and furnished in contrasting styles. A great deal of care has gone into the renovations and this is also reflected in the varied and reasonably priced menu, which changes each day.

There are some tables outside the Tavern and a grassy area where children can play. A table and a chair has been placed in the Ladies, and a baby can be changed there in comfort.

This is an excellent family restaurant with good food and a pleasant atmosphere and it is open every day of the week.

✗ £1–5: Buckie prawns, haddock, lentil & spinach pots, lasagne, steaks
Children: own menu, half portions
Open 12pm to 2.00pm & 6pm to 9pm; Sunday 12pm to 2.00pm & 5pm to 9pm
Licensed. Access/Visa
No smoking in dining rooms
Ⓟ own car park

TYNDRUM, CENTRAL
Ⓡ CLIFTON COFFEE HOUSE, Tyndrum
Tel: 083 84 271.
On the A82.

On a main tourist route, this is a busy and efficient restaurant with a shopping area which offers quite a wide range of craft and souvenir goods, clothing, and Scottish delicacies.

The restaurant is large, well-organized and sparkling clean. The pine ceilings, bright Formica-topped tables and the many plants and flowers add to the welcoming atmosphere.

The lavatories for the disabled have shelves ideal for nappy-changing, and the owner will find a quiet spot for a mother wishing to breastfeed her baby. The staff are very happy to warm bottles and baby food.

There is an excellent range of freshly cooked food, both hot and cold, served in generous portions at reasonable prices. A good enough recommendation for anyone and especially for families on the move. The various shops include a new gift shop, a specialist food and whisky shop and an outdoor clothing shop. As in the restaurant, the emphasis is on items of good quality.

✕ £1–7: tuna salad, fresh salmon salad, lamb curry, steak pie, venison
Children: half portions
Open every day 8.30am to 5.30pm. Closed early January to 1 March
Access/AmEx/Diners/Visa. No music
Large no-smoking area. Licensed
℗ own car park

Wales

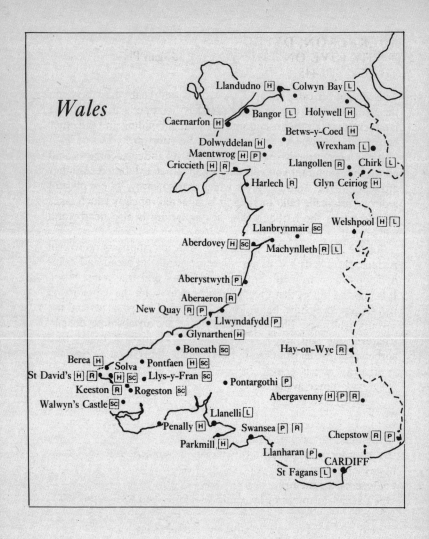

Wales

Llandudno [H] Colwyn Bay [L]

Bangor [L] Holywell [H]

Caernarfon [H]

Betws-y-Coed [H]

Dolwyddelan [H] Wrexham [L]

Maentwrog [H] [P]

Criccieth [H] [R] Llangollen [R] Chirk [L]

Harlech [R] Glyn Ceiriog [H]

Welshpool [H] [L]

Llanbrynmair [SC]

Aberdovey [H] [SC] Welshpool [H] [L]

Machynlleth [R] [L]

Aberystwyth [P]

Aberaeron [R]

New Quay [R] [P]

Llwyndafydd [P]

Glynarthen [H]

Boncath [SC] Hay-on-Wye [R]

Berea [H]

Solva Pontfaen [H] [SC]

St David's [H] [R] [H] [SC] Llys-y-Fran [SC]

Pontargothi [P]

Keeston [R] Rogeston [SC]

Abergavenny [H] [P] [R]

Walwyn's Castle [SC]

Llanelli [L]

Penally [H] Swansea [P] [R]

Chepstow [R] [P]

Parkmill [H]

Llanharan [P] **CARDIFF**

St Fagans [L]

ABERAERON, DYFED
ⓇTHE HIVE ON THE QUAY, Cadwgan Place
Tel: 0545 570 445.

This delightful café, situated on a converted coal wharf between the two harbours; the inner harbour has been pedestrianized to a large extent. Half the restaurant is in a stone building and the other half in a conservatory. You can eat in the courtyard.

It is a most attractive place, amid colourful and neat cottages, and above the restaurant you will find a honey-bee exhibition. Another attraction is the Aeron Express which starts nearby. The replica of a device originally built in 1885, it is an aerial ropeway which takes people across the harbour. The sea aquarium is also nearby and will appeal to the children.

All the food is freshly homemade with an emphasis on Welsh recipes; the salads are always interesting and the bread and cakes delicious (they are made from organic flour and free range eggs). It is good to report that the children's menu is not the usual dreary fish fingers and chips, but a proper offering of soup, salads and hot savoury pancakes. The honey ice creams are an absolute delight, whatever age you are, and there is also a range of honey fruit sorbets, all made from fresh fruit, and yoghurt ices. Across the courtyard there is a fresh fish shop and the restaurant therefore has a wide range available.

If you wish to change a baby there is a shelf in the Ladies.

✗ £1–7: cracked crab salad, local prawns, spinach & cream cheese cannelloni, hot savoury pancakes
DINNER (6pm to 9.30pm) £8: smoked salmon, Aberaeron huss, honey ice cream
Children: own menu
Open 10.30am to 5pm May, June & Sept; 10am to 9.30pm July & Aug
Closed end Sept to spring bank hol. Access/Visa
⌑ Ale: Wadworth's. No music
Ⓟ ample street parking

ABERDOVEY, GWYNEDD
Ⓗ BODFOR HOTEL, Aberdovey
Tel: 0654 767 475.
On the sea front.

This tall, double-fronted Victorian hotel has a lovely position over-looking the sea front of this attractive and relatively unspoilt seaside resort. The owners have undertaken an exhaustive refurbishment programme, which is now complete. Most of the bedrooms have their own bathrooms and there are three family rooms. There is a paddling pool and a swing park opposite the hotel.

The hotel offers excellent accommodation for families at a reasonable price – a very good reason for recommending it. The rooms at the front of the hotel have lovely views of the Dovey Estuary and of the hills beyond.

Nearby: like the other hotels which we recommend in Aber-dovey, the Bodfor can secure concessionary rates for its guests at the golf course. Several water sports can be done from the beach including wind surfing and sailing, and there are sandy beaches all along this coast. Railway buffs should be in their element with the Talyllyn, Fairbourne and Vale of Rheidol all within easy reach. The Coed-y-Brenin Forest has several waymarked trails to walk, and you can visit the Llanfair Slate Caverns, and the Maes Artro Tourist Village. Portmeirion is a little further north.

✕ DINNER (7pm to 9.30pm) £13: smoked salmon roulade, escalope of pork, pudding
Children: own menu, half portions
£ medium
Best Bargain Break: £70 per person, 2 nights – dinner, b&b
Children: £2 for a cot; £11–16 thereafter
Facilities: 2 cots and 2 high chairs; baby listening to every room.
16 rooms, 3 family. Open all year. No music
Ⓟ street & car park opposite. Access/Visa

ABERDOVEY, GWYNEDD
Ⓗ HARBOUR HOTEL, Aberdovey
Tel: 0654 767 250.
On the sea front.

Here is a hotel which makes a special effort to make all members of the family feel at home. It is a charming Victorian property which has been restored in a stylish and comfortable way. Amongst the ten rooms are four smart and comfortable family suites, which comprise two separate bedrooms and a bathroom. Three of these are especially quiet, since they are at the back of the hotel.

Their family restaurant, Rumbles, is open all day from mid-morning and offers a good range of food including vegetarian dishes, main courses and snacks at reasonable prices. The hotel dining room is reserved for the adults in the evenings, and the basement wine bar offers an excellent choice of food, wines and beers.

Nearby: There are five miles of sand on the doorstep, and a public play area a hundred yards away. There are many other excellent beaches nearby, and that lovely golf course just up the road, with concessionary rates for guests. There are many attractions within reach including the Centre for Alternative Technology, the Coed-y-Brenin Forest, the Llanfair Slate Caverns, the Maes Artro Tourist Village, steam railways at Talyllyn, Fairbourne and the Vale of Rheidol, and Portmeirion to the north.

✗ RUMBLES (10am to 10pm) £1–9: plaice & chips, seafood platter, spicy vegetable chilli, lamb cutlets, steak;
DINNER (from 7.30pm) £15: king prawns, rack of Welsh lamb, pudding or cheese
Children: own menu, half portions
£ high
Best Bargain Break: 10 per cent discount for 3 or more nights
Children: £5 under 3 years; £12.50 from 4 to 9; £17.50 from 10 to 15 years
Facilities: 3 cots and 3 high chairs; a baby listening system to all rooms
10 rooms, 4 family. Open all year
Ⓟ public car park opposite hotel. Access/AmEx/Diners/Visa

ABERDOVEY, GWYNEDD
H SC TREFEDDIAN HOTEL, Aberdovey
Tel: 0654 767 213.
On the A493 west of the village.

This appealing hotel has an enviable position just outside Aberdovey and it overlooks the lovely Aberdovey golf course, a great favourite of Bernard Darwin, who wrote: 'about this one course in the world I am a hopeless and shameful sentimentalist and I glory in my shame'. The hotel naturally offers its guests concessionary rates there. Beyond the links you can see the sandy sweep of Cardigan Bay.

Apart from the golf, a vast expanse of beach, and the sea, there is plenty more at the hotel: a large and well-designed indoor heated pool with a separate paddling pool for children (the area is surveyed by closed circuit television); an all-weather tennis court; a 9-hole pitch and putt course, table tennis and pool in the games room; a children's play room; and a snooker table. The hotel also has its own speed boat, and water skiing can be arranged.

There is a play area for children up above the hotel and alongside the tennis court. It has a large wooden climbing frame, a swing and a slide and a safe surface underfoot.

There is a stretch of garden in front of the hotel, and a putting green. It's a lovely place to sit on a summer's day and look across the links below to the vast expanse of sea.

It is an excellent hotel in a very pleasant seaside resort.

Nearby: there are long stretches of beach on which to laze, and a wide choice of watersports: sailing and canoeing, wind surfing and water skiing. Railway enthusiasts have plenty to see: the Vale of Rheidol, Fairbourne and Talyllyn railways. Castle Nant Eos is worth a look, as is the Corris Craft Centre. Pony trekking can be done in the vicinity, and river, sea and lake fishing are available.

✕ LUNCH (12.30pm to 1.45pm) £8: spinach & prawn roulade, cold buffet or a hot dish of the day, pudding or cheese;
DINNER (7.15pm to 8.30pm) £16: smoked salmon salad, ravioli, saddle of Welsh lamb, pudding and cheese
Children: high teas, half portions
£ medium
Best Bargain Break: £84 per person, 2 nights – dinner, b&b
Children – cots £9; extra bed £21 (includes breakfast and high tea or dinner)
Facilities: 6 cots and 6 high chairs, and baby listening
46 rooms, 4 family, 3 sets interconnecting
Closed January to mid-March. Access/Visa
No smoking in dining room and one lounge. No music
℗ own car park
Self-catering: The hotel has a house which overlooks the golf course and the dunes. With four bedrooms (including bunk beds for children) it can sleep up to ten people and the price includes linen, heating and electricity. The bungalow, which is also in the hotel grounds, has three bedrooms and can sleep up to seven people. The hotel also has a flat in Aberdovey itself and it sleeps up to four people. All the hotel facilities can be used and the rents are between £240 and £500 per week.

ABERGAVENNY, GWENT
Ⓗ℗ LLANWENARTH ARMS HOTEL, Abergavenny
Tel: 0873 810 550.
On the A40 towards Brecon.

The hotel is more or less halfway between Abergavenny and Crick-howell, and sits in a splendid position above the River Usk. It is a

large roadside inn and hotel which has its origins in the 16th century but has been substantially altered and extended in the last two decades.

This is a hotel which has excellent facilities for families, who will find a spacious restaurant alongside the bar, and there are several high chairs available. Down a few stairs there is a sizeable conservatory where they are also welcome to settle. It is appropriately furnished with cane furniture and from here you have a lovely view of the river below – down a steep bank which is crowded with bushes and small trees. On warmer days you can sit on the paved terrace which has the same views of the Usk Valley. The hotel has two stretches of salmon and trout fishing which are available to guests.

Nearby: this is a lovely part of Wales and you could do no better for scenery than to follow the Usk south. There are a great number of castles to see. The ruined one at Abergavenny has a museum on site; Tretower Castle; Raglan; and the three castles of Gwent which form a triangle – Grosmont, Skenfrith and the White Castle. The area is a splendid one for walkers, golfers, fishermen and horse riders, and plenty of other sports are available.

✕ BAR SNACKS (12pm to 2pm & 6pm to 9.30pm) £3–13: smoked chicken breast, poached salmon, mushroom stroganoff, loin of pork DINNER (6pm to 10pm) £18: fresh crab cocktail, rack of lamb, loin of pork, pudding or cheese
Children: own menu, half portions

£ medium
Best Bargain Break: £49 per person, 2 nights – b&b
Children: half price
Facilities: 2 cots and 4 high chairs; no baby listening
18 rooms. Open all year
Access/AmEx/Diners/Visa
🍺 Ale: Bass, Wadworth's
🅿 own car park

NR ABERYSTWYTH, DYFED
🅿 HALFWAY INN, Devil's Bridge Road, Pisgah
Tel: 097 084 631.
On the A4120 between Devil's Bridge and Aberystwyth.

One of the finest views, of the Rheidol valley surrounded by hills, awaits you at this appealing old pub – a long, white-painted two-storey building. Just down the road are the well-known Mynach Falls, and it is a lovely part of the world.

Even lovelier for real ale drinkers when they see the stillage in the bar; it holds four barrels and the licensee will serve over 40 different ales during the course of a year. It is a nice bar too, with a slate floor, stone walls, scrubbed wooden tables and pews and huge wooden beams.

Families can use a spacious room alongside; it has plenty of tables and comfortably padded bench seats, and through a window you can see the trickle of a small waterfall. A small snug, with one table, is off to one side.

There are tables outside the pub, and up above it a long grassy terrace where the children can play. The views from here will delight you.

The pub is open throughout the day on Saturdays and there is music on Friday evenings.

✗ (12pm to 2pm & 7pm to 9pm) £2–11: sirloin steak, chicken & ham & mushroom pie, brie & broccoli pithivier, plaice & chips, spaghetti Bolognese
Children: own menu, half portions
🍺 Ale: Felinfoel and a range of 40 brews
🅿 own car park

NR BANGOR, GWYNEDD
Ⓛ PENRHYN CASTLE, Bangor
Tel: 0248 353 084.
On the A5122 just east of Bangor.

Penrhyn is properly described as a fantasy castle, a huge building in the Norman style and, in its way, the masterpiece of Thomas Hopper. It was commissioned around 1820 by G.H. Dawkins-Pennant, who had made so much money from quarrying and the West Indian sugar trade that he could indulge his fantasies. Lucky man, indeed.

The rooms are on a massive and lavish scale and the Great Hall was modelled on Durham Cathedral and has a remarkable carved staircase. There is a fine collection of paintings and a fascinating museum of industrial railways and engines.

Finally the gardens are huge and full of rare shrubs and plants. There are lovely walks with views long the coast to Puffin Island and Great Orme, and an adventure playground will amuse the children.

The pleasant tea rooms offer a reasonable choice of snacks and salads, and there is a children's menu and several high chairs.

Parents with young children are very well looked after here. Both of the Ladies' toilet areas have shelving, a baby care unit, nappy disposal unit, a chair and washbasins.

A family can have an interesting and varied day out here in marvellous surroundings.

Open: April to 31 October, 12 to 4.30pm; from 11am in July and August. Closed on Tuesdays.
Charges: adults £4.20; children £2.10; under 5s free (1993 prices)
Baby changing: two mother and baby rooms
Ⓟ ample

NR BEREA, NR ST DAVID'S, DYFED
Ⓗ CWMWDIG WATER GUEST HOUSE, Groesgoch
Tel: 0348 831 434.
Off the A487 a few miles north-east of St David's.

The house is less than a mile from the Pembrokeshire coastal path, and guests are therefore well set for excellent walks in the area. The guest house was converted from a 17th-century farmhouse and its adjacent barns, and offers very comfortable accommodation in rooms which mostly have views towards Abereiddy Bay.

The useful facility of a small kitchen is provided so that you can make snacks and drinks there, and there are two sitting rooms: a large one with a beamed ceiling and an open fire and a good selection of books, and a smaller television room. There is a separate dining room and a small bar. We stayed here last year and were impressed by the excellent value offered; the food was particularly good, cooked with skill and generously served. The restaurant is open for coffee, light lunches and afternoon tea, as well as dinner.

Nearby: Pembrokeshire has so much to offer the holiday maker and the lovely town of St David's is just five miles away. There are many good beaches along the coast; Abereiddy Bay and Whitesand Bay are close, and the latter is particularly good for surfing. Children will no doubt be keen to visit the Wildlife Park at Cardigan, and there is a Marine Life Centre near St David's. There is quite a choice of museums and castles: at Scoton Manor, Haverfordwest, Pembroke, Manorbier, Tenby and so on.

✗ DINNER (7pm) £10: pear & cheese salad, steak paprika, pudding and cheese
Children: own menu, half portions
£ low
Children: babies free; £3.50 from 2 to 5 years; £7 from 5 to 7; £10.50 from 8 to 12 years
Facilities: 4 cots and 4 high chairs; baby listening system
12 rooms, 2 family Open all year except Christmas
Access/AmEx/Diners/Visa. No music
No smoking in dining room
Ⓟ ample

BETWS-Y-COED, GWYNEDD
◫ TY GWYN HOTEL, Betws-y-Coed
Tel: 0690 710 383.
On the A5 just south of Waterloo Bridge.

This handsome stone hotel, partly built in the 17th century, was one of our earliest finds for *The Family Welcome Guide* and remains a firm favourite. It has a stylish interior with antique furniture scattered about, comfortable armchairs, highly polished oak furniture and old prints on the walls.

There are several rooms in which to settle, including a very attractive beamed lounge with comfortable chintzy armchairs and a small room alongside with a lovely carved antique pew. You can eat bar meals here or in the bar itself, most appealing with its low-beamed ceiling, polished oak furniture and old cooking range set in a huge fireplace. Wherever you look there are antiques and bric-a-brac – china, prints, lamps, brassware and other curios; it is a fascinating place.

The bedrooms are beautifully furnished and decorated in varying styles and include two superb family rooms at the top of the building under the rafters. One has a four poster bed and a separate children's bedroom and has the advantage of a little balcony; and the other also has a four poster and a single bed for a child. Several of the other rooms can easily accommodate an extra bed or a cot.

You will find some excellent food here, both in the bar and in the charming, low-ceilinged restaurant – there is always a good selection of fish dishes, and the three-course Sunday lunch is a real bargain at around £10. The hotel is very much a family affair. It is owned and run by the Ratcliffe family, which is one of the keys to its great charm and individuality.

Nearby: Four main valleys converge at this town, which is the gateway to the beauties of the Snowdonia National Park. The great mountain is not far away and you can travel close to its summit on the mountain railway, which starts at Llanberis. Enthusiasts can also sample the Ffestiniog Railway. There are many attractions within easy reach, including Gwydyr Forest and the Cwm Idwal nature trail, the slate caverns at Blaenau and Portmeirion. The north coast can be reached quickly, where there are many sandy beaches; at Llandudno, for example, a traditional seaside resort with a pier, donkey rides, Punch and Judy shows, etc, plus the Great Orme Country Park.

✘ BAR SNACKS (12pm to 2pm & 7pm to 9.30pm) £2–9: moules marinière, fresh seabass, sirloin steak, wheat & walnut casserole
DINNER (7pm to 9.30pm) £17: fresh grilled sardines, braised pheasant, pudding or cheese
Children: own menu, half portions
£ low
Best Bargain Break: £69–110 per person, 2 nights – dinner, b&b
Children: free up to 3 years; 75 per cent off from 4 to 6; 50 per cent from 7 to 12; 25 per cent from 13 to 16 years
Facilities: 3 cots and 2 high chairs; baby listening system
13 rooms, 2 family. Access/Visa
Open all year
⊞ Ale: Theakston's
Ⓟ own car park

BONCATH, PEMBROKESHIRE, DYFED
ⓈⒸ FRON FAWR, Boncath
Tel: 0239 841 285.
Off the A478 south of Cardigan.

The first thing you will notice at Fron Fawr is the tranquillity of the place, and then the spectacular views.

The three cottages were converted by Mr and Mrs Cori from a huge barn and each contains three bedrooms (a double and two singles), an open-plan living area, a kitchen and bathroom. The bald description does no justice to the excellent design of the cottages, into which much has been packed without any hint of strain.

The furnishings are stylish and comfortable and are nicely in harmony with the decorations. As well as easy chairs you will find pine tables and the occasional rocker. There are cushions in plenty, interesting water colours on the walls and bright flowers on the tables. It seems like home, not rented holiday accommodation, and it is no surprise that Fron Fawr is in the Welsh Tourist Board's top grade.

The kitchens are superbly equipped with all a cook would need, down to a food mixer and a microwave oven. The same goes for the rest of the rooms with nothing forgotten: even first aid kits are supplied. The sloping ceilings of the bedrooms on the upper floor are particularly attractive, and each cottage has its own patio.

Fron Fawr has sixty-five acres of land and this includes seventeen acres of woodland. There is a beautiful lawned garden which the whole family can enjoy and some children's swings are set up here. You can gaze up the slope, past an old barn, to the wood beyond. It is a great haven for wildlife of all kinds including badgers and buzzards (Boncath is Welsh for buzzard). If you have an interest in the natural world this is a great spot to be.

On a more practical level you will find a bottle of wine and a meal waiting for you when you arrive, and there are no hidden extras in the price. You can even have your clothes laundered (£2 per load).

When you want a change from cooking, Mrs Cori has a most impressive list of frozen meals, all home cooked from fresh local ingredients.

Nearby: This is wonderful walking country and you can start nearly two hundred miles of the Pembrokeshire coastal path at nearby Cemaes Head. Sailing and pony trekking are available, and a good choice of fishing either in the sea or on the River Teifi. The sea is not foo far; Poppit Sands is only a few miles and the lovely bay at Mwnt is an alternative. The children will no doubt urge a visit to the wildlife park at Cardigan; there are the falls to see at Cenarth and the ruins of Cilgerran Castle.

Units: 3
Rent: £160 to £480 per week
Other costs: electricity is metered
Central heating: provided
A cot and a high chair for each cottage
Open all year

CAERNARFON, GWYNEDD
Ⓗ GORFFWYSFA, St David's Road
Tel: 0286 2647.
Just off the A487.

The house was built in the late 19th century, and has an imposing look to it as you would expect of a former rectory. The owners have retained many of the original features such as the fireplaces, stained glass windows and pine staircase. They offer good facilities and a real welcome to families, and the bedrooms are spacious and have views of the sea. Very useful for families is the suite which comprises a double room, an adjoining room with bunk beds and space for a folding bed, and a bathroom. They are also willing to arrange baby listening and sitting, and high teas are included in the reduced price for children, if parents are having dinner. It is good to know that vegetarian meals can also be provided, if you let the owners know in advance.

The house is built on three storeys and you enter into a spacious tiled hall and reception area with leaded light windows. Toys and books are made available in the guests' lounge, and there is a pool table. Children can play in the rear garden which has a swing and a paddling pool in the summer. The large front garden overlooks the Menai Strait, and Anglesey.

The hotel is situated in a quiet residential area, and yet is within walking distance of the centre of the town.

Nearby: Caernarfon is not a 'bucket and spade' town, but there are excellent beaches nearby: Llanddwyn, with its adjoining nature reserves, on Anglesey; and further south Traeth Penllech and Porthoer. Dinas Dinlle, an EC safe beach, is only a couple of miles away. This is also the land of castles, in Caernarfon itself, Dolbadarn, and Penrhyn. The many attractions of Snowdonia lie close at hand, as do Llyn Padarn Country Park, the Cwm Idwal Nature Trail, and Gwydir Forest with its many walks.

✗ BAR SNACKS (6pm to 8pm) £1–3: baked potatoes, burgers, salads, omelettes;
DINNER (7pm) £8: soup, roast Welsh lamb, fresh fruit salad
Children: own menu, half portions
£ low
Children: free up to 2 years; half price from 2 to 12 years
Facilities: 2 cots and 2 high chairs; baby listening by arrangement
7 rooms, 3 family, 1 set interconnecting. Open all year except Christmas and New Year
No credit cards. No smoking in dining room
Ⓟ own car park and on street. No music

CHEPSTOW, GWENT
P R PIERCEFIELD, St Arvans
Tel: 0291 622 614.
On the A466 in the village of St Arvans.

Smartly painted in cream, this large pub is not far from Chepstow race course and contains excellent facilities for families.

There is loads of space inside, as is apparent as soon as you enter and see the bar stretching along one side of the pub. There are several interconnected areas and the occasional alcove, and the wood panelling and good quality carpets give the whole place a comfortable look.

The family eating area is very welcoming with wooden tables and chairs and curved padded settles, and is no-smoking territory. There is a children's play area, with a ball swamp and other items, at one end. Nappy changing facilities are provided, as are several high chairs.

Outside you will find a large lawned garden with some shady trees. There are bench tables here and it is safely enclosed; the well-equipped children's play area has a bark surface and there is also a bouncy castle.

Its facilities make the Piercefield a very useful family pub and it has the extra bonus of providing food and drink throughout the day.

✗ (11.30am to 10pm; from noon on Sundays) £2: smoked trout, roast chicken, plaice & chips, lasagne verde, steak hoagie
Children: own menu
Ale: Bass, Boddington, Flowers and guests
Access/Visa. No smoking in half the pub.
P plenty

NR CHIRK, CLWYD
L CHIRK CASTLE, Chirk
Tel: 0691 777 701.
Off the A5 and B4500 west of Chirk.

The castle is a superb example of a Marcher fortress, built to a traditional design for Edward I. It has a rectangular shape with huge drum towers at each corner and commands superb views of the surrounding countryside. It was bought in 1595 by Thomas Myddleton, an adventurer who made his money on the Spanish Main with Walter Raleigh, and has been occupied by the family ever since.

There are some fine rooms with interesting paintings and tapestries, and the collection of arms and armour will certainly interest the children, as will the dungeon and the servants' hall.

The garden covers five acres and includes an avenue of oaks and a Hawk House, a conservatory converted into a mews for falcons.

The restaurant is housed in what was the main kitchen and is cheerful enough with its white walls and pine furniture. The food is made on the spot and ranges in price up to about £4. There are two high chairs.

Open: 1 April to 26 September, except Monday and Saturday; and weekends in October; Castle – 12 to 5pm; garden – 12 to 6pm
Charges: adults £4; children £2
Baby changing: a table in a small bathroom
Ⓟ ample

COLWYN BAY, CLWYD
Ⓛ WELSH MOUNTAIN ZOO AND GARDENS,
Colwyn Bay
Tel: 0492 532 938.
Off the A55 and well signposted in Colwyn Bay.

The zoo stands on a site of around forty acres which was originally designed as a garden by the Victorian landscaper, Sir Thomas Mawson. High above sea level the gardens make a wonderful setting with superb views of Snowdonia, the Conwy Valley and Anglesey.

Although this is not a large zoo there are many different animals, including elephants, lions, bears, chimpanzees, monkeys and leopards. The great attractions for children are the free flying displays of eagles, the feeding of the sealions and the indoor 'chimp encounter' presentation.

The Jungle Adventureland and the Tarzan Trail make up a wonderful complex of play equipment, which would keep a child of any age happy for hours. It is all set in natural woodland, and indeed there are plenty of wooded and garden areas where the adults can relax, too.

The spacious Safari Restaurant has loads of high chairs and a glorious view out over the bay. There is a range of snacks and hot meals on offer. Alongside there is the bistro and bar, mainly for adults and with a different menu – a cold buffet, lasagne and chicken curry. It has the same lovely views over the bay. There is a mother and baby room with a large shelf, wash basin, bench seating and baby care packs.

Any family would have an enjoyable time here, helped in no small way by the friendly and cheerful staff.

Open: every day, 9.30am to 5pm (until 4pm in winter)
Charges: adults £4.95; children £2.95; OAPs £3.65; family ticket £14.30
Baby changing: mother and baby room
P ample

CRICCIETH, GWYNEDD
Ⓗ ⓇMOELWYN RESTAURANT, Mona Terrace
Tel: 0766 522 500.
By the sea front off the A497.

The hotel/restaurant is housed in a Victorian building which is framed with creeper. It is bright and welcoming and the dining room itself is smartly decorated with patterned wallpaper and pink tablecloths. There is an excellent range of food on offer here, including a special menu for children and smaller portions of most dishes. The restaurant is open every evening, and for lunch on Sundays and during the peak holiday periods. It offers splendid value at around £9 for a lunch of three courses.

From many of the windows you have splendid views of Cardigan Bay, the hills and in the distance Harlech Castle, and especially so from the small garden, which is a delightful place to sit on a summer's day. The public rooms include a charming bar and lounge with a bay window and a residents' lounge on the first floor; it has a video machine, table football and a piano. The bedrooms have been decorated and furnished to a very high standard and all have their own bathrooms. Most of them have delectable views of the bay and are very comfortable.

Nearby: There is a wealth of things to do and see in this part of Wales. There are good beaches to be found all along the coast line of Cardigan Bay and many other attractions for the holiday maker. The ancient castle of Criccieth is worth a visit simply for the view, while the extraordinary village of Portmeirion is very close. Harlech Castle, the Ffestiniog Railway, the Lloyd George Museum, and the slate caverns at Blaenau are all nearby, and the beauties of Snowdonia are not too far away.

✘ DINNER (6.30pm to 9.30pm) £15: smoked Welsh trout, supreme of chicken provençale, pudding or cheese
Children: own menu, half portions
£ low
Best Bargain Break: £60 per person, 2 nights – dinner, b&b
Children: cot free; £7 thereafter up to 12 years
Facilities: 2 cots and 3 high chairs; and a baby listening service
6 rooms, 1 family. Open Easter to Christmas
No smoking in dining room. Access/Visa
Ⓟ on the street

DOLWYDDELAN, GWYNEDD
Ⓗ ELEN'S CASTLE HOTEL, Dolwyddelan
Tel: 06906 207.
On the A470 south west of Betwys-y-Coed.

This charming stone hotel, its walls hung with ivy and Virginia creeper, dates back to the 18th century and was once part of the Earl of Ancaster's Welsh estate. It was once a village alehouse and later a coaching inn.

It is a comfortable and relaxing hotel with a welcoming little bar, with an ancient stove, in what was once the kitchen; the game hooks are still in place. The lounges are comfortably furnished, and the bright dining room has windows on to the garden.

The bedrooms are furnished and decorated in a functional and unfussy style and this is reflected in the very reasonable prices.

It is a pleasant place to relax, especially in the large and attractive garden alongside the hotel. It is safely enclosed and rises on three levels, each separated by rambling roses and flower beds. Children can play in an adjoining field, which contains the legendary Roman well, which is reputed to have healing qualities.

Nearby: The hotel is situated in the lovely Lledr Valley in the middle of the Snowdonia National Park. It is a splendid spot for walkers, climbers and fishermen. The hotel is a starting point for many walks, including the popular one to the summit of Moel Siabod. Fishermen can try their luck for trout and salmon in the nearby river, and coarse fishing is also available to hotel guests. Pony trekking can also be arranged locally. Dolwyddelan Castle, built in the 12th century by Llywelyn the Great, is well worth a visit, as are Gwydir Castle, Gwydyr Forest with its many walks and the Cwm Idwal Nature Trail. Bodnant Garden and the Great Orme Country Park are close, and you can easily reach the sandy beaches of the north coast.

✕ BAR SNACKS (11.30am to 2pm & 6pm to 9pm) £2–9: liver & herb paté, poached halibut, Bulghur wheat & walnut casserole, sirloin steak, grilled Conwy plaice;
DINNER (8pm onwards) £12: egg & prawn mayonnaise, noisette of lamb, pudding
Children: own menu, half portions
£ low
Children: free up to 3 years; half price from 4 to 8; three quarters from 9 to 14
Facilities: 2 cots and 1 high chair; a baby listening system
10 rooms, 2 family, 1 set interconnecting. Open all year
No smoking in dining room. Access/Visa
ℙ own car park

GLYN CEIRIOG, NR LLANGOLLEN, CLWYD
Ⓗ GOLDEN PHEASANT HOTEL, Y Glyn Ceiriog
Tel: 0691 718 281.
On the B4500 west of Chirk.

This country hotel is a welcoming sight. Set in the beautiful Ceiriog Valley, the hotel has its own flower-filled garden, two tiled patios and a play area for the children, and it includes a swing, a slide and a climbing frame. There is also a paddling pool, a pets' corner and an aviary.

Inside a very comfortable lounge looks away to the hills. The splendid Pheasant Bar has dark wooden settles, stuffed game birds in glass cases, many items of militaria, an old stove with the original tiles on the fireplace surround, and a fine, carved wooden mirror. A lovely place to have the odd tincture or two.

At lunchtimes and in the evening you can eat from the bar menu and the dining room offers a full menu. If you are keen on country pursuits, such as fishing and shooting, the hotel provides excellent facilities; and they have their own riding centre as well.

Nearby: This is a lovely part of the Border country and naturally there are interesting castles to see, at Chirk and Powis for example. The mansions of Erddig and Plas Newydd are worth a visit, and the Llangollen Steam Railway will take you on a trip through the delightful Dee Valley. Pistyll Rhaeadr and the Lake Vyrnwy Visitor Centre are both within easy reach.

✗ BAR SNACKS (12pm to 9.30pm) £2–5: lasagne, chilli con carne, Ceiriog trout, gammon & egg;
LUNCH (12pm to 2pm) £10: soup, sauté of chicken, pudding
DINNER (7pm to 8.30pm) £18: prawn salad, casserole of local pheasant, pudding or cheese
Children: own menu, half portions
£ high
Best Bargain Break: £90 per person, 2 nights – dinner, b&b
Children: free up to 18 years
Facilities: 3 cots and 2 high chairs; baby listening to all rooms
15 rooms, 4 family. Access/AmEx/Diners/Visa
Open all year. No music
Ⓟ own car park

GLYNARTHEN, NR CARDIGAN, DYFED
Ⓗ PENBONTBREN FARM HOTEL, Glynarthen
Tel: 0239 810 248.
Off the A487 north of Cardigan. There is a sign on the road.

Great care has been exercised in the conversion of these old stone farm buildings. The bedrooms, most of which can take an extra bed and a cot, have been built in what were once the stables, the granary and the barn. The three family rooms are on the ground floor and contain a double and a single bed, and a bathroom. They are attractive rooms under their sloping roofs and look out to the countryside. The whole project has been done in a stylish and charming way and it deservedly won an award as the best farm conversion.

The public rooms are on either side of the courtyard. There is a very pleasant and comfortable restaurant, with stone walls, pine tables, a wood-burning stove, a grandfather clock and a fine Welsh harp. Alongside is a spacious lounge, very light by dint of its skylight and French windows lead out to a small terrace.

Mr and Mrs Humphreys also have an interesting museum, which contains an old farm tractor, pottery and many other artefacts; there is also a nature trail on the surrounding land.

Nearby: The hotel is in a marvellous spot for walking, riding and fishing; and there are some excellent beaches nearby – Penbryn, Tresaith and Mwnt, for example. There is a wildlife park at Cardigan, and a splendid stretch of coastline leads down to St David's with its famous cathedral.

✕ DINNER (7pm to 8pm) £12: smoked fish terrine, country beef casserole, pudding
Children: own menu, smaller portions
£ medium
Best Bargain Break: £80 per person, 2 nights – dinner, b&b
Children: free up to 16 years
Facilities: 2 cots and 2 high chairs; baby listening on 2 lines
10 rooms, 3 family. Access/Visa
Open all year
No smoking in dining room
Ⓟ own car park

HARLECH, GWYNEDD
Ⓡ PLAS RESTAURANT, High Street
Tel: 0766 780 204.
In the town centre.

A smart and welcoming café in what was once an inn and then the summer house of the Earl of Winchelsea. His second son (later to be played by Robert Redford in *Out of Africa*) probably ran in and out with his bucket and spade. The exterior is stone, with attractive bow windows at the front.

The main dining room stretches the full width of the building; it is an elegant and well-proportioned room which seats about forty people in comfort. Beyond this is a verandah which has been enclosed in glass and has cane and pine furniture and a lovely display of plants and flowers. From here, and from the delightful garden, you have enthralling views of the bay, the golf course and the famous and very imposing castle.

There is a craft shop attached to the café.

✕ (9am to 8.30pm) £1–7: herring salad, plaice & chips, lasagne, sirloin steak
Children: own menu, half portions
Closed early Nov to mid-Mar. Access/Visa
Licensed
Ⓟ public car parks

HAY-ON-WYE, POWYS
Ⓡ THE GRANARY, 20 Broad Street
Tel: 0497 820 790.

The café is situated near the clock tower in this appealing town, whose position on the borders of England and Wales has ensured more than its fair share of bloody mayhem over the centuries. It's quite peaceful now and the town has become a notable centre for second-hand books.

The restaurant certainly was a granary (and also a wool collection warehouse in its time), as the machinery and pulleys which are still in place will confirm. It's a relaxed and welcoming place, with an excellent choice of freshly cooked food available, including an extensive vegetarian menu.

There are several high chairs and, if you need to change or feed a baby, facilities can be made available.

✕ £2–6: houmos and aubergine paté, feta cheese salad, game pie, hare casserole, spicy pork
Children: half portions

Open each day 10am to 5.30pm, to 9pm during Easter and summer holidays
Closed at Christmas. Access/Visa
No smoking in the dining room
🍺 Ale: Bass, Hancock's
Ⓟ plenty of street parking except Market Day (Thursday)

HOLYWELL, CLWYD
Ⓗ GREENHILL FARM, Holywell
Tel: 0352 713 270.
On the Holywell to Greenfield road, almost opposite the Royal Oak.

This is a most attractive farmhouse, built of stone on a timber frame in the 16th century and the façade is a mass of bright flowers during summer. The original beams and pillars are much in evidence in the comfortable lounge, which also has an open fire and a little alcove with window seats. The dining room was built about a century later and is notable for its partly oak-panelled walls and the sturdy beams on its ceiling.

The bedrooms are delightful, also with their share of oak beams and pillars, and with fascinating views of the estuary. The rooms are spacious, especially the family room which has a double bed, two bunk beds and its own bathroom.

From the farm you will have superb views of the Dee Estuary and Hilbre Island; and just beyond the Island you will perhaps be able to see the great golf course at Hoylake. You can sit on the spacious lawns and admire it all, and the children can head for the play area with its swings, slide, Wendy House and climbing frame. Guests are welcome to roam the 120 acres of the farm, which supports a herd of pedigree cattle. If the weather is unkind there is a games room with snooker, darts, toys and board games. On a more utilitarian front the Jones family also provide a washing machine and dryer.

This is a wholly delightful place to stay, full of charm and character. A large family could occupy all three bedrooms and the prices charged are very reasonable indeed.

Nearby: There is much to see in this part of the world. The Greenfield Valley Heritage Park is on the doorstep, and there are castles to see at Rhuddlan, Ewloe and Flint. Just a bit further on you can visit Loggerheads Country Park (near Mold), and there is a sports and water centre in Holywell, and the Sun Centre in Rhyl.

✗ DINNER (6.30pm) £7: homemade soup, steak & kidney pie, pudding
Children: half portions
£ low
Children: cot £2; half price up to 10 years
Facilities: 1 cot and 1 high chair; baby listening can be arranged
3 rooms, 1 family. Open 1 March to 31 October
No credit cards accepted. Unlicensed
Ⓟ ample. No music

KEESTON, NR HAVERFORDWEST, DYFED
Ⓡ KEESTON KITCHEN, Keeston
Tel: 0437 710 440.
On the main A487 – not in the village.

Converted from an old farm cottage, this roadside restaurant is cosy and welcoming and has a little sheltered terrace by the front door. Coffee is served from about 10.30am and a good selection of reasonably priced snacks is served at lunchtime. There's plenty to suit a young palate and, if required, half portions are available as they are for dinner, although the owners prefer that the dining room is clear of smaller children in the evenings, so that the adults can enjoy themselves.

The owners can find some space in their own accommodation where a mother could feed or change a baby.

The owners now have two self-catering flats available in the house next door, and these can be booked for single nights as well as longer periods.

✗ LUNCH (12pm to 2pm) £1–5: Welsh rarebit, vegetarian lasagne, salade nicoise, spicy chicken;
DINNER (7pm to 9.30pm) £14: hot avocado & Stilton, Dover sole, banana split
Children: own menu, half portions
Access/Visa
🍺 Ale: Bass (during the summer season)
🅿 own small car park

LLANBRYNMAIR, POWYS
SC BARLINGS BARN, Llanbrynmair
Tel: 0650 521 479.
Off the A470 east of Machynlleth. Take the road to Pandy and after one and a half miles there is a sign to Barlings Barn.

This delightful, 18th-century stone farmhouse has a wonderful position in the hills above Llanbrynmair and commands superb views of the valley below. The owners have renovated the house and restored the adjoining barn, The Wanws, and the latter is one of the self-catering units. Like the farmhouse, roses and honeysuckle cling to the walls and the original features have been retained wherever possible: stone walls and an oak-beamed fireplace, for example. The kitchen has a stripped pine table, old pews and chairs and a Welsh dresser, and is very well-equipped; there is a microwave oven as well as a cooker, a washing machine and a dryer. There is a twin and a double bedroom, both with en-suite showers.

The two 'Barling Barnlets' are recently built suites of two storeys. The bedroom is downstairs and from the living room up above you have magnificent views of the hills and the valley.

This is certainly a place to get away from it all and there are excellent facilities available at Barlings: a heated swimming pool encased in a plastic bubble, a squash court (and Terry Margolis is a qualified coach so you can improve your game with a few lessons), a sauna, a solarium and a pool table. Alternatively you can sit at your ease and enjoy the beauty of the surroundings while the children can run freely in the paddock.

' Terry and Felicity Margolis have thought of everything to make your stay an enjoyable one. There are no hidden extras; the rent pays for everything including the central heating, the squash court, swimming pool and sauna. Groceries can be ordered in advance of your arrival; as can a good range of meals, cooked on the spot at Barlings.

It is a delightful place where you will be looked after in a very friendly and relaxed fashion.

Nearby: There is much to see and do in this beautiful part of Wales – riding, walking, fishing and golf for a start; and the beaches at Tywyn, Aberdovey and Borth can easily be reached. Northwards lies the Snowdonia National Park and the Coed-y-Brenin Forest, with its many waymarked trails. The Centre for Alternative Technology is well worth a visit, as is the Lake Vyrnwy Visitor Centre. Railway buffs can visit the Fairbourne and the Talyllyn Railways.

Units: 3
Rent: £180 to £460 a week (short breaks available)
Other Costs: none
Heating: Central heating
2 cots and 2 high chairs
Open all year

LLANDUDNO, GWYNEDD
Ⓗ AMBASSADOR HOTEL, Grand Promenade
Tel: 0492 876 886.
On the promenade near the pier.

We wanted to recommend some hotels in this famous and traditional North Wales resort and this well-maintained hotel stands out among the many sea-front establishments. It is a pleasant Victorian building with a corner position and marvellous views of Llandudno Bay, and of the promenade and its gardens. A great asset is the presence of two conservatories along the front of the hotel, and there is a sizeable and comfortable lounge bar.

The hotel certainly caters for families, as the presence of sixteen family rooms and a good supply of cots and high chairs will attest. The bedrooms are spacious and functional, decorated and furnished in an unfussy way. The hotel has no garden of its own, but you hardly need it with the great sweep of the beach almost at your feet. There are donkey rides, Punch and Judy shows and all the other attractions of a traditional seaside resort. Above all (literally) is the Great Orme Country Park, with its fine examples of wildlife. You can get to the top by car, cable car, Victorian tramway or even on foot, and magnificent views await you.

Nearby: There are many things to do and see in this part of Wales: the castles at Conwy, Penrhyn and Gwydir; the zoo at Colwyn Bay and Llyn Padarn Country Park; Bodnant Gardens; the Gwydir Forest; and the great expanse of Snowdonia itself.

✕ BAR SNACKS (12pm to 1.30pm) £1–5: chilli con carne, plaice meunière, spaghetti Bolognese, pizza;
DINNER (6.30pm to 7.30pm) £11: prawn cocktail, roast duck, pudding or cheese
Children: half portions
£ low
Best Bargain Break: £142 per person, 7 nights – dinner, b&b
Children: free up to 5 years; £12 from 5 to 8; £15 from 9 to 11; £16 from 12 to 14 years
Facilities: 4 cots and 4 high chairs, but no baby listening
68 rooms, 16 family. Open all year
No credit cards accepted. No music

No smoking in restaurant and in one lounge
Ⓟ own car park

LLANDUDNO, GWYNEDD
Ⓗ ST TUDNO HOTEL, The Promenade
Tel: 0492 874 411.
On the promenade opposite the pier.

We are firm fans of this excellent seaside hotel, which is furnished with great style and care, and welcomes all the family, from babies to grandmothers. The St Tudno sets a standard to which few hotels in the traditional seaside resorts aspire. It is not an inexpensive hotel, but it offers marvellous value for money.

Alice Liddel, Lewis Carrol's Alice, stayed at the hotel when she was eight and was no doubt pleased that it was situated opposite the pier and close to the beach. There are donkey rides and Punch and Judy shows on the beach.

The hotel has a small indoor heated swimming pool near the coffee lounge which, like all the public rooms is elegantly furnished and comfortable. The Garden Room restaurant is particularly appealing with its dashing wallpaper and hand-painted panels, and has the benefit of being air-conditioned and a non-smoking area. It is a lovely setting in which to sample the excellent food which has a deserved reputation for quality, based as it is on the best available local produce. Older children can join their parents for dinner, but the younger ones are served high tea in the coffee lounge at 5.45pm. They have a varied menu too; fish fingers appear on it, but they are homemade.

We looked at several bedrooms, all furnished and decorated in fine style and many with lovely views over the bay. The family rooms are spacious, especially a top floor room under a sloping ceiling; it contains a king-size bed and a double bed which pulls down from the wall.

St Tudno is a most impressive family hotel, which is run with great style and sympathy.

Nearby: Llandudno has its own long and sandy beaches and there are many others to enjoy along the coast. The Great Orme Country Park rises nearly 700 feet from the sea and has a wide variety of wildlife. You can reach the top on foot, by car, cable car or Victorian tramway. There are several castles in this part of Wales: Conwy, Penrhyn and Gwydir – and Bodnant Garden is a wonderful sight. The children will no doubt like to visit the Welsh Mountain Zoo, Gwydir Forest and the Cwm Idwal Nature Trail. There is also a dry ski slope and a toboggan run about half a mile away.

✖ BAR LUNCHES (12.30pm to 2pm) £3–12: smoked chicken salad, local plaice, Welsh fillet steak, poached local salmon; DINNER (7pm to 9.30pm) £24: crab mousse, soup, soup, noisettes of Welsh lamb, hot Bakewell tart with egg custard, Welsh farmhouse cheese
Children: own menu, half portions
£ high
Best Bargain Break: £112–154 per person, 2 nights – dinner, b&b & Sunday lunch
Children: £7.50 for cots; from £12.50 thereafter (including breakfast)
Facilities: 4 cots and 4 high chairs; 4 baby listening lines
21 rooms, 3 family, 2 suites. Access/AmEx/Visa
Open all year. No music
No smoking in the sitting room and the restaurant
Ⓟ own car park

LLANELLI, DYFED
Ⓛ WILDFOWL AND WETLANDS CENTRE, Llanelli
Tel: 0554 741 087.
Three miles east of Llanelli, off the A484.

The centre spreads over 150 acres of saltmarsh and is a part of the Wildfowl and Wetland Trust founded by Peter Scott.

Anyone with an interest in wildlife can spend many fascinating hours at this well-organized centre, laid out in splendid countryside. Special hides and walkways enable visitors to see rare and beautiful birds at close quarters: Hawaiian Geese, Caribbean Flamingoes, white-winged Wood Ducks, flocks of Curlew and Oystercatchers, Pintails, Kingfishers and short-eared Owls. The Summer Duckery is a great favourite with everyone, especially children.

You can have a relaxed picnic in the grounds or take advantage of the meals and snacks in the Coffee Shop, where high chairs are provided. Its wide windows look out over the centre and you can choose from a menu of basic snacks such as soup, salads and baked potatoes.

Open: 9.30am to 5pm (until 4pm in winter); closed 24 and 25 December
Charges: adults £3.20; OAPs £2.40; children £1.60; under 4s free (1993 prices)
Baby changing: mother and baby room
Ⓟ own car park

LLANGOLLEN, CLWYD
Ⓡ GALES, 18 Bridge Street
Tel: 0978 860 089.
In the town centre.

The renowned international Eisteddfod takes place each year in this picturesque town in the Dee valley; in the heart of lovely hilly country it is guarded on one side by the famous Horseshoe Pass.

This restaurant has a catholic mixture of tables and chairs, some stout and splendid; there are pews from a church in the back room and from a chapel in the front. The rooms are panelled, with an even board floor and oak pillars and beams. It is all very appealing, and classical music plays softly; and there are prints for sale on the walls.

The patio is enclosed by brick and trellis and there is a vine-covered arbour, with wooden benches and tables.

The building dates from 1775, though some parts are a bit older. It has great charm and atmosphere, and the food is reasonably priced. A mother could use a spare bedroom if she needs to feed or change a baby.

✕ (12pm to 2pm & 6pm to 10pm) £1–5: mushroom & trout Mornay, tuna & tarragon mousse, beef & paprika pie, Hawaiian pork, spicy vegetable casserole
Children: small portions
Closed on Sundays. Access/Visa

One high chair only. Licensed
P 5 spaces and on street

LLANHARAN, SOUTH GLAMORGAN
P HIGH CORNER HOUSE
Tel: 0443 238 056.
On the A473 in Llanharan.

This large Victorian pub, with prominent bay windows, has been
converted to provide excellent family facilities. The interior is very
spacious but a more intimate atmosphere has been provided by
varying the level of the floor and by the use of alcoves here and
there. There is an attractive fireplace at one side, and bright carpets.

The special family room is a no smoking area, and has a children's play area, a nappy changing facility and high chairs. Outside
there is a small enclosed garden with several bench tables.

High Corner House has the extra bonus for families of being
open all day with food available at all times.

✕ (11.30am to 10pm; from noon on Sundays) £2–8: hot
mushrooms, sirloin steak, sole bearnaise, vegetable harlequin,
chicken masala
Children: own menu
⊟ Ale: Bass, Boddington's, Brain's, Flowers
No-smoking areas. Access/Visa
P own car parking

LLWYNDAFYDD, DYFED
P CROWN INN, Llwyndafydd
Tel: 0545 560 396.
Off the A487 or the A486 near New Quay.

This is a very popular pub especially on summer days when the
terrace is packed with families having food and suitably long drinks.
Above all, the children can have a lot of fun in the playground with
its slides and a climbing frame.

Your eye will be caught by the good proportions of this long and
low building, smartly painted white with black trimmings. There is

plenty of space, too, in the family room which is off the main bar and has a good quota of tables, benches and so on.

An enterprising choice of food and of real ales is available, and the pub is now open seven days a week.

✗ (12pm to 2pm & 6pm to 9pm) £2–9: garlic mushrooms, haddock, steaks, lamb pie, lasagne
Children: own menu
⊟ Ale: Bass, Flowers and guest beer
Ⓟ own car park

LLYS-Y-FRAN, NR HAVERFORDWEST, PEMBROKESHIRE, DYFED

SC IVY COURT COTTAGES, Llys-y-Fran
Tel: 0437 532 473.
North-east of Haverfordwest off the B4329 or B4313.

Ivy Court sits in the middle of beautiful Pembrokeshire countryside and, to add to its considerable appeal, the Llys-y-Fran Country Park is alongside. You hop over a stile and there is the lake and the wooded valley of the park.

There is excellent fishing in the lake, well stocked with trout, and anglers can hire boats. You can use sailing dinghies and other craft with permission from Welsh Water on-site staff. If you are feeling fit you can do the seven mile hike around the lake's perimeter and enjoy the huge variety of wildlife.

The eight cottages have been built from early 19th-century stone farm buildings. Some are single-storied and some are on two floors but all have been converted with great care and with an eye to retaining as much of the original materials as was practicable. For example we saw how a part of the old wooden manger has been kept as a kitchen screen in one of the cottages. It is nicely complemented by the wooden beams and attractive doors.

The kitchens are all very well-equipped, too, with full sized cookers and refrigerators; microwave ovens are supplied in two of them. Central heating is laid on and some cottages have log burning stoves. There is a service area with washing machines, driers and a deep-freeze.

The cottages are of varying sizes and can each accommodate between four and seven people. The linen is provided and the beds are made up for the guests' arrival.

We were not surprised to hear that the three acres of gardens had recently won a 'Wales in Bloom' award. They are organized in a most attractive way, with smooth lawns and arrays of flowers, trees and shrubs. There are alcoves here and there where you can enjoy the tranquillity of it all.

All ages are catered for and the children, for example, have their own play area. It is safely enclosed and has swings, a climbing frame, and a slide. All the family can play croquet and badminton on the lawns.

The owners, Tim and Cathy Arthur, offer a range of oven-ready meals and you can order these in advance for your arrival.

In summary we were most impressed with the stylish accommodation and excellent facilities offered at Ivy Court. All the cottages have been graded by the Wales Tourist Board as '4 Dragon' or '5 Dragon', the two top categories.

Nearby: Apart from the amenities of Llys-y-Fran Country Park, the Preseli Hills are nearby and it is an easy drive to safe and sandy beaches: Newport and Newgale, for example. If you fancy some sightseeing, Haverfordwest has a ruined castle and you could take in the Graham Sutherland Gallery, Scotton Manor and St David's Cathedral.

Units: 8
Rent: £110 to £300 a week (sleeping 4); £140 to £420 (sleeping 6)
Other costs: some fuel is metered
Central heating: provided
Several cots and high chairs
Open all year

MACHYNLLETH, POWYS
Ⓡ Ⓛ CENTRE FOR ALTERNATIVE
TECHNOLOGY, Machynlleth
Tel: 0654 702 948.
Off the A487 just north of Machynlleth.

This centre was propagating the 'green' message long before it became so fashionable and anyone who cares about the future of our much abused planet will find it a rewarding place to visit.

The centre occupies the site of an old slate quarry and it is a fairly steep climb to it. A community of around thirty work at the centre and about a third of them live there. The essence of the project is to live in harmony with nature and be as self-sufficient as possible.

Electricity is produced by harnessing wind and water power, and solar panels trap and store heat. You can see how organic gardening methods are used and wildlife is conserved; and you can also get lots of tips on how to conserve energy in your own home. Recently, a wonderful new attraction was initiated: it is a water-powered cliff railway which carries visitors up 200 feet of cliff from the car park to the centre.

It is never too early to put the conservation message across to children, and they can also amuse themselves in the adventure playground. There is another playground for smaller children.

The self-service restaurant is nicely furnished with pine tables and chairs and there are lots of pot plants scattered about. The wholefood vegetarian menu offers very good value and several high chairs are made available.

Open: every day, 10am to 5pm
Charges: adults £3.20; OAPs £2.70; children £2; under 5s free (1993 prices)
Baby changing: changing tables and chairs in the Ladies and Gents toilets
Ⓟ own car park

MAENTWROG, BLAENAU FFESTINIOG, GWYNEDD
Ⓗ THE OLD RECTORY, Maentwrog
Tel: 076 685 305.
Just off the A487 as you enter the village.

Built in the mid-18th century as a dower house for a local family of landed gentry, this is a handsome house of Welsh stone, and has the great bonus of a very large lawned garden which stretches away at the back and is encircled by trees and bushes. Children are welcome to play here. A river runs nearby and eventually joins the sea at Tremadog Bay.

Several of the rooms can accommodate a family and especially a huge suite on the first floor which stretches the width of the house and has delightful views of the countryside. The annexe on one side of the hotel has eight rooms, comfortable and well decorated and all with their own bathrooms. They are also slightly cheaper than the rooms in the main house, and a family room includes a double bed and a separate bunk bedroom (as well as a spare folding bed, if required).

In addition to conventional food, the owner provides an excellent vegetarian dinner menu at around £9. Children are offered smaller portions of the adults' food – no junk is served here, we are glad to report.

Nearby: There is a play area in the village, and many other attractions in this lovely part of Wales: the slate caverns near Blaenau Ffestiniog; the famous village of Portmeirion; the Ffestiniog and Snowdon Mountain railways; the Coed-y-Brenin Forest; Gwydyr Forest and Gwydir Castle, which is one of many in the locality, including Harlech, Caernarfon and Dolwyddelan. There are many safe and sandy beaches in the area, especially Black Rock Sands and Harlech.

✕ DINNER (7pm to 9.30pm) £9
Children: half portions
£ low
Children: free (a linen charge of £10 per visit)
Facilities: 2 cots and a high chair
12 rooms, 3 family. Open all year
Access/Visa
Ⓟ own car park

MAENTWROG, BLAENAU FFESTINIOG, GWYNEDD
Ⓟ THE GRAPES HOTEL, Maentwrog
Tel: 076 685 208.
Just off the A487 as you turn into the village.

Wooded hills rise steeply across the road from this grey stone building dating from 1853, though the cellars are 13th century, and hanging baskets and pretty window boxes brighten the facade. At the back the large verandah, safely railed along the front, overlooks a pretty garden with trees, shrubs and a small pond with a fountain (the garden is private).

The verandah room with its sliding window is an ideal place for summer meals and looks away to the hills. In addition, there is a sizeable family room alongside; it is a charming room with its stone walls, nice wooden tables and padded settles. The two bars are very appealing, with stone walls, wooden pillars and pews and a collection of pewter tankards. An old Wurlitzer juke box sits in the front bar. The whole place has a lovely atmosphere.

This pub has elected to open all day (except Sunday) and food is available most of the day. In the afternoon during summer cold food is available on the verandah.

✗ (12pm to 9.30pm) £2–9: wild mushroom stroganoff, aubergine moussaka, beef en daube, local dressed crab, leek & ham bake
Children: own menu, half portions
⚑ Ale: Bass, Worthington and guest beer
Ⓟ own car park

NEW QUAY, DYFED
Ⓟ BLACK LION HOTEL, New Quay
Tel: 0545 560 209.
Follow the one way system to 'Harbour and Beach'.

Of 17th-century origin, but added to in 1830, this stone hotel is close to Newquay harbour, down a narrow road. You can walk straight into one of the bars off the street and very welcoming it is with oak beams, lots of brassware and two fireplaces – one used as a 'sit-in' area, the other housing a wood-burning stove. There are two small rooms at each end, one of which houses a pool table and the other a bar-billiards table. The latter has windows which look out over the bay.

The dining room is dedicated to Dylan Thomas, who was a regular in the Black Lion in the mid-1940s. The comfortable room has a portrait of him and over fifty fascinating photographs.

The long and grassy garden, with several bench tables, has a fabulous position overlooking Cardigan Bay, the beach and the harbour, all ringed by protective hills. There is a children's slide here and an 'enchanted tree', and a boule pitch. Barbecues are laid on during the summer and there are Punch and Judy shows for the children at Saturday lunchtimes in July and August.

During the months of June, July and August the pub is open all day from Monday to Saturday.

✗ BAR SNACKS (12pm to 2.30pm & 6.30pm to 10pm) £2–8: plaice & chips, steak and ale pie, spaghetti Bolognese, chicken dhansak, pizza
Children: own menu, half portions
🍺 Ale: Boddington's, Brains, Courage
🅿 own car park

NEW QUAY, DYFED
Ⓡ THE HUNGRY TROUT, 2 South John Street
Tel: 0545 560 680.
In the town centre.

The restaurant has a marvellous location, and from the bay windows you can look out over the harbour and the sweep of Cardigan Bay. The little terrace is a lovely spot to sit on a summer day.

The interior contains a pleasant bar area with a few round wooden tables and the main dining room has chintzy wallpaper and curtains, some wooden pews, and those superb views.

There is a great variety of dishes available here; they range from farmhouse scramble to a full à la carte dinner menu. You could eat a modest lunch for around £3, or spend over £10 on an evening meal. The roast of the day, with all the trimmings, represents very good value at just under £4, and there is, as you would predict, plenty of fresh fish on the menus. Children are provided for with a Boatman Bill's menu.

✗ £1–8: crab salad, plaice & chips, poached scallops, boozy lamb, Brazilian chicken
Children: own menu
Open 10am to 10pm March to Nov; weekends only in winter
Access/Visa. Licensed
No music. One high chair only
Ⓟ public car parks

PARKMILL, WEST GLAMORGAN
Ⓗ PARC-LE-BREOS RIDING AND HOLIDAY CENTRE, Penmaen
Tel: 0792 371 636.
Off the A4118 west of Swansea.

A spacious Victorian farmhouse which is situated on the delightful Gower Peninsula. It is surrounded by woodland which gives the place a quiet and secluded atmosphere, but the many attractions of this popular holiday area are within easy reach.

Parc-Le-Breos is a pony trekking centre and is primarily aimed at horse-mad youngsters and, therefore, there are no frills; the bedrooms, with many family rooms with extra bunk beds, are functional, as are the dining room and various lounges. There is plenty of space and it is an excellent place for a family which wants to have an active outdoor holiday. The facilities include a television lounge, a games room with table tennis and a pool, and a delightful lawned garden, a paddock and a small lake. The food will be fresh, since much of it is grown on the farm.

Nearby: There is a long stretch of excellent beaches: Port Enon, Oxwich Bay, Three Cliffs (with the ruins of Pennard Castle up above), Pwlldu Bay and Caswell Bay. Two nature reserves add to the interest: the South Gower Coast Reserve stretches from Port Eynon to Worms Head at Rhossili and further east is the Oxwich National Nature Reserve. A little further afield you can visit Penscynor Wildlife Park, Aberdulais Falls, Afan Argoed Country Park, Margam Country Park and the Glamorgan Nature Centre. Nature lovers are well catered for, and so are those interested in fishing, golf and water sports.

✕ DINNER (6pm) £7
Children: half portions
£ low
Best Bargain Break: £47 per person, 2 nights – dinner, b&b
Children: half price to 8 years; two thirds thereafter
Facilities: 2 cots and 2 high chairs, and baby listening by arrangement
10 rooms, 7 family. Open all year
No credit cards accepted. No music. Unlicensed
Ⓟ ample

PENALLY, NR TENBY, DYFED
Ⓗ PENALLY ABBEY HOTEL, Penally
Tel: 0834 843 033.
Just off the A4139 west of Tenby.

This delectable 18th-century stone manor house, built on the site of an ancient abbey, sits high above the coast road and from its windows and gardens you can see Tenby golf course and Carmarthen Bay beyond. Indeed, the sandy beach is a ten minute walk across the links (reduced green fees available).

The stone walls and gabled windows house some beautifully proportioned and spacious rooms, made even more interesting by the pointed arches of the windows and the doors; an unusual and very effective design. The highly attractive lounge has comfortable sofas and chairs, and a piano, and the elegant dining room has splendid views. The pleasant bar has a conservatory alongside which also takes advantage of the panoramic views out to sea.

If you fancy a swim, there is a small indoor heated pool; or you can relax in the five acres of mature lawns, garden and woodland. It is a lovely spot and has the added attraction of a ruined 13th-century chapel within its confines.

The owners try to keep a blance here between families and other guests and most of the bedrooms are spacious enough to take extra beds and cots. Some of them contain sofa beds and all the double rooms have splendid four-poster beds. We were greatly impressed by the great care which has been exercised in furnishing and decorating the rooms; they are comfortable and stylish. The top floor contains two very attractive bedrooms; the double room has high wooden rafters and there is a twin-bedded room along a short corridor (plus two bathrooms). A family could use the rooms as a self-contained suite and enjoy great comfort and seclusion.

The old coach house has now been converted to form four rooms and the high standards of comfort and decoration have been maintained. Each has a four-poster bed and a bathrooma and the rooms on the upper floor have terrific views over the bay.

There are several extra facilities, which are unusual and welcome; for example, breakfast is served until 11 o'clock in the morning. Yunger children (under 7) are encouraged to have their evening meals at 5 o'clock, so that the adults can linger undisturbed over their dinner.

The Penally Abbey is an exceptional hotel in a delightful part of Wales.

Nearby: Tenby is a busy seaside resort with sandy beaches, of which there is a wide choice including Manorbier Bay, Barafundle Bay (owned by the National Trust) and Broad Haven. There are several castles to see: Pembroke, Tenby, Manorbier and Carew, for example; and the children will relish a visit to Manor House Wildlife Park. Caldey Island, with its abbey and Cistercian monastery, can also be visited.

✗ DINNER (7.30pm onwards) £22: crab thermidor, rack of Welsh lamb, pudding or cheese
Children: half portions
£ high
Best Bargain Break: 10% discount from 1 November to Easter
Children: free to age 6; half price from age 6 to 14
Facilities: 3 cots and 2 high chairs; baby listening system
12 rooms Access/Visa. Open all year
ℙ own car park

PONTARGOTHI, DYFED
P CRESSELLY ARMS, Pontargothi
Tel: 0267 290 221.
On the A40 between Llandeilo and Carmarthen.

This appealing pub is very smartly turned out in its coat of white paint with black trimmings, and sits alongside the River Cothi. One of the bonuses of visiting the pub is that you can sit in the lovely garden alongside the river. The children are well catered for, too, with a safely enclosed play area with swings, an enchanted tree and a dinosaur slide.

Inside you will find a very pleasant bar area, with a small restaurant to one side. Up some stairs from the bar there is another attractive room, comfortably furnished with well padded seats and copper-topped tables, and families are welcome to settle here.

The landlord emphasized that families are very welcome in his pub and form an important part of his trade. Another of the advantages here is that food is available for most of the opening hours, and there is always a good selection of fish.

✗ (11.30am to 2pm & 6.30pm to 9.30pm) £1–6: plaice & chips, beef curry, lasagne, steak & kidney pie, hake & chips
Children: own menu, small portions
⊕ Ale: Flowers, Marston's
P own car park

PONTFAEN, NEWPORT, NR FISHGUARD, DYFED
H SC GELLI FAWR COUNTRY HOUSE, Pontfaen
Tel: 0239 820 343.
Off the B4313 south of Fishguard; the brochure has clear directions.

A series of winding country lanes will take you to this old and well-established Welsh hill farm, converted into a hotel with ten bedrooms, and there are self-catering apartments built in the original coach house and mill house. The old mill wheel is still in place.

It is in a lovely spot in the Gwaun Valley at the base of the Preseli Hills and is situated in the Pembrokeshire National Park. It has its

own large stretch of pasture and gardens, twelve acres in which the adults can relax and the children can play. There are plenty of grassy areas, an abundance of trees, picnic and play areas, and goats, dogs and cats – a paradise for young children. There is also the great bonus of a heated swimming pool, with a paddling pool alongside, and this is located in the middle of the courtyard.

There are two family rooms here and plenty of cots and high chairs, as well as a plug-in baby listening system. There is a nice big bar, and a very spacious dining room which looks out on to the terrace and garden and a comfortable lounge, where guests will find board games and a good selection of children's books. The accent is on informality at Gelli Fawr and one of the marks of this is that children's meals can usually be rustled up at most times during the day. The food, both traditional and vegetarian, is of a high standard; the owners run cookery weekends and have won 'Taste of Wales' competitions on two recent occasions. The wines are organic, from France, Australia and New Zealand.

Nearby: This is a splendid place for fishing in the many rivers and lakes and in the sea, and for riding, surfing, rough shooting, walking, bird watching and other country pursuits. There are some excellent beaches along the Pembrokeshire coast and a wealth of other things to do and see. Wildlife enthusiasts have several parks in the vicinity: at Cardigan, at St David's (the Marine Life Centre), and further afield at Tenby. There are castles to see at Tenby, Manorbier, Carew and Pembroke, and railway enthusiasts can make a trip to the Gwili Steam Railway near Carmarthen. Oakwood Park Narberth offers lots of entertainment for the whole family.

✗ BAR MEALS (12pm to 2pm & 5pm to 9.30pm) £3–5: plaice & chips, lasagne, beef & vegetable pie, Welsh rarebit & salad; DINNER (7pm to 9.30pm) £18: deep fried crispy vegetables, lamb steaks, treacle tart & custard
Children: own menu, half portions
£ medium
Best Bargain Break: £80 per person, 2 nights – dinner, b&b
Children: free up to 12 years
Facilities: 3 cots and 3 high chairs; and a baby listening system
10 rooms, 2 family. Open all year
Access/Visa
Ⓟ plenty
Self-catering: The Coach House, an attractive stone building, overlooks the swimming pool and has two apartments, each with three bedrooms. There are another seven apartments in the Mill House, another lovely stone building. Some have two and others three bedrooms and several of the apartments have bed settees as well. The decorations and furnishings offer no frills; the accent is on the functional, not the luxurious. The cottages are designed for families who want a relaxed and active country holiday together. Cots and high chairs are provided, as is central heating, but an additional charge is made for electricity. The utility room has a washing machine, drier and ironing board. The rents are very reasonable: from £100 to £530 a week.

ROGESTON, NR HAVERFORDWEST, PEMBROKESHIRE, DYFED

[SC] ROGESTON COTTAGES, Rogeston
Tel: 0437 781 373.
Two miles off the A487 to St David's.

The owners of Rogeston Cottages, Mr and Mrs Rees, give full and accurate directions in their brochure and you will need them because they are hidden away in the delightful coastal countryside of Pembrokeshire, and just over a mile from the sandy beach of Druidston.

If you want peace and quiet in beautiful surroundings, this is an excellent choice; and, as a base, Rogeston offers much to do and see in the surrounding area.

The cottages were made from 18th-century farm buildings and are grouped round the old cattle yard in two blocks. With one exception they are all single storey and the original stone walls are complemented by wooden beams and panelling, pine furniture and fittings. The cottages have been converted in a generous style. For example, the dried flowers and herbs which appear in abundance and the skilful decorations make such a difference. A great effort is made to ensure that guests feel at home.

The cottages all have a combined sitting and dining room and a bedroom. A couch converts easily into an extra double bed. The kitchens are extremely well-equipped and central heating is provided. The Old Granary, built towards the end of the 19th century, has accommodation for larger families or groups. Each of the two floors has three double bedrooms.

A fully equipped laundry room is provided, and if you tire of cooking a good choice of cooked meals is available: chicken & broccoli crumble, lamb rigatoni, cauliflower & pasta bake for example. All the dishes are low in fat.

Each house has its own private patio but the communal gardens are delightful with smooth lawns and wonderful views of the encircling countryside. There is plenty to do: there is an excellent grass badminton court, swing ball and even a boule pitch. Behind the Old Granary there is another lawn with a children's sand pit. Above all, the children will enjoy the spacious grounds and they can made friends with the animals: the ducks and hens and the Jersey cows.

Nearby: All the pleasures of the countryside lie at your feet – walking (Mr and Mrs Rees can help you to plan your routes), horse riding, fishing in sea or stream and facilities for water sports, golf, swimming, tennis and squash are all available. The nearest beach is Druidston Haven, which is a lovely sandy bay. There are castles galore to see, Pembroke, Manorbier and Carew, for example, and St David's Cathedral is close. There is a small Marine Life Centre at St David's and a butterfly farm.

Units: 7
Rent: £154 to £487 per week
Other costs: none
Central Heating: provided
A cot and a high chair for every cottage
Open all year

ST DAVID'S, DYFED
Ⓗ WARPOOL COURT HOTEL, St David's
Tel: 0437 720 300.
Close to the centre of the town; the brochure has clear directions.

This hotel has been recommended in *The Family Welcome Guide*
since the very first edition. It is an appealing place, built of grey
stone, has extensions here and there and was built in the 19th
century as the St David's Cathedral choir school. It is a comfortable
hotel and has a remarkable collection of 2500 antique armorial and
pistorial wall tiles.

It is certainly not lacking in charm and it has a magnificent
position on the unspoiled Pembrokeshire coast, adjoining stretches
of which are owned by the National Trust. There are wonderful
views of St Bride's Bay, especially from the large lawned garden,
a delightful place to loll on a warm day. It is notable for the statuary
dotted around.

There are excellent facilities here including a covered and heated
swimming pool, a gymnasium, a pool table and table tennis, an all-
weather tennis court, a croquet lawn and an outdoor play area for
children. Free golf can be arranged at the nearby St David's Golf
Club.

The menu is strong on fresh local produce, especially fish: crab,
lobster, sewin and sea bass are caught nearby. A vegetarian menu
is available, and local Welsh farm cheeses are served.

Nearby: There are lovely beaches here – Whitesand Bay,
Newgale Sands and Marloes Sands for example – and the Pembrokeshire Coast path can be followed. The famous Cathedral is
within walking distance and the Marine life Centre is just down
the road. There is a wildlife park near Cardigan and another near
Tenby; and lots of castles to see including Carew, Tenby and
Manorbier.

✕ BAR SNACKS (12pm to 2pm) £3–7: smoked salmon, minute steak, Court salad, Glamorgan cheese sausages;
LUNCH (12pm to 2pm) £19: cheese & nut salad, noisettes of Welsh lamb, pudding or cheese;
DINNER (7pm to 9.30pm) £19: smoked salmon, mignon of pork, pudding, cheese
Children: high teas, half portions
Facilities: 4 cots and 3 high chairs; and a baby listening system £ high
Best Bargain Break: £100 per person, 2 nights – dinner, b&b
Children: free up to 14 years
25 rooms, 6 family. Access/AmEx/Diners/Visa
Open all year except January
🍺 Ale: Bass
🅿 own car park

ST DAVID'S, DYFED
🆁 CARTREF RESTAURANT, Cross Square
Tel: 0437 720 422.

This is a busy and enterprising family restaurant in the centre of the town, and is built around a 17th-century stone cottage. It has been a tea room since 1870. The four rooms have rough stone walls, ceiling beams, and varnished pine furniture, and it adds up to a welcoming atmosphere.

The range of food on offer is very wide and you will find something to your taste at any time of the day from snacks and sandwiches to a fillet steak, and it is also good to see some interesting vegetarian dishes.

There is a patio at the back of the restaurant, with a self-service bar, which looks out to the Cathedral. This area is open from May to September and is a very pleasant spot for a quick drink or a snack. If a baby needs to be changed or fed the helpful staff will find space upstairs.

✕ £1–12: pork satay, supreme of chicken, lentil Bolognese, sirloin steak, grilled trout
Children: own menu, half portions
Open 11am to 5pm and 6pm to 9.30pm. Closed Jan and Feb

Licensed. Access/AmEx/Diners/Visa
No smoking in three of four rooms
Ⓟ car park near Cathedral

ST FAGANS, CARDIFF
Ⓛ WELSH FOLK MUSEUM, St Fagans
Tel: 0222 569 441.
Four miles west of Cardiff. From junction 33 of the M4, take the A4232.

The museum was packed with parties of schoolchildren when we visited; not surprisingly since it illustrates so many aspects of Welsh history.

St Fagans castle and park were given to the National Museum of Wales in 1947 by the Earl of Plymouth. The castle dates from 1580 and has an archetypal Elizabethan design. The Great Chamber and the Long Gallery are notable rooms with some fine furniture and tapestries.

A fascinating aspect of the museum is the collection of rural buildings, which have been carefully re-erected in the grounds; farmhouses of different periods, a corn mill, a pig sty, a tollhouse, a bakery, a smithy and so on. Recently opened buildings include a terrace of six cottages from the industrial valleys of South Wales, a Victorian shop complex, and a Celtic village settlement where a primitive way of life can be seen.

The museum galleries are contained in a modern concrete building and include an agricultural section, costume and musical instruments.

There is a large cafeteria on the first floor of the gallery building and it has a terrace with a few tables. There are two high chairs and a children's menu is served. Down below is a coffee shop and it has a picnic area with bench tables.

A new toilet block was opened a couple of years ago and it contains a well-equipped mother and baby room.

Open: 10am to 5pm, every day; except Sundays between 1 November and 31 March, Christmas and New Year, and Good Friday
Charges: adults £3.50; OAPs £2.60; children £1.75

Baby changing: mother and baby room
P ample

SOLVA, NR ST DAVID'S, DYFED
H SC LLANDDINOG OLD FARMHOUSE, Solva
Tel: 0348 831 224.

Follow the signs to the farmhouse from the A487. They start at the top of the hill on the east side of Solva village; you take the signs to Llandeloy and then the Llanddinog signs. O.S. map reference SM831 271.

Tucked away in the peaceful countryside the farmhouse can give you a family holiday away from it all. The attractive stone farmhouse was built in the 17th century and the delightful lounge, with its ancient beams and huge inglenook fireplace, is very much in character; as is the equally attractive dining room which has an antique high chair. Both the family rooms contain bunks and cots and baby listening can be arranged with the owner. A good selection of board games and books is provided.

From the charming dining room you look out through french windows over the extensive gardens, about five acres of lawns and paddocks. There is plenty of room for the adults to relax and for the children to play; impromptu games of cricket and football are easily accommodated. In the grounds there is a large pond and some wild garden, some rope swings, and many small animals including two ponies, sheep, calves, poultry and pigs.

Nearby: If you want an active holiday there is plenty to do in the vicinity – fishing, pony trekking, walking, golf, swimming, sailing and surfing, and there are many beaches along the coast. If museums and castles interest you there are many of these: at Scolton Manor, Haverfordwest, Manorbier, Pembroke and Tenby. There is a wildlife park and a Rare Breeds Farm near Tenby, a Marine Life Centre near St David's and a science museum at Milford Haven. The Oakwood Leisure Park near Narbeth offers a lot of family entertainment too.

✗ DINNER (7pm) £8: homemade soup, Welsh lamb, apple crumble & cream
Children: own menu, half portions

£ low
Children: cot £1; half price thereafter
Facilities: 2 cots and 2 high chairs; baby listening can be arranged
2 rooms, both family. Unlicensed
Open all year except Christmas and New Year. No music
No smoking in dining room or bedrooms
Ⓟ ample
Self-catering: Three attractive cottages are available and form
an open courtyard. The smallest can sleep four people and the
others six; one of them has a small enclosed garden and the other
an enclosed forecourt, which makes them very suitable for
families with very young children. Wee looked at the Tach Room
which has stone walls and, in contrast, pine ceilings and fittings.
The sloped wooden ceilings in the bedroom are very agreeable
and there is a double and twin-bedded room and a bunk bedroom
for children. Cots and high chairs are provided and the inclusive
rental varies between £115 and £385 a week. Short breaks are
also available, and meals can be taken in the farmhouse by
arrangement.

NR SWANSEA, WEST GLAMORGAN
Ⓟⓡ COMMERCIAL INN, Killay
Tel: 0792 203 980.
On the A4118, about 3 miles west of Swansea at Killay.

If you are on your way to the Gower this is an excellent place to
break your journey, especially if you have children in tow.

The pub is open all day, provides food throughout most of its
opening hours and offers a full range of amenities for families.
There is a special family room, which is a no smoking area and has
a play machine for children; high chairs are provided; and there is
a nappy changing facility. In addition the large, safely enclosed
garden has a well-equipped play area on a bark surface and a
bouncy castle. You can watch your darlings from the safety of the
terrace.

The interior of the Commercial Inn is a cheerful and well-
designed place, with a long L-shaped bar, wooden tables and chairs,
padded benches, the occasional alcove, and pleasant stained glass

screens and windows. When we had lunch there it was busy and the staff coped cheerfully and efficiently with their many customers.

✗ (11.30am to 10pm; from noon on Sundays) £2–8: crispy vegetable parcels, steak & kidney pie, fillet of salmon, lasagne verde, Spanish omelette
Children: own menu
Access/Visa. No smoking areas
🍺 Ale: Boddington's, Flowers, Marston's
🅿 plenty

WALWYN'S CASTLE, NR HAVERFORDWEST, DYFED

ⓈⒸ ROSEMOOR, Walwyn's Castle
Tel: 0437 781 326.
Off the B4327 south-west of Haverfordwest.

It would be a difficult task, even in lovely Pembrokeshire, to find a more attractive spot for a holiday than Rosemoor, which is situated in the Pembrokeshire Coast National Park, with its scenic variations from sandy beaches and lakes to the Preseli Mountains.

Mr and Mrs Lloyd moved here in the mid-1970s and have eight cottages and two flats. The cottages, with their thick sandstone walls and slate roofs, form an open square and offer a variety of accommodation from one bedroom to three, to sleep from four to seven or eight people. The two flats can sleep four people (Holly Tree) or up to ten (Rosemoor House). Cots and high chairs are available in every property plus other essentials such as baby baths, potties and safety gates for the stairs.

The kitchens are equipped to a very high standard with fridge-freezers, microwave ovens and cookpots, and the only items you need to take with you are towels and bedding for cots. As well as a television, you will find games (scrabble, jigsaws, and chess sets) in your cottage, books, guide books, maps and the Radio Times. There is a laundry in Rosemoor House.

The gardens surrounding Rosemoor are delightful. The cottages back on to an enclosed lawned garden and there is loads of space for children to play and the parents can keep an eye on them from the patios, which most of the cottages have. From another stretch of garden alongside the house, you see the lake below. This is part of a nature reserve, which was created by Mr and Mrs Lloyd and covers around twenty acres. There is a great variety of bird life to watch and a family of otters has occasionally been seen.

We were struck by the peaceful atmosphere of Rosemoor and also by the great care (and efficiency) which the Lloyd family apply to the running of it. Their prices, as they rightly point out in their informative brochure, offer excellent comparative value, especially in the off-peak periods.

Nearby: You can have a very active holiday here, if you wish, since there are so many amenities within easy reach. You can tackle the Pembrokeshire Coastal Path; go riding; play golf; and fishing is available on sea, lake or river. All sorts of water sports can be arranged and there are plenty of safe and sandy beaches in the vicinity: at Broad Haven and Marloes Sands for instance. Sightseers can have their fill of ancient castles, at Pembroke, Carew, Manorbier and Tenby; and St David's Cathedral should also be seen. There is a Marine Life Centre at St David's and a butterfly farm, and Manor House Wildlife Park is near Tenby. Oakwood Park, twenty minutes from Rosemoor by car, is an excellent amusement park.

Units: 10
Rent: £110 to £452 per week
Other costs: none
Plenty of cots and high chairs
Open all year

WELSHPOOL, POWYS
Ⓗ MOAT FARM, Welshpool
Tel: 0938 553 179.
On the A483 just south of Welshpool.

This is a very busy dairy farm of 250 acres, with 200 cows to be milked, morning and evening. There is, needless to say, plenty to interest visitors, especially children, who are welcome to watch all the farming activities. They must of course be in the care of an adult.

The farmhouse was built of brick in the 17th century and has had various additions over the years. The oak-beamed dining room has antique furniture including a Welsh dresser, and the very comfortable lounge overlooks the large and pretty garden, which reaches down to the meadow. There are tables set out here and the views across the countryside towards Long Mountain are very pleasing. Beyond is the River Severn, which is quite narrow here.

You can play tennis and croquet in the garden, and the games room has a pool table. The river offers excellent fishing, and this is wonderful walking country, especially through the Severn Valley to the Breidden Hills and Long Mountain.

This is a relaxing place to stay in lovely surroundings. All the bedrooms have their own bathrooms and the prices are eminently reasonable.

Nearby: There is Powis Castle, the Welshpool and Llanfair Light Railway, and market day in Welshpool is worth a look (Mondays). Further afield lies the delightful countryside of south Shropshire where Clun, Ludlow and Church Stretton are well worth a visit. To the north of Welshpool you can reach Lake Vyrnwy and Pistyll Rhaeadr, 'spout waterfall' in Welsh.

✗ DINNER (6pm) £10: soup, roast leg of lamb, pudding and cheese
Children: smaller portions
£ low
Children: one third up to 6 years; half rate from 6 to 12 years
Facilities: 1 cot and 1 high chair; baby sitting can be arranged
3 rooms, 1 family. Open March to October
No credit cards. Unlicensed
Ⓟ own car park

NR WELSHPOOL, POWYS
Ⓛ POWIS CASTLE, Welshpool
Tel: 0938 554 336.
Between the A458 and A483 on the outskirts of Welshpool.

The original 13th-century buiding was a basic stone fortress, but Sir Edward Herbert bought it in 1587 and set about creating something more elaborate. Succeeding generations, especially the 3rd Baron Powis in the late 17th century, added to it and embellished it until it became the huge mansion of red stone with battlements and towers and turrets, which stands today.

The 3rd Baron created the magnificent gardens; terraces lead down to the formal garden, a Villa d'Este in miniature as it has been called, and on to the 'wilderness' with its walks through the woodland. Above you looms Castell Coch, the Red Castle.

The castle has many treasures, a great proportion of which were brought here by Lord Clive, the son of Clive of India, who married into the family. The Clive Museum was instigated a few years ago.

The old stable block contains the restaurant within its huge, thick walls, which are freshly painted white. There is pine furniture and seating for well over a hundred in the two rooms, one of which is a no smoking area. Two high chairs are provided.

This is perhaps a place mainly for adults and older children and the slopes of the gardens could be dangerous for younger children. The many steps would make a push chair hard work, but baby slings are provided.

Open: 1 April to 31 October, every day except Monday and Tuesday (also open on Tuesday in July and August); Castle – 12 to 4.30pm; gardens and Clive Museum – 11am to 6pm
Charges: adults £5.80; children £2.90
Baby changing: mother and baby room in the courtyard with a chair and a changing table
P ample

NR WREXHAM, CLWYD
L ERDDIG, Wrexham
Tel: 0978 355 314.
South of Wrexham off the A534.

The building was begun in the late 17th century and cannot be described as the most beautiful or grandest of great houses, but it is full of interest. The house contains a fine collection of 18th-century furniture and ceramics, for example.

But its greater interest lies in the tour through the outbuildings and servants' rooms. This gives a wonderful insight into the workings of a great house: of life 'below stairs' and the self-sufficient nature of such a place. You can see the joiner's shop, the smithy, the saw mill, stables, bakehouse, laundry, kitchen, the house-keeper's room and the servants' hall. There is a remarkable collection of pictures of the staff during the 18th and 19th centuries.

The self-service restaurant is housed in an old barn, long and narrow and with pine furniture; a couple of high chairs are available.

The parkland covers 2,000 acres and includes picnic areas, one of which is in the orchard. There are various walks through the woods and the park and a beautiful 18th-century walled garden to be seen.

Open: 3 April to 3 October, every day except Thursday and Friday; house – noon to 5pm; outbuildings and garden – 11m to 6pm

Charges: adults £5; children £2.50; family ticket £7.50

Baby changing: a baby changing unit with changing mat, chair, etc

P ample

Index

science centre, 121–2
Scone Palace, 423–4, 433, 459, 467–8
Scotney Castle Gardens, 218
Scotton Manor, 487, 510, 525
Sea Life Centre
  Barcaldine, Oban, 427, 429–30, 455, 464
  Weymouth, 129, 134, 138, 151–2, 161, 164–6
  see also marine, museums
Seal Sanctuary, 43, 65–6, 82–3, 429
Sezincote, 254, 262, 284
Shakespeare play performances, 391–2
Shandy Hall, 410, 418
Sheldon Manor, 118, 288
Sherbourne Abbey, 135
Shuttleworth Collection (aeroplane museum), 229–30
Skenfrith Castle, 263
Sissinghurst Castle Gardens, 218
shire horse *see* horses
shooting, 423, 459, 497, 519
  clay pigeon, 46, 87, 135, 276, 284, 450
Shugborough Hall, 270
sing songs, 45
skating; 434
ski centre, 427
  slope, dry, 133
skittles, 36, 41, 48, 51, 61, 69, 127
Skye, 448, 450
slate caverns, 482–3, 490, 497, 512
Snape Maltings, 293
snooker, 28, 38, 43, 48, 67, 69, 79, 90, 99, 138, 182, 288, 294, 327, 347, 372, 375, 412, 466, 470, 482, 501
Snowshill Manor, 254, 262
solarium, 103, 150, 187, 401, 503
Southwick Hall, 329
spa bath, 24, 31, 48, 79, 103
space invaders, 36, 49, 466
sports centre, 46, 501
  hall, 69
squash courts, 48, 55–6, 60–1, 64, 67, 69, 85, 90, 103, 129, 138, 147, 192, 288, 334, 343, 349, 375, 423, 427, 459, 464, 466, 503, 521
stairgates *see* safety gates
Stapeley Water Gardens, 354
Stonehenge, 131
Stourhead House and Garden, 118, 135, 147, 149
Stratford-upon-Avon, 266, 328
Stump Cross Caverns, 413
Sudbury, 310
  Gainsborough's House, 310
Sulgrave Manor, 328
sun bed, 41
Sun Centre, Rhyl, 501
surfing *see* water sports
Sutton Bank, 415
swimming pools:
  England: children's, 28, 36, 67, 115, 138, 375, galas, 41, 69; indoor, Cornwall, 25, 28, 31, 43, 57, 61, 65, 67, 70, 79, 83, Devon, 34, 36, 38, 40, 46, 48, 50, 85,

90, 101, 103, Dorset, 115, 138, 150, Hereford and Worcester, 261, 275, Norfolk, 294, Northumberland, 392, 401, Nottinghamshire, 335, Somerset, 128, Yorkshire, 410; Scotland, 427, 434, 470; Wales, 482, 503, 505, 519, 522
  England: outdoor, Cornwall, 56, 61, 65, 67, 70, 79, 81–3, Cumbria, 349, Devon, 35, 38, 41, 52, 85, 88, 103, Dorset, 45, 134, 150, Gloucestershire, 271, Hampshire, 182, Hereford and Worcester, 260, Northumberland, 390, Sussex, 187, 192, 200, Wiltshire, 118; Scotland, 423, 435, 460; Wales, 525

Tarka Trail, 99
Technology, Centre for Alternative, 481, 503, 511
teenagers' room, 41
Tenby, 487
tennis:
  England: Cornwall, 24–5, 28, 31, 43, 54–5, 61, 67, 69, 76, 79, 81–2; Cumbria, 349, 351, 379; Devon, 34, 48, 41, 46, 48, 51, 85, 89–90, 103; Dorset, 129, 138, 147, 150; Gloucestershire, 288; Hereford and Worcester, 260, 275; Northumberland, 390, 401; Somerset, 128; Sussex, 187, 192, 200; Wiltshire, 412
  Scotland, 423, 427, 433, 435, 459, 465–6
  Wales, 482, 522, 529
tennis, short, 138
tennis, table:
  England: Avon, 163; Cornwall, 43, 57, 61, 64, 67, 69, 75, 79, 83; Devon, 30, 35–6, 38, 40–1, 46, 48–9, 52, 63, 90, 99, 101, 103; Dorset, 115, 135, 138, 150; Gloucestershire, 254, 288; Norfolk, 294; Northumberland, 401; Nottinghamshire, 335; Somerset, 128; Wiltshire, 118
  Scotland, 366, 470
  Wales, 482, 515, 522
Tetbury, 266
Theme Parks
  Alton Towers, 247–8
  Blackgang Chine, 185
  Flambards, 43, 65–6, 82–3
  Lightwater Valley, 406–7
  Pleasurewood Hills American, 311
  Thorpe Park, 186
  see also Adventure parks, Wildlife parks
Thirks (Darrowby in James Herriot's novels), 415
Thorburn's Edwardian Countryside, 59
Threave Garden, 430–1, 469
Thurleston, 15, 49
Tinturn Abbey, 276
Tintinhull House, 154
toboggan run, 506
Torridon Mountain Centre, 448, 450
Tower of London, 208–9
Townend, 361

READERS' COMMENTS

Please use this sheet to recommend establishments which you think should be considered for the next edition of the Guide. The basic facilities we look for are:

- hotels with cots, high chairs and a free baby listening service
- pubs with separate family rooms
- restaurants with high chairs
- theme parks, zoos, museums etc with mother and baby rooms and high chairs in their cafés

Comments, adverse or otherwise, are welcome about any of the current Guide's entries.

To: The Editors, The Family Welcome Guide 1994, c/o Hamer Books Ltd. Freepost, London SW13 9BR

Full name and address of establishment:

....

....

....

Phone number: ....

Comments:

....

....

....

....

Name and address of sender:

....

....

....

We regret that we cannot acknowledge these forms, but they will be properly considered.

THE FAMILY WELCOME GUIDE
HELPING TOMMY'S CAMPAIGN TO
MAKE BRITAIN PARENT FRIENDLY

The Family Welcome Guide is supporting Tommy's Campaign to help promote a more positive and welcoming approach towards parents with young children.

Are you tired of struggling every time you take your children shopping? Do you get the cold shoulder when you and your children go to a restaurant? Is travelling by train with your children an ordeal? Now is the time to fight back and help Britain become more Parent Friendly!

If you want more information on Tommy's Parent Friendly Campaign or any other aspect of Tommy's Campaign please complete this page and send it to Tommy's Campaign at the address below:

TOMMY'S CAMPAIGN, LONDON SE99 6RD

NAME . . . .

ADDRESS . . . .

. . . .

. . . . POST CODE . . . .

TELEPHONE NUMBER . . . .

TOMMY'S PARENT FRIENDLY CAMPAIGN

Parent Friendly is run by Tommy's Campaign, a national charity which funds research and treatment in the fight against prematurity, childlessness, stillbirth and miscarriage.

Tommy's Campaign is dedicated to caring for babies both inside and outside the womb. Though Parent Friendly it aims to make Britain an easier place for parents with young children.

Tommy's Campaign in support of The Baby Fund, Registered
Charity number 1001362
Patron, Her Royal Highness The Duchess of York
President, Lord Palumbo of Walbrook, Joint Chairmen Ian Fergusson FRCS,
FRCOG, Anthony Kenney FRCS, FRCOG
Tommy's Campaign, 7th Floor, North Wing, St Thomas' Hospital, London SE1
7EH. Telephone 071-620 0188. Fax: 071-928 6628